USS NEW JERSEY (BB-62)

TURNER PUBLISHING COMPANY
Paducah, Kentucky

Members of K Division, USS New Jersey at King's Palace, Paris, France, August 1952. (Submitted by Michael J. Bakos)

TURNER PUBLISHING COMPANY
412 Broadway, P.O. Box 3101
Paducah, KY 42002-3101
Phone: (502) 443-0121

Turner Publishing Company Staff:
Publishing Consultant: Keith R. Steele
Project Assistant: David P. Figge
Book Design: Trevor W. Grantham

Copyright © 1996, Turner Publishing Company. All rights reserved. Additional Copies may be purchased from Turner Publishing Company.

Library of Congress
Catalog Card No.:96-060247
ISBN 978-1-63026-968-5
Limited Edition. Printed in the U.S.A.

Cover: USS *New Jersey* (BB-62). Copyright © 1993 James A. Flood.
Endsheets are courtesy of Stuart Chalkley.
Feature Article: *From Philly to Tokyo, War Cruise of the USS New Jersey (BB 62)*. Copyright ©Charles W. Frank, 1993

This book or any part thereof may not be reproduced, electronically or mechanically, without the written consent of the publisher. This publication was produced using available material. The publisher regrets it cannot assume liability for errors or omissions.

Table of Contents

Association Message 3

Publisher's Message 4

General History - USS New Jersey (BB-62) 6

USS New Jersey: A Chronology 15

From Philly to Tokyo, War Cruise of the USS New Jersey 16

USS New Jersey Veteran's Biographies 65

Index 104

Association Message

*General Chairman
Director-*
Russell Brown
1414 South Western Avenue
Champaign, IL 61821
(217) 356-6253

*President
Director-*
James C. Martin
501-F Waters Edge Drive
Newport News, VA 23606-4102
(804) 599-6628

*Vice-President
Director-*
James J. Schatzman
201 Sunray Rd.
Del Haven, NJ 08251-3233

*Secretary-Treasurer
Director-*
Edwin M. Fogelson
281 Autumn Trail
Port Orange, FL 32119-7802
(904) 788-1459

Assistant Treasurer
Richard McDowell
83 Queens Way
Port Orange, FL 32119
(904) 756-1144

*Legal Council
Director-*
George H. Elwood
10 West Main Street
Hancock, NY 13783
(607) 637-4791

The USS *New Jersey* Veterans, Inc. would like to dedicate this book to all deceased shipmates, spouses and friends of the USS *New Jersey* BB-62 and to Russell Brown, who had the idea to form the *New Jersey* Veterans. Russell formed a group of seventy-five former shipmates and wives at his home in Urbana, IL in June 1981 with wife Marge and it went from there.

The first reunion was held at the Hyatt, in Long Beach, CA in January 1982 at which time they were to attend the recommissioning of the *New Jersey*. However, President Ronald Reagan had the recommissioning held at Christmas time as he was in California on vacation at the time. The reunion went on in January with Russell and his wife Marge, and Dr. Frank Blair and wife Ruth as co-chairpersons. The event drew about 150 ex-crewmen and wives. The ship was visited by all and many a tear flowed that day.

Today, between 525 and 680 attend the reunions. Edwin Fogelson, the reunion coordinator, staged the 2nd reunion along with his wife, Marylyn in Atlantic City, NJ. He helped with the 3rd reunion in Indianapolis in 1986 with Dick Powers as chairman. O'Neil Leonard and his wife Pam chaired the 1988 reunion in New Orleans. Ed Fogelson put on the biggest reunion in 1990 at Daytona Beach with 680 in attendance. This reunion was billed as a family reunion and children and grandchildren attended with Grandpa to have a great time on the beach.

Ed, Marylyn, Russell and Marge ran the Nashville event in 1992. The 50th Anniversary in 1993 was held in Cherry Hill, NJ with Ed and Marylyn chairing. The 1994 reunion in San Diego was chaired by Larry Kalakauski with help from Ed. The 1995 reunion was held in Norfolk, VA with James C. Martin and Ed as co-chairmen. It was a great event at the Naval Base with Vice Admiral Douglas J. Katz, Commander of the US Atlantic Fleet attending. The 1996 reunion with Robert Munsey, Jr. and Ed co-chairing will be held in Ft. Mitchell, KY. The 1997 event will be held in Boston. John Walsh and Carl Butts will chair this reunion. The members attending these reunions have a great time meeting old shipmates they haven't seen in over 40 years or more.

The first officer was Russell Brown who was in charge of all offices. The present officers are: General Chairman, Russell Brown; President, James C. Martin; Vice President, James Schatzman who filled in the office after the death of member Charles Gasser in 1993.; Secretary/Treasurer, Edwin Fogelson; and Legal Council George Elwood. All are directors as is O'Neil Leonard. The officers hold their positions for 4 years. This year, 1996 is an election year.

The purpose for the Veterans, Inc. is to promote reunions for former crew members of the *New Jersey*, provide scholarships for two outstanding people, and to bring back the USS *New Jersey* (BB-62) to the State of New Jersey where she would be on display for all to have the opportunity to view the greatest battleship and most decorated ship in the Navy.

USS *New Jersey* Battleship Commission

Commission Mission Statement
The USS *New Jersey* Battleship Commission was created in 1980 under New Jersey Law to be an operational commission to provide for the preservation of the battleship *New Jersey* as a historical monument, memorial and museum once returned to New Jersey.

The commission consists of 13 members appointed by the Governor and confirmed by the State Senate to 5 year terms and two ex officio members, the State Treasurer and the Commissioner of the Department of Environmental Protection. Meeting once a month, the commission actively follows a working business plan for the return and preservation of the *New Jersey*. The commission's plan of action is divided up into three distinct areas of operation:

Phase 1: To secure and prepare a site for the *New Jersey* that will provide maximum accessibility, visibility and preservation: The proposed site is in Liberty State Park. With over 3 million visitors a year, Liberty Park would provide the attendance needed to maintain and operate the ship. The site must be tested, dredged, bulkheaded and finished to Navy, EPA, and NJDEP standards to minimize the effects on the environment and to provide for the ship's preservation.

Phase 2: To acquire the *New Jersey* from the Navy, provide for its return trip home and recondition her for viewing and preservation: The *New Jersey* currently sits in Bremerton, Washington and is maintained by the Navy. Once the Navy sees that the State of New Jersey has diligently prepared a secure berth and has arranged for her return trip home, they will give her to us. In tow, the return trip from the Pacific Northwest to New Jersey will take over 2 months going through the Panama Canal. Once back in *New Jersey*, BB-62 will need to be completely overhauled to prepare her for a new life as a museum.

Phase 3: To manage, maintain and promote the *New Jersey* and run her like any other self-sustaining business, once in her final resting place: The commission, along with the *New Jersey* Division of Parks & Forestry and the Battleship *New Jersey* Historical Society will be responsible for the success of the New Jersey being the biggest and hopefully the most memorable attraction in the Garden State.

The USS *New Jersey* Battleship Commission is not funded under the state budget and must conduct its own efforts to raise the estimated $25 million to provide for her return, berth, and preservation.

Publisher's Message

Dave Turner, President - Turner Publishing Company

Among the most famous battleships in the history of the US Navy, the USS *New Jersey* (BB-62) is certainly one of the most colorful. From her commissioning on May 23, 1943 and her brave service throughout World War II, Korea, Vietnam, and Beirut to her final decommissioning in February of 1991, the USS *New Jersey* traveled the world in the name of freedom.

This book is dedicated to those of you who proudly served aboard the *New Jersey* and defended those persecuted by aggression over the decades. It was you, the veterans, who selflessly gave yourselves, heart and soul, and risked your lives. It was you, who through your actions, created the history of the USS *New Jersey* that is held in such high esteem today.

I would like to thank all of you who submitted your photos and biographies to be included in this history book. I would like to personally thank Mr. Ed Fogelson, Secretary-Treasurer of the USS *New Jersey* Veterans, Inc. for his efforts in making this volume possible. Also, I would like to thank Mr. Charles Frank for providing his detailed account of his service aboard during World War II. Finally, I would like to thank Mr. Keith Steele, publishing consultant, whose dedication to publishing Naval history helped make this volume a success.

Dave Turner
President, Turner Publishing Company

History of the USS *New Jersey* (BB-62)

The Battleships

Billy Mitchell thought he had buried the age of the battleships beneath the Atlantic waves with his experiments in the early 1920s, and generally was credited with such. That judgment proved premature, to say the least.

The fabled dreadnoughts for many years were the undisputed royalty of the world's oceans. They reigned in the age when a nation's military might was measured not by missile range and nuclear warheads but in the number of capital ships and the size of their gun bores. International arms treaties were written around that very concept.

It was a battleship, as often as not, that came to symbolize some epic event. Mention the *Maine*, the *Arizona* and the *Missouri*, and most Americans make an immediate association. "Sink the *Bismark*" became the rallying cry of the British early in World War II, as though the fate of the empire itself depended upon that act.

The American experience in World War II started with the sinking of the *Arizona*, which still rests in the mud of Pearl Harbor, and ended with the signing of the surrender document aboard the *Missouri* in Tokyo Bay.

The *Missouri* is the younger sister of the *New Jersey*, two in the last class of battleships ever built. The first was the *Iowa* and the last was the *Wisconsin*, and together those four warships proved the point, in firepower and staying power, that the obituary of the battleship was written much too early.

To return to the Mitchell affair, that World War I ace and apostle of air power was a true visionary who took a courageous stand for what he believed, but he did not quite accomplish what he set out to do or claim that he did. His premise was simple: An airplane could sink a battleship, which in 1921 bordered on heresy in military circles. So he had some hulks towed out to sea and dropped bombs on them until they sank, which proved virtually nothing except there is a limit to watertight integrity. The ancient ships could neither maneuver nor fight back. They more resembled toothless old lions than anything else.

Nevertheless the Mitchell legend took hold and later would contribute to the myth that the aircraft carrier, which came into its own in World War II, had rendered the battleship not only obsolete but virtually useless.

That idea was reinforced at Pearl Harbor where Japanese air power dealt a near knockout blow against the American battleship fleet, but those were the last of the U.S. Navy's battleships ever sunk and, let's not forget, they were old ships caught dozing in their berths. As World War II progressed, many battleships, including the four new ones, would see much action, take punishment from bombs and kamikazes, and still remain afloat and fighting back.

The post-World War II history of the battleship is confined to the four *Iowa*-class vessels, each of which has undergone multiple incarnations. The typical cycle was peacetime mothballing, presumably forever, and recommissioning in the face of a new war or threat of one that no one quite expected.

This happened first in Korea, where all four ships saw action on a rotating basis. The *New Jersey* came back for Vietnam and again in the early 1980s in the Middle East. The *New Jersey* thus was the only battleship to have fought in four wars, and for that matter was the only American man-of-war ever to do so. It was during those later conflicts, Korea, Vietnam and Lebanon, that the value of the big guns in hitting shore targets was demonstrated again, contradicting the assumptions of 1945 that the surface battles with the Japanese and the bombardment of Pacific islands represented the last time warfare would require the services of a battleship's main battery.

Finally, two battlewagons, the *Missouri* and *Wisconsin*, by then upgraded with missiles but still carrying the 16-inch guns, fought offshore in the Persian Gulf war.

Thus the Navy kept finding uses for these heavyweights of the fleet. Their high speed, thick belt of protective armor and lethal punching power made them formidable machines of war, regardless of their age or the technological advances in methods of combat.

Desert Storm occurred 70 years after Billy Mitchell pulled off his demonstration. It's too bad he couldn't have been there to see it. The jet aircraft would have been beyond the imagination of the man who had flown the rickety biplanes over France in 1918. But most amazing of all to him might have been the sight of a couple of 50-year-old battleships engaging in the same fight as state-of-the-art aircraft.

The ensuing chapters will trace the history of one battleship, the USS *New Jersey*, BB 62, in its participation in four wars and duty between wars. The New Jersey story, 1940-91, epitomizes

USS New Jersey *in the late 1940s. (submitted by Helen Leverton)*

the saga of the American battleship, that versatile, durable dreadnought whose regal bearing made her in any company and any circumstances the Queen of the Sea.

Construction

From the conception to the birth of the USS *New Jersey*, three dates are pertinent: Sept. 16, 1940, when the keel was laid at the Philadelphia Naval Yard, Dec. 7, 1942, when the ship was launched, and May 23, 1943, the day she was commissioned as a part of the United States fleet.

With war on the horizon in the late 1930s, the United States made the decision to build a new class of battleships. The hull design for which was conceived by the venerable shipbuilding firm of Gibbs and Cox. Though the main battery- nine 16-inch guns- would be patterned after the most recent battleships, such as the *South Dakota*, *Washington* and *Alabama*, the hull would be considerably longer and have distinctive lines.

Two ships each were awarded the Navy shipyards at New York and Philadelphia. The first one, BB 61, the *Iowa*, would be built at New York. At Philadelphia, the *New Jersey* and the *Wisconsin*, BB 64, were to be built side-by-side. The *Missouri*, BB 63, was the second New York ship.

The *New Jersey* had a number before it had name. Battleships, of course, were named for states and it was a matter of great pride for any state to be chosen for the honor. Lobbying naturally was intense, and the state of *New Jersey* made itself heard on the subject as early as 1937.

As it happened, Charles Edison, son of the great inventor, was Assistant Secretary of the Navy on July 1, 1939, when the contract for the BB 62 was awarded to the Philadelphia yard. Six days later, the Secretary of the Navy died and Edison was elevated to acting secretary. In that capacity, he exercised his prerogative to name the new battleship for his own state. Edison was elected governor of New Jersey in November 1940.

Two months earlier, on Sept. 16, Edison did the ceremonial honors at the keel-laying of the new ship on ways that had had to be lengthened in order to accommodate its size.

Planning and building a ship of this size and complexity is not a static process. Adjustments and revisions in design are a constant, and these were compared back and forth between the *New Jersey* and the *Iowa*, which was started and finished three months ahead. Some of the changes were made as a result of the actual combat situations being encountered in the fleet. For instance, the 1.1-inch anti-aircraft guns originally planned were shelved in favor of 40- and 20-millimeter weapons.

In charge of the construction were two lieutenant commanders, Francis X. "Savvy" Forest, and Allen L. "High Pockets" Dunning, both experienced and accomplished in their craft. They supervised a huge work force and complex operation, which included the subcontracting of component elements in many localities. Overall, it is estimated that 6,000 to 8,000 men and women were involved in the building of the *New Jersey*. In time of war, building a ship, as with a tank or an airplane, was a special endeavor calling for the best in workmanship. After all, other Americans would have to fight in these machines and their lives might depend on the fit of a rivet or the tightness of a weld.

Competition between the New York and Philadelphia yards was spirited, in part out of the urgent need to claim scarce parts. Finally launch date came for the *New Jersey* on Dec. 7, 1942, a year to the day after Pearl Harbor. The *Iowa* had gone down the ways on Sept. 6.

Mrs. Edison, wife of the governor, swung the traditional bottle of champagne against the mammoth bow, and the hull began its one-minute slide toward water for the first time, reaching a speed of about 20 miles per hour. The principal address was given by James Forrestal, then Under Secretary of the Navy.

At 36,447 tons, the *New Jersey* was the largest ship ever launched in the United States from inclined ways. The *Iowa* weighed 36,346 tons, 101 tons less, so the two ships, though sisters of the same class and essentially the same, were not identical, at launching anyway.

The enormous water displacement in the Delaware River had the effect of a small flood on nearby shores, including those at Camden, N.J., directly across from Philadelphia.

When complete, the *New Jersey* would displace 45,000 tons, and be capable of speeds of 33 knots, an important improvement over the 27-knot, 35,000-ton battleships completed in the late 1930s. The additional speed would allow the *Iowa*-class ships to keep up with the fast carrier task forces that were then carrying the war to the Pacific enemy.

The *New Jersey's* length was 887 feet, 7 inches, and at the beam she measured 108 feet, 1 inch in width. That maximum beam dimension, incidentally, allowed the Iowa-class battleships to squeeze through the 110-foot-wide Panama Canal locks with just under a foot to spare on either side. In profile the new battleships made a sleek appearance. It was characteristic of the warships of that era, those that were built for and during World War II, to have graceful lines, a quality that was magnified at sea as they cut through the water. This was true of the Fletcher and Sumner-class destroyers and the Baltimore-class heavy cruisers. The Iowa-class battleships had the same style, which gladdened any sailorman's heart just to watch.

The ship drew 28 feet, 11 inches. Armor up to 17 inches thick protected the hull and the 16-inch turrets down through the barbette.

The main battery was nine 16-inch, 50 caliber guns, three each in three turrets, two forward and one aft. Other armament included 20 5-inch, 38 caliber rifles set in 10 twin mounts, five to a side, 16 quad 40-millimeter guns and 49 20-millimeter machine guns. The main battery was strictly a bombardment and surface-engagement weapon, the 5-inchers were dual purpose anti-aircraft and bombardment and the 40s and 20s anti-aircraft. The caliber reference on the larger guns denoted the ratio of the barrel length from breech to muzzle to the diameter of the bore. Thus the 16-inch guns were 800 inches long (16 times 50), or approximately 66 feet. The 5-inch guns were 190 inches, or 15 feet, 10 inches, in length.

The 16-inch guns were capable of hurling a 2,700 pound shell 20 to 22 miles. The 5-inch guns had a range of about eight miles.

The *New Jersey's* power plant consisted of eight Babcock and Wilcox boilers and four Westinghouse turbines. Her four propellers produced 53,000 shaft horsepower each.

The ship initially carried three Vought OS2U Kingfisher float planes.

After the *New Jersey* was launched, there was still much work to do topside and below to make the warship ready to carry out its wartime purpose. When the keel was laid in September 1940, United States involvement in global war was but a near-certain prospect. It became a reality at Pearl Harbor where the decimation of the battleship fleet and the challenge from such a maritime power as Japan added urgency to the job at hand. Ship-building had to be expedited. It was. The ship was commissioned a year before the originally scheduled completion date.

As work was being completed, men who would make up the *New Jersey's* first crew began to arrive and take up residence in barracks at the Philadelpia Navy Yard. As this happened, the influence of the Navy men on the final construction increased. Even though the yard staff remained in control during the pre-commissioning period, the workers gave a certain amount of deference to the officers and sailors who would have to live in, sail and fight the battleship in the months ahead.

Commissioning day came less than six months after launching, on May 23, 1943. The man chosen as the first captain was Capt. Carl F. Holden, a member of Admiral Ernest King's staff, a fact that might have positioned the captain favorably for the plum assignment. The 47-year-old Holden had already seen action in the current war as executive officer of the battleship Pennsylvania when it was attacked at Pearl Harbor.

Rear Admiral Milo F. Draemel, commandant of the Fourth Naval District and the Philadelphia yard, read the authorization and at 12:38 p.m. directed that the USS *New Jersey* be placed in commision. The American flag, the union jack and the commissioning pennant were raised and the first watch was set. The battleship thus joined the active fleet, her control passed from the shipyard to the commanding officer and his men. At a cost of about $100 million, the ship over the next five decades would prove to be quite a bargain.

Some of the words of Capt. Holden on the occasion are worth relating: "This new existence, this new warrior of the deep, yesterday was an 'it', a mere structure of steel, a stout hull powered by mighty engines and studded with cannon. Today this inanimate 'it' becomes 'she', a being endowed with the living character of personality with a soul and with a purpose. A lovely lady, but a lovely lady who will have her angry moments....

"This is going to be a smart ship. By smart I mean clean, trim, alert, disciplined. That is synonymous with an efficient ship. It is already a powerful ship. It is going to be a fighting ship."

Captains

The commanding officer of a battleship is a captain by rank, a four-striper of senior status.

For most naval officers, there could be no greater seagoing honor than to be tapped for command of a battleship, especially a new one like the *New Jersey*. Carl Holden epitomized the kind of officer who rose to become the skipper of such a ship. A Naval Academy graduate, he served in a series of smaller ships and in shore and staff positions of increasing responsibility. He eventually retired as a vice admiral. Indicative of the quality of officers who served as captain of the *New Jersey* over its lifetime is the fact that virtually all of them later achieved flag rank.

The typical tenure of a battleship captain was less than two years and often less than one. Holden's was one of the longer ones. After assuming command at commissioning on May 23, 1943, he served until Jan. 26, 1945.

His successors in order were: Edmund Tyler Wooldridge, Jan. 26, 1945-Nov. 17, 1945; Edward M. Thompson, Nov. 17, 1945-Aug. 5, 1946; Leon J. Huffman, Aug. 5, 1946-May 23, 1947; George L. Menocal, May 23, 1947-Feb. 14, 1948.

Joseph W. Leverton, Jr., Feb. 14, 1948-June 30, 1948; David Tyree, Nov. 21, 1950-Nov. 17, 1951; Francis D. McCorkle, Nov. 17, 1951-Oct. 20, 1952; Charles L. Melson, Oct. 20, 1952-Oct. 24, 1953.

John C. Atkeson, Oct. 24, 1953-March 18, 1955; Edward J. O'Donnell, March 18, 1955-May 31, 1956; Charles S. Brooks, Jr., May 31, 1956-Aug. 21, 1957; J. Edward Snyder, Jr., April 6, 1968-Aug. 27, 1969.

Robert C. Peniston, Aug. 27, 1969-Dec. 17, 1969; William M. Fogarty, Dec. 28, 1982-Sept. 15, 1983; Richard D. Milligan, Sept. 15, 1983-Sept. 7, 1985; and Walter L. Glenn, Jr., Sept. 7, 1985-Aug. 8, 1987; Douglas J. Katz, Aug. 8,1987-May 19, 1989; and Ronald Tucker, May 19, 1989-Feb. 8, 1991.

Shakedown

The commissioning did not mean the *New Jersey* and her crew were ready for war, or even for sea. The official complement for the ship had been set at 117 officers and 1,804 enlisted men, but the actual number aboard after the *New Jersey* was commissioned was closer to 2,400. Many of the enlisted men were new to the Navy, either fresh from boot camp or service schools. Some of the officers were seasoned. Among those who knew what war was about was Lt. Roman V. "Rosy" Mrozinski, a turret officer. The previous fall he was aboard the cruiser *San Francisco*, which saw heavy action off Guadalcanal and absorbed terrific punishment.

The first weeks were spent in place finishing detail work, allowing the men to familiarize themselves with their equipment, duties and living quarters. For men who had never been to sea before, learning to live in the close quarters aboard ship required adjustments.

Finally on July 8, the USS *New Jersey* got under way on its own power for the first time, heading down the Delaware River to Delaware Bay and into the open Atlantic. The first trial of the power plant went well enough to propel the mammoth haze gray bulk nearly 33 knots.

Two weeks later, it was time to test the guns, the very reason for the battleship's existence. First to fire, one barrel at a time, were the

C.O. Leon Huffman: August 5, 1946- May 23, 1947 (submitted by Helen Leverton)

(L-R): Adm. McLean, Capt. Menocal (C.O. May 23, 1947- February 14, 1948), Adm. Connolly, and King Haakan of Norway - July 2, 1947. (submitted by Helen Leverton)

16-inch rifles. Then came the 5-inch secondary batteries, followed by the 40s and the 20s. In all, 142 barrels erupted in fire, from the roar of the 16s, the crack of the 5s, the rhythmic pattern of the 40s to the staccato of the 20s. Most of the crew did not know what to expect, but that day they learned one thing. When the 16-inch battery fired, loose gear needed to be secure.

Sea trials, shakedown in the Caribbean, drills and training, the process continued the remainder of 1943. Finally, in January 1944, the *New Jersey* was ready for war and set sail for the Panama Canal and the Pacific beyond. The *New Jersey* caught up with the battle fleet on Jan. 23 and was on hand for pre-invasion activity at Kwajalein in the Marshall Islands, but did no firing.

On Feb. 4, Admiral Raymond Spruance raised his Fifth Fleet flag in the *New Jersey*, which for much of the remainder of the Pacific War would serve as the flagship alternately of the Fifth Fleet or Admiral William Halsey's Third Fleet. These fleets were essentially the same ships, but their designations changed when the two admirals exchanged roles. While one was actively prosecuting the war, the other was drafting plans for the next phase. The *New Jersey* also served at times as the Battleship Division flagship.

The first combat gunfire ever to originate from the *New Jersey* occurred Feb. 16 off Truk, a Japanese stronghold, when the ship shot at an enemy aircraft menacing the Iowa. A short time later, the *New Jersey's* guns destroyed a Japanese trawler and sank a destroyer.

Members of 9th Division during WWII (submitted by Joseph A Dinell)

Members of 9th Division during WWII (submitted by Joseph A Dinell)

The battleship encountered hostile fire for the first time on March 17, during a practice bombardment of the Marshall island of Mille. Japanese were ashore and their batteries put a shell through the deck of the *New Jersey*, but there were no casualties. Throughout the war, in fact, all the men wounded aboard the *New Jersey*, about four, were hit by fragments from friendly fire, in one case from the battleship itself and another from a nearby aircraft carrier.

After the Marshalls, the next major campaign for the fleet, and the *New Jersey*, was in the Marianas - specifically Saipan, Tinian, Guam and Rota. In June 1944, the *New Jersey* participated in the heavy bombardment of Saipan and Tinian and in what World War II historians officially called the Battle of the Philippine Sea and unofficially the "Marianas Turkey Shoot." On that day, June 19, the Japanese air fleet was decimated by American fighter planes and anti-aircraft fire from the surface fleet.

Next came the liberation of the Philippines and the air-sea battles offshore. It was here in October 1944 that the Japanese introduced a diabolical new weapon, the suicide plane. The *New Jersey* was never hit by a kamikaze, but the battleship was credited more than once with shooting them out of the sky as they headed for nearby aircraft carriers.

The *New Jersey* was engaged with enemy aircraft off Leyte, where landings were made on Oct. 20, and off Luzon, which was invaded in December.

That fall, the *New Jersey* also hit the Japanese-held island of Formosa (Taiwan) and ventured as far north as Okinawa for a preliminary strike against what would be the last major island target in the Pacific six months hence.

Not only did the *New Jersey* undergo nearly relentless combat through most of 1944, but was forced to ride out two of the worst typhoons ever to hit the Pacific. The first was in October and the second in December., when three American destroyers capsized with heavy loss of life.

In February 1945, the battleship joined the fleet softening up Iwo Jima for that epic landing and subsequent battle, and also went north with the carriers to hit the Japanese main islands. She was on hand the day in March when the carrier Franklin was nearly mortally damaged by Japanese bombs with the loss of more than 700 crewmen.

Finally came Okinawa, which was invaded by the American Army and Marines on April 1. Offshore the American Navy endured its greatest ordeal as the kamikazes swept down from Kyushu and up from Formosa in maximum force. The *New Jersey* participated in that great battle until April 16, when she was ordered to Bremerton, Washington for rest and repairs.

In July, the *New Jersey* returned to the western Pacific, where Spruance again made the BB 62 his flagship. There was little fighting left to be done, however, as the war ended on Aug. 14.

The official surrender on Sept. 2 in Tokyo Bay would have taken place on the decks of the *New Jersey* as the Fifth Fleet flagship but for the fact that the president, Harry S Truman, was from Missouri. Thus the ceremonies were switched to the battleship named for his state, while the men on the *New Jersey* could only watch from a distance in the bay.

The *New Jersey* remained in Japan on occupational duty for a few months and headed home with about 1,000 veterans of the Pacific war aboard as passengers. The battleship, docking in San Francisco on Feb. 10, 1946, was home from the war. The big ship compiled an excellent combat record, winning 11 battle stars. The *New Jersey* was credited with shooting down 20 enemy planes and assisting in the sinking several of Japanese ships. The *New Jersey's* crew also was credited with saving the lives of a number of downed airmen.

The battleship remained an active part of the fleet until she was decommissioned on July 30, 1948, at Bayonne, New Jersey.

Korea

The United States in June 1950 learned to its distresss it was not finished with war nor with the need for battleships ready to fight. Alone among the four *Iowa*-class battleships, the *Missouri* had remained activated. It was soon flexing its considerable muscle off the shores of Korea where the war in the latter half of the year was a bloody series of dramatic successes and crushing defeats. That Asian peninsula, with hundreds of miles of shoreline and key coastal locations, was a place where heavy bombardment capabilities could be put to good use.

The Navy wasted little time starting the reactivation process of the other three battleships, including the *New Jersey*. The BB 62 was ready first, and on Nov. 21, the ship was recommissioned under the command of Capt. David Tyree.

Shakedowns, equipment testing and training reminscent of 1943 were necessary and on April 16, 1951, the *New Jersey* stood out from Norfolk, Va., on its way to war once again. As the ship passed through the Panama Canal, she met the sister ship *Missouri* on its return trip from the Korean war zone.

On May 12, the *New Jersey* sailed into Yokosuka, the big naval base in Tokyo Bay that was to become the American Navy's principal logistical support installation during the Korean War. A second one was at Sasebo on the island of Kyushu, which was considerably closer to the scene of action.

Eight days later, the battleship, which served as the flagship of Seventh Fleet commander Vice Admiral Harold M. Martin, was off Wonsan Harbor. That night, May 20, her 16-inch guns roared in anger for the first time since 1945.

Wonsan consistently was the hottest spot for the Navy. About 60 miles north of the front lines on the east coast, the harbor remained under constant naval siege for the duration of the war, and the New Jersey called there several times.

The second day on the line, the ship learned what a dangerous place it could be. During the *New Jersey's* firing mission on May 21, crewmen noticed splashes to port coming steadily closer. Enemy shore batteries were at work from a jut of land known as Kalmagak. The forward 16-inch turret took a direct hit, which caused little damage and no casualties. However, as the crew was responding to the call to battle stations, a near miss off the port quarter sprayed shell fragments onto the weather deck. One piece of shrapnel penetrated the life jacket of Seaman Apprentice Robert Osterwind and hit him in the chest. He was dead by the time he reached the wardroom aid station. Three other sailors, Joseph H. Dzekon, J. E. Schaniel and J. A. Bailey, were wounded. Osterwind, who had entered the Navy about six months earlier, was only 17 years old. He was the only man ever to lose his life to enemy action aboard the *New Jersey*.

The *New Jersey*, often in the company of destroyers, ranged up and down the Korean coast, firing at enemy targets at places with names such as Kojo, Hungnam, Songjin and Chongjin, the latter the northernmost port on the east coast and not far from the Siberian border.

Considerable attention was given to an area called the bombline. That was where the front line met the Sea of Japan and was the only locality where naval gunfire could be employed in direct support of friendly troops. Some of the *New Jersey's* most effective fire was done there, specifically against positions on Anchor Hill where Republic of Korea infantry often found itself engaged.

Late in August, the *New Jersey* took part in a feigned invasion behind enemy lines, a tactic designed to take pressure off ROK troops. In company with the destroyers *Marshall* and *Wedderburn*, the *New Jersey* moved into position and commenced firing as though in prelanding bombardment. The ruse gained credibility by the presence of landing ships standing off farther at sea.

The *New Jersey* made one foray to the western side of the Korean peninsula to shell enemy installations, but most of the naval activity was

Members of 5th Division during WWII (submitted by H.G. Wolochok)

"R" Division 1950-1952 (submitted by Arnold Millman)

off the east coast. That is where the fast carrier task force operated, typically 15 to 20 miles offshore. Task Force 77 ordinarily consisted of two to three Essex-class carriers, one or two heavy warships, a cruiser or the battleship in the theater, and about a dozen destroyers in the screen. The heavies were frequently detached for bombardment missions and spent most of their time within gun range of Korea's rugged coast.

The *New Jersey* concentrated main and secondary battery fire on a variety of targets, including gun emplacements, bunkers, tanks, truck convoys, supply dumps, railroad marshaling yards, trains, bridges and troop concentrations. Fire was spotted and called either by ground observer teams or from the air. Sometimes the spotter observed from the *New Jersey's* own helicopter. Most night-time shelling was harassing fire directed at pre-determined coordinates. The shore fire sometimes encountered, usually came from 76, 90 or 120 millimeter pieces, often hidden in caves. Mines were another potential hazard. When sighted, they usually were sunk by rifle fire.

The ship's helicopter was used for pilot rescue, and it was on such an occasion early in the first tour that the chopper ran out of fuel while trying to find an airman and went down among the ridges near the coast. For three days, there was no word, but eventually the helicopter pilot, Lt. George Tuffanelli, and the crewman, J. B. Williams, hiked out of the hills safely.

In October, while the *New Jersey* shelled the Hamhung-Hungnam area, Tuffanelli rescued a Task Force 77 pilot who had been shot down near Wonsan to the south. The chopper pilot was decorated with the Distinguished Flying Cross.

The battleship was back in Yokosuka on Nov. 17, the Korean tour over. During the six months on line, interrupted only by occasional provisioning trips to one of the Japanese ports, the *New Jersey* fired more than 3,000 rounds of 16-inch ammunition and 39,000 5-inch projectiles. In the process, the battleship made the enemy pay a fearful price in casualties and material damage. The appraisal of observers was that the *New Jersey's* fire was accurate and effective.

While the ship was in Yokosuka, Capt. Tyree was relieved as commanding officer by Capt. Francis D. McCorkle, who would take the big ship home.

#2 Engine Room, 1968 (submitted by Earl Bigelow)

A battleship rotation for combat duty now had been established so that one of the four was in the theater at all times. Next up was the *Wisconsin* to be followed by the *Iowa* and then the *Missouri* again.

Upon the *New Jersey's* return to the United States, the ship went into the Navy yard at Norfolk for overhaul, resumed training and shakedown procedures in the Caribbean and took midshipmen aboard. The *New Jersey* set sail for Europe, making port calls in Cherbourg, France, and Lisbon, Portugal.

The *New Jersey* returned to Korea on April 10, 1953, again relieving the *Missouri*. Only those two battleships among the four made two combat tours during that conflict. The locales for shelling were the same as those during 1951 - the bombline, Kojo, Wonsan, Hungnam and Chongjin, among others. The *New Jersey* also shelled positions on the west coast on the Chinampo peninsula where it came under enemy shore-battery fire.

As before, it was Wonsan where the greatest communist activity was evident. The *New Jersey* pounded a particularly troublesome peninsula called Hodo Pando that guarded the harbor on the north.

The truce talks taking place in the spring and early summer of 1953 did nothing to make the North Koreans and Chinese more docile. Their shore gunners were unusually active at times, but the mere presence of the *New Jersey*, it was found, induced the enemy to hold its fire against smaller warships closer in.

During this tour, the *New Jersey* made port both in Pusan, on the southeast coast of South Korea and Inchon, on the west coast. Both times, South Korean President Syngman Rhee and his wife came aboard.

The negotiators at Pammunjon finally agreed on the terms for a truce, establishing the dividing line between the two warring countries at the existing front lines, which were approximately where they had been in June 1951, somewhat north of the 38th parallel on the east, and south of that latitude on the west. For the signing of the armistice, the *New Jersey* sent a delegation led by Lt. (j.g.) R. G. Spencer.

The *New Jersey* had an even more distinctive honor associated with the end of the fighting, that of firing the last shots. The cease-fire was scheduled for 2200 on July 27, 1953, a fact announced 12 hours earlier. Since the flight of a 16-inch shell was calculated to be one minute at the range involved, the *New Jersey* fired a full nine-gun salvo toward Wonsan, appropriately enough, at precisely one minute until 10 p.m. so that the shells landed at the exact moment the truce took effect.

Those 2,700-pound projectiles were added to the approximately 4,000 fired by the *New Jersey's* main battery during the second tour off Korea.

The end of hostilities before the normal seven-month rotation gave the *New Jersey* time to visit Taiwan and Hong Kong before returning to Pusan in September where Mr. Rhee came aboard and awarded the entire Seventh Fleet the Korean Presidential Unit Citation.

Peacetime duty took the battleship to the Mediterranean before she was decommissioned a second time on Aug. 21, 1957.

Vietnam

Ten years later, the United States was engaged in another major shooting war, in Vietnam, and military leaders recognized the need for firepower only a battleship could provide. None was in commission at the time.

Inspection of the three berthed side-by-side at the Philadelphia Naval Yard - the *New Jersey*, the *Wisconsin* and the *Iowa* - led to the conclusion that the *New Jersey* could be reactivated at the least expense. In June 1967, the process began. It involve removing the preservatives and doing what was necessary to get the machinery and ordnance operating again. The electronics were updated, the 40 millimeter guns removed and a helicopter pad added. As an economy measure, only two of the four engines were placed on line. The emphasis off Vietnam would be on gunnery, not speed.

The complement was much smaller than the 2,400 men who manned the battleship in World War II and Korea. This time, 1,556 enlisted men and 70 officers would form the ship's company. The Navy had no trouble finding them. Volunteers quickly made themselves available for what they considered some of the sea service's most prestigious duty. Even some of the *New Jersey* veterans of the two previous wars asked to come back for another tour of combat duty, but the Navy did not require the services of the retreads.

The captain selected to lead the recommissioned *New Jersey* back into war was Capt. J. Edward Snyder, Jr., Annapolis Class of '45, whose first seagoing assignment had been aboard the battleship *Pennsylvania* in the latter stages of World War II.

New Jersey's third commissioning ceremony was held on April 6, 1968, at a time when the Vietnam War was at or near its peak in ferocity. The fleet had been offshore nearly from the start, but carrier air strikes and the lighter bombardment ships, destroyers and cruisers, were not sufficiently effective against the deeply dug-in North Vietnamese and Viet Cong engaging allied ground troops. The battleship's 16-inch guns were needed.

On May 29, the world's only active battleship left the dock at Norfolk, Va., and headed for the Panama Canal. The fit through the locks was even tighter than usual, because of fenders along the sides, but with the help of mules - an incongruous sight - the great ship emerged into the Pacific.

After stops in Long Beach, Calif., the ship's new home port, and then Pearl Harbor and Subic Bay in the Philippines, the *New Jersey* arrived off Vietnam on Sept. 29 prepared to fight her third war.

The place was the Gulf of Tonkin at the Demilitarized Zone dividing North and South Vietnam. At this point, along the 17th parallel, the country narrows down in such a way that the *New Jersey's* main battery could reach much of the ground combat area where the American 3rd Marine Division was fighting. When the *New Jersey's* big guns roared that day, it marked the first time in 15 years that an American battleship had fired in anger. It was the *New Jersey*, remember, that fired the last shots off Korea in 1953.

For the first day, the expended ammunition was 29 rounds of 16-inch, and 45 rounds of 5-inch, which reportedly achieved good effect against entrenchments, gun positions and supplies. The bombardment was concentrated on the area north-northeast of the U.S. outpost of Con Thien.

Snyder observed that technology had improved the accuracy of the 16-inch guns from times of the *New Jersey's* earlier life. Furthermore, the advantages of such a ship in the kind the war the United States was fighting were obvious. The main battery delivered bomb-like destructive power akin to that of a B-52, but could remain on station and hurl the 2,700-pound projectiles almost indefinitely. It was said that a 16-inch barrage of just a few minutes was the equivalent of half a B-52 bomb load.

The 16-inch shells were capable of burrowing deep into the soft soil of Vietnam, or even into solid rock, before exploding, which gave them a terrible aspect against entrenched troops.

The *New Jersey* remained in and around the DMZ, including North Vietnamese territory to the north, throughout October, but a presidential halt to bombing and shelling of the enemy country forced the battleship to move south down the coast in search of targets of opportunity near Hue, Nha Trang and other places.

Shore batteries could be active off Vietnam, but the communists tended to remain in awe of the big ship and only occasionally sent shells its way. Figuratively, these guns represented little more than bee stings to a ship the size and having the armor protection of the *New Jersey*. However, the Russian-made missile, Styx, was another matter. That 20-foot weapon was capable of inflicting important damage on the battleship, but none ever made an appearance.

Christmas that year brought a top-drawer diversion that had been and continued to be a grand tradition anytime Americans were fighting a war anywhere in the world. The tradition's name is Bob Hope. He and his troupe came aboard the *New Jersey* in 1968 offshore in the South China Sea. They entertained not just the crew of the battleship, but as many ground personnel as could be accommodated on the ship's decks.

After the holidays, the *New Jersey* left the war zone for trips to Yokosuka, Japan, Subic Bay and Singapore. The latter cruise required the crossing of the Equator and therefore the conversion of erstwhile pollywogs into shellbacks in the humiliating and discomforting methods that are in keeping with the age-old tradition of mariners.

The trip from Yokosuka took the *New Jersey* through what was probably the heaviest weather the ship experienced since the typhoons of late World War II. The battleship took green water over its huge bow, causing some topside damage.

The *New Jersey* was back on the firing line Feb. 10, 1969, in support of South Vietnamese Marines south of Da Nang.

By contrast to Korea, naval bombardment off Vietnam was oriented more toward direct support of friendly troops ashore and less toward interdiction of static installations. That is because of the different nature of that conflict, which had no front lines. Thus American and Vietnamese ground units might be engaged with enemy forces anywhere inside the long coastline. In Korea, it is recalled, that was true only in one location.

In Vietnam, for instance, Marines specifically requested as much heavy fire as the *New Jersey* could provide against tunnels where they suspected Viet Cong were hiding. This was done effectively.

A more dramatic mission occurred on Feb. 23 when a contingent of Marines was in danger of being wiped out by a force of about 130 Viet Cong before the *New Jersey* went to work about 1 a.m. The battleship poured main and secondary battery fire into the enemy positions through the remainder of the night. Piles of empty shellcases, the pungent odor of gun powder and the overheated gun barrels told their own story. But the enemy was mauled and the Marines survived. The major in charge of the outpost explicitly credited the *New Jersey* with saving his men.

Capt. Robert C. Peniston, USN departing USS New Jersey *after decommissioning on December 17, 1969, Bremerton, WA (submitted by Robert C. Peniston)*

As the *New Jersey* was about to close out the war-zone tour, the 3rd Marine Division commander put in an urgent call for help, to which the battleship responded by steaming 280 miles to the DMZ and pounding enemy targets for three days. The last shots were fired on March 31.

The output of ammunition during the tour was 5,688 rounds from the main battery and 14,891 from the 5-inch guns. That was a higher ratio of 16-inch to 5-inch than had been demonstrated off Korea, and also represented a much heavier concentration of main battery fire generally than in the earlier war. For instance, in two Korean tours plus midshipment crews, the expenditure of 16-inch shells came to 6,671, while Vietnam's volume occurred essentially in a total of about four months on line.

The value of the *New Jersey's* presence along the Vietnamese coast during those months of 1968-69 was enormous, beyond any question. It could be measured in the number of Americans who survived the war. The Marines and Army personnel ashore, who came to call the *New Jersey* "Big Mama" and to welcome the sound of her shells going overhead, estimated that the battleship saved 100 of their lives for every day she was on station. That is impressive.

When the *New Jersey* left Vietnam and headed back to Long Beach, there remained nearly four years of war and many assumed the BB 62 would make a second appearance off those hostile shores. However, the national administrations had changed and the new Secretary of Defense was Melvin Laird, who as a congressman had opposed spending money to reactivate the *New Jersey*. So in August, he ordered the decommissioning.

Because the battleship had proved itself so effective in support of ground troops, many were disappointed she would not be returning to the war zone.

The *New Jersey* docked in Long Beach on May 5 after a delay in her arrival caused by an unscheduled turnaround while en route. When the North Koreans shot down an American surveillance plane over the Sea of Japan, the *New Jersey* was hastily dispatched to that new point of tension and remained on station for three days before the crisis eased and the homeward journey resumed.

A change in command in August brought Capt. Robert C. Peniston aboard as the new skipper. As a young fourth class midshipman in 1943, Peniston had sailed on the *New Jersey*, then a brand-new ship about to go to war. In 1946, as a freshly minted ensign, Peniston's first assignment was aboard the *New Jersey*. Now he was the ships' captain - but unfortunately not for long.

In September, the *New Jersey* headed for Bremerton, Wash., and mothballs. The veteran of three wars was decommissioned on Dec. 17.

Lebanon

Despite the longest hiatus yet, 13 years as it turned out, permanent retirement still was not in the cards for the USS *New Jersey*. The new presidency of the defense-minded Ronald Reagan in 1981 revived the fortunes of all four Iowa-class battleships. Recognition was general that despite their age, the ships remained the most formidable instruments afloat for the delivery of a surface punch against targets ashore.

Thus for the *New Jersey*, resurrection day came on Dec. 28, 1982, with President Reagan presiding at the recommissioning ceremony. It was not quite the old *New Jersey*, however. Upgrading included removing four of the five-inch mounts and the addition of missile systems - Harpoons and Tomahawks. Four Phalanx Close-In Weapons Systems also were added.

The following summer, while the *New Jersey* was sailing the Western Pacific on a planned three-month shakedown cruise, more urgent business was at hand. The chronic Middle East violence was boiling over and U.S. Marines were in a vulnerable position.

The *New Jersey* was in port in Thailand when the word came: expedite in sailing eastward. The ship passed through the Panama Canal, the Caribbean and into the Atlantic and Mediterranean, arriving off Lebanon on Sept. 25, 1983.

The mission to Lebanon became the fourth shooting war for the *New Jersey* on Dec. 14, 1983, when the ship fired 11 16-inch shells at Syrian gun positions. It was the first shots from the ship against hostile forces since the spring of 1969 off Vietnam.

The next night, the secondary battery of 5-inchers opened up against positions firing on the American Marines. Intermittent fire support efforts continued through the early part of the following year, the heaviest barrage occurring on Feb. 8 when 288 16-inch rounds were directed toward the hills behind Beirut.

The *New Jersey* was relieved by the *Iowa* on April 2 after having spent 170 of the previous 191 days on station in the Eastern Mediterranean. When the battleship docked in Long Beach on May 5, 1984, it was the 15th anniversary of her arrival home from Vietnam, and at the same port.

The *New Jersey's* fighting days were over, but she remained in commission for nearly seven more years. Finally, on Feb. 8, 1991, in Long Beach, the old battleship was decommissioned for the last time. The man of war had been awarded 16 battle stars, the most ever for a U.S. Navy ship, from her four wars.

The ship now rests in the Bremerton naval yard alongside the mothballed *Missouri*. Across the continent, in Philadelphia, are the *Iowa* and the *Wisconsin*.

The four ships' names also have been removed from the Registry of Naval Ships. It is the hope of two organizations, the Battleship Commission and the Battleship *New Jersey* Historical Museum Society, that the *New Jersey* some day can be brought around to the East Coast and serve as a floating naval museum in Liberty State Park in Jersey City, N.J.

At least one, preferably, all, of the Iowa-class battleships should be preserved, so that present and future generations can appreciate what arguably were the greatest naval warships any nation ever built were like.

To review: Their active service spanned almost a half century each and one or all fought in every war from World War II to the Persian Gulf. To put it in perspective, that is the equivalent of a ship built in the 1890s still able to perform front-line duty with the fleet in World War II.

There was hardly a sea combat function in which the battleship did not demonstrate its unique value. The 16-inch guns were unparalleled weapons for surface engagement and shore bombardment. Because of the sheer volume of anti-aircraft fire the ships could throw up, they were ideal for carrier task force protection. And they had no trouble keeping up. Finally, when missiles became the primary weapons of war, no better platform for launch could be found than those heavily armored dreadnoughts.

The wistful belief of battleship sailors, indeed Navy men of all descriptions, is that even at 50 years old, the *New Jersey* and her sisters were forced to retire before their potential usefulness in their nation's service had expired.

USS New Jersey, *Long Beach, CA, 1987 (submitted by B.J. Klein)*

USS *New Jersey*: A Chronology

1940, September	Keel laid
1942, December	Launched
1943, May	Commissioned at Philadelphia Naval Shipyard
1944, January	Joined the Fifth Fleet in the Pacific
1944, August	Became ADM "Bull" Halsey's flagship
1945, August	Became ADM Spruance's flagship
1947 June-August	Part of the first training squadron in the North Atlantic since the beginning of World War II
1948, June	Decommissioned at Bayonne, NJ/ assigned to the Atlantic Reserve Fleet
1950, November	Recommissioned at Bayonne, NJ
1951, May	Became Seventh Fleet flagship off Korea
1953, April	Rejoined Seventh Fleet as flagship off Korea
1955, September	Joined the Sixth Fleet in the Mediterranean
1957, August	Decommissioned at Bayonne, NJ
1968, April	Recommissioned at Philadelphia Naval Shipyard
1968, September	Began tour off the coast of Vietnam
1969, December	Decommissioned at Puget Sound Naval Shipyard, Bremerton, WA
1982, December	Recommissioned by President Reagan at Long Beach, CA
1983, June-1984, May	Deployed to the Western Pacific, Central America, and to duty with the Sixth Fleet in support of U.S. forces of the Multi-National Peace keeping Force in Beirut, Lebanon
1985, May-October	Deployed to the Western Pacific as centerpiece of the first Battleship Battle Group to deploy to the Western Pacific since the Korean Conflict
1987, February-October	In dry dock, Long Beach Naval Shipyard
1988, July-November	Deployed to the Western Pacific to stage pre-Olympic presence operations and to participate in the Australian Bicentennial
1989, September- 1990, February	Participated in PacEx and deployed to the Western Pacific and Indian Oceans as flagship for Commander, Cruiser Destroyer Group One, becoming the first battleship to enter and operate in the Persian Gulf.
1991, February	Final decommissioning

Statistics

Class:	IOWA- class battleship
Length:	887 feet, 7 inches
Height:	209 feet
Beam:	108 feet, 1 inch
Draft:	38 feet
Displacement:	57,200 tons fully loaded
Boilers:	Eight 600 PSI Babcock and Wilcox
Main Engines:	Four geared Westinghouse turbines
Horsepower:	212,000 shaft horsepower (total all four shafts)
Propellers:	Two five-bladed 17 feet 5 inches (inboard)
	Two four-bladed 18 feet 3 inches (outboard)
Rudders:	Two 21 feet high
Speed:	In excess of 33 knots
Tank Capacity:	2,402,922 gallons of fuel oil (F-76)
	64,966 gallons of diesel oil
	32,644 gallons of aviation fuel (JP 5)
	209,076 gallons of fresh water
	132,133 gallons of boiler feed water
Anchors:	Two anchors, port and starboard bow, each weighing 30,000 pounds. Each anchor chain is 12 shots or 1,080 feet long and each link weighs about 110 pounds.
Armor:	The main armor belt is encased in the hull from the aft turret to the second forward turret. It is 13.5 inches thick and tapers vertically to 1.62 inches. Aft, the steering machinery is boxed in 13.5 inches of armor. Other armor thicknesses are:

Conning tower sides	17.3 inches
Turret faces	17 inches
Turret backs	12 inches
Turret sides	9.25 inches
Turret tops	7.25 inches
Second deck	6 inches

Personnel:	WWII:	134 officers, 2,400 enlisted
	1991:	Navy: 70 officers, 1,400 enlisted
		Marine Corps: 2 officers, 61 enlisted

From Philly to Tokyo, War Cruise of the USS *New Jersey* (BB 62)

By Charles W. Frank, Capt., USNR (Ret.)

Foreword: From Philly to Tokyo

Fifty years have passed since I stood on the fantail of the USS *New Jersey*, BB 62, a bright eyed and eager young ensign, fresh out of Tulane University, with a DEVG (deck and engineering, volunteer general) Commission from the N.R.O.T.C. and a degree in Chemical Engineering tucked under my arm. The *Jersey* was moored starboard side-to, in the Philadelphia Navy Yard. For the past weeks we had worked around the clock to clear the ship of "yard birds" and their welding torches, trying to bring some semblance of order to a man-o-war. She was a sleeping, gray, steel, giant swathed in the coils of shorebased power lines with air driven spray guns spitting paint at her massive hull. Finally she was ready for Commissioning.

Charles Edison, Governor of the State of New Jersey, was piped aboard to deliver the Commissioning address to the crew. Smartly turned out in dress whites we stood at attention under a broiling sun. It was a blistering day, that May 23rd. Pitch bubbled from the caulking of her teak decking. As Captain Carl F. Holden, U.S.N., took command, the commissioning pennant was hoisted, a slim red, white and blue streamer that fluttered from the peak of the main mast. The colors were hoisted, a bugle sounded, a band played the National Anthem and we were a part of the Fleet.

What a mixed emotion that memory brings. This effort to recall those days of service brings to mind not bloody combat, but the memory of friendships forged in common dangers shared. The *New Jersey*, for all her steaming in the South Pacific and the North Atlantic, was remarkably lucky to have avoided any serious casualties. The thoughts that are paramount as I reach seventy-four years of age, are of friendship, of a lifestyle that the sailor of the WWII era lived, and of lessons that the regular Navy drummed into the heads of a bunch of "muddy water sailors."

I've never been much of a drinker, but the night before commissioning, I celebrated with a bunch of young officers at the Bellvue Stratford Hotel. The Officer's Club there was a scene of revelry that seamen have indulged in since the Vikings set forth in their longboats for an uncharted new world. Laughter and shouts, as young shipmates vied with one another to buy another round of drinks.

Young Philadelphia society girls were in bright cocktail dresses. There was candlelight on the white table cloths and fresh flowers lent a touch of spring to the surroundings. Beautiful young women shared the evening with equally young officers, resplendant in dress whites - shoulderboards and gold braid reflected in sparkling eyes. It was an era when we forgot for a moment that the fates might snatch us away, and we lived for the moment in an aura of pleasure at just being young and alive.

Charles W. Frank, Capt., USNR (Ret.)

This is not a tale of thunderous battles fought in the bloody Hell of Naval combat. It is the recollection of the memories of a young commissioned officer, on a ship that with God's blessing, came through the eye of a typhoon, and nine major engagements with the Japanese fleet untouched. We were one of the lucky ones. I've taken liberties with my memories, perhaps stretching the facts and misplacing events, but by and large those of you who served on the *Jersey* from 1943 until she sailed for home in 1946 will know the basic truths of what I've recorded.

The morning of May 23, 1943 was time for me to pay for my sins. My night of celebration with Ensign Bob Parker, a Tulane University classmate, at the Bellvue Stratford, left me with one grand hang-over. I remember fragments of the Governor's speech, the ranks in pressed whites, the officers standing proudly before the admiring glances of civilian guests. More vividly a spinning sun and flashing lights as I held on grimly to a 20-mm gun tub, praying I wouldn't disgrace myself. When Commander Pete McDowell, U.S.N., the Executive Officer, gave the order for Division Commanders to dismiss their men, I was one sick sailor. Somehow I made it to my quarters and as I washed my face in tepid water, heard my name called on the 1MC to report to the Gunnery Officer's office.

I checked my dress whites, squared my hat and presented myself to the "gun boss", Commander Rufus Rose, U.S.N. He requested that I report to the Captain's cabin to escort one of the young lady visitors, daughter of a New Jersey Senator, about the ship. She was a cute young thing and bubbling with enthusiasm until I mentioned that I had just gotten married and my wife was joining me in another few weeks. Most of the rest of the short tour was rather subdued. I was reeling with a sick headache and she had only too obviously lost all interest in my company. Finally, with great relief on my part, she disappeared into the Captain's quarters. My head splitting, I vowed "never again."

Some forty odd years later the sun again brightened a tranquil bay. The *New Jersey* lay alongside a dock, across a continent, and an eon in time from Philadephia. The *New Jersey* was in the Long Beach Naval Shipyard and had just completed her fourth commissioning ceremony.

She had served in three wars and once again a new crew was preparing to take her out on "shake-down". Her brightwork gleamed, dull burnished gold in the sunlight, and I looked at another generation of youngsters whose lives would be forever imprinted by service aboard her. Her deck watch and her sailors looked so very young.

I was a retired Captain in the Naval Reserve and was escorted aboard to meet her latest Commanding Officer. Captain William M. Fogarty was part of the new Navy. An N.R.O.T.C. graduate of Georgia Tech, he was one of many officers given a major command and slated for flag ranks in what had been an exclusive Naval Academy Club during WWII. Her crew was less than half of the WW II compliment. Her 40mm and 20mm batteries had been replaced with four Phalanx rapid fire weapons capable of target acquisition and tracking we had never dreamed of.

The smokeless powder catapults that had hurled her OS2U float aircraft aloft as spotters during WWII are gone. Her catalpults are replaced with a helipad and her Kingfisher float planes are long ago retired, relics of an era that has passed. The Pacific Ocean and the skies of my generation were of another world. The airplane crane that lifted planes aboard after a mission and the gun tubs that housed a battery of two 40-mm quads stuck on her fantail, are missing. Where are the smiling faces of her aviators- Harris, Ethridge, Charlie Nobel and Goodpasture? Walking her decks, the men of past crews who were on board again seemed subdued, lost in the reverie of fierce air battles when Kamikazes swirled and dove at the Fleet. The thunder of the 5-inch battery and the sharp reports of 40 and 20-mm weapons was in the back of their minds. Their footsteps wandered about the walkways and passages they had run through generations ago. Faces and names kept coming back. Were these old men the youngsters who served together and became men aboard this battle wagon? Another crew of "feather merchants" and a cadre of regulars will once again take her to sea, serving our Nation and maturing - better men, as Navy discipline leaves its mark.

Yes, the 40-mm and 20-mm weapons are gone. One half of the 5-inch thirty eights are missing, but the new technology, allows a projection of firepower that is awesome.

Phalanx machine guns, capable of firing thousands of rounds a minute, are mounted on each quarter. Satellite navigation antenna bristle from her yardarms. Telecommunications gear hooked into orbiting units permit defenses and power projection unheard of in World War II. I feel a pang of regret that we could not join her on this next cruise - to feel again her gentle roll, her bow slicing through uncharted waters.

She's a grand lady, wearing a new gown, and ready to dance with her latest paramours. The great adventure begins again, and a task as demanding as any she's ever faced.

The sailors of yesteryear were just beginning to venture into the world of high technology. The sailor of today must be computer literate, and knowledgeable in marlinspike seamanship if he is to survive. Target acquisition and target tracking are more fully automated. As I hear words like "Tomahawk" and "Harpoon", a feeling of wonder steals over me. What awesome power these young warriors command. MIRV'ed (multiple intercontinental rockets, programmed for as many as ten nuclear targets), warheads tipped with nuclear weapons that could destroy targets a hemisphere away.

The odor seems the same. Diesel oil leaves its imprint. The smell brings back memories of sailors and marines scrambling to General Quarters, the claxon screaming and the Bos'un piping "Now all hands to General Quarters. Man your battle stations." A bugle sounding Torpedo Defense over the MC, the rush to man the secondary battery. These are the thoughts those odors evoke. The smell of smokeless powder and the piles of brass cases to be kicked overside after an engagement, residue of thousands of rounds she hurled skyward in moments of air attack. I dream of the awesome blast of a 16-inch broadside, each barrel pushing 2,700 pounds of high explosive and steel, enough recoil to push her massive 86,000 tons sideways some 18 inches.

Memories are softened by the years, but I dream of signal halyards flapping as the Jersey swings her bow to starboard, racing into the wind to launch aircraft. The smell of salt air fills my dream, and we steam at flank speed toward an invisible foe, long vanquished.

Looking through Officers' Country for the cabin I shared for several years with Lt. L.L. "Larry" Moorman, I find it has been converted into a storage locker. So much for dreams of glory. In front of the locker, two Warrant Officers share the cabin the Fourth and Fifth Division officers occupied those years ago.

Her complement today is 1,500 men and 67 officers. In WWII she was manned by 2,500 blue jackets, 167 officers and a staff of some 60 to 80 additional personnel if a Flag Officer was aboard. Admiral William F. Halsey, Admiral Raymond Spruance, Admirals O.C. Badger and Willis A. Lee, all chose her for their flagship during her tour in the South Pacific.

The day I reported aboard in early 1943, I was her most junior Ensign. It began a learning process that I shall always cherish. As it did with me, the Navy, and the *Jersey* have trained four generations of young Americans, helping them to serve with pride and honor, fitting an order and discipline into their lives. It has made us better men. She has more than justified her cost!

I pray that she will serve her succeeding tours of duty defending the principles on which our Nation is founded. Her's is the spirit on which freedom hinges.

The officers and men who served on her shakedown and first wartime patrols (1943-45), epitomized a dedication to service that was and is her hallmark. Speak to her veterans of WWII, Korea, or Vietnam, of her patrols off Honduras and Lebanon and they uniformly reflect the pride and dignity of their service. It puts to shame those who question or berate the services for their burden to the taxpayer. If we are to continue to man the ramparts for peace and the dignity of all mankind, we must pay the price, preparing for a battle we hope we'll never have to fight.

The armaments, offensive and defensive, that the *New Jersey* and her sisters have been re-equipped with, may well be the means to negate hostilities. We have been the unique wardens of past generations. Never has the overwhelming power we control been used to seek self aggrandizement. Frequently we have exercised a restraint that no other nation in history has matched. Quick, sometimes too quick, to self criticisms, we still have been the beneficent patron of many less powerful and less affluent nations. If the billions we spend on foreign aid were to be applied to our military we would forever dominate the power structure of world politics.

Historian and author, Herman Wouk, whose epic novel *The Winds of War*, became a national best seller, commented on the events that precipitated WWII. Touring our Minute Man missile sites and our fleet equipped with sophisticated guidance programs and powerful rockets with multiple re-entry nuclear war heads, he was depressed to see how little the world has learned from history. The state of the art electronics for surveillance of our possible foes and a number of weapons that could deliver unbelievable destruction to pre-programmed targets, were manned by men no older than his son. His revulsion was profound, but he missed the lesson we have hopefully learned. The deterrent force we have used so judiciously these past years stands between the free world and Armageddon. The Russians, in spite of their new image have been longtime practitioners of power politics. The world still lives by the dictum, "The price of freedom is eternal vigilance." Herman Wouk served in the Navy during WWII and his son served in the Israeli Navy. The training and discipline this service engenders is priceless. The literary success of Wouk is no accident. Those who would lead must first serve.

The Mongols, the Tartars, the Huns and the Nazis could not have overrun the world, except for the weakness of men of good will. Perhaps someday we'll find a way out of the closed loop of an arms race, but until then be grateful for ships like the *New Jersey*, and the young men who sail her.

I dedicate this saga to the young men of her new crew, their greening, like mine, will hopefully lead to a happier time. A time when we will recognize that "service" is the most wonderful word in the dictionary.

I've used names that were invented in some cases to avoid any possible embarrassment to those who were the butt of pranks they might want to forget. This might be especially true when the pranks might not reflect the "highest traditions of Naval service." Some of the dates and events may vary by a day or so from action reports officially recorded, and if this is so, remember a diary during those hectic times wasn't always done on a daily basis. Fatigued from frequent calls to General Quarters it is easy to make errors of this kind. What I've tried to do is to record the reaction of a reserve officer on his first tour of duty. It was a great experience, one that has served me well.

There have been several books published about the *New Jersey*. What am I trying to do by writing another? I think a record should be made of more than just the revelations of battle. A time and place where so many of us look back and hope that faith and values we took for granted can somehow be restored. I know this is a dream, but it is a dream I find worth hoping for. Can it somehow be made a reality? Quoting an old friend, "We must record the past to shape the future."

These recollections were frequently enhanced by officers and men from past crews of the *New Jersey*. Many the shipmate I met with at reunions or heard from on their passage through New Orleans. Quite a few are gone to their reward and I can only hope they'll look down with a smile at the days when we were all so very, very young.

I'd like to thank George Morse, Captain Tim Wooldridge (Son of Captain later Vice Admiral E.T. Woolderidge), Lt. Jim Evans, Lt.Cmdr. Harry Reynolds, and Captain Jack McCormick, John Rossie, Capt. Thompson, Capt. Penniston and a host of others for details, memorabilia and recollections that were always welcomed.

I have used the term "JAP" frequently in this tale. Today the ethnic sensitivity of our society will perhaps frown on this term. However, this was the way we spoke during the great conflict that was WWII. American servicemen and women were engaged in a life and death struggle with a brutal and courageous enemy. It was a time when our national existance was on the line and to change the sentiments that led to victory would be an injustice to those who gave their lives in defense of our freedom.

History of Ships Named New Jersey

The USS *New Jersey*, BB 62 was not the first to bear the name. A lot of Naval history is buried in the dusty archives of the Navy Department. When I began to research this work, I was delighted at the vast amount of data relating to this and every ship that has proudly borne our colors, available in the ships' history section of the Office of the Chief of Naval Operations. I was pleased at the willingness of the staff, to furnish at nominal cost, any and all data requested. It made my task a lot more enjoyable and refreshed my seventy year old memory with facts in which I might very well have erred.

This chapter is an excerpt from those files, shortened, but extremely interesting.

In April of 1902, the keel of *New Jersey* BB -16 was laid. She was built by the Fore River Shipbuilding Company, of Quincy, Massachusetts. Launched 10 November 1904, she was placed in Commission 12 May 1904. The time of construction, some 20 months was just a few months longer than the 16 months between laying the keel and the launching of BB-62. Captain William W. Kimball, USN was her first Commanding Officer.

With an overall length of just 441 feet, she was one half as long as her sister in 1943. Her beam was 76 feet, one third less than her later sister BB-62. Her draft was just short of 24 feet, her designed speed of 19 knots surprisingly close to the cruising speed of the *New Jersey* (BB-62) during her War Cruise of 1943-1946.

A complement of 40 Officers and 772 men was roughly one third of our WWII complement. Most of the difference was in the anti-aircraft batteries, needed to man the WWII close in fire support furnished by her 40 mm and 20 mm weapons system. Four 12 inch 40 caliber guns, eight 8-inch 45 caliber guns, twelve 6-inch 50 caliber guns, twelve 3-inch 50 caliber guns, twelve 3-pounder, two 1-pounder, six 30 caliber guns and four submerged 21 inch torpedo tubes made the old behemoth literally bristle with weaponry. Her armored box was 12 inches thick, her shaft horsepower listed at 19,000. The *New Jersey* of the 1940's developed 108,000 shaft horse power.

After a review in Oyster Bay by President Theodore Roosevelt, BB 16 trained along the New England Coast, home porting first in Providence and later in Boston.

In September of 1906 she was stationed in Havana, protecting American lives during the Cuban insurection. In mid October she returned to the continental United States, training in Boston, Newport, and Norfolk, and sailing for battle practice in the Caribbean.

As a part of the Great White Fleet, she stood out of Hampton Roads the morning of 16 December 1907. Passing in review before President Thedore Roosevelt on the *Mayflower*, her sailors manned the rail while a 21 gun salute was fired. Thus began the cruise that established the beginning of our dominion of the oceans of the world.

Circling South America, she stopped at almost every major port, Trinidad, Rio, Buenos Aires, Punta Arenas, Valpariso and Callao. She was welcomed with open hearts and minds wherever she stopped.

On 7 July 1908 the Great White Fleet stood out of San Francisco making calls in the Hawaiian Islands enroute to Auckland New Zealand.

Everywhere the *Jersey* sailed she was greeted with a landscape covered with wildly cheering throngs. The Star Spangled Banner was played over and over for a crew proudly at attention.

A destroyer comes alongside for refueling. This was in the South Atlantic, summer of '43. Note the long sleeves and early configuration of the bed-spring radar. Also, the radar on Sky-1 lacks the rocker arm that was added to give an angle of elevation on incoming aircraft.

In Sydney, Australia the Prime Minister welcomed the Great White Fleet and hosted a dance for the crews in the Town Hall. The Prime Minister remarked: "No other flag but that of Great Britain would receive such a welcome as we are extending to the United States Fleet. May our cordiality convince our King that the great strength of battleships counts for less than the invisible ties drawing us together, united in our affection in our heritage of freedom and in humane ideals."

On 19 September 1908, the Fleet visited in Manila and on 18 October the Fleet with the *New Jersey* entered Tokyo Harbor. The following day her Officers visited Tokyo where a reception was held in the favorite garden of the Empress. Thousands of Japanese bowed respectfully and repeated the only English phrase they knew-"We are glad to see you.".

School children had tried to master the Star Spangled Banner but found it easier to sing Hail Columbia. "Welcome" blazed from electric lights and whale oil lamps in every town and hamlet.

Next stop was Amoy, China where huge pavilions had been constructed to seat some five hundred sailors in each tent. Thousands of men were employed to construct two huge Chinese theaters. Here the crews of the Fleet were regally entertained.

Returning to the Philippines the Fleet fired on target ranges, before departing for the Suez Canal enroute to Port Said in Egypt.

Calls at Naples, Italy, Villefrance and Gibralta concluded, the fleet finally headed for a grand review in Hampton Roads, Virginia. President Theodore Roosevelt welcomed the Fleet. Her epic voyage was over.

The *Jersey Bounce*, newsletter of the *New Jersey* Veterans Association recently reported that Jennings Berttheard who served on the BB -16 from October 1917 to May 1918 as a Quartermaster 3rd Class, is 91 years old and resides in Carrierer, MS. He may be the last veteran from our illustrious forbearer. The tie that binds us to the past is a bond that will insure the future.

Chapter 1: Pre-commissioning and Shakedown

Our *New Jersey* was born in the drafting rooms of the New York Shipyard in Brooklyn. Her design started in the thirties, and some of her officers were vintage Mustangs from that austere time. One of these men was Lt. Harry Reynolds, U.S.N. He came aboard as a part of the fledgling Engineering Department in 1940, when the *New Jersey's* keel was laid in the Philadelphia Naval Shipyard. His title was Assistant Engineering Officer from 1940 until 10 May 1943 when the *New Jersey*, BB62 was commissioned.

I can laugh now about my first impression of Harry. A dour little man, he was a reflection of the best of the peace time Navy. All business and with a mind as sharp as any I've ever known, we all revered him, but thought he was older than God. He was one of those men who looked like he was always dressed for Captain's inspection- and he probably was. I asked him at a reunion in 1984 how old he was when I came aboard in 1943. He gave me a wry smile and said, "I was forty." Damn it, he hadn't changed a lot but some of us sure had. He wore his 80-odd years with that same look of confidence that was evident to all the young men he taught in '43.

Reporting for duty, we had a whole new world to adjust to. "Roger, WILCO" became second nature, and the language of old salts and the phonetic alphabet were quickly "de regeur". We struggled manfully to learn strange sounds

Transfer by breeches buoy for personnel and mail sacks was the order of the day whenever new ships joined the formation. A heavy sea and rolling and pitching decks could make a transfer quite an adventure. Seamen strained on line tending details to keep the transfer dry.

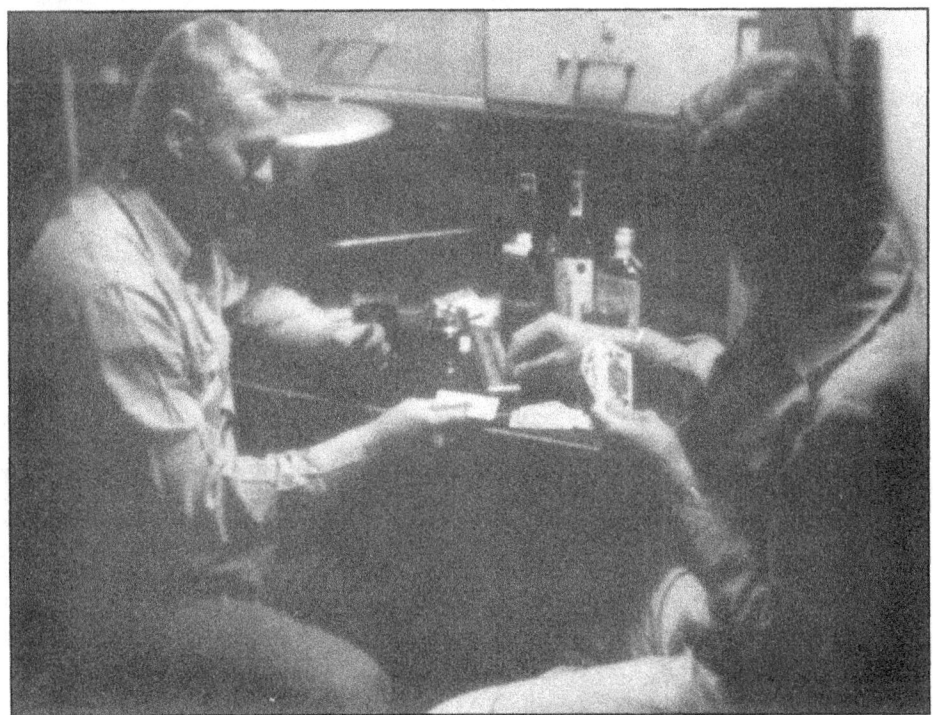

Larry Moorman and Charles Frank play cribbage before the evening alert. Note the bottles of Boca Chica Rum. Neither one of us were drinkers, but the illegality of a jigger mixed with a Coke (ice supplied by John Rossie) was too great a temptation to resist.

from the boatswain's pipe and to react to bugle calls, blasted out from the ship's PA system from reveille to taps.

Summoned to tasks night and day, we slowly became a crew. Uniform of the day, plan of the day, and the ship's newsletter became paramount. We shifted to dress whites from dress blues as the temperature in Philadelphia soared into the high nineties. Admiral "Bull" Halsey was in the Pacific, and had set the tone of war there. No dress whites, uniforms with ties off, short sleeves, dungarees and khakis. A far piece removed from the Atlantic Theater. The Jerseyman, in the Philadelphia Navy Yard, stood Officer of the Deck watches in dress whites, a .45 cal. Colt on his web belt, and carried a long glass under his arm. Sailors on deck watch looked like they could pose for a recruiting poster. Smartly turned out in whites, still using the front buttoned trousers and with few of the amenities in the berthing spaces that todays sailors take for granted.

I remember standing a Junior Officer of the Watch with my Colt .45 slung a bit low so that I could do a normal fast draw. The tight belt position and a holster design that originated in WWI was too high for practical use. The Officer of the Deck, a Trade School type, about six months my senior, gave me a snotty look and said "Two block that weapon Mister." He'll never know how much I wanted to kick his ass over the side. It was tough sometimes to shed our civilian habits, but the Trade School boys, and the Chiefs and Warrants (lifers) taught us and we quickly learned. A W*atch Officer's Guide* was kept on the Quarterdeck in case honors were required, or a question of protocol needed a quick look. Sailors studied the *Blue Jacket's Manual* and drills were constantly repeated. We loaded stores and tried to clear the ship of "yard-birds" as quickly as possible. A four hour deck watch in dress whites left you limp and exhausted. It was so hot that the tar used in caulking the teak decks stuck to white shoes and sweat stained the collars of dress whites.

We were still civilians in a Navy uniforms, and one beautiful summer evening, in the Philly Navy Yard, I was making my evening check of crews quarters with a CPO named Connally. He was a real salty character, a man who would have been commissioned long ago- but, the rule of the day made an indiscretion years ago, a mark that no "officer and a gentleman" code could forgive. Like the great character he was, Connally never seemed to regret his inability to be commissioned. Suddenly the bugler sounded off. Connally snapped to attention, smartly rendering a salute. Puzzled, but not to be caught wanting, I saluted with him. "Wasn't that call 'Watertight doors', Chief?" "Yes Sir." he replied. "Chief, do you always salute on that call?" "No Sir." He smiled, "Sometimes I do and sometimes I don't." I never saluted on "Water-tight doors" again.

The New York Shipyard was the design center for the *Iowa* class battleships (*Iowa* BB62, *New Jersey* BB63, *Missouri* BB64, and the *Wisconsin* BB65). This class was officially listed as a 45,000 ton battleships and was and is the most advanced naval platform for the projection of sea power. Her actual gross tonnage when carrying full bunkers and full ammunition magazines, was closer to 84,000 tons. Her main battery was nine sixteen inch rifles, each hurling a projectile weighing 2,700 pounds for an accurate delivery at ranges to 25,000 yards. Her secondary battery of ten five inch thirty eight twins, and her eighty 20mm and twenty forty mm quads could hurl so much anti aircraft fire skyward that a night engagement from a topside station felt as though you were standing in the middle of Hell.

There was a healthy rivalry between the crew of the *New Jersey* and the *Iowa*. It started with the keel laying of the *Iowa* in Brooklyn some three months before the *Jersey's* keel was laid in Philadelphia. The race, to see which yard could put their wagon in commission first, began.

The months passed and the New York yard was leading the way. Her plans and design changes were tied to the Navy's need for more capital ships. This encouraged a constant pressure to get the ships commissioned. Our Philadelphia yard personnel picked up mistakes and changes in plans and worked in close concert with the engineers and draftsmen in Brooklyn, but this took a bit more time. It was an excellent system, and expedited the progress of what had become a race to the wire. Brooklyn was very touchy about the progress being reported from the Philly Navy Yard, and Harry Reynolds, Assistant Engineering Officer, saw a wonderful opportunity to insert a "burr under Brooklyn's saddle."

What Harry and his cohorts did was to persuade the Ship's Lieutenant to install a small upright donkey boiler in the forward stack. A whistle was installed on the fore structure and a steam line rigged to actuate the whistle. When the *New Jersey* slid majestically down the ways a few months later, smoke poured out of the stack and the whistle signaled to New York that the *Jersey* had power and a boiler on the line.

New York was furious and accused Philadelphia of withholding material manufactured in their yard but pre-consigned to the *Iowa*. Priorities had apparently been ignored and things for awhile got out of hand. After the launch, the pranksters assured their rather crestfallen friends that no priorities had been violated, the whistle signaled nothing and a good laugh was enjoyed by all.

The 1983 reunion of the *New Jersey* in Los Angles brought together a number of plank owners (men who had put the ship in commission the first time). We decided to informally survey the ship and see what modifications had been effected over these past forty years. The engineers noted that the ship was burning distillate instead of the thick black bunker oil used in 1943. This allowed the boilers to operate a lot longer and more maintenance free. The distillate has almost the same viscosity as diesel fuel and could be burned without pre-heating. It could be used at room temperature, and is cleaner burning and a lot less dangerous around the boiler fronts.

After three wars and a lot of time laid up in mothballs she could still match or slightly exceed the engineering standards her original commissioning crew had established on trial runs off Rockland Maine in 1943. Her sea keeping qualities and speed of 33 to 34 knots make her a match for any of her newer sisters.

Harry Reynolds recalled: "One thing I'll never forget was that in heavy weather no ship could match her performance. Her handling in gale force winds was superior to any of the carriers or cruisers in her Task Group. If the weather got heavy we had to slow down in order for the rest of the Fleet to keep up with us. Once when we were laying off Guam, the Admiral on a carrier rang up thirty knots. The *Alabama*, a *South Dakota* class battleship had a flank speed of 27 knots. The ships in the Task Group started to pick up speed, and the *Alabama* was quickly left astern. When the Task Group reached thirty knots the *Alabama* was a speck on the horizon. We literally ran away from her."

On 10 May of 1943 I reported to the precommissioning detail in the Philadelphia Navy Yard. My first day was spent being interviewed by a crusty (I thought) chief engineering officer and a gun boss who was a spit and polish Naval Academy type. To my surprise I was given an offer of assignment from both. I had to make a decision as to deck or engineering duty. My commission was DEVG, which translated into "qualified for deck or engineering duty, volunteer, general." I hardly felt qualified for anything, but thought I'd like to learn more about gunnery. I knew my degree in chemical engineering would allow me to request EDO (engineering duty only), a classification in short supply. I was given a stack of ships organization manuals and plans to begin my familiarization. Sipping hot coffee in the wardroom, I spent the next couple of days trying to familiarize myself with the ships anti-aircraft battery.

Assigned by the gunnery officer to the Fifth Division, the starboard 5 inch battery, I found myself working about as many hours as I could stay awake, and enjoying every minute of it. Most of the officers in my division were back from a tour in the war theaters of the North Atlantic or the South Pacific and all they wanted was a chance to relax, get to Washington or New York for the weekend and raise as much hell as possible. Since my bride of some eight days was in New Orleans finishing her junior year in college, I was happy to take the duty every week end. In a few months, I learned a great deal. Setting myself the chore of walking every compartment on the ship, I spent almost a full week checking off each compartment from the ship's plans we were issued. This was no small task. She was bulkheaded every few yards and the passageways below deck were rather small for my six foot four inch body. I left a lot of skin on those hatches.

Junior officer accommodations were filled and I was assigned a berth in warrant officer's country. This was a break for me. Here, I got to know the best qualified men aboard ship. Their years of service were long and we jokingly referred to them as "lifers." The warrant officer's bunk room was in the forward section of the *Jersey*, just abaft the sail locker. Here my bunk was separated from the ocean by one thin sheet of steel. Voids (compartments in which fuel oil and water could be stored, forming a protective outer defense against torpedo damage) didn't begin until much further aft. It took a bit of getting used to. The sound of waves washing against the bulkhead was rather disquieting when I thought about U-boats on the prowl. But, after a few restless nights I found it rather soothing and slept like a babe in arms.

One of my first assignments as personnel officer of the Fifth Division was to select one hundred and fifty odd men who would make up our complement. Setting off for the receiving pool with a list of parameters I felt were necessary, my idea of what the average sailor looked like and what his educational background should be was to be sadly off the mark. There were 3,900 mostly seamen recruits, right out of boot camp in the pool. I wanted a physical individual, weighing 175 pounds or more, with a high school education. After going through 3,900 service records, I was forced to lower minimum weight and high school education to 155 pounds and some high school. There were more minor scrapes with authority than diplomas in the records. The men selected were thrilled to be a part of the *Jersey's* crew and their enthusiasm was infectious. But it was a shock to try teaching recruits to read dials in minutes and seconds of angle when many only knew these words to denote time. A gun pointer or trainer was selected quickly if he knew the difference.

I teamed up with Chief J. Connally, U.S.N., a Gunner's Mate. A professional Navy man, he was one of the finest men I have ever been privileged to serve with. He was preparing the data for the firing cut out cams on the starboard five inch battery and I asked if I could work with him. We would train and elevate the mounts in manual, recording a bearing several degrees short of the line of fire striking the superstructure. This was recorded by angle of deflection and elevation. The machinists in the Philadelphia Navy Yard cut the cams for us to install and check. These devices electrically broke the firing circuit on any bearing that could endanger the ship's superstructure or personnel. Although not normally an officer's task, I learned a great deal about the weapons and the men who would man them- and, a lasting admiration for Connally.

Time flew by and in June, my Jean joined me. What an eye opener to finances this posed! Ensigns were getting one hundred and twenty five dollars a month and a married officers allowance of another fifty dollars. Seaman recruits were drawing about $60.00 a month and quite a few of them were married. This was not enough to board at the Bellevue Stratford at seventeen bucks a night. Most of us just weren't smart enough to figure this out. We were heading for a big problem. One evening, gazing with the look of newlyweds at one another, I handed her a love letter, a one way ticket to New Orleans and a twenty dollar bill. She understood- when our funds ran out she was homeward bound. The next liberty I drew, she was waiting for me in the lobby of the Bellevue Stratford. We had a room in the St. James Annex a few blocks away. Teddy Roosevelt probably slept there. George Washington may even have stabled his horse at the St. James. We were definitely the first couple to spend the whole night there in years. The furniture and the decor were depression era dirty, but in a few days Jean had our thread-bare quarters spotless. Scrubbing with Ivory Soap and liberal dosages of Lysol did it. To this day, I get excited whenever I smell Lysol disinfectant. Jean must have used a gallon getting that musty odor out of carpets and walls but no two newly-weds ever had a more wonderful honeymoon.

In better days the room had been a suite. A dumb waiter yawned at us in the ante room. The draft coming through this opening smelled of kitchen odors but we put newspapers across it. This wouldn't hold so we finally gave up. Jean laid a pathway of news print across the room and we closed it off, using it as a passage. Knowing we'd be separated again soon, we loved every minute of it and laughed at the reaction we expected when my Mother came to visit.

My Mother, poor thing, was appalled and frightened. She begged to sleep in the room with us, promising to take a sleeping pill every night. The open chute from the dumb waiter was a particular fright. She had visions of some drunken wild man climbing into the room. But lady like, lady treated, and Jean and my Mother became the special wards of the St. James staff. No queens could have been watched over or treated with greater deference. Mother even remarked that they were lovely young men when she left for home a week later.

Drills and checklists were endless, spare parts for the weapons systems and loading drills for the gun crews. And there were calls to General Quarters and mock casualties and meetings in the Wardroom to critique our performance. Loading machines on the short deck between stacks clanked hour after hour and we timed the drills, over and over. Finally we could load and fire some 21 rounds a minute.

The firing cut out cams were installed, a big improvement over the pipes that had been used to limit the angle of fire on older vessels.

Transportation to and from the Navy Yard was another learning experience. The subways were quite a bit more crowded than the street cars in New Orleans, and the people were hard to understand, at least for this "good ole' southern boy."

Since I was due on board at 0700, I hit the subway platform in downtown Philly at 0615. The start of the ride was never crowded but as we got closer to the yard, it was standing room only. One morning, I gallantly rose to give my seat to a young lady, swaying on a strap near me. As I offered her my seat, a crummy looking yard-bird sat down in it. I was mad as hell. "Get out of that seat bud, or I'll throw you out." He scurried away thinking I had lost my mind (I think I must have), and I once again proffered the young lady my seat. She turned up her nose, and retreated to the far end of the car looking back at me like I must be as "mad as a hatter." So much for Southern courtesy in Philadelphia, the city of brotherly love. It was difficult to do, but I never offered another seat on that subway.

There was another incident that caused a great flap and still is cause for smiles when we look back on it. I had been going to the Officers' Club in the Bellevue Stratford for supper while waiting for Jean to finish college. The Club was staffed with young society girls who were doing their bit to cheer up lonely young officers. I spoke with a number of them but even then, had a very poor memory for names. "Honey," seemed to fit everyone.

I came off duty, one evening shortly after Jean's arrival, to a rather frosty greeting. "Roslyn called." she said.

"Who the hell is that?" I asked in all innocence.

"She wants us to spend the weekend at her Country Club, and seems to know you quite well."

In righteous pique, not knowing who Roslyn was, I said "That sounds like fun, tell her we'd be delighted."

The weekend was a long way off and we seemed unable to communicate. At long last we arrived at the Club. An ebullient Roslyn, who I still couldn't place, greeted us. The weekend was great and Jean and Roslyn got along wonderfully, so much so that they continued to correspond all during the war. Do you understand women?

Oh, we had a lot of things that puzzled us. The officer's wives decided that their protocol required that they enter and leave transportation in order of the seniority of their spouses. Jean was never a blushing Southern violet. Lady-like, but a steel magnolia, she correctly concluded that she would defer to age but she was not in the Navy and saw no reason to defer to an officer's wife of her own age. Very few of the officers were not senior to me, but the gals loved her and most of the senior ones thought she was great to stand up for what she believed.

One evening, I was standing the evening watch as Officer of the Deck. Commander Jack McCormick, the Assistant Engineering Officer had the Command Duty watch. Now, it was Captain Carl F. Holden's pleasure to invite some of the young wives to have supper at his table, an honor most eagerly sought by most. Nothing wrong with this. He was just being sociable and their husbands were on watch. Well, Commander McCormick came on the quarterdeck to inform me that my bride was disrupting tradition again. It seems she had declined the Captain's invitation, saying she would prefer to wait for her husband to complete his watch so that she might dine with him. Jack, a Trade School type, was in a tizzy.

"Mr. Frank, please explain to your wife the protocol. She doesn't understand that a request from the Captain is tantamount to an order."

I explained to Commander McCormick that my wife had every right to select a dinner partner and to convey my regrets to the Captain.

The Skipper was a great guy and, lucky no doubt for me, had a wonderful sense of humor. One night, months later, as we steamed on a very lonely ocean, he put his arm around my shoulder, and whispered, "Well kid, just don't let anyone aboard know, but you're a better man than I am."

Just before we left the Philly Yard on our shakedown, I received a new set of orders to permanent engineering duty on the U.S.S. Wyoming, an old WWI battle wagon. She was serving as an underway training station out of Norfolk. I was fit to be tied. Fortunately, all of those weekend duties I stood for my division officer came to roost. He had asked that I be retained and told the Exec I was indispensible. Commander McDowell sent for me and asked if I wanted to remain aboard.

"I didn't join the Navy to be tied up dockside, Sir. I want to stay with the *Jersey*."

McDowell smiled, and shook his head, "Damn, what are we coming to, an *indispensable* ensign."

The next thing I knew, he was calling Bupers, and asking a classmate of his from the Naval Academy to have my orders changed. "Yes, he said, that's what I said, an *indispensable* ensign." Still laughing, he told me to get lost for the next three days, and when I returned to duty, sure enough, my orders to the *Wyoming* had been canceled.

About the time we were winding up our yard activities, a Chief Commissary Steward made a screwup that could have been catastrophic. Anxious to get ashore, for a last big liberty, he sliced a number of hams hot from the ovens, for the evening mess, still hours away. By the time the ship had completed the evening meal, one third of the crew were falling down, dizzy and sick with food poisoning. What a sight: sailors forming ragged lines to Sick Bay, vomit everywhere. For a few hours we had no idea what had been the cause. I got Jean off the ship as rapidly as I could, afraid that we might have some sort of epidemic. By morning young bodies had recovered, but the Commissary Steward did not sail with us.

7-8-43- Our activities at sea began. We were underway at 1348 and steamed down the Delaware River anchoring off Cape May in Delaware Bay and had our first smell of salt water. Drills in July and August were complicated with a thousand small problems in internal communications. The sound power phones were not battle ready and to make things harder to sort out, telephone discipline was very poor. Telling young men accustomed to unregimented conversation, to use circuits only as needed, was a hard thing to get across. As flying fish leaped in the Gulf Stream and the Atlantic Ocean, huge hammerhead sharks lazed just beneath the surface. The sailor, latent within his civilian cocoon, began to emerge. The metamorphosis steadily changed the men into disciplined seamen. Division formations as smart as any would wish emerged. Nowhere was the smartness more apparent than watching the men leaving the ship on liberty. They were proud to be "Jerseymen." Hats squared and dress blues smartly creased, they were now a proud part of the best ship in the United States Navy and ready to fight anyone who thought otherwise. This caused a lot of trouble with the Shore Patrol.

From an anchorage in Hampton Roads, we steamed to Wolftrap, Virginia on 26 July 1943 for deperming and degausing. This procedure reduced the magnetic field of the ship and made her less susceptible to magnetic mines. Then we were off to Annapolis, the Naval Academy, and a chance for Midshipmen to visit the *Jersey*. They came aboard and we proudly escorted them on a quick tour. Like every first time visitor they were awed by the *Jersey*. She was really something special and her crew had now bonded to her. The odor of welding torches and of diesel fumes was now replaced with the fresh clean smell of salt water, and her teak decks had a golden glow in the summer evening.

8-8, 8-9- We moored portside to the dock- Pier 5 in Norfolk. We had a last check of yard modifications and took aboard a team that was to monitor our shakedown in Trinidad.

Armed and with a full complement of men, we were underway at last. As we steamed out of the harbor, the *Alabama* and the *South Dakota*, fresh from the Solomons, steamed in company with several transports loaded with European prisoners of war. It was strange to wonder what these men were thinking. Their war was over, ours was just beginning. The feeling of victory was beginning to seem within reach. We would steam a distance equal to going around the world ten times, but only today seemed real. The horizon was as far as we wanted to see. The ocean swallowed us, the routine of watch standing became a way of life, dawn and evening alerts another detail to put behind us. Will any of us ever forget the aroma of freshly brewed coffee and salt air as we gazed over those long low swells of the Atlantic Ocean?

Drills and more drills, observers watching each evolution with stop-watch in hand. OS2U's catapulted into azure skies, search patterns first, then simulated air attacks from low on the water. Zooming in at masthead height, we tracked them and learned to get computer solutions in moments. Gunnery practice, our first with live ammunition, fired as we passed Culebra Island gunnery range. Our float planes spotted for the main and secondary batteries. Destroyers towed targets that were used to fire offset shoots. Maneuvering boards and stadimeters became extra arms as watch keepers learned the seamanship we would live by in the coming months. And sleeves, my God we knocked down those towed aerial targets so quickly the fly boys couldn't keep up with us. Gunners learned to lead the target, and cheers went up as we splashed one after another.

New sights had been installed on the twenties and the forties. These sights determined the lead by using the precessing of the gyro, a force in proportion to the speed the pointer swung his weapon to keep on the target. This was a great improvement over the old spider web sights gunners had used just a few short months before.

We were good and getting better and the crew loved the "Old Man." Captain Holden's idiosyncrasies were quickly made a part of the ship's lore. He frequently found his favorite man with the hand lead in the brig for some wild drunken behavior ashore. Since the Captain didn't trust the fathometer in shoal water, the miscreant posed a dilemma. Holden would swear softly under his breath, and tell the Master at Arms to get the bugger out of the brig. Into the chains he'd go, sounding for our entry into any shallow harbor. Having sentenced the bos'n at Captain's mast, it was an aggravation to release him, but nothing overrides a sailor's superstition, not even if the sailor is a Captain. A cheer from the crew always greeted "Blackie" as he blinked bleary eyes and swung the lead. After we dropped the hook, "Blackie" would get his stripes back, only to lose them on the next liberty.

Halcyon days on the shakedown- liberty in Port of Spain, Trinidad on the weekends, rum and "Coke" to the sound of steel drums, forest covered hills for a backdrop. I remember the sunsets and the cement scallop shell band stand at the Officers Club- lush palms and lianas dropping into the Gulf de Paria, natives fishing from dugout canoes, bright tropical birds adding a splash of color. Cute gals, walking arm and arm with "Jerseymen" down dusty streets in the gathering darkness. This in stark contrast to the Battle of the Atlantic, being fought not too far offshore. LTA craft (lighter than air) patrolled for German subs, and the *Jersey* crew continued to drill, drill, drill.

We were put on alert for what could have been WWII's most unusual assignment for a battleship. A German U-boat (U-615) was sighted by an LTA craft. A Martin Mariner was dispatched and dropped her depth charges on the sub. Her diving planes jammed and her rudder was damaged. She steamed in a tight circle, helpless. Helpless? She had been first damaged by an Army B-18 out of Aruba, but her crew manned their deck guns and shot down the attacker. Now one Mariner after another was dispatched from Trinidad for what became the damndest dog and pony show in the Caribbean. The German submariners had been under attack since 29 July and here, on 6 August, she was still fighting back, her decks a bloody mess with casualties. It was decided to send the *New Jersey* to sink her. The Admiral finally thought better of this and dispatched the destroyer *Walker* from Port of Spain to administer the 'coup de grace.'

Just as we were ready to leave the area, an outbreak of amoebic dysentery broke out aboard

Drills in Chesapeake Bay.

ship. Partly this was from the contaminated water of the Gulf de Paria we used for a daily hose down of our weather decks.

Discussing this incident years later, John Rossie, who was an engineering division officer feels the problem was finally traced to a small salt water to fresh water cooling device which was installed in the discharge piping of the fresh water pumps. These pumps took their suction from fresh water storage tanks in the bottoms and pressurized the system. Because there were times when no fresh water was being taken into the system, it was necessary to have a pressure relief valve in the pump discharge to recirculate water back to the pump suction. To prevent overheating the pump when no water was being used from the system and all the pump work was going into heating up recirculated water, it was necessary to carry away this heat by means of a small radiator cooler which drew salt water from the fire main. One of these coolers sprung a leak and the contaminated water of the Gulf de Paria entered our fresh water.

Sick Bay was quickly filled to overflowing with some pretty sorry looking sailors. I drew a bottle of sulfa quiuanadine from Sick Bay and spent a miserable few weeks, losing weight the hard way. By the time we arrived State-side, I had gone from 205 to 175 pounds and felt weak as a kitten. Fortunately young bodies and fresh ocean air quickly helped us to recover rapidly.

7-31- We left the Gulf, still unblooded, for Hampton Roads, having passed shakedown requirements with flying colors. We were a proud ship with a crew that were well trained and we knew it.

As we approached Chesapeake Bay we were enveloped in a pea soup fog. Ghostly fishing boats slipped by and moisture formed droplets on our faces as we searched for the sea buoy. Only an occasional seagull or the forlorn sound of our fog horn broke the gray shroud.

I was standing watch as a J.O.O.D. (Junior Officer of the Deck), and found myself next to the navigator on the wing of the bridge. As we strained our eyes for sight of the sea buoy, the ship slowly pressed through the mist. I turned to the navigator with a suggestion.

"Sir, why don't we hail one of those fishing boats? They could take us right to the buoy."

The look I got was enough to melt steel. Can you imagine the mighty BB 62 being led into Chesapeake Bay by a fishing smack?!

8-4- We dropped our observers at Hamp-

The gunnery department was managed by left to right Lt. D. Davis, III, Ltcdr. W.C.Abhau, Ltcdr. E.W.Taylor, Ltcdr. E.C.Spencer, and Lt. Charles Dancy. They did a great job turning a bunch of feather merchants into sailors.

ton Roads and returned to the Philadelphia Navy Yard for several modifications. Imagine my delight to find Jean was due to arrive in Philadelphia in the morning. Her friends included the Navigator's new bride. The word was out, and all hands had somehow managed to get word to loved ones, or had the loved ones managed to invade the sanctity of naval communications? So much for secrecy, wives of officers and enlisted personnel had their networks. Thank goodness the Germans never studied their system.

Late September began a most unusual assignment. The flank speed of the *New Jersey* was a closely guarded secret. We were dispatched to Portland, Maine and began a month-long charade that had us weekending in Portland and steaming past the sea buoy on Monday mornings.
The weather was dull and overcast with constant light sleet mixed with flurries of snow. Bands of pelagic ducks, scoters and brant, parted as we sliced through the mist. Sailors on lookout, pea jackets buttoned against the chill manned the wings of the bridge. Officers in greatcoats stood their watches, eyes straining to part the half light of fall evenings. As soon as we passed the sea buoy and the fishing fleet, we bent on all the power we could and sped toward an imaginary chop line in mid Atlantic.

This was the longitude that would allow us to intercept the German battleship *Tirpitz*. She and her sister ship the *Scharnhorst* were a constant threat to the North Atlantic convoys so vital to the British. Their commerce raiding was costing the Allies dearly. If she would only venture out far enough and we were on station, we could catch her before she could retreat to her lair in Kaafjord, Norway. She had proven herself so well protected by anti-aircraft fire and torpedo nets, that the RAF had been unable to do more than damage her. We were even sent into Argentua, Newfoundland in order to be closer, but no luck. This was the coldest spot most of us could have ever dreamed up. High winds gave a chill factor that numbed the bones and ice formed on the rigging. On one watch, the temperature dropped to 23 degees below zero C. We waited and waited for the *Tirpitz* to show herself. Finally after several heroic attempts, the RAF on 12 November 1944, dropped a string of 6-ton 'Tallboy' bombs on her and the *Tirpitz* was sunk. Maybe we were lucky.

In the harbor at Rockland, Maine, Captain Carl F. Holden received a dispatch warning of the possible use of German swimmers armed with limpet mines. This had been the cause of some problems in Scapa Flo, where these magnetic charges had caused damage to ships of the Royal Navy.

Always an admiral-striker, our Captain had junior officers manning a whale boat, with crew of coxswain, engineer and bow hook. These little spit-kits patrolled the ships waterline from an hour before sunset until one hour after sunrise. Armed with a Reising .45 cal. submachine gun and a .45 semi-automatic pistol, suited as best you could against sub zero cold, and carrying a thermos of hot coffee, I spent many a miserable night on this fruitless exercise. But the event was not without its moments of excitement.

One night a vessel loomed out of stygian blackness and a low ground fog. Huddled against the cold we looked at this intruder, all thoughts of the discomfort vanishing as the possibility of heroic defense of the *Jersey* pumped adrenalin through our veins. I hailed her without response. Standing in the stern, cold and soaked with freezing spray, I hailed her again. By now the outline of her pilot house was dimly illuminated. Her binnacle and a small light that could have come from her chart table cast a yellow glow through the cold night air.

I said to the Coxswain, "If that SOB doesn't answer my hail I'm going to give him a burst through his stack."

"Give it to him Mr. Frank." my cox'n and engineer chorused.

Greatly encouraged by this support, I cocked a round into the chamber and was just about to fire when a head poked out of the wheelhouse and a bearded face shouted, "This is the Yard Garbage Scow, where in hell is the damned *New Jersey*?"

So much for what was almost our first taste of shots fired in anger.

On another watch, as my crew waited impatiently to take the duty, Ensign Robert Parker, the officer I was to relieve, didn't appear with the whale boat and his frozen charges. I stayed at the forward accommodation ladder with my crew for an hour and finally got permission from the OOD to secure.

When day broke I went topside to see what had happened. No sign of the whale boat. I asked for permission to lower the second boat and search the area. I had a hunch my friend had gotten out of the wind and taken shelter behind one of the small islands not too far removed from our anchorage. Sure enough, the tide had gone out and there was one very embarrassed young officer. High and dry, it was several hours before the tide let him float clear. With his frozen charges he limped up the after accomodation ladder.

12-15- We were in Boston Navy Yard for further modifications, a reunion, and Christmas with wives and sweethearts. Transportation was difficult to arrange but somehow the wives found a way to get to Boston or any other port we might spend a few weeks in.

The scramble for housing started another round of worries. We knew the Copley Plaza in Boston or the Bellevue Stratford in Philadelphia would not fit junior officer's budgets. Jean was a wonder, stretching our funds and finding accommodations. It was impossible to get reservations on planes and trains were almost as bad, but somehow she always arrived in port on schedule. This from a southern belle who before the war didn't study at the Tulane University Library without an escort.

Accommodations were the biggest problem. Each move from Philly to Boston to Portland and back to Boston was a difficult one. Somehow the girls found rooms. Portland, Maine was particularly tough. With the Portland Navy Yard a very busy place in a rather small town, Jean lucked out on a lovely garret that rented for about twelve bucks a week. It was colder than we were accustomed to, with snow a white blanket wherever we looked. But the house was warmed by a roaring log fire and we had wonderful fresh lobsters and baked potatoes in small restaurants and heavy down coverlets at night. The thought of imminent separation also helped to keep us warm. Walking the streets at night under a cloudless starlit sky seemed as close to heaven as we could get.

Our little nest on Boston Commons was a gem. We occupied a third floor walk up- no hardware remained on any of the doors. The owners had sold the old brass locks and door knobs to contractors, desperate for this sort of treasure. The three story house looked like every other brownstone on the Commons and we had to be very careful not to get in the wrong house or the wrong room.

To cut costs, we were always at the end of our financial tether, we'd shop at the market and keep deviled ham, crackers and soup in our room. One evening, after a late night snack, Jean placed a half can of ham in the snow on the window ledge. Next evening I decided to finish it and ended up with the damndest case of food poisoning you ever saw. The sun had melted most of the snow during the day and the ham had spoiled. It was great to be young- by midnight I was feeling better but at least ten pounds lighter. No more window ledge refrigerators for us!

Our accomodation with no locks made everything very sociable- sometimes a bit too sociable. Friends and neighbors drifted in and out, forgetting to knock. We kept a case of soft drinks under the bed and since the room was very cool, the drinks were just right. We'd wake up in the morning and see some of the neighbors' kids at the foot of our bed, waiting patiently for me to open my eyes to get them a "moxie." For newlyweds this can be rather disconcerting.

Then it was back to the ship at dawn in a wildly rocking and pitching motor launch, her canvas cover thick with ice- a constant threat to capsizing in the frigid bay. Our fingers and faces tingling from the cold, officers and men would rush to the coffee pots before turning in. I think the *New Jersey* may have set some sort of record for gallons of "Joe" consumed in that port.

Time ashore was running out. We had brought all of our gear up to date with Nav Mods (Naval Modifications to equipment in place) in each yard stay, and it was time to join the Fleet in the Southwest Pacific. On 28 December, I bid Jean a tearful farewell, and we debarked for Hampton Roads. Heavy weather clothes were offloaded and ammunition replenished. Stores were brought aboard in an endless stream. We knew we were headed South, but where? "Scuttlebutt" had us going to North Africa, then it was the far East, and on and on.

On 2 January in company with the *Iowa* and a screen of Destroyers we sortied. The course was due South. Once again we watched the light-ship at the sea bouy of Boston harbor rolling and pitching in gale force winter winds. What a miserable duty this must have been.

The southerly course sent us into delightful temperate climes. Now flying fish, gannets and sharks in the Gulf Stream replaced the windbirds and dolphins escorting our entry into the South Atlantic.

Drills and a never ending effort to erase the debris of yard workmen were topics in the plan of the day. Water conservation was called to our attention daily. Every gallon consumed depleted the bunker oil required to extend our cruising range. We were exhorted to wet down, soap up, and rinse. No more the luxury of running water while we showered. Slowly the *Jersey* began to take on the bearing of the man-o-war she was meant to be. Her crew were "rounding out" as well trained seamen and her officers and crew were learning to effectively handle all of the complexities that combine to operate a combatant vessel of the United States Navy.

Chapter 2: Virgins No More - Flintlock and the Ellice Islands, Truk, Kwalajein, and Mille

Uncle Sugar Able disappeared at 1430, 7 January, 1944. The sight of our wives waving from the Hotel Chamberlain and Old point Comfort was in many a dream that night.

It was a day to remember. A soft breeze wafted the odor of new mown hay, perhaps from a barnyard some where, a land odor that added

A group of gunnery officers taken in the Marshall Islands in 1944. Sitting, left to right: Capt. Francis X. Regan, Ltcdr. Matt Landers, Ltcdr. Spencer, Lcdr. Sampson, Lt. Benny Raat, Second row: 2nd Lt. Cuisner, Lt(jg) S.M. Weyburn, 1st Lt. E.H. Greason, Ens. Boose, Lt. Cruise, Lt. Gregory McMahon, Third row: Ens. Allen Cooney, O'Malley, Bullard, Lt(jg) John Yeager, 2nd Lt. Al Topham, and Lt. (jg) Ford.

its fragrance to the fresh smell of salt air. Rolling gently, we passed through the South Atlantic passing the Bahamas to port and threaded our way through the Windward Passage. Cuba to starboard and Haiti to port, an occasional dim light flickering from lowering rain clouds.

We were caught in a melancholy mood that tried to hold on to the wives and sweethearts we were leaving behind. The night was lit by a million stars- only the sailor on a darkened ship will see such a magnificent display. The Caribbean was a sparkling mirror of bluegreen at sunrise, flying fish leaping across the surface, a path of iridescence in their wake. Dawn and dark alerts were a routine that didn't seem necessary on this tranquil sea but shortly we would learn the value of repeated drills.

1-7-44- We dropped the hook off Cristobal in the Canal Zone and awaited the dawn ritual of a passage through the Panama Canal.

The hook came up with all hands at General Quarters and the first rays of sunlight caught us transiting Gatun Locks. Crew at attention, white uniforms freshly pressed for the deck divisions, dungarees for the engineers. Signal flags snapping at the halyards, our colors at the fore peak, our grey camouflage paint a counterpoint to the gay colors adrift in a spanking breeze.

Rapidly we were lifted to the level of Gatun Lake. I watched a saucy little mine sweep, heading home, swing towards the *Jersey*. A seaman semaphored from her bridge, the message received by the quartermaster of the watch. The Captain shook his head and smiled as he handed the message to me. It was from an N.R.O.T.C classmate: "Happy hunting to Ensign Charles Frank and Ensign Robert Parker. Give the Japs hell." It was signed- Ensign Robert Turchin, U.S.N.R. The regular Navy had to have a lot of patience getting used to the irreverence of the reserves.

Then it was through Culebra Cut and Miraflores Locks, the sheer banks of the cut covered with verdant forests. Only the outposts of G.I.'s, stationed to guard this most vulnerable pass, marred emerald green walls of tropical foliage. Olivedrab tents and an occasional wisp of smoke marked a cook tent. An occasional wave from a lonely sentry to the *Jersey's* massive bulk and then they dissapeared astern.

The *New Jersey* and the larger carriers had all been built with the width of the Canal a limiting factor. Sparks flashing, the hull of our ship scraped it's 108 foot beam and massive bulk through the locks. The flight deck of a carrier that followed in our wake knocked down light standards like tenpins. It was a beautiful day, billowing white clouds slipping through an azure sky, looking like square rigged clippers bound for the devil knows where.

The last locks were at Pedro Miguel and we were shortly moored dockside in Balboa. We were given an eight hour liberty, and a race was on to cram twenty four hours into eight. I had an old family friend who had been with the Panama Canal Company for many years. I called him and with his wife we enjoyed a delightful dinner at the Balboa Gardens.

It was a time when the wonder of each passing day was an adventure. Most of the crew had never been more than a few miles from home and the Navy offered a new world. The sights and sounds of a foreign country were exciting and a bevy of beautiful young Panamanian girls circled about the sailors. Their white uniforms, freshly pressed for the occasion, were surrounded by the bright colored skirts and olive skinned beauties of the "entertainment district."

Night sounds were all too soon replaced with the clarion call of the bugler sounding reveille, and the bosun in the crews quarters shouting "Rise and shine sailors, loose your xxxx and grab your socks. It's reveille." And the morning ritual, "Now a clean sweep down fore and aft. Sweep down all weather decks and ladders." General Quarters and special sea details set, we

The engineering department. The back row: Ed Stafford (Ensign,B-Division), Rasmusson (Machinist,A-Division), Nultemeir (Machinist,M-Division), Love (Ch.Electrician,E-Division), Stu Miller (Lt. Fuel Officer), unknown, unknown, Louis Erickson,(Lt.E-Division), Leo Hicks (Chief Machinist), Fred Geisendorf (Ensign M-Division), front row John Rossie (Lt.j.g. A-Division), Maurice Jackson (Lt.A-Division), Durham (Lt. E-Division), Jack McCormick (Ltcdr. Assistant Engineering Officer), G.Ogle (Cdr.G.Ogle Engineering Officer), Herb Blackwood (Lt.Cdr. Engineering), Harry Reynolds (Lt. M-Division), Tim Rogers (Lt. B-Division), Dave Harpster (Lt.j.g. B-Division).

sortied into the Pacific, our home away from home for the next two and a half years.

Our first hours in the Pacific- motor torpedo boats flashed across the ocean from the Coastal Defense Forces. Flying from one white crested swell to the next, they looked like tiny predators about to attack their prey. Torpedo Defense sounding on the MC, men racing to Battle Stations, heavy machine guns rapidly training and elevating to repel the simulated attack- these memories are still vivid. A squadron P-59 Aircobras, twin booms giving them a Buck Rodgers look, swept out of the sun and caught us off guard. A grim reminder that a good look-out and a seaman's eye were as important as early warning radar. While we were engaging the MTBs, the air attack had come in undetected.

The calm blue waters of our first days in the Pacific stretched to the horizon. Day after day passed. Battle stations, torpedo defense and endless casualty drills, all designed to make response routine. The ship's newspaper, remember-"THE JERSEYMAN", and the plan of the day were our only contact with the world we had left behind.

1-13- We crossed the line, zig-zagging across the Equator, setting a Guiness Book record for crossings in a twenty four hour period. Wartime threat of subs belayed any initiation and we became "Shellbacks and Golden Dragons" rather painlessly.

1-18-It had been rumored for days that we are heading for Funafutti in the Ellice Islands and today it is confirmed.

The sun rises and sets in breathtaking glory. We are overwhelmed. Rays of light, untouched by urban pollution, fan out of an orb of brilliant red and gold. Clouds that billowed white in an azure sky turn to outrageous shades of pink and mauve. The sea is the deepest blue and the contrast with the somber grays of the North Atlantic lifts our spirits.

1-22- We sailed into a coral atoll called Funafutti.

Beautiful sandy beaches, a palm fringed lagoon, natives paddling about in sarongs and longboats, everything was there but Dorothy Lamour. I sat atop Sky Four, my 5 inch gun director station, during general quarters, and in my leisure hours sketched the scene. Palm trees swayed in gentle breezes, white coral sand and a touch of surf breaking on the seaward shore, a second line of surf on the outer edge of the coral barrier reef- blues and greys and rich greens gave everthing a mystic aura to which most of us had never been exposed.

Watches were one in three, a routine that gives you a rather restricted view of life. Each third night you were blessed with eight hours of sleep, then six hours the next night and four the third. This was the routine if you weren't interrupted by calls to drills, division musters and assorted lectures and critiques in the Wardroom. At first we were exhausted- in a few weeks the routine had become an accepted ritual.

I watched the sunset one evening with my roommate, "Dial Damage" Deal. The anchorage was a forest of masts and antennae, of ships in wartime gray, lights darkened except for the flash of blinkers signaling the developing operation.

Tojo would have had nightmares if he could have seen this assemblage. Sailors who had spent their adult lives in the service were awestruck. Eight new battleships, more carriers, cruisers and destroyers than we knew existed assembled for *Operation Flintlock*, the invasion of the Marianas.

Strange that this deepest penetration to date of the Japanese Empire should take place over the Marianas Trench, at 36,198 feet, the deepest part of any ocean and just two hundred miles SW of Guam.

It was D minus seven and the operation was beginning to take form. Task groups were assigned and missions defined. Then I watched the strangest sight. A procession of swab handles were floating by on an outgoing tide. Interspersed were thousands of cans of Solarine brightwork polish. Like an army of Chinese mandarins, they were drifting past in orderly ranks, row after row, as far as the eye could see.

"Deal, my friend,", I remarked, "We can't lose this war. The industrial capacity of the United States is producing swabs and brightwork polish faster than the "swabbies" can throw them over the side."

We sortied a few days later, headed North, brightwork polished by reluctant hands. Passing the "Bloody Gilberts", the lessons learned at Tarawa would hopefully save many G.I.s in the operation now labeled *Flintlock*, the capture of the Marshall Islands.

We were part of TG 58.3 under Rear Adm. Forrest C. Sherman. Overall command was vested in Adm. Raymond Spruance, who was determined to lessen the cost in lives for the landings scheduled to secure Kwajelein.

This atoll was needed to prepare a landing strip, moving us closer to the Japanese mainland. Air reconnaissance showed a bomber strip partly completed on the South end of Kwajalein Island. Majuro and Wotje were also to be taken. Majuro, a great palm studded atoll had a wonderful deep water anchorage. It was to be our first objective.

The Japanese fields on Eniwetok, some 360 nautical miles Northwest, were to be neutralized by bombing from carrier based aircraft. We departed Funafuti as part of TG 58.5, Admiral Sherman as O.T.C., but were shortly formed into a part of Task Group 58.3 with the carrier *Bunker Hill*.

We supported her air strikes against Kwajelein and Efate in the Marshalls, retiring to an intercept station off Eniwetok Atoll. The Japanese had lost control of the skies. The only sign of Jap resistance was an occasional crippled aircraft from one of our carrier squadrons, splashing near the formation. The air crews were quickly picked up by destroyers assigned as plane guards. The *New Jersey* was stationed in the center of most formations, with destroyers screening the front of the Task Group, and carriers either astern or abreast the *Jersey*. Our secondary battery was awesome. Jap planes that came into range of the five inch, or heavy machine guns (forty mm and twenty mm) didn't last very long.

The next phase of our operations involved support of Admiral Spruance's raid on Truk. This Jap bastion was thought to have been the place where Amelia Earhart was lost. A heavily fortified atoll, it boasted formidable air and shore batteries. But, it could not equal the power that Task Force 50.9 and the carriers *Enterprise*, *Yorktown*, *Essex* and *Bunker Hill* had, Spruance's surface attack force of the *New Jersey*, the *Iowa* and their screen would bring to bear.

The raid was an unqualified success. The

Japs lost over 200,000 tons of shipping and one of their major staging bases was effectivly eliminated. Also destroyed were most of the four hundred aircraft defending Truk. In the three Task Groups supporting the operation only the *Intrepid* sustained battle damage. At 22:11 17 February 1944, she took a torpedo from one of eight Kate torpedo bombers launched from Parram Field on Truk. They flirted with the screen, like tiny fireflies, finally scoring a single hit on the *Intrepid*. The effectiveness of fleet training was beginning to show the professionalism that marked the sea battles from this point on. Combat Air Patrols, and more effective anti-submarine tactics by the screen were making the fleet seem invulnerable.

2-16- From the *New Jersey's* war log: "Participated in support group for air strikes against Truk Atoll, Caroline Islands. **1127** detached from Task Group 58.3 to become Flag of Task Group 58.9, striking force, composed of *Iowa*, *New Jersey*, *Minneapolis*, *New Orleans*, and four DD's, with orders to proceed around Truk to destroy shipping and cripples. Truk considered the Japanese Gibraltar. **1315** first action against the enemy. Fired at Zeke attacking the *Iowa*. **1440** fired on enemy Val to port. **1520** sunk a small enemy trawler to port with 5 inch fire. **1527** opened fire on enemy DD Asashio class. DD sank **1541**."

One of the most memorable events of the Truk operation occurred on a bright sunny afternoon. The *Jersey* was steaming with the *Iowa* on her stern, Condition II was set (Air defense) when General Quarters called all hands to battle stations. We quickly closed on two Japanese destroyers and a small craft. When we opened fire (the *New Jersey* and her screening cruisers), the ships literally disappeared. The small craft was hit by our five-inch secondary battery, and a cloud of paper seemed to float down as though we'd struck a huge "pinata" with a stick. The rangefinder operator in Sky-1 turned to me and said "My God Mr. Frank, I think we hit the Gunnery Office."

The Japanese destroyers managed to get off a spread of torpedoes that passed between the *Iowa* and the *Jersey*. This and a dive bomber, that managed to drop a single stick on the Starboard side of the *Iowa*, was the closest we came to trouble. We were surprised by the dive bomber but managed to get off 34 rounds from the starboard five inch battery before the plane disappeared into the clouds. The CAP (Combat Air Patrol) splashed it a few moments later.

Carrying Admiral Spruance, we circled Truk with his Task Group. A potent display of the disdain we were developing for anything the enemy could throw at us. Our main and secondary batteries both performed well, destroying considerable warehouse stores and barracks.

I was still a junior officer in the Fifth Division, my duties now expanded to include J.O.O.D. underway and Catapult Officer on the Starboard catapult. The *Jersey* and the *Iowa* developed a rivalry to see who could launch their float planes first, when Flight Quarters sounded. This made the catapult officers bend every effort to insure a fast and trouble free launch. These stations and my battle station in the forward five inch gun director, Sky-1, made a run from one to the other a real track meet. The

Drinking a few beers and waiting for the motor launch was a rather infrequent pleasure, but you couldn't tell it by the look of this weary bunch.

ship was 887 feet long and one heck of an obstacle course. The level of Sky-1 was four levels above the main deck and I kept in good shape running between stations. When Condition III was set and flight quarters sounded, it was an even longer run. Air Defense was in the peak of the foretop some 12 levels above the main deck, and my Condition Three watches were located there. Even during Condition III, I got my exercise.

Training programs, sessions with stadimeter and the maneuvering board were mixed in with the daily routine. To maneuver the Task Group under all conditions, with a zig-zag pattern of constantly changing courses, to confuse an underwater attacker, required precise range and bearing on adjacent ships. To make a major change in course, the screen had to be re-oriented. This called for the finest seamanship. The repetitive drills proved that "as you train so will you fight."

We exercised with medicine ball games and weight lifting and went through weeks of sailing without a sign of the Japanese fleet. And then, as we approached another island, and our intentions to take it became obvious, there was a flurry of activity heralded by lamp lighters (Jap float planes dropping flares), and intermitant attempts at penetration of CAP and screen by torpedo planes. These were usually splashed by far ranging scouts (combat air patrol) before they could penetrate the screen.

2-18- The occupation of Majuro was completed by a landing party of a few Marines. They were advised by natives that the Majuro atoll was almost free of the enemy and in fact only three men were captured when the sweep was completed. The Japanese had decided to let their troops in the Marshalls fight a delaying action without attempts at reinforcement. Except for the heavily bunkered force on Kwajalein and a few picket submarines that's what they did.

Majuro was one of the finest harbors and anchorages in the Pacific. The fleet used it after completing offensive operations to replenish ammunition and stores and for a brief liberty for all hands. We spent many a pleasant hour swimming on the beaches. Each one of the little islands that rimmed the harbor was a beautiful contradiction to the violence of war. Sea-bees had constructed a shelter for a bar that dispensed hot beer to thirsty sailors and shelter from the tropic sun to drink it. The mahogany bar was the longest I've ever seen, possibly a hundred yards, and lined with sailors from a hundred ships at anchor in the harbor.

Being twenty-one and eager for combat made the whole thing seem rather exciting, but I remember a conversation one evening on the bridge with a forty year old lieutenant named Joseph Francis Murphy. He asked me how I was sleeping, and I told him just fine. I was still berthed in Warrant Officers country and the swishing of the ocean against the bulkhead next to my bunk had become a delightful lullaby. He sighed and said "Kid you don't know how lucky you are. I keep thinking of my wife and kids at home. What would they do if something happened to me?"

That made a lot of difference in how you looked at the war. Liberty in a beautiful South Sea atoll was the stuff that Navy recruiting posters were made of before the war started. Only the young could still appreciate them, forgetting the danger.

2-22- We stood in to Kwajalein Atoll. The size of the fleet was by this time unbelievable. Battleships and carriers, cruisers, destroyers and supply ships by the score were anchored in this wonderful, protected anchorage. Ships were scattered in azimuths as far as the eye could see. Small craft scurried about transferring stores and replacements from transports to the fleet. But, it's hard to imagine the desolation ashore. Scarcely a palm tree was standing.

Marines were living in small tents with the damndest Rube Goldberg washing machines clanking away in the prevailing westerly trades. The originator of this device was a mechanical genius. It consisted of a small windmill that rotated to face the breeze. This turned a pulley that actuated a plunger in a bucket of sea water set in the sand. Clothes were scrubbed clean while the owner sat idly by cleaning his weapons or smoking a cigarette- this, with the smell of the dead everywhere.

We were overwhelmed with the cloying, sweet, sickly odor- appalled at the toll of enemy and our own dead. Only a little over six square land miles, but it took eight bloody days and thousands of casualties to secure it.

The Navy poured thousands of rounds of high explosive ammunition into each landing area and it seemed that no man could survive the bombardment. Naval air bombed and strafed targets of opportunity day after day. The Japanese burrowed into the coral and somehow survived. Wave after wave of Marines went ashore. The Japanese came out of the rubble to defend every inch of land until the last soldier died for the Emperor. There were few prisoners taken.

The sky, a brilliant blue, the mild breeze blowing across the sand, the deeper blue of the ocean with waves caressing the reef were a counterpoint to the desolation and thundering barrages that raked the island a few short days before. It was a strange feeling to spend day after day on a gentle sea. Our only activity was the routine of drills and the dawn and dark alerts, then to go through a few hours of tension, planes diving into the formation and the bedlam of air defense. Aircraft damaged in combat miles away from the screen, limping in to splash alongside other Naval air coming in to carrier flight decks, bombs hanging at a crazy angle, sometimes to explode with frightful casualties to deck hands trying to save the pilot.

We ventured into concrete pill-boxes, enemy soldiers frozen in the rictus of death. A small Japanese tank, gutted from the fire of a flame thrower looked like a child's toy, burned and left to rust in the sand. Twisted metal rods and concrete revetments bore mute testimony to the care with which the Japanese had prepared their defenses. It was all to no avail. Flame throwers and satchel charges, AP shells from the fleet and bombs from the air tore them to bits.

We were warned to watch out for booby traps, left by the enemy to reward the ever-eager American souvenir hunter. No one seemed to give the warnings a thought. I examined a light machine gun, a hand-made replica of the old .30 caliber Lewis gun I'd practiced with on the Wyoming in prewar NROTC training cruises. Like the Arisaka service rifle parts, they were duplicated in home workshops, each painstakingly filed by hand to a pattern furnished by the government. The parts were hand fitted by gunsmiths and were not interchangeable. Our mass production was light years ahead of this system!

The most ridiculous casualty on the ship was in the cabin of a Lieutenant Craig Leedom (a Naval Academy graduate, no less). He brought aboard a live round from one of the Japanese knee mortars. Deciding it would make a wonderful table lamp, he attempted to disarm it. After taking the powder out, he was trying to remove the primer when it detonated. For weeks we thought he would lose his sight. No one brought live ammunition aboard after this incident.

I limited my activities ashore to snorkeling on the reef and making knives in the ship's machine shop from discarded files. A Chief Warrant I'd bunked with on the shakedown taught me to heat and anneal the blade in the ships forge. South Pacific sea shells were another intriguing activity for those sailors venturesome enough to brave the undertow and the sharks on the reef. Swimming with face masks we made from plexiglass and rubber, we collected shells more beautiful than we ever knew existed. The problem was getting the little critters that inhabited the shells out. The odor when they died was really a bit much for your room-mate, unless he was also a shell collector.

2-26- Underway to Majuro again. Four drills a day and night tracking of the Combat Air Patrol on radar of the Combat Information Center- this was the routine for several weeks.

3-18- We steamed due South for a scheduled "exercise", a bombardment of Milli Atoll. This little sand spit had a small Japanese garrison we had bypassed. It had no tactical or strategic significance at this time. It almost caused our first casualties.

5-19- was a beautiful day- sun sparkled on white caps, and a school of pelagic fish splashed across our bow. I was sitting on top of Sky-1 and watching the beach as our main battery fired broadside after broadside into the island. We were at 17,000 yards and closing. Black smoke from burning supplies hit by broadsides of high explosive shells towered like crinolated castles.

It was almost time for the five-inch 38s to commence firing when I saw a splash on our port beam. I casually informed the rangefinder operator that the Japanese were firing at us. The splashes walked to us but it wasn't until one whistled overhead that I reacted. I heard a piece of rigging snap. With a shout I dropped through the hatch on top of the range finder operator. If I'd had spurs, he'd have been marked for life. Some thirty seven salvos were fired at us but the *New Jersey* was a charmed ship. One shell dropped on the Starboard side no more than thirty yards or so abeam. We were engaged to Port. The *Iowa*, astern of us, was less fortunate. She took two hits from what was estimated to be a 5.7 inch rifle. We promptly went to full speed and performed that well known naval maneuver known as "Let's get the hell out of here."

The enemy had one little weapon capable of reaching us and it was mounted on a narrow gauge railroad track. As fast as our spotter air sent in corrections, they'd move her along a hundred yards, fire again and be ready to move forward or back as soon as they saw a flash from our batteries. It was a tough little fly trying to bite an elephant on the ass, and it came pretty close to doing it.

Like the G.I. looking for souvenirs, the *Jersey* was looking for battle stars. A very foolish and unnecessary evolution. Had the Japanese waited until we closed to the scheduled 10,000 yards, we would not have been so lucky. With the main and secondary batteries pouring in salvo after salvo, the dust and smoke soon obscured the island completely. Then the wind would blow the debris away and a flash would let you know another round had your address. Fortunately the enemy fire control radar was never as accurate as our own, and we watched splashes in our wake as we increased the range. We had gotten in a crap game with a full wallet and with an enemy already broke.

Now we steamed for Majuro. A few days of cleaning up the ship and taking on stores in preparation for the invasion of New Guinea were scheduled- drills and fine tuning the reaction time of Departments in preparation for any contingency. More hot beer and swimming off the reefs of Mog-mog.

While reading in my cabin one morning, a couple of petty officers from the Fifth Division knocked on the bulkhead. "Can we ask you a few questions Mr. Frank?"

"Sure," I naively answered.

The questions involved building a still. I drew a schematic diagram, proud of my recently acquired degree in Chemical Engineering, and cautioned them about the danger of fusil oil distilling into the "white lightning," if temperatures were not very carefully monitored. I was positive they would be afraid to proceed with the threat of blindness pointed out if heat in the still exceeded allowable limits. Also where the heck could they find the components to ferment? Seemed innocent enough. Just sailors exploring a pipe dream.

A few weeks later a very red faced sailor reported I'd better check the space under the airplane crane, before Captain's inspection on Saturday. To my horror, I found mash splattered in every corner and the space smelling like a bar room after a drunken orgy.

One of the men assigned to clean the place suggested that we dog the hatch cover with long dogs, and replace every one in sight with short dogs. Now a dog wrench is a piece of pipe used to get additional leverage on a fastening of the watertight doors throughout the ship. We followed his suggestion, and when the hatch was approached during inspection, the Master at Arms strained valiantly, but he couldn't open that hatch. He was a potbellied old Chief- I can still remember his frown as he strained to open that hatch for the Skipper.

It took a month of airing before the odor of beer was replaced with diesel oil fumes. The Division got a note in the Captain's report, telling us that no long dogs were in place near the hatch, and warning that we should have them in place before the next inspection.

A misconception as to my valor occurred about this time. When the Japanese on Mille threw a few shells at us, my telephone talker, "Gedunk", panicked. As a flash from the beach heralded another incoming round he kept crying, "Let's get out of here Mr. Frank."

I tried to say something to him but my voice wouldn't come out. I laughed and watched the second hand on my watch trying to keep control of myself by timing the flight of incoming freight. Later I heard "Gedunk" saying how fearless I was.

"Hell", he said, "I wet myself but the bastard was laughing and looking at his watch to see when the shells would land." You can't beat good press. I thought I'd best let this one pass.

Chapter 3: New Guinea

We left Majuro on 20 March 1944 for what was the first phase of the invasion of New Guinea. Crossing the Equator on 24 March we headed Northwest, just above Hollandia (Dutch New Guinea). The transit was a quiet one. Calm seas and a routine that we now found quite comfortable. The men had mastered their ratings. Honed to a fine point, we rushed towards the war zone confident with our Captain, our crew, and our ship.

Guadalcanal, in the Solomon Islands, was to the southeast of our station, and their radio broadcasts (Armed Forces Radio) put out a strong signal and some great recordings of the big bands then popular in the States. Glenn Miller with Tex Beneke singing "Chattanooga Choo-choo" and Tommy Dorsey playing "Marie" were favorites. Now secured after months of bloody fighting, the Slot was no longer a graveyard for this new generation of seamen.

But Tokyo Rose was something else! Her pidgen English accented what we associated with the Japanese. We listened, the crew whistling and hooting as she described the pasteing the Japanese fleet was giving us. The *New Jersey* was sunk several times, and we lost enough carriers to create another fleet. Self-delusion was a fine art, and Tokyo Rose was a master practitioner. Her sucess in spellbinding her countrymen was illustrated by the lack of information possessed by the Japanese public on the true status of her armed forces.

When the war was over many Japanese could not comprehend the defeat of the Imperial Armada. Much better to show the people the true events; warts and all. We sometimes had a problem with controlling the press, but all in all, they did a responsible and accurate analysis of the battles of WWII in the Pacific. There was a spirit of cooperation between military and press that, although sometimes strained, was far better than in later conflicts.

The fast carrier Task Forces were clobbering Japanese airfields, destroying many of their planes, parked in neat rows on air fields painstakingly constructed on Hollandia. The momentum of the war shifted more and more to the rapid destruction of Japanese air power. Islands were isolated and subjected to intense pre-invasion bombardment. From sea and air, strikes destroyed the ability of the Japanese to defend the territory they had conquered in the early days of the war. Task Groups and Fleets were shifted in name, the Third Fleet (Halsey) to Fifth Fleet (Spruance).

The illusion allowed a staff to plan an operation at Fleet Headquarters in Pearl Harbor, while the fleet and the opposite staff pounded the Japanese on a continuous schedule. Halsey was flown into San Francisco with a few young staff officers. Headlines read, "The Third Fleet rests while the Fifth Fleet pounds the enemy." This disinformation was extremely effective, more than convincing the Imperial General Staff that they were fighting two great armadas. We envied the lucky stiffs shown in a nightclub in `Frisco with Admiral Halsey, who was obviously enjoying the charade.

The next few weeks were spent supporting

Sky four gun director was a lofty perch for the duty watch during condition three.

a fast carrier Task Force in the area of Humboldt Bay. Days on the *New Jersey* were occupied with refueling destroyers of the screen and replenishing stores for the "small boys." The *New Jersey* was a vast repository of every imaginable service and supply. Our machine shop and our capacity for bunker oil were used to keep the Task Group at peak efficiency on missions that frequently exceeded a month.

I was now assigned to a starboard refueling station, and we shot a line carrying projectile across to the destroyers. Using this light line as a leader, a hawser could be secured to tend hose that would transfer fuel, carefully monitored by the *Jersey's* "Oil King", "Stew" Miller. We laughingly referred to ourselves as a floating service station, AO 62 (Fleet oiler).

The nights were another matter. Although the Japanese were unable to meet the fleet air arm in even combat, the cover of darkness made the armada a tempting target for lamp lighters and their flares. These lone planes flew in at midnight and disturbed many a restful sleep with the call: "General Quarters. All hands man your battle stations." Many a sailor heard the sound of the claxon and the shrill call of the bosun's pipe in their dreams, long after the war had ended.

And speaking of dreams: about this time one of the J.O.'s went to Sick Bay with a complaint that he had been having repeated wet dreams. His problem came from petroleum jelly amply squirted on his privates every time he dozed off. His room-mate, in collusion with a medical officer, who will also remain anonymous, directed him to give up eggs for breakfast. Now the J.O. loved a morning ritual, debating just how he wanted his eggs prepared. Shell eggs were one of the perks that the Officers Mess enjoyed for a few weeks after the crew were eating dried, powered eggs. This punishment went on until the J.O. was certain his problem had been cured. Confessing to his roommate that he had eaten eggs for breakfast, brought on another series of very embarrassing "dreams". The poor guy went to the Medical Officer to confess and ask for advice. "No meat for at least a month.," was the prescription. If the duo hadn't tired of the game, the poor guy might have starved.

It seemed at times we were constantly at air defense. Flares silhouetted the ships for enemy torpedo bombers coming in fast and low. Flying at wave head height, the planes were difficult to pick up on radar. Even more difficult to vector combat air to a bogey. It was a last minute fire fight that usually splashed a bogey close aboard. When one of those babies penetrated the screen it was like being on the inside of a barrel of flame. Tracers spewed forth from the *New Jersey* like some gigantic fireworks display. Carriers on our beam, ever the primary target and the most vulnerable with their huge supply of av-gas, frequently fired into our superstructure inflicting minor structural damage. Twenty mm and forty mm shells exploded on impact like giant fire-flies. Miraculously, they never killed anyone on the *New Jersey*.

The tempo of the war continued shifting more and more our way. ComAirPac, in a report to CincPac, said: "Carriers are no longer an expensive weapon for dealing single sharp blows, but have become efficient machines for keeping aircraft constantly in motion against enemy targets from dawn to dark."

Daylight attacks from small groups of enemy torpedo planes were our biggest threat. The big bed screen radar antennae rotated silently above us, picking up bogies far enough out that enemy planes were welcomed by our CAP, and splashed well outside the range of their torpedoes. But enemy pilots pressed some aircraft through. Avoiding the destroyers and the cruisers of our screen and their anti-aircraft fire, they went for the carriers.

To avoid the error of shooting at friendly planes, IFF (Identification friend or foe) was installed. This allowed the radar operator to get a pulsing blip, on his screen from friendlies. Sometimes this device malfunctioned or was damaged in combat, so a secondary defense against mistakes was the daily publication of a safe relative bearing for friendly planes to return to their Task Group. Many a ship jokingly had an arrow painted on top of a gun turret with the message: "THIS WAY TO THE CARRIERS."

It was not unusual to see considerable AA fire from the screen and the main body of the Task Group. One morning the sky was rather cloudy, huge nimbo-cumulus thunderheads towering into the heavens. Gray bursts of five inch anti-aircraft shells still lingered in the air from our defense against sporadic flights of the enemy. Diving from high altitude, they attacked the carriers. They dove in as single units, weaving and twisting to evade our fire. Heroically, they pressed the attack home. This allowed the fire of the Task Group to focus on a single bandit.

With voids filled with high octane gasoline and a thin flight deck, the carriers could become an inferno from a single five hundred pound bomb. Several times, the *New Jersey*, in the center of a diamond formation of four carriers, watched as more than one CV fought fires from a Kamikaze attack. Too often we watched crewmen battling blazes on flight decks. The carriers wheeling like stricken whales placed the wind across their line of advance, trying to clear the deck of black smoke billowing from ruptured fuel lines.

We had been given 270 degrees relative as a safe bearing for returning friendlies. Suddenly dive bombers dove through the clouds. The carrier on our starboard beam was the target. This was a hostile bearing, and I gave the order to commence firing with the 40mm battery I commanded. The planes disintegrated, crashing into the ocean on the port beam of the carrier. Only then did I hear air defense shouting, "Cease fire, friendlies."

It was over in a moment and I felt terrible. To make matters worse, a conference was called in the Wardroom and the "Gun Boss" started chewing us out for poor firecontrol discipline. I couldn't take the undeserved rebukes in silence, so I stood up to say my piece:

"Commander, those planes were diving out of thick clouds on a hostile bearing. If the situation occurred tomorrow I'd have to do the same thing."

He glared at me but didn't reply. I was chided by one of my fellow junior officers for being damned foolish to say anything, but I felt better about it a few hours later.

I returned to my cabin very disturbed by the thought that I had helped to destroy those "friendly" air crews. What had caused them to dive at the carrier? There was a knock on my stateroom and Photographers-mate, 1st class, Shad, parting the curtains, held out a shiny black and white photograph. Three Corsairs diving on a fourth plane. The meat ball on the lead aircraft looked as big as the sun. The unfortunate incident had occurred when the CAP, in hot pursuit, had followed the Jap to the deck, in an attempt to prevent damage to the carrier. One of those sad but unavoidable incidents that I will never forget.

3-30 to 4-1- We escorted the carriers to bombing runs on Palau and Woeai. There were evening alerts, the sky sporadically illuminated with the flash of anti-aircraft fire from the screen. Probably one of the most awesome views of battle are over-the-horizon gun flashes-bursting AA projectiles providing a crescendo of sight and sound- rumblings as though from the bowels of Hell, the crimson streak of tracers accenting the deeper scarlet and magenta of muzzle flashes. Tons of steel hurled at darting fire-flies attacking the fleet. No artists pallet can recreate the grandeur of those pyrotechnics.

The Pacific command was a rather loose amalgam of conflicting egos. In retrospect, after reading Sam Elliot Morison's fifteen volume *History of United States Naval Operations in WWII*, it is apparent that Admiral Nimitz was primarily interested in destroying the Japanese fleet. MacArthur had a much broader objective, and his ego was directing him to a first priority: regaining the Philippines! Again in retrospect, if we could have arrived at a quicker realization that island hopping was a dreadful waste of lives and many of the islands had little tactical and no strategic significance, the war effort would have shifted rapidly to the conquest of mainland Japan. The strangest alliance of the brass was the patrician pro-consul General MacArthur and the plebeian Admiral "Bull" Halsey. No two men could have been more unalike. Yet, their minds meshed in what was one of the most powerful bondings of upper level tacticians. They were both fighters who cared deeply for the men under their commands. They were both brave to the extreme. Their credo of battle was as dissimilar as their personalities. MacArthur, the ultimate tactician, deciding his moves like a boxer choreographing each blow. Halsey, meeting with the staff he called the "dirty tricks department", "Let's close with the bastards and wipe them out." MacArthur would defend Halsey in his blackest moments. And, "The Bull" was always quick to back the General's plans. A paradox that worked well. They were a mismatched pair of cuff links that just seemed to mesh when it counted.

Our runs off Palau netted the *New Jersey* one possible; a night run by a torpedo plane that I think was splashed by Sky-4's battery of five inch thirty-eights, although the fire of several ships were brought to bear on her.

Another incident I recorded in my "illegal" diary was a possible sub attack off Palau. We had just turned to port to launch a Kingfisher. The port catapult was trained outboard and I stood on the launcher, over the water, as the damn thing was temporarily trained in. Check list in hand, trying to ready the Starboard plane for launch as soon as the port plane was airborne, I was outboard, with nothing but foaming wake to look down on from my perch on the catapult.

We were making about twenty five knots, with a twenty knot breeze. The water sparkled in the sunlight. Torpedo Defense sounded over the MC and all hands ran for their battle stations. There was a submarine contact to starboard. It was picked up by one of the cans in the screen. Then, I heard a talker on my sound power phone sing out, "Torpedo, bearing 160." I looked out on the quarter, and saw a white streak passing across our wake fifty yards astern. I'll never know if it was a dolphin or another more lethal fish, but when the port plane was launched I was quick to train outboard and jump down to the fantail, and signal the pilot for first warm-up. In a few moments that seemed eternal, the Kingfisher was flying off to join our other plane, as spotters for a main battery shore bombardment.

Leaving the area, my log shows we crossed the Equator on 2 April, 149-50 East longitude and again on 6 April at 159-45 East. The return to base was uneventful.

4-6- We were back in Majuro for three days and some well appreciated time on the beach. We dove for shells and swam on the reef, watching tropical fish nibble on our arms and feeling as though the war was a million miles away. The water was so clear you had the feeling you were suspended in air.

Baseball games and inter-division boxing matches were part of "Happy-hour," and a thousand and one trinkets were being manufactured as the crew gravitated to the pastime that seamen have traditionally enjoyed. Trinkets hammered out of silver and copper coins, for loved ones, knife making and acey-ducey. Acey-ducey is a game very similar to backgammon, and canvas from the sail locker was in great demand. Ship's artists fashioned boards that could be rolled up quickly if action threatened. The search for washers in brass and steel for the pugs in the game, drove the machinists mad. There was an acute shortage of brass washers for some months as the games expanded into the wardroom.

We climbed palm trees and drank the milk from coconuts we shook down. We watched clouds in a blue inverted bowl overhead, and thought of loved ones so far away. Diving among the coral heads in the shallows of the reef we collected tropical shells- coweries and spider conchs, terribra, cats eyes and a dozen types of coral and sea urchins all to be fashioned into bracelets, rings and ear pendants for girl friends and wives an ocean away. It helped young men to forget that death might include them. It was always the fleet on the horizon that took the hits. Truly the *New Jersey* seemed to have a charmed life.

Another activity that always seemed to get started on the beach was a poker game called "Red Dog." A wild and unpredictable way to lose your money. Loose piles of dollars changed hands on games atop barrels of av-gas. One of the games I watched had a *New Jersey* warrant officer with a streak of luck that just wouldn't stop. He was winning no matter how he bet. So drunk he could hardly stand, his jacket, his pants pockets and his hat so stuffed with bills he looked like the scarecrow in the *Wizard of Oz*. We helped him back to the motor launch and up the gangway to the *New Jersey*, where he straightened up to salute the colors and the OD, before staggering to his stateroom.

4-13- The ill-fated *Indianapolis*, a heavy cruiser, came alongside to transfer Admiral Spruance and Flag to the *New Jersey*. Little did we dream what the fates had in store for her. She was to be sunk by a Japanese submarine in the closing hours of the war, with great loss of life. Through a mix-up in communications, her loss was not discovered for several days after she went down. Sharks and the tropical sun killed many of her survivors.

The great tragedy was caused by the failure of communications at Fleet Headquarters in Pearl. It caused her crew to drift for several days before any action to save them developed. The lucky sighting of a few survivors by a passing Mariner aircraft on patrol, alerted the Fleet to her sinking.

4-16- We were sailing south by west to the Gilberts and Tarawa six hundred miles due East. The vast reaches of the South Pacific could make logistics a nightmare. It was over two thousand miles between Palau and the Gilberts- thirty five hundred statute miles from Truk to Oahu in the Hawaiian Islands. These distances were made even longer by the need to steer a zig-zag pattern to make a torpedo solution more difficult for Japanese submarines.

We were heading for the support of landings scheduled for Hollandia, with refueling of the screen underway a continuing necessity. The big boys were amply bunkered, but the destroyers of the screen were always thirsty on long pitches. We supported the landings on Hollandia, Aitape, and Tana Maru Bay, strange names and spots on the map that none of us had heard of before- a grim urn for the burial of comrades who perished there. Completing the establishment of control through these landings, we had defeated the enemy on New Guinea and had neutralized the big base he had at Raboul. Only a month earlier, this base was an almost impregnable extension of Japanese might. Their air interdicted our supply routes over a goodly portion of the South Pacific.

4-23- Our forces were ashore in Hollandia and had overcome what little resistance the Japanese could offer. Day and night, the carriers launched air strikes that controlled the tactics of the area. The northern coast of New Guinea was ours. Bogies were on the screen frequently, and we were at General Quarters for endless hours. Day after day passed in this fashion with the control of air and sea secured by the fast carrier strike forces. The *New Jersey* was now part of Task Force 58.1 under Admiral Marc Mitscher.

4-29- We were at GQ most of the night, lamp lighters dropping flares several times but no serious attempts to attack were made. The enemy was trying to keep us off balance, without committing his rather meager reserves.

4-30- My diary shows that there were bogies all over at evening alert, but again no attack was pressed home.

In the morning, while at dawn alert, a few planes came in. The air was filled with the bursts of five inch AA fire. From Sky-1 I watched the task group splash four planes in less than a minute. When hit, they turned into flaming meteors, heading for the nearest ship in an attempt to die for the Emperor in a last blaze of glory. The courage of these young pilots can never be questioned. They were a valiant but misguided foe, and with the new and improved radar and the concentration of fire from the secondary batteries, die for the Emperor they did.

We'd pick them up on fire-control radar long before visual contact, and the five inch thirty-eights would begin to bark, barrels pointing at the seemingly empty sky. Then they were in optical range and closing fast. The forty mm quads grunted out their streams of tracers and finally the twin twenty mm joined their sharp refrain to the chorus for the grand finale. The sheer volume of fire from the integrated response of a Task Group must have been a most fearsome cauldron of death to fly through, even more fearsome as VT's (proximity detonated five inch rounds) were loaded for every fifth shell.

5-1- My first anniversary was a double one. I had been married and commissioned the same day, and a year later here I was half way around the world, on the fantail of the *New Jersey* launching an OS2U to spot a bombardment off Ponape. I lay awake that night with a heart full of longing for the bride I'd left behind. So many thoughts of hearth and home. It was a very blue day.

The little island of Ponape looked so peaceful and green. It was an emerald set in a turquoise-blue sea, hills of jade, rising against a lovely summer sky.

Halfway between Truk and Majuro, the island looked uninhabited, but as our planes located targets, smoke began to billow up in sinuous, black columns. Our fire had found its mark. Occasional flashes at the base of the smoke told of exploding ammunition and gasoline stores. At 1450, one of our lookouts spotted a periscope, then the *Iowa* with Com. Task Group 58 aboard, spotted another. Our withdrawal was ordered and we made a Cast recovery of our birds further out at sea.

This recovery was always an interesting maneuver. We would steam into the wind, and the float plane would begin to circle us about 300 yards outboard. As he passed our port beam we would commence a turn to Starboard with the new course at right angles to the wind. Our wake would be flattened, the white caps disappearing and a vast slick created. A sled of hemp would be towed a few yards astern and the OS2U would, by this time, be approaching our fantail, to alight in the slick our hull created.

Like a giant gooney bird with feet outstretched, the pontoon of the float plane would gently touch down, seeming to glide from one wave crest to the next before settling in the water. Delicately gunning his motor, the pilot would run the pontoon onto the sled. A hook on his keel would engage the mat as he cut the power. The mat would be pulled under the airplane crane on the tip of the fantail. Hooks would be lowered on steel cables engaging in lifting shackles, one ahead of the cowling- by the pilot, and one abaft the cowling, by the radioman. Gently, we'd swing the bird back to the catapult. Sounds simple, but we lost several planes when sea conditions were a little too much for the aircraft to handle.

One new aviator was rooming next to me. When the plane guard destroyer had picked him and his radioman out of the briny, he had splashed his plane in our wake, he found a note on his bunk, "Dear Mom: I hope you are buying a lot of War Bonds. I just washed out an OS2U and we need a replacement. The Captain says just four more washouts and I'll be a Japanese Ace. Love, Dilbert." Dilbert was an imaginary aviator who was always screwing up, but the new Ensign was his clone. To top off his embarrassment, Admiral Halsey and Admiral Carney were both on the fantail watching the performance. We didn't make much of an impression on Ponape, but she made a big one on us, and we headed back to Majuro to resupply.

5-4 to 5-14- We caught our breath and replenished ammunition and stores. Drills were back to four per day but with the Japanese air neutralized, we watched movies on the fantail instead of evening alert at gun stations. One favorite we watched over and over starred Louie Prima, a New Orleans orchestra leader and Keely Smith, a shapely singer and rather amply endowed. A B-grade movie, "That Old Black Magic," was a favorite. The sailors whistled and screamed every time Keely appeared. The film had been shown so many times in the Fleet that it had gotten brittle. It would break and a groan would go up from the crew. The movie operator would try to splice it before things got too far out of hand. Stomping feet and catcalls were directed at the projectionist until Keely returned to the screen. Films were supposed to be swapped about, but this one stayed in the *Jersey's* film locker.

About this time, I made a couple of diving masks out of rubber and plexiglass, and snorkling in the shallows of the atoll reefs became an even more enjoyable pastime. The light reflected from fish and coral in a thousand and one iridescent flashes. My diary was filled with attempts to identify fish and shells I'd never seen before.

5-15- I was in charge of a recreation party to the beach. All hands got two cans of hot beer and you'd have thought we'd been given the world. Strange how important small details like this can affect morale. Majuro was a haven where baseball and football replaced watching the sky for bandits. How quickly our young minds could forget the stress and bounce back to battery.

The Japanese had built barracks on Majuro that now housed our machine shops and the SeaBees were busy building roads and barracks for the Navy. The island looked like a small village in rural America from the nineteenth century, except for the Jeeps racing about and the sound of machinery in the shops. There were mountains of supplies stacked in every direction, the tarmac covered with fighter aircraft, bombers in revetments dug into the coral. Planes were landing and taking off in countless numbers from a strip at one end of the island. I managed to scrounge two more beers for the liberty party and we played baseball with the Fourth Division. We lost, but returned to the *New Jersey* in high spirits.

We managed to get ashore several more times but I was feeling down for some reason and spent my time walking the beach to the most remote section I could find. Just getting away from everyone seemed to be what I wanted to do most. The palms waving in the tropical trades and the sound of surf crashing on the reef were a background to dreams of home. I felt the war was never going to end.

The Marines had again constructed their little washing machines. Lining the windward side of the island, their plungers pounded up and down in an empty ammo can and the clanking sound of their windmills played a refrain that seemed to say "Let's get home, get home, get home."

We lay at anchor until 6 June. Monotony replaced all other emotions. Finally we weighed anchor and headed out to sea again. Exiting that palm fringed atoll we left her surf drenched beaches behind, and Condition III watches and "fine tuning the rig" began again.

There were some humorous aspects to the stress we were under. That evening when the alert was sounded, a bogey was spotted by our lookouts, and a closing range rate reported by CIC. We opened fire and the sky quickly filled with the dark gray bursts of 5 inch shells, the whole task group joining in. Suddenly there was a call to "Cease fire." A conference was called in the Wardroom and there was a lot of explaining about how the planet Venus could show a closing range rate. I wonder what that little screw up cost the taxpayers?

Chapter 4: The Marianas-Saipan, Tinian and Guam

6-6- We left Majuro for the invasion of Saipan, Tinian and Guam. Admiral Willis Lee shifted his flag to the *New Jersey*. We were now a part of Task Group 58.2. Course westerly, we sailed a quiet ocean, with trade winds softly capping a brilliant blue ocean with white. The routine of Condition III readiness was maintained, but for days on end we seemed a disembodied force, sailing like the ancient mariner- "a painted ship upon a painted ocean." And it was hot. Once again pitch bubbled between the teak planks of our weather decks.

The task group stretched its camouflaged men-o-war from horizon to horizon. CAP lifted from the decks of carriers on our beam and we stood endless Condition III watches. One third of the ship's complement was on alert, one third on stand by for drills and one third trying to relax in sweaty bunks.

Gray-blue skies and light breezes matched a featureless ocean. No pelagic birds broke the monotony, the only sound was the soft swish of radar antennae, rotating in endless search for the enemy. The throb of our power plant buried with her watch standers, deep in the bowels of the ship, lived in another world. Forced draft blowers pushed hot air at them for four long hours-then the snipes would rush topside to feel the "cool breeze."

The temperature reached 115 degrees on the main deck and quite a few men suffered in parts unmentionable with heat rash. Sailors hosed down weather decks, trying to keep the lower spaces a bit cooler. Salt spray caked in white runs, almost like snow. I hear again in the distance, the boatswain's pipe, and the call: "Now hear this. Sailors man your brooms, a clean sweep down, fore and aft. Sweep down all weather decks and ladders." Then the gentle roll turned us to a view of the horizon that stretched to eternity.

6-10- Our first contact in weeks was a Betty, shot down by search planes from TG58.2. At a range of sixty five miles, the only record her pilot left was a watery grave far from the sight of his fellow men and the enemy he tried valiantly to destroy. Then a bos'n piping: "Now secure from General Quarters. Carry out the plan of the day."

We supported carrier air strikes against enemy bases on Saipan. General Quarters were manned most of the next several nights. Contacts on radar showed bogies shadowing our movements, sporadic single plane attacks, breaking off at ranges just out of reach. Sleep, a sort of fitful daze with half awake gun crews, ready to jump to action stations if the enemy got past the CAP.

6-12- The starboard 20mm battery splashed a Betty close aboard, bearing 010 degrees. A ball of flame and a loud "womp," then a rapidly spreading sheet of burning fuel was the end of another Samurai. We were up all night, at battle stations, securing just before dawn. A quick cup of black coffee and back to the gun director for dawn alert. All night long, bogies surrounded our Task Group. Flares dropped constantly. The ghostly Fleet illuminated, is for a moment silhouetted against a black ocean. Night fighters lifting off from the carriers on our bow and stern, the glow of their exhaust like fireflies disappearing in the dark.

The men in CIC, Combat Information Center, or the Center of Intellectual Confusion, take your pick, vectoring planes to targets at fifty and sixty thousand yards. We had entered a phase of "the war of the wizards," as Winston Churchill phrased it. More and more our superior air control rested on the dramatic improvement of electronics. Advances in acoustics and sonar also continued to aid us in the destruction of the enemy's submarines. The Japanese knew we

Apra Harbor Guam with Quonset huts supplying Sea-bees everything they needed to build a naval presence on a coral strip.

were coming but were powerless to stop our advance. Our technology had leaped beyond the Japanese industrial potential. We were mass producing the implements of war with interchangeable parts- the Japanese were still using a great deal of homefront labor to craft items that had to be hand fitted at an assembly station. Their standard field rifle that I picked up on Saipan showed the marks of hand filing on many of the small parts.

At morning muster, Ensign H. was missing. A query from me brought a snicker from the 5th Division's leading bos'n. Seems Ensign H. had been catching men dozing on gun watches. Rushing from starboard to port he tried to catch additional miscreants. Now the athwart ship walkway Ensign H. was rushing through was very dark, and the crew placed a heavy mess bench across the passage. On the far side a bunch of buckets half-filled with water awaited him. Ensign H. hit the bench and landed in the buckets. The gun crew helped him down to Sick Bay and he never reported another man for sleeping on watch. He limped for a month.

The following morning, we launched aircraft to spot for the main battery bombardment of Saipan. All hands went to General Quarters and the first broadside was fired at a range of twenty thousand yards. That's ten nautical miles! We were hurling a group of high explosive shells, each weighing twenty seven hundred pounds. A broadside moved the ship some eighteen inches across the axis of the flight of the shells each time we fired.

As the range closed we began to see smoke and then flashes of fire as the rounds found their targets. The OS2U's directed each load to its mark, flitting about over the target like dragon flies. A pall of smoke seemed to hide most of the shore and we could see no sign of an enemy response. Then suddenly, a spotter aircraft was hit by enemy AA fire (not one of ours). We watched through binoculars as she went down in a spiral of smoke and debris. Until you take casualties, action seems very remote. Even the loss of planes and ships close aboard didn't seem to involve us as directly as hand to hand combat would have. The weapons were so awesome, the action seldom lasted for long. Well trained crews cleared the damage as quickly as it occurred.

A few splashes from what appeared to be three inch enemy shore batteries raised plumes of spray near some of the cans but I saw no damage to the Task Group from the beach. Forty-eight hours of continuous bombardment by the old battle-wagons covered the landing areas. We stayed further out and it was quite a sight to watch the Task Group execute an "Emergency 9 turn."

Halyards snaping taut, signal flags as stiff as boards in the wind, the sea a blue backdrop, white wakes and spindrift sparkling in the summer sun. Skies blue, and the towering, pristine white of cumulus clouds formed a backdrop. Sub contacts and fighter aircraft shouting: "Tally-ho!" into the VHF as contact was established. It was a very busy time. Sky 1,2,3 & 4, the five inch gun directors, swinging about. Radar antennae moving up and down, looking like giant beetles, animated toys of the Red God of Battle. The 40mm and 20mm gun crews with life jackets and battle helmets manned the barrels that were our close-in fire support. Many a young sailor, still in his teens, playing a deadly game, had to grow up fast. Trajectory controlled by the precessed angle of the new gun sights, determined by the rate at which the gun pointer swung ahead of the target. This required a steady hand and a cool head. A good pointer literally grew into his Mark 14 gun sight, ignoring the friendly fire that frequently bounced off the gun shields or the superstructure. With evening alert, more bogies closing and solutions generating in fire control computers- only to hear- "Hold fire! Friendlies!"

Flaming enemy planes splashing in the formation. Three that night, splashed by our night fighters. Streams of tracers flashed from the screen as the enemy tried desperately to close.

6-19- At 10:00, we were alerted again. The claxon horn, the bos'uns pipe and the MC blared, "General Quarters. All hands man your battle stations!"

Streams of men were running fore and aft, forward to starboard and aft to port: the organized chaos of men at war. Joseph Campbell, the philosopher who penned *The Power of Myth*, said man creates a myth when he says, "Here's a soldier suit, we've got a job for you."

The air waves were filled with transmissions as we maneuvered to launch aircraft and defend against a massive number of bandits. Closing from a range of one hundred odd miles, Combat Information Center informed all secondary batteries that our fighter air was tangled with a massive air armada launched from enemy carriers. Our torpedo planes were being launched when the first enemy planes appeared. Closing low, Tonys, Bettys and Jills came in.

Enemy bombers and torpedo planes carried these Anglicized names since Japanese nomenclature was more difficult for our lookouts to remember, and impossible to pronounce under the stress of combat. They flashed into the formation with anti-aircraft batteries pouring out shells. Pieces of exploded five-inch shells were bouncing off the decks and occasional twenty-mm rounds from our "friends" exploded against the bulkheads, looking like fireflies in the darkened superstructure. Planes were splashing in the formation and then with the Fleet wheeling in radical turns in evasive action, the firing stopped as suddenly as it started. Amazing, but again we took no casualties.

The planes attacked in two waves. Soon another group was picked up and closing fast. Firing started again, building rapidly to a crescendo of sound that was deafening. My tin hat felt very inadequate. I remember writing my Mother that I was just eighteen inches from the safest place on the ship. This gave her great comfort during the war she later told me. What she never realized was that I referred to the top of turret three, on whose mighty armor my gun director and my feet rested.

The *San Francisco*, a cruiser on our beam suddenly began to pour smoke into the air. She had taken a hit. A Japanese plane had dived into her fantail, igniting her smoke pots. Damage was minimal but, my God, what a lot of smoke poured out. I'm sure accompanying enemy planes reported her as being in big trouble, probably sinking.

In the morning, we were detached from Task Group 58.2 and ordered to join Task Group 58.7. This was comprised of the Battleships *New Jersey, Iowa, South Dakota, Indiana, North Carolina, Massachusetts, Washington* and *Alabama*. Escorted by a screen of Cru Div 6, and Des Divs 12, 89, and 106, we proceeded to a position some one hundred and fifty miles West of Guam. Land based planes were said to be forming and an attack seemed imminent. The Task Group topped off from AO's (fleet oilers) and we escorted them some four hundred miles to a station out of harm's way.

At about 1500, a report came from one of the screen that a bogie was closing, bearing 270 true. We picked it up on optical, the range finders reporting a closing range rate. First one ship, then another commenced firing. I could see a bright spot in the heavens, but too far away for the 40mm battery. The air was filled with gray-black bursts as hundreds of five inch shells exploded. Suddenly the cry, "Cease fire!" rang out. The whole Fleet was firing at the planet Venus again. Plenty of red faces in C.I.C. where they had confirmed a closing range rate on Venus for the second time this month.

6-18- From the ship's log: "Cruising 250 miles West of Rota. Enemy planes attack formation but are shot down by CAP. Jap force 350 miles SW.

6-19- From the ship's log: "Cruising 150 to 250 miles West of Rota. Various small groups and single planes detected during early morning. **0553** single plane shot down by screening DD. **0915** received information regarding a large enemy force (surface) bearing 250T, 350 miles- composed of 4 BB, 7 CV, 8 CA, 20 DD. Radar contact on large group of enemy planes 258T, 122 miles. **1007** General Quarters. **1035** enemy planes 40 miles West closing rapidly. The *New Jersey* opened fire on a Zeke and two Jills on port quarter.

1153- Fired on two Tonys approaching ship. Formation subjected to almost continuous air attacks from **1045** until **1205**. During this time there was not a noticeable lull. From **1205** until **1320** enemy planes were in our area and under fire from our batteries and other ships in the Task Group.

"**1319**- A single Tony taken under fire by the *New Jersey*. The Jap seemed to be launching planes (from the carriers) on a one way trip over the Task Force, then flying to Rota or Guam to land for refueling and reammunitioning.

"**1600**- Task Group launched fighter sweeps against Rota and Guam.

"**1730**- Colors were put at half mast while the Fleet buried their dead. Divine services on the fantail were heavily attended. Thanks given to the Supreme Protector of us all for His mercy.

"**1955** Unidentified plane fired on by ships of our Task Group.

"**2200**- Base course for night 260T. Speed 23 knots to intercept Jap Fleet. For the *New Jersey* one probable, one assist. For the CAP over 220 planes shot down. Fighter sweeps over Guam and Rota destroyed another 100 planes. Superficial damage to *San Francisco*. **1500**- Search planes reported Jap force 290T, 250 miles. **1600**- Carriers launched all available planes to attack enemy formation. **2000**- strike returning, took Easterly heading to recover planes. Steamed east for approximately three hours which let the Jap forces escape. Distance too great and time too late for easy recovery. Several planes attempted to land on DD's in the dark. Searchlights were turned on and flares dropped but many planes lost in dark and confusion. Primary problem, shortage of fuel in aircraft after long strikes. **2257** changed course to northwest speed 16 knots to overtake 20 knot enemy force."

A very courageous act by Admiral Marc Mitscher was his decision to turn on the landing lights on carrier flight decks. This helped many a flyer find a haven as fuel expended on raids extended to the max, ran tanks dry. Pilots landed on the first carrier deck they could find. If a Japanese sub had been able to get into the formation, Mitscher would no doubt have been severely sensured.

The time lost in maneuvering into the wind to recover aircraft and the urgent need to refuel the destroyers of the screen may have resulted in the escape of the enemy force and a prolongation of the war. It was a tough break.

6-22- From the ship's log: "Chase abandoned, picking up survivors from aircraft ditched in the turkey shoot. Japs ships sunk: 1 CV, 1 DD, 2 AO. Damaged 3 CV, 1 BB, 2 DD, with additional reports of 1 CA, 3 AO, and 3 more DD of which one probably sunk. Jap planes lost 373. American planes lost 70. Japs damaged 2 CV, and 1 BB. Fleet returning to vicinity of Saipan."

One of the pilots picked up on a can we were refueling reported several Jap oilers in flames and sinking, several carriers in flames. It was tough for the fly-boys to watch the crippled enemy slip away, knowing they'd have to fight them again.

6-27- Bogies! General Quarters until 2200. One snooper flew directly overhead but we were ordered to hold fire because our night fighters were being vectored in. We heard the soft buzz of the fighter's machine guns, saw the tracers, fire-flies converging on the target, and heard a dull "whump." The sky lit up and the pilot reported, "Splash one bandit."

The nights were filled with General Alarms and battle stations were manned at midnight several times during the next few days. I wondered what the Japanese must have felt when their young pilots were sent out night after night and so few returned? The vectoring of the Task Group's CAP had now reached a degree of professionalism that cost the enemy dearly.

7-1- Two alerts and a mid watch. I was pooped. Watches and alerts blended into one another until we were bleary eyed. The second alert was the scene of night fighters splashing another Betty in flames. An incandescent flash of burning AV gas and an oily slick at dawn were the only markers for a fallen enemy.

7-2- I was asked to conduct Jewish divine services for some of the crew members. I'm afraid they knew a great deal more of the ritual than I did, but their devotion and the feeling that any communion which the Almighty gives to men in the forward area is always inspiring. "There are no atheists in a foxhole."

I heard recently from Jerry McCormick, wife of Capt. Jack McCormick, that Father J. Goode, the Catholic Chaplain that had endeared himself to many, had passed away the 15th day of May 1992. A wonderful old time Jesuit, he comforted many a crewman of many a faith on the *New Jersey*.

7-6- We entered Saipan's rather unprotected roadway. Destroyers patrolled the outer perimeter constantly to interdict any enemy submarines in the area. We had been underway from Majuro for about a month, but Saipan gave us little opportunity to rest. Stores had to be replenished, ammunition and fuel bunkered. The DD's needed all the help our working parties could give them and we worked around the clock.

An ammunition ship moored alongside was manned by merchant seamen. They were having a labor dispute and picked this time to go on strike. A closing bogie broke the strike. The Captain posted Marines to stop them from casting off, and the General Alarm called all hands to man their battle stations. They decided to help offload the ship and did so at a very rapid clip.

Only one eighth of Saipan was still in enemy hands, but the resistance was stubborn. The distant rumble of artillery and fire support from sea borne batteries was a refrain played over and over as we worked the enemy over. The end of the island still in Japanese hands was illuminated at night with star shells from cruisers and destroyers. Tons of high explosive shells roared into the enemy lines. A dull purple glow bathed the night sky and occasional flashes from our warships or from exploding munitions on the beach gave the scene an eerie look.

It was a month before the last pockets of resistance and snipers could be cleared. Tinian was temporarily bypassed. Guam was bombed day and night.

Ex-governor of Minnesota and future presidential candidate, Harold Stassen, a Naval Reserve Commander, came aboard to look over Flag Plot and the staff quarters preparatory to Admiral Halsey joining us with his flag in Pearl. Another flag for the *Jersey*. Spruance had been aboard for Truk and Palau.

The inner harbor of Apra, Guam was a seething mass of small boys scuttling back and forth between their ships and supply vessels. Moored to anchor buoys like fat slugs, they seemed to be feeding a never ending stream of drones. LST, LCI, LCT, LCVP and YPC were ferrying their cargo to huge supply dumps, rapidly converting the landing beach into a supply center.

Dive bombers hovered over the enemy, falling in on call from Marine forward observation posts. Further out at sea a constant patrol of aircraft from the land based squadrons kept watch for any effort to reinforce the Japanese. Army Thunderbolt fighters flew over us from strafing runs, and a procession of Catalina flying boats patroling for submarines formed an endless chain. Many of them were built in New Orleans, on Lake Pontchartrain.

7-10- All resistance ceased. A final suicide attack; Japanese jumping from cliffs, rather than surrender, marked their final hours. The intensity of one last charge by the Japanese, forced our lines back almost two thousand yards before it was repulsed. Japanese bodies were stacked like cord wood in the rictus of death.

7-19- First mail call in over a month. What a thrill! Everyone in his own dream of hearth and home. Some sad young men getting the first "Dear Johns" that were a part of almost every mail call. Separations over the months began to stretch bonds made in haste. This was the second mail we had received in two months. It's been a busy time, and mail was frequently stacked on islands left far behind. One parcel was a cake my Mother baked for me. It arrived about five months late. I thanked her and told her it was great.

1400-1600- Catapult watch, **1600-1800** on watch in Sky-1, and a mid watch in Air Defense. I didn't get to sleep before the mid. It was a long, long night.

From my diary: "Big green bottle flies have come aboard- a product of the thousands of unburied dead. When the wind is off the island and the hook is down, the odor and the flies pervade everything. The revolting little pests remind us how fortunate we are to be seaborne. Yet, I talked with a Marine on the beach and he was relieved to get off the transport that brought him to Saipan. 'God', he said, 'I thought when we were at sea, we'd take a torpedo. The only time I could sleep was when I had a life jacket on and was able to get topside and out of that stinking hold.' I guess it all depends on your perspective.

7-21- Guam- more troops landing, the beach is a shell blasted, burning rubble. Littered with wrecked tanks and all terrain vehicles, most of which appear to be ours, the chaos is Orwellian. Planes returning today were marked by the enemy's "light fire," predicted in the op-order. Wings shot full of holes, landing gear in half retracted positions, tail surfaces showing huge holes, mute testimony to the close fire support those carrier fly boys were giving the Marines. One Avenger, taking off from the Hornet, crashed directly in front of her bow. There was a burst of flame and a dull noise of her exploding bombs. A pilots requiem. Another Avenger launched seconds later, flying through the smoke of her funeral pyre.

7-23- Landings started on Tinian.

From the ship's war log- "**7-8 to 23**- Cruising in vicinity of southern Marianas. Anchored off Saipan **7-23** through **7-30**."

We got ashore for a few hours with the Admiral's party and were amazed at the mass of men still pouring in. No chance here of another Tarawa.

7-18- We rejoined Task Group 58.3. **7-25** through 27 and supported air strikes against Palau, Carolines. **7-27**- Air strikes and photo reconnaissance completed, we withdrew.

We rejoined TG58.4 on 30 July in the Southern Marianas and were ordered to proceed to Pearl Harbor.

8-2- We detached from TG58.4 and formed TG50.12 *New Jersey*, *Hunt*, *Hickox*, and *Lewis Hancock*. Departed for Hawaii. Signal flying- 4th Repeater-Mike- Corpen-090 (My course 090 True).

8-4- We anchored in Einewetok Atoll. Nissen huts covered the atoll on both sides of the channel. Since our last visit, net tenders had been stationed to prevent the entry of Japanese midget subs. Coronado flying boats were hauled out, gleaming in a merciless sun. The palm trees looked like woebegone relics of a horror movie and had been totally destroyed during the fighting. Most were just blackened stumps or a single shaft with fronds hanging like wilted salad.

Flights of Liberators in squadrons of twenty and thirty were flying overhead enroute to further bomb the atolls of Truk, Yap and Woleai. The harbor was covered with LSTs. Supply ships of every possible configuration were pouring in. The growing size of the Fleet was still hard to believe. The old battleships had been modernized as platforms for shore bombardment and the fast carrier striking forces were splitting and expanding with the addition of one new carrier after another. Heavy cruisers with their eight inch rifles looked as big as the old wagons. Sleek and forbidding, with the grace of greyhounds, they seemed to be multiplying in amoeba-like fashion in each new island harbor.

The next day, on 5 August, we crossed the 180th meridian, 14-00 N.latitude, in calm sea with only an announcement to mark our passage. Golden Dragons now, but initiation was waived because of the threat of enemy submarines.

8-9- We steamed into Pearl, past Hickam Field, Ford Island, and the remains of the *Utah* and the *Arizona*- moored starboard side to *Maryland* and the sub base. "**1100**- Allen Lill, waving from the flying bridge of the *Maryland*, Bruce Baird also aboard, N.C. Cromwell and Ben Dart on the *Mississippi*, the Tulane NROTC was well represented."

Seeing females after nine months of monastic life among coral and sea gave us a strange feeling. Liberty in the bustle of an urban community and the sights and sounds of civilization were great for morale. The city was awash with sailors and soldiers from all over the United States. I saw a dozen classmates from Tulane and several of the N.R.O.T.C. Staff who had just a year ago been instructors in the program. We exchanged sea stories, and had delightful reunions at Don the Beachcombers. David Spizer was a doctor at Aiea General Hospital. Bob Parker was the Officer in Charge of Transport at the Officers Club in Honolulu. Ralph Schwartz was in a gunnery division on the *Maryland*, and Allen Koltun was the newly appointed C.O. of a sub chaser.

He recently reminded me of a very humorous incident when he was first assigned to the SC. They were about to depart for the South Pacific from the West Coast of Uncle Sugar Able. Newly commissioned and assigned as supply officer, he had to figure the amount of stores required to get the ship over with enough surplus for any unexpected delays. Now, the old supply manual issued the SC, listed toilet paper by the sheet. Allen figured number of sheets per man per day, and then number of days to cross the Pacific, allowing a ten percent margin of error (he is today a very respected New Orleans CPA). Brilliant planning, right? Wrong! The new Navy Supply Manual had changed sheets to rolls, and SC's were pretty far down on the pubs list for updating. The next day a huge truck, almost as long as the SC, pulled out on the pier. A sailor brought Koltun the manifest, a look of awe on his face, "Mr. Koltun," he said "My God, we have enough toilet paper to wipe the ass on every sailor in the Fleet. What will we do with

This was the Mark 1, Mod. 1 "Skimmer", built expressly for Admiral Halsey. The Admiral loved it. The sail locker later made a canvas top for the passengers and decorated it with beautiful turksheads and other nautical knots.

it?" Koltun thought for a moment and answered, "We'll have to tell the Skipper to off load the ammunition." One thing about the N.R.O.T.C, you learned fast.

Prostitution in Pearl was controlled to some extent by the military. Lines of soldiers, sailors, and marines cued outside the houses and prophylactics were issued by the Shore Patrol as the sailors exited. Not a pretty memory, but that's the way it was. The advice to the crew from the medical staff, "If you're going to play in the sand, wear a raincoat."

There were huge numbers of newly commissioned transports, destroyers and cruisers. The industrial might of the United States was building ships and planes in numbers that produced an ever widening number of Task Groups for each succeeding operation. The Punch-Bowl had become Staff Headquarters where Admiral Spruance and Admiral Halsey alternately planned successive operations. The logistics of each thrust called for meticulous attention to detail. Estimates of enemy capabilities had to be balanced against vast amounts of data gathered in search and reconnaissance missions and correlated to mesh with offensive plans. A problem of converting sheets to rolls of toilet paper was a microcosm of the problems a misplaced decimal point could cause when torpedoes or incendiary ammunition was involved. Multiply this by the hundreds of thousands of sailors and troops engaged under the umbrella of CINCPAC (Admiral Nimitz, Commander in Chief Pacific), and remember there were no computers to simplify the compilation and sorting of data.

Huge piles of mail again- love letters from my bride and sad news from my folks- Jack Gordon, a boyhood friend, was missing in action. He was a pilot on the *Tennessee*. I found out in Pearl, his OS2U was rear ended by an Army Moth, spotting for a Marine Division on Tinian. He had joined a growing list of classmates, casualties of the bitter struggle for islands most of us had never heard of a few short years ago.

I was transferred to the 7th Division, the

"The Bull" and staff officers on the "Skimmer". Note the short pants and open collar that were Halsey's trade mark in Sou-Wes-Pac.

starboard division of 40mm quads. New Condition III watch station, a lot closer to the Starboard catapult, and hence a lot less running when Flight Quarters sounds.

We found Honolulu overwhelmed with a huge influx of service personnel, but made the best of it. We went to the Royal Hawaiian Hotel for lunch, then swam on Waikiki Beach. The view of Diamond Head and the Outrigger Club made a magnificent backdrop, but we were rather disappointed with the coarse sand of the beach. Food was a high priority. Chinese food, steaks and ice-cream seemed quite elegant and we could never get filled. The food on the *Jersey* was really quite good, but the change was just what the doctor ordered. Seeing flowers and birds, after looking at wrecked landing craft and shredded palm trees was like being in heaven. Sitting on the beach and looking out over the lagoon at sunset, I was lost in another world. Mynah birds, doves and lush vines, tables lit by candle-light, how I wanted Jean to be with me.

I was assigned to Fire Fighter's School. A

mock up of the engineering spaces of a man-o-war was turned into a blazing inferno for a classroom. A fantastic experience. Worked our buns off for two days, and learned that oil fires could be controlled, if you knew how. Being lead man on a high pressure hose, with a second hose spraying your body, flames surrounding everything in a blanket of red, was quite a show. Several casualties were sent to the hospital during this training. Learned to breath through my nose, not my mouth. It was painful, but the only way to survive. The instructors impressed us to RFM (read the f—ing manual). Returned to the *Jersey* black with soot and feeling the time spent well worth the effort. One more orgy of ice cream before we got underway.

My roommate, Larry Moorman, still one of my closest friends, and I emptied every Coke machine on the pier. Hoarded, with a bottle of Boca Chica Rum, we'd open a Coke and lace it with a bit of rum, after each evening alert. Then we'd play cribbage for what we deemed the "SouWesPac Championship." These are the bonds of shipmates that have no counterpart in civil life.

8-24- We received Admiral Halsey, Com3rd Fleet, and Staff aboard, and the word was 150 days at sea for the next operation.

At 0930, we were under way. The roll of the ship as we hit the open ocean was a pleasant way to sleep off the excesses of our brief sojourn ashore. Then came the mid-watch, as JOOD, to return me to the reality of shipboard routine.

Throughout 25-28 August, we took part in continuous underway training- gunnery exercises with off-set shoots for the main battery and the five inch rifles- towed sleeves for the forty-mm and twenty-mm batteries.

Admiral Wm. F. Halsey was aboard, and every officer and man aboard felt his presence. He cut quite an impressive figure, thick-set, with a size 17 neck, craggy browed- he exuded an air of confidence that was infectious. His staff was rather numerous, about sixty odd yeomen and some twenty officers made berthing an added complication. We quickly learned that having Halsey aboard meant a sizable delegation of reporters. He was a news maker and the press knew it.

Once again, we neared the 180th meridian and were about 10 degrees south of Johnson Island, steaming in formation, with three DD's heading south by west.

I stood on the bow in a 20mm gun tub and watched the waves part in sibilant harmony and dreamed of home. Looking back at the massive superstructure of the *Jersey*, her antennae silhouetted against the rapidly receding highlands, pulled me back into the reality of dog watch on the bridge.

Chapter 5: The Philippines and a Typhoon

In the past weeks we sailed three thousand six hundred miles, transiting the Pacific from Pearl Harbor to the coast of New Guinea. We crossed the Equator again at 152 degrees east and the 180th meridian at 09-20 north latitude. We were a part of Task Group 30.1, carriers surrounding the *Jersey* and a screen of destroyers, like hounds on a tether, covering our advance with sonar and evasive course changes. The ships maneuvered in a choreographed ritual that seemed to bind each to the other as though by invisible strings. The weapons of each interlock to fashion an impenetrable umbrella of steel.

9-4- We dropped the hook in Seeadler Harbor, Manus Island, a tiny atoll in the Admiralty Islands, palm fringed shores and white coral beaches gave it an idyllic appearance. Lightly defended by a small detachment of the enemy, it was quickly taken. With its excellent harbor it was a staging area for the Pacific Fleet.

About this time a new duty as boat officer for the Admiral's Barge came about, and makes another memory of those strange events that military service seems to generate.

A notice was posted on the bulletin board. "Junior Officer with small boat experience report to the Executive Officer for possible assignment."

The prevailing attitude of the "Trade School" JO'S was "Don't volunteer for anything." I never felt that way. After all, what could the Navy do if I rejected the duty? Send me home? So I reported to the Exec to see what the "assignment" might be.

Turned out that Admiral Halsey didn't like the barges that had been used since the days of Admiral Horatio Nelson. Too slow. About the only change made was the addition of gasoline engines to replace oars. The barges, round chined and heavy, pushed through the water at about twelve knots. Sluggish and uncomfortable, not particularly sea worthy, their day had passed.

Since I had been fooling around with small boats all my life, and I was the only "Volunteer," I got the job. Commander McDowell, the Exec, told me to pick out a smart looking crew and check the new craft out, reporting to him on speed and seaworthiness.

The "Skimmer," Mark 1-Mod-1 from BuShips was a beauty. A 25 foot hull with a modified V bottom, and lots of beam, she could make about 35 knots. I picked two crews, each with a cox'n, a bowhook and an engineer. We spent the first morning in Manus running about and practicing docking drills. The skimmer was a great little craft, very responsive and fast. I knew the Admiral would be pleased.

For the next several weeks I raced about the harbor training the crews, mixed with swimming on remote beaches and visiting native villages. Finally, the MC blasted out- " Now, Lt. Frank report to the Executive Officer's Cabin."

"Well Frank, what do you think of the barge?"

"Great, Sir." I answered.

"And just when did you expect to tell me about it?"

"Not till you asked Commander."

He laughed and I became Admiral Halsey's Barge Officer.

About noon, a few days later, as we came alongside the after accomodation ladder, Bill Kitchel, the Admiral's Flag-secretary was waiting for me. Could I take the Admiral and a small party ashore for a swim? Of course I told him we'd be ready. The Admiral also asked that I run over to the hospital ship B*enevolence* to pick up a group of nurses who would join the swimming party. I was beginning to like the job better and better.

At 1430 Admiral Halsey, Admiral "Mick" Carney and a few of the staff piled aboard for the maiden voyage of the skimmer. We took them to Los Negros where just a few months ago the Army had landed. The small Officers Club was awash with brass- Captains, Commanders and LTJG. Frank. I saw Captain E.T. Eves, C.O. of the repair ship *Dixie*, who had given me my orders at Tulane University a little over a year ago. I had always admired him, in fact, I still think of him as epitomizing the best of what a regular Naval Officer represented to "us feather-merchants". When he heard I was Halsey's Barge Officer, he remarked that he'd like to shake hands with the Admiral. I was delighted to take him over and introduce him. It made my day.

The Admiral loved swimming, and at dusk, the beach on Manus was cleared of all but his party. When he finally got out of the water, the sun was dipping below the horizon. Bill Kitchel had asked me how long it would take to get the party to a staff meeting on Pier Able, where a meeting was scheduled with the newly arrived British Task Group Commander. I checked the chart and told him it would only take a matter of minutes.

As the sun began to dip below the horizon, the Admiral shook hands with the Colonel in charge of the area and we zipped out into the lagoon. About a third of the way across, the motor sputtered and died. We tossed about in the most God forsaken part of the anchorage. Not a single small boat in sight. I watched the "engineer" look at the motor for a few moments, and asked him what the problem was. It turned out he had been to a class B school in diesel engines, was a damn poor student and had the mechanical skills of a book-keeper.

I took off my shirt and crawled into the engine compartment. It was hot as Hades. I discovered we weren't getting any gas. The problem was why? At this point I looked up as an LCVP was passing. I shouted at him to come alongside. Telling him to take a line and start towing us to the pier was humbling, but I was determined to get the Admiral to his meeting in spite of my pride. Imagine my surprise when the coxwain of the LCVP told me he was due back to his ship and we'd have to make it on our own. I chewed him out and threatened him with the consequences if he left the Admiral adrift. Sweating and grease covered, I stole a look back at the Admiral who had a grin on his face from ear to ear. I was covered with oil from the engine, no shirt on and must have been a heck of a sight. Grudgingly, we were taken under tow and I continued to tinker with the engine. Finally found a clogged filter and the motor roared to life. Thanking the cox'n, I cast off. But that was not to be the end of my sorrow.

As the LCVP chugged away in the gathering darkness, the motor coughed and quit again. I shouted at the LCVP and saw the little bastard look over at us several times before he finally came about. He kept mumbling about getting his ass chewed if he didn't tow us and getting it chewed by his O.D. if he came back late with the "cockamamy" tale that he had towed Admiral Halsey. Once again we started on a slow drag

35

towards the meeting. I found a second filter, also clogged, but I wasn't about to let that Cox'n get away again. The Admiral was very late for his meeting.

I was standing forlornly by the skimmer when Bill Kitchel came over. "Charlie", he said, "take the skimmer back to the *Jersey* and check that motor out before we use it again." And, "Oh yes, the Admiral said to tell you not to feel bad. This is one thing Navy Regulations never has been able to cover." Quite a man, that Halsey.

Got back to the ship at 2020, just in time to shower and shave for the mid-watch. What a day. At dawn we sortied to rendevous with the Task Group.

9-6- From the ships log, "Joined TG38.5"

9-9- "Participated in air strikes against Palau."

9-11- From my diary- "We are now some three hundred odd miles from Manila, and about four hundred miles from Palau."

9-12- Dawn alert, more firing from screen- fighter aircraft splashed another couple of bandits. At 1030, we saw the Philippine Islands for the first time, just low shadows on the horizon, a range of mountains in the background. But, we were getting closer, operating in an area centered some 300 miles from Samar.

"Participated in support of air strikes against Visayan Group in the Phillipines. Have joined TG38.2, Admiral Bogan CTG in *Bunker Hill*. Received several Jap prisoners aboard, from sunken DD Natori, for interrogation. Unidentified aircraft approached within 6 to 8 miles of formation, not taken under fire."

9-13/17 "Continued support of air strikes."

9-14- We were patrolling the eastern Philippine Sea just 30 to 50 miles offshore from Samar, Suragio, and Mindanao. In spite of continued squalls, carrier air mounted heavy strikes against airfields on Davao, Cagaya, and more northern strips. Our losses were reported as light but over 200 Jap aircraft claimed destroyed. We again approached Palau. Tomorrow- D-day in the Philippines!

9-15- "We are expecting to be back in Manus for a D+5 conference. The recapture of the Philippines is said to hinge on this first phase, although so far there seems to be little opposition. A Dinah was shot down during evening alert by the CAP and three others probed but escaped.

"One of the Japs we picked up was an arrogant little bastard who spoke English. Halsey saw him from the bridge and shouted down to the Marine guard, 'Make that little son-of-a-bitch look up, I want to see him.' The Marines had him walking a straight line in short order.

"There were several bogies during evening alert. Hope we get back to Manus as planned. No mail for some time."

2130-A bridge game in the Wardroom was interrupted by call to General Quarters. Four bogies closed to 11.5 miles but by 2220 we had lost them in the darkness and heavy rain. We secured from General Quarters, lightning flashing and rain squalls lashing the weather decks. The ship rolling in heavy seas. A feeling of oppression in the air portended a storm. All weather decks and light machine gun batteries were secured on the main deck. Green water was coming over the bow, and, as we pushed into moun-

A cast recovery on the port catapult in calm seas off Trinidad.

tainous waves, the ship shuddered as though in pain. Some gun shields on the bow, inch thick armor, were bent out of shape by the force of the waves. Although the *New Jersey* and her sisters could proceed at cruising speed in heavy weather, the smaller ships of the screen were catching Hell. Task Group speed was reduced again and again until we were barely keeping our bows into the winds.

0530- Dawn alert with bogies all over the screen again. It was hard to imagine the difficulty of launching aircraft from those pitching decks. Some distant firing, several planes splashed by CAP.

9-17- We moved into a fleet of transports, landing craft and supply ships. Dive bombers were working over pockets of resistance. Eight or ten planes regrouped overhead and were on call from the Air Wing Coordinator. Phosphorus shells were detonating on the beach and several old battleships were operating as close to the beach as their draft allowed. Cruisers and destroyers added to the bombardment. The Japs were catching Hell.

We dropped the hook at 7,000 yards and I was told to get the barge ready. At the last moment the Admiral's plan to go ashore was canceled and we got underway at 1500, rejoining TG38 at sea. The weather was beautiful again and the sunset left you wondering, "What the Hell are we doing here? We're messing up one of the most beautiful places left on earth.".

9-20- My watch on the bridge was uneventful. Course 340T, speed, 24 knots. We were scheduled to support air strikes against Manila. The formation was a diamond, with the *New Jersey* at the center of four carriers. The flat tops were the primary target of Jap air. We were overflown by Japanese planes that could have done some real damage to us. Time and again the enemy pressed on to the carriers, passing over the ships that defended them. Flying low, they had to run through a hail of light machine gun fire (20 and 40mm). They were splashed in a ball of fire, just short of their objective, sun-drenched spray rising like the plume of a spouting whale, flame substituted for arterial blood. We were in the midst of numerous small islands, each with a squadron or more of Nip air. The CAP shot down an estimated seventy of their planes and bombed air strips wherever they found them. Merchant ships and support craft were secondary targets and the Imperial losses had to be hurting their field support badly.

9-22- From my diary: "Had the 0400 to 0800 watch. Wind speed 80 knots relative- that's a lot of breeze. All main deck quads were secured, life lines rigged but no one was safe on the main deck. Green water in greasy swells rushed over everything. Several broken legs and arms in Sick Bay. General Quarters was a little late and stations that could be manned were watching four radar contacts and wondering how flight operations could be handled in this heavy sea. Winds abated a bit and a little after dawn (0700), some flights were launched. In spite of the threat of a typhoon, the Japanese continued to probe the screen, and the gray, cottony puffs of five inch anti-aircraft fire were seen all morning as the DD's on the screen gave them Hell.

"To get some idea of the difficulty of defending against these attacks, try shooting from the back of a pickup truck on an unpaved country road, the target a diving twisting mourning dove. The CAP was able to splash most of the bandits and the DD's somehow got many of the survivors, but the ones they missed, came through with awesome determination to die for the Emperor. When they hit the damage could be massive. At 1200 we secured from GQ drenched with spray from rising winds, wet and exhausted."

When the swells were on the beam, a 30 knot wind could drench the main deck gun crews on the windward side with a salt coating that left you feeling as though coated in wet sand. Eyes burning, it was great to get a quick shower and hit the rack.

"The seas picked up even more and rolled across our bow in long, even rows. They were at least twenty feet high from trough to crest. Some, reinforced by simple harmonic motion, were much larger. These were the ones you had to watch out for. There were no white caps on these mountainous swells. The wind whipped the crests into a spume of fine mist that coated ship and sailors in salt, till we looked like we were frosted in snow.

"I finally got to the Wardroom for the first hot meal in the past twenty four hours. Little information on the air strikes against Manila, except that there were quite a number of barrage balloons up. This was an attempt to keep the torpedo planes as high as possible. But, weaving and twisting they pressed home on a fleet bottled in the harbor like sitting ducks."

9-23- "We missed the worst of the typhoon by changing course and increasing speed slightly. All day we had Baker two-blocked and refueled destroyers. As fast as one was finished another was alongside. Heaving lines and line throwing guns established first contact, followed by a traveler with a lead to a heavy rubber hose. The deck hands and bos'uns have become real pros, using the drum of a large winch on the fantail to tend lines. It was quite a sight to see half a dozen seamen playing a 3 inch hauser, the cans, rolling and pitching alongside refueling even in these heavy seas. We were moving in quietly on Cebu and Samar to support a carrier strike. The last report on Manila was received today. The harbor took an awful pounding. Jap losses were reported- 144 planes in air battles, 140 aircraft destroyed on the ground. Forty oilers and transports, two destroyers and landing fields and docks heavily damaged. Our losses were 17 planes. You couldn't help wondering how long they could absorb this terrible beating. When our casualties are reported as light, I wondered how this news was received by the loved ones of those 'light casualties.' When you think of the reaction to a tanker grounding today, you wonder why we never gave pollution a second thought when we sank forty oil tankers in Mamila Harbor in one week." Nature's restorative powers are somehow overlooked.

Dawn alert was scheduled for 0445, and scuttlebutt had us scheduled for States-side in January. Rumors were rife, and it was all we talked about.

A rather cruel joke was pulled on one of the gunnery division officers today. He was a real bastard, and had managed to aggravate just about everyone. Well, one of the communicators sent him a fake dispatch, transferring him to recruiting duty in his home town. Elated, he rushed into the Wardroom to announce his good fortune. Handing out cigars he had been hoarding, he proceeded to make a real ass of himself. The Gun-boss looked at him like he had flipped, and asked to see a copy of the order. On finding out the dispatch was a joke, he was crushed. I almost felt sorry for him. All kinds of efforts were made to find the prankster. He remained unknown, except to a privileged few.

9-24- We supported air strikes against harbors between Luzon and Mindanao. The CAP shot down three snoopers, a Tony, an Oscar, and a Dinah. We left the islands and headed in the general direction of the Marianas.

9-25- Cruising off Samar, we continued support of air strikes. Battleships *Washington*, *Massachusetts*, and *Alabama* joined the Task Group and we departed for Saipan.

9-28- **0615** anchored at Saipan. I had the barge in the water while the ship was still underway. Spent the morning sight seeing, while we checked out the motor that was giving fuel problems again. Holding docking drills with a new cox'n, we stopped in the middle of the lagoon to swim for a few minutes, only to have the cox'n almost drown. He was a big midwestern country boy who had somehow managed to evade swimming instruction in boot camp. He had never learned to swim! When he saw the rest of us dive in, he followed. Thrashing about and going under a second time he almost drowned before I realized he wasn't joking. I managed to drag his 240 pound ass aboard, choking and scared to death. I'd have had a heck of a job explaining what we were doing swimming in the middle of the atoll.

1500, Captain Holden and Admiral Curtis Badger took the barge for an evaluation of our prior bombardment. We found what was left of a Jap dispensary, sani-tubes and mercurous oxide all over. A battery of enemy six inch rifles tilted at a crazy angle in a nearby revetment were proof positive of the lives saved in pre-invasion shore bombardment. The Japs had mounted some of their weapons on a narrow gauge railroad track, and had apparently been doing their usual number, firing a round or two and man-hauling the guns a hundred yards down the line for another salvo. Made the use of the Kingfisher spotter planes very important.

1815- Took Admiral Halsey and his party out to the seaplane landing area. He flew off, probably for Hollandia, and a visit with General MacArthur, his good friend and one of his staunchest supporters.

When the plane returned she was loaded up with a number of sailors who were suffering with terrible "jock-itch," the Navy equivalent of "jungle rot." Half way to Pearl, the medical officer accompanying them found a dramatic improvement in their condition. The plane returned with the very dissapointed sufferers. Instead of a trip to Pearl and the tender ministrations of pretty nurses, they got to use the aircraft, whenever one was available. Taking some of the worst sufferers for a ride, the high altitude semed to help keep the malaise under control.

Managed to buy a dozen cans of hot beer from a SeaBee, and returned to the *Jersey* in time for supper, a cat nap and the mid-watch.

9-29- The hills of Saipan were a beautiful setting for our tranquil anchorage. What a change from the scene of death and destruction we witnessed here a few short weeks ago- landing craft and G.I.s blown apart on their approach, heavy resistance on many of the beaches. There were still roughly two thousand Nip defenders alive in the hills, who refused to surrender. The Marines were rooting out about 200 men a week, but sadly, another six or seven G.I.'s died each week in the effort.

9-30- At 1700 we got underway for Ulithi, recently taken without much resistance. A wonderful anchorage, located north and east of Yap.

10-1 -Anchored in Ulithi Atoll. A mountain of stores was swung aboard from a supply ship and the fantail looked like a huge open-air warehouse. Ran into Malcolm Peters, another NROTC classmate on Mogmog. His destroyer has been credited with another Jap sub since I saw him last. The threat of a typhoon cut short liberty. All stores were secured and we prepared to sortie to ride it out.

This storm continued in varying degrees through the 8th of October. It was really heavy weather, reminded us of what we'd experienced in the North Atlantic. With mountainous waves and the ship rolling slowly some 23 degrees in each direction, I stood my watches on the bridge and in air defense with a rather queasy stomach. Had a lot of company.

10-3- Back in the harbor overnight, then under way 0715 some 48 hours later. Glad I had a day to run around the harbor in the Admiral's barge before we left. Saw Billy Minor, Bob Cole and David Levy on the beach. Beer drinking was never my favorite way to spend a day ashore, and I decided to go looking for shells on the outer reef of Ulithi Harbor.

Swimming on the coral reef with two of my friends, Larry Moorman and Alan Cooney - we had a real narrow escape. We had been diving on the outer reef for shells many times. But this time the tide started in. The coral on the outer edge dropped off into unfathonable deep green and blue depths. As we felt the increased pressure of the flooding tide, we started back by a shallow route we had used the past. Suddenly, we were in trouble. The water was moving swiftly and the drift would pass the end of the atoll where prior tides had scoured a channel. As we passed the end of the beach, I put my head down and tried to make it ashore. No go! Larry and Alan were even further out and we watched the island dropping further and further astern. By now we were quite exhausted and I dropped a bag of coweries I'd tied to my waist. Kicking off my tennis shoes to make swimming a little easier, I was threading water and wondering how much longer we would keep afloat. The memory of warnings in the *New Jersey* Plan of the Day of GIs being drowned in just such a fashion made things look pretty grim.

Then fate intervened. My feet touched a large coral head five feet below the surface. Holding on, I shouted to Larry and Cooney that I'd found bottom. They were specks on the lagoon and I really wasn't sure they heard, but all I could do was hang on and hope the tide would slack off.

After what seemed an eternity, it did, and I slowly swam towards the palm lined haven of the beach. As the water became shallow, I was too exhausted to stand. I crawled on the coral sand and watched as my two companions slowly worked their way in. Our knees were badly cut from that last stretch of broken coral, but we returned to the ship grateful to be alive.

The next day the weather worsened. Three destroyers moored alongside and the tender *Dixie* had torn loose at night and went aground. The open sea was the place to be.

Waves at sea were tough on us, but hell on the little boys. 40 to 50 foot troughs, 100 feet from crest to crest- we rolled some 23 degrees again. It was a slow roll and as green seas washed over bow and main deck, you wondered as she shuddered in the maelstrom, if she'd ever right herself. Rain squalls were almost horizontal. Sheets of water lashed at topside watchstanders and lookouts- shrieking winds of gale force, a constant roar as they passed through the rigging.

The storm was much more severe than we had expected. I played bridge in the Wardroom after supper but was glad to leave the game to go topside and get a little fresh air. My next watch was in the peak of the foremast in Air Defense, all watches on weather decks had been secured. Our primary responsibility was to act as lookouts for any errant small boys in trouble.

At dawn the air was filled with VHF transmissions from carriers with flight decks secured, hanger decks with loose planes sliding about. A steering casualty on one carrier caused her to veer across the base course of the formation. With visibilty limited to a hundred yards or less it was a bit hairy for ships with turning radius restricted by slow speeds and heavy winds. We lost more aircraft in that storm than the Japs accounted for in the past month.

In the half light of early morning the skies were a leaden gray, the formation separated. Some ships fought to keep their bows into the wind, some tried to come about to put the swells on their quarter. Essex class carriers took a beating. Flight decks twisted from waves that curled them up like a giant can-opener. *South Dakota* was taking spray as high as her Air Defense stations. The *Iowa* and the *New Jersey* performed magnificently. Their improved bow design lifted them into one huge comber after another. The destroyers should have drawn submarine pay. Bows plowed into one wave and rode up the next, their sonar domes out of the water.

We tried to take on fuel from a tanker, but the seas were just too much. We parted a couple of fuel lines as the tanker yawed in the heavy swells and she finally sheared off into the mist.

A DD came alongside and attempted to transfer mail. We had about 75 men of the Seventh Division tending the line, but they spent more time on the deck than on their feet. This was the monsoon season and we had more than enough of it.

The rain came in solid sheets. I'd never seen anything like it. You couldn't see across the fantail when a gust hit us and that was only 108 feet. Life lines were mandatory on the main deck and several times I was knocked off my feet by swells that washed across us, only the hook of the safety line keeping me from being swept over the side. The fantail had the Admiral's barge in a cradle, well secured, but a staff car broke loose, and we managed to secure it by the narrowest of margins.

At last the howling winds abated and the sea slacked off into long heavy swells. The battered Task Groups reformed and traced a track back to the harbor of Ulithi.

After a subsequent typhoon had inflicted even more severe damage on the Fleet, Adm. Nimitz issued a directive that in part summed things up: "A hundred years ago, a ship's survival depended almost solely on the competence of her Master and his constant alertness to every hint of change in the weather. To be taken aback or caught with full sail by even a passing squall might spell disaster. Seamen of the present day should be better at forecasting weather at sea, independently of the radio, than were their predecessors. The general laws of storms and the weather expectancy for all months of the year in all parts of the world are now more understood, more completely cataloged, and more readily available in a number of publications. Stress of the foregoing is no belittlement of our aerological centers and weather broadcasts, but just as the Navigator is held culpable if he neglects 'Log, lead and lookout,' through blind faith in radio fixes, so is the seaman culpable who regards personal weather estimates as obsolete."

What Admiral Nimitz failed to address was the Navy and the Task Force command structure. No ship's Captain wanted to make an independent course change except in "extremis." Perhaps some of the carrier flight decks could have been saved if the ships had taken the winds on their quarter, but what Captain wanted to risk censure for breaking clear of the formation?

The Fleet took a greater battering from this typhoon than had been sustained in any engagement since Pearl Harbor.

And thus the first phase of the plan to invade the Phillippines was completed.

Chapter 6: Okinawa, the Philippines and more heavy weather

10-10- The weather abated and with clearing skies we supported air strikes against Okinawa Jima and Ryuku Retto. Reveille was at 0345 each morning and dawn alert was at 0500, one in three watches were scheduled, and drills, drills, drills. We were "too weary to worry." The anti-aircraft batteries at General Quarters most of the day became the norm. Bandits on the screen after dark constantly kept the crews of the secondary battery running from bunk to battle stations.

The islands of the Okinawa chain, are only about 350 to 400 miles from Kyushu, the southernmost island of the Japanese archipelago. The operation was code named *Stalemate* and was in support of D-Day for the Philippines.

For the first time since we sailed into the Pacific, we enjoyed a touch of cool weather. We were in 30 to 40 degrees N latitude and the change was a welcome one. Forty degrees in the early morning hours and mid sixties by noon gave all hands a lift. The tedium of watches and alerts seemed somehow less burdensome in the cooler air.

The Task Group air strikes were very successful. Fourteen planes were shot down and seventy five destroyed on the ground. Japanese support craft, oilers and supply ships, yard craft and landing craft, several DD's and one CL badly damaged or sunk, had cost the Japanese badly needed support. Our own losses were nothing, a few planes damaged by anti-aircraft batteries and small arms fire from ground troops.

Admiral Sam Elliot Morison, in his *History of Naval Operations in World War II* phrased it well: "Okinawa, in Japanese, can be loosely translated as 'Long rope.' Halsey appears to have fastened it into a noose." Although this was the furthest penetration of Japanese home waters, we saw very little action. Dawn and evening alerts were canceled.

10-11- There were a few bogies and a midnight General Quarters. We refueled and started in towards Formosa (Taiwan). The air strikes against the Northern tip of the Philippines were planned to fool the Japanese into thinking the landings would occur there. I wondered?

Stayed at GQ until 0345. Our "bird men" enjoyed a field day. Reports were 124 planes shot down and 94 destroyed on the ground.

10-12- At 2100, enemy planes attacked the formation. Dropping flares, the lamp lighter gave an eerie illumination to the Task Force. As we wheeled and took evasive action, guns sent lines of tracers heavenward and the deep sounds of the secondary battery counterpointed the sharper rattle of heavy machine-guns. Five attackers were splashed by surface fire. The radar ranges and the gunnery were superb. Several planes were flamed by CAP but the *New Jersey* was a spectator- we never had to open fire. We did take several rounds of "friendly" 40mm fire and a lot of close misses. The carriers were rather jumpy and not too careful when a torpedo plane was anywhere in the vicinity. Can't really say I

A broadside fired in anger was quite an impressive sight. The ship's 80,000 pounds moved sideways some eighteen inches from the recoil.

blamed them. Our only casualty to date was one "sight see-er" hit by shrapnel while "lolly-gagging" on the fantail. Appropriately he was shot in the butt. Hope his Purple Heart will show this.

10-13- Friday. Well, I had only five hours sleep in the past forty eight. Watches and GQ just seemed to catch you with the hours scheduled off watch for sleep interrupted. My log showed bogies began to appear at 1805 and the night was a busy one. I had a rather narrow escape on this Friday the thirteenth. Friendly fire put several rounds of 40mm into a winch about 50 feet from our gun crew on the top of turret number three. We didn't know about it until dawn. Saved a piece of the shredded canvas cover and the plan of the day for a souvenir. It's quite a sight to see converging lines of tracers peaking a few yards overhead. Ship's log, "0153 *New Jersey* opened fire on plane crossing astern. Shot down in flames."

10-14- My log: "Last night, TG 38.1 was almost constantly under attack. Nine planes have been shot down in flames (by TG gunfire) within our formation. We picked up a few pieces of shrapnel but again God had his arms around us. Five inch shells were bursting directly overhead from the batteries of the carriers. Red lines of tracers from the heavy machine guns looked like incandescent streams from a garden hose. When we opened fire after dark, you had the feeling you were in the cone of a volcano that had erupted."

Last night the tracers looked close enough to touch and with a line of tracers coming at us, we hit the deck. Picking himself up, my pointer looked at me and said, "Mr. Frank, I was a track man in high school, and I thought I was pretty fast. But, when I hit the deck, I landed on top of you!" In 1989, I got a nice letter from him (James McFarland, now a grandfather) asking if I'd be at the 45th ship's reunion in Los Angles. He wanted to know if I remembered him. I wrote back, "Mac, I don't remember too many grandfathers, but I sure as Hell remember a fuzzy cheeked kid who landed on top of me one night in the air action off Okinawa." It's hard to recall how young we all were. I can see the gun crews standing in the light of dawn, helmets at a rakish angle, sound powered phones on the talkers. Most of them still didn't need to shave.

Flares that night seemed to have been dropped directly overhead. Drifting down ever so slowly, we felt stripped naked, our privacy invaded. I was exhausted when we secured from GQ, and knew the dog watch was to follow.

Dawn, and I was checking the quad ammo racks. We had taken a hit from what appeared to be a 20mm round. Scraps of 40mm casings and the smell of half burned smokeless powder were all around our mount, but somehow we were again untouched.

McFarland, G/M 3rd, again had the quote of the day- "Mr. Frank the evening prayer ought to be a dilly!"

10-14- My log-"Early reveille, secured from dawn alert at 0645 with orders to chow down fast. A quick bite and back to GQ- bogies all over. Heavy fighter strikes were launched. Jap dive bombers made several passes on the Hancock off our Port beam. She fired wildly, two near misses by attacking Jap dive bombers have her gun crews understandably nervous. She almost shot down a flight of her own Hellcats. Didn't secure until 1840."

10-14- Ship's log- 1518- "*New Jersey* opened fire on plane crossing stern- splashed in flames. 1526 opened fire on bomber that splashed near Hancock after dropping a bomb that just missed her."

During evening alert eight planes were shot down by AA fire within the formation. CAP reported numerous kills outside our visual range. The cruiser Houston was torpedoed. She was reported listing and dead in the water. Taken under tow, she retired from the area. Damage control proccedures and the quick action of rigging tows, salvaged a lot of ships that would have been abandoned a few years ago. Classmate Ed Addy lost an arm when an explosion on the *Houston* wounded a group on the fantail of the *Pittsburgh*, alongside to help fight the fires that were raging on the damaged cruiser.

GQ at 1709, 2146, and 2314 on reports of enemy planes.

10-15- Mail call was most welcome. A DD came alongside and we exchanged mail sacks and sent over a couple of tanks of ice cream from the "gedunk" stand. We are roughly between the Philippines and Formosa.

Evening alert and the carriers were lit up like Christmas trees to speed up launching and recovery. Planes were re-armed and serviced at an unprecedented rate. Signal lights were blinking and the air waves were filled with TBS transmissions (talk between ships). We were under continuous attack or surveillance for three days.

10-16-Ship's log- "Several planes approached our formation but concentrated on *Houston* (under tow) and Canberra group. 1425 received report of large Jap force, 2 BB, 1 CA, 2 CL, 8 DD 280 miles Northeast. Changed course to intercept, launched search planes. Results negative. *Houston* took another torpedo."

10-17- "Search for enemy force abandoned. Supported air strikes against Luzon."

10-18 to 10-21- We continued support of air strikes against Jap forces on the mainland, steaming in vicinity of San Bernardino Strait, air attacks by carrier strike force on Visayan Group in support of landings on Leyte. CAP splashed one twin engine bomber.

General Douglas MacArthur landed in the Philippines. Our GI's have returned and it's the Japs turn to retreat. Father Goode, a great man of the cloth, gave a most inspired prayer of thanksgiving after the evening alert was secured. In his Irish brogue he once told me "The worst mistake of the Catholic Church is the damned vow of celibacy." His small frame hunched against the wind, walking topside with his tin hat squared, he was a source of strength to the ship's complement during many a moment of stress.

10-22- We received four Jap POW's from a downed Betty.

10-24- From ship's log- "Cruising off Samar. 0228 CAP shot down Betty, first of nine during day. 0810 report of Jap force received. 4 BB, 8 CA, 13 DD off Mindoro, 240 miles West. Entered San Bernardino Strait. 0942 - Carriers launched large flights against Jap force. Returning planes reported heavy damage. During the day reports were received of two other groups of Jap ships to the North. One group one was comprised of- 2 CV, 1 CVL, 3 CL, and 3 DD. Group two consisted of- 4 BB, 5 CA, and 6 DD."

2000- We withdrew from support group and changed course to 000 degrees T.

10-25-Ship's log- "0742 Steaming North. Jap force reported 030 T, distance 125 miles. Changed course to intercept. Speed 20. Carriers launched strike against Northern Jap fleet. Received urgent request for assistance from Admiral Olendorf Commander of the 7th Fleet in the Leyte Gulf. 1114- We reversed course to assist Southern group, and to intercept reported 14 enemy ships steaming into San Bernardino Strait. Slowed to top off DD's and increased speed in moderate to heavy seas to 28 knots. Leaving screen and all but Iowa behind. Force to North was reported crippled. TG 34- *Iowa* and *New Jersey*, CRUDIV 14, Biloxi, and DESDIV 104 raced to assist the 7th Fleet."

10-26- Ship's log- "0041 Steaming at flank speed. Arrived vicinity of San Bernardino Straits. Formed battle line, *Iowa*, New Jersey screened by DESDIV 104. Cruisers in van. 0100 cruisers opened fire on enemy ship presumed to be Jap cruiser. 0105 explosions and dull glow on horizon. Target believed sunk. *New Jersey* passing targets in haste to get to Strait. Probably a CL or CV crippled by air on preceeding day. 0624 passing through area covered with survivors clinging to rafts. Picked up several American pilots sighted and some Japanese POW's. Jap fleet suffered grievous losses in Strait from PT's and the battle line of the 7th Fleet."

My diary - "General Quarters sounded as a late afternoon sun made the waters of the Philippine Sea sparkle. We steamed North with the largest set of colors streaming from the peak of the main yard that any of us had ever seen. Admiral Halsey was ready to fight the greatest naval battle of his career. The stars and stripes never looked more thrilling than they did at this moment. Scuttlebutt had us closing on a large fleet crippled by carrier planes earlier in the day. Snoopers were on the radar screen and the scenario looked more like Hollywood than the battle that was shaping up. Sleek men-o-war steaming with a bone in their teeth. Sailors with life jackets buttoned and tied, helmets on, eyes straining to find the enemy before dark. All hands were on station, weapons manned and ready. We had closed the range to about 100 miles and the main battery was limbering up. Huge muzzles swung right and left as fire control exercised the turrets."

Then a bombshell- MacArthur was in trouble, the Japs were pasting the landing force, a dispatch from CINPAC - "The whole world wants to know, where is the 3rd Fleet ?" Admiral Halsey was in a rage. He left the bridge and retired to his cabin. Admiral "Mick" Carney, his Chief of Staff, ordered the detachment of the *Iowa*, the *Jersey*, a couple of cruisers, and several DD's. We reversed course and at flank speed proceeded on a reverse course through the night to San Bernardino Strait.

During the 0000 to 0400 watch we picked up several "gadgets" on the radar. All hands manned their battle stations at 0230, but, all we could do was watch. Cruisers and destroyers changed course, their tracers screaming out to

39

enemy ships. The *New Jersey* steamed on at flank speed, leaving the action in our wake. The night sky was alight with the flash of the cruisers main batteries and on the horizon the dull glow and flash of detonations as high explosive war heads found their targets. A final huge light as enemy magazines exploded and streamers of red and gold, like giant sparks from a bonfire- then a soft amber light, fading as bunker oil burned out, and the sea claimed a once proud Japanese man-o-war.

We raced on through heavy swells and a night as pitch dark as the caves of Hell, refusing several targets (later identified as enemy CAs crippled by our air). At early morn we were steaming through thousands of Jap survivors, floating about in groups, and clinging to life-rafts. It looked like Coney Island on a hot summer day. The sea was covered with Jap swimmers as far as the horizon. Fortunately for them, the sea had calmed, as though an omen that the hectic night was over.

Scuttlebutt had it that Admiral Halsey sent a dispatch to the screen that caused a great flap among the Chaplains: "Recover a few of the more intelligent and cooperative survivors. Help the rest to join their honorable ancestors." I've tried to affirm this without success, but a Staff Officer told me Admiral Halsey made the decision and felt there was a choice of finishing a crippled foe or allowing them to swim ashore and rearm to fight again. One thing I remember, there were a lot of depth charges going off in San Bernardino that morning and I don't remember any reported submarine contacts.

This was a war where the Kamikazi and the Baku human bomb made dying for the Emperor the supreme sacrifice. Surrender was a word the Japanese abhorred. Sailors from sunken Japanese ships preferred death to capture and many were the tales of stabbings to fend off the proffered hand.

In the early morning hours a second "gadget" had been picked up fleeing south and was confirmed by the *Iowa*. Although the target appeared a large vessel we steamed by without engaging. Admiral Halsey had been so disturbed by the dispatch, nothing was going to stop his getting to the Strait. It had been a day and night of missed opportunities and mistaken priorities.

Admiral Olendorf and the Seventh Fleet, old battleships whose keels were laid during WWI, had performed magnificently. Capping the T, their guns raked and destroyed the best the Japanese could muster. It was the last great battle of a naval era. Nothing like it will ever occur again.

Shortly after steaming into the Strait, Admiral Halsey dispatched a destroyer to pick up a few of the Japanese survivors for interrogation. Possibly this is were the rumor of the depth charge attack started. At any rate, the DD came alongside with one of our downed aviators and a frightened and bedraggled group of Japanese sailors. Most of them were dazed, one had to be sent over in a coal sack instead of the breeches bouy. The poor devil, on being released from the sack tried to dive over the side. Fortunately for him one of our Marines tackled him. He came at his captors, and although the "Gyreens" could have clubbed him with rifle butts, they handled him as though he was a child misbehaving. With great restraint he was dumped in the middle of a circle of his captors. He decided to be still.

An interesting use was later made of one captive, a radar rating. We needed information on how effective the enemy radar had become. The POW was brought to sick bay and handled like an honored guest. He loved ice cream, and in two weeks looked like a fat, smiling Buddha.

Now Admiral Halsey had a Commander on his staff who spoke fluent Japanese. He visited the POW daily and developed a nice relationship with the little fellow. One morning all this changed. He informed him that his shipmates had been brutally beaten and starved. He was going to ask some questions and he wanted straight answers. One slip and his fat little butt would be placed in company with his friends. He looked at his clean face and spotless uniform in a mirror and he knew what conclusions his shipmates would draw. He sang like a canary. In fact if he didn't know the answer he tried to improvise. I wonder what happened to him after the war?

10-29- We supported air strikes against Luzon again. The Jap fleet had been badly mauled and Adm. Kurita and Adm. Ozawa, two of Japan's most brilliant commanders had been crushed. Still, land based air harried our formation.

From my diary- "General Quarters at 1230. Bogies converging on formation. CAP reports downing 2 Zekes, 2 Judys, and three Tonys. One Oscar dove on carrier *Intrepid*. We opened fire but she sailed thru a wall of tracers and crashed

Moorman and Frank in front of the Intramuras in Manila. Note the breached wall in the background, thru which our troops stormed the last Jap defenders.

The New Jersey's *fantail was always a busy place. Aircraft, the skimmer and the Captains land transport were stored and secured during underway activities. The auto transport was only added after our sojourn in Bremerton.*

onto the flight deck of the *Intrepid*. 20 and 40mm shells from the *Intrepid*'s AA battery hit the *New Jersey*'s superstructure. Two men were hit on the deck below my quad. Fortunately the wounds were superficial.

The *Intrepid* heeled into the wind and soon had the fire from the Kamikazi under control. Six of her men were killed and 10 wounded in the attack. The carrier, though soot blackened and singed from the heat of the blaze, was not too badly damaged."

Colors were put at the dip and burial at sea completed on those ships that had taken casualties, all of us thinking how lucky we had been again. At 1645 two groups of planes, sixteen in all, attacked the formation. We were at GQ until 1745 and the screen AA fire accounted for five. The rest retreated. Reports came from the tanker support force that the Japs were using suicide tactics again.

10-31- A banner day. First mail for some time. Read letters from my bride at least a dozen times. Mail Call was the happiest sound a ship's crew could hear.

11-1- "Last few days have been hectic. Downed planes from our Task Group are all over the ocean. They have been extending their range, trying to knock out the enemy's air support, and are deserving of every effort made to rescue pilots and crew. Colors have been dipped as burial services are conducted on *Cabot*, *Hancock*, and *Independence*. We have been blessed. That's the only explanation that can account for our good fortune. The carriers are of course doubly vulnerable. The prime target of any attack, many of her casualties are due to badly shot up planes crashing on their flight decks. We have sent our doctors and corpsmen over several times to help with a casualty load their personnel in Sick Bay couldn't handle."

11-2- A snooper (an Irving) was shot down after chasing in and out of the formation for several hours.

11-3- Ship's log- "Half masted colors, following motion from *Cabot*. Cruising in vicinity of Luzon. *Reno* torpedoed. Taken in tow."

11-4- Ship's log- "Destroyer *Callahan* lost steering control while trying to refuel. Collided port quarter of *New Jersey*. Beading on side of *Jersey* carried away, *Callahan* lost Starboard anchor. Reno torpedoed during mid-watch.

"Operation *Pulverize* commenced. TG 38.1 hit South Luzon. We hit Manila area again as part of TG 38.2, while TG38.3 struck the North end of island."

11-5- My log- "Six alerts, everyone ready for and expecting heavy attack. CAP reported eleven snoopers splashed so far today. AA battery to Condition One at 1945. Stayed at alert till 0930 on following day. General Quarters almost continuous for 48 hours. Admiral McCain's death march from Manila? We were walking around like zombies."

Ship's log, same day- "Supporting air strikes against Manila. Suicide attacks in earnest. Several planes dove on TG 38.3 but none closed with TG38.2. *Lexington* hit, but damage superficial."

11-6,7- Another typhoon. We rolled and pitched like a giant toy. A slow roll made it very hard to stay in the bunk. Straps across the chest kept you from falling out but restricted breathing. Finally fatigue takes over and you dozed fitfully. The crew was far from peak performance, but fortunately the Japs were grounded and there was little danger of air attack.

11-8- Wind speed abated to 55 knots. We were scheduled to anchor in Ulithi Atoll the next day. We had been underway for 33 days and steamed 14,789 nautical miles.

11-9- We dropped the hook in Ulithi Harbor at 1130. Stores came aboard in an endless stream. Fantail looked like a giant ant hill, lines of sailors carrying crates and ammunition below.

11-10- Stores continued pouring aboard. Eddy Peabody and a troop of Hollywood types came aboard and put on a magnificent "Happy Hour." The fantail was filled with sailors not on watch and the stage for Peabody was the top of Turret 3. Peaboby was one of the great banjo players of this era and the ovation he received was thunderous. What a thrill those performers must have gotten. I never heard such cheering. Admiral Halsey came out of the crowd and thanked the troop for sharing the evening with us. Quite a moving evening. It brought our thoughts of home and loved ones into focus. We slept well that night.

I got ashore several times during the next few days, wandered about the beach and swam in the lagoon. This was a calm before another storm, but the beauty of the South Pacific never seemed to pale. Waving palms, crashing surf on the outer reef and a steady breeze were a welcome relief from the heat of steel gun shields and closed compartments. Just getting away from the smell of bunker oil was a pleaure we reveled in.

11-14- Underway, westerly course.

11-14 to **11-19**- The *Jersey* returned to the vicinity of the Philippines. We supported air strikes against central Luzon. 0220 on the 19th, at GQ, we splashed one Emily. Numerous alerts during morning. The CAP was active keeping the Japanese at bay. One plane from the *Hancock* exploded on her flight deck after returning from a mission. Flames shot up and black smoke hid everthing, but damage control parties had the fires out quickly, and damage was light. Burn victims had our Medical people transferring to assist in emergency treatment of the wounded.

0530 - Dawn alert, CAP splashed 8 Japs. One Hellcat was lost. The screen fired at enemy aircraft several times during the day. Nothing got through.

11-20- We received a report of three Japanese midget subs getting into Ulithi Harbor. One tanker was hit, the *Mobile* got one sub with 40mm fire. The biggest danger was from wild counter battery fire from our own ships. Two mini-subs apparently got away. Several torpedoes were fired in the harbor but somehow nothing else was hit. (The subs were found by divers after the war. It was apparently a one way attack). Glad we were at sea.

11-25- My diary- "General Alarm went off at 0415. A single bogie closed on TG. Screen fired and drove him away. Supporting strikes against Luzon. Flights of torpedo bombers and fighters leaving in waves from carrier flight decks all day. General Alarm again at 0945. CAP reported splashing 18 enemy planes but in spite of this, at 1235 first Jap air got through. One scored on the *Intrepid*. She was on our Port quarter. It was a Kamikazi attack. This tactic was a level of combat that Americans could never quite understand. All out effort we could reason with, but always, try for survival! No matter how slim the chance. To the Jap though, dying for the Emperor was a sure ticket to heaven.

"Oily black smoke poured out of the strickened *Intrepid*. Firefighters occasionally could be seen through flashes of exploding small arms ammunition. We watched sailors push several damaged planes over the side. A short time later a second Kamikazi dove into the *Intrepid*. Only her bow was visible through the smoke and flames. She lost way and the fires seemed to be gaining, as more explosions wracked her hull.

"Another Jap tried to home in on her but our secondary battery blew him apart. Part of his plane fell on the carrier, but he had ejected just before impact. A bomb he released fell close aboard the carrier *Cabot*.

"Another Jap bomb just missed the *Miami*. The *Hancock* was blazing again, another hit, possibly a Kamikazi. It appeared that the Jap dropped his bomb and when it missed, he dove into the *Hancock*, just astern of the *New Jersey*."

1430- The CAP reported another 6 bandits were splashed.

1500- "All fires in the Task Group are out. All ships in the Task Group keeping station. During the action not one ship was out of the formation. Station keeping no doubt accounted for minimizing the damage. Covering fire was designed to interlock and increase the effectiveness of AA batteries against enemy air. The *New Jersey* was credited with two kills, 3 probables and six assists in this fracas. Fire control discipline was the best performance to date. GQ from 1750 till 0300 but no further action."

11-27- We entered Ulithi harbor. Anchored in the midst of a huge battle fleet and an ever expanding train of oilers, repair vessels and supply ships.

The *New Jersey's* log of 25 November makes an interesting comparison with my diary: "Supported air strikes against Luzon. 0435 GQ. Screen opened fire on unidentified plane. 1010 GQ Raid driven off by CAP. 1235 3 planes shot down by CAP. Plane dropped bomb, narrowly missing *Hancock*. 1240 to 1357 Attacks frequent. 1252 *New Jersey* fired on two low flying planes. One crashed in water, one crashed on flight deck of *Intrepid*. 1254- Plane attempted suicide attack on *Cabot*. Overshot target but wing tip caught flight deck. 1255- *New Jersey* fired on another bandit which crashed on *Cabot's* port beam. 1259 *New Jersey* fired on another plane that crashed dived into the *Intrepid's* flight deck. 1300 to 1415 three planes splashed by CAP. 1919 one of returning planes (ours) crashed on deck of *Independence*. *Intrepid* seriously damaged."

The ship's log shows the intensity of the action on the 25th. Even though their planes were shot to pieces, the Japanese pilots continued to press home their attacks. The Japs were making what many thought was an all out attempt to win the war. The number of pilots and crews they lost in these months must have been staggering. Pilots and air-crews can't be replaced overnight, and the relative losses and replacement ratios were all very much in our favor.

11-28 through **12-11**- We spent the next days alternately drilling and getting ashore for R&R on Mogmog Island. This little palm covered coral speck in the middle of the beautiful Pacific Ocean is quite a change for us after the past months at sea. There is a large bar where you can get all the beer and spirits you want, but that has never been my thing. It's a great place to look for hometown sailors and I seldom went ashore that I didn't run into someone from New Orleans.

The Officer's Club was a concrete slab, covered with a thatched palm frond roof. The bar must have been one hundred feet long and was crowded with young men from all over the United States, each looking for hometown shipmates in the hopes of a brief update on local news and a reunion with classmates who were so close and yet so far away.

The island had the remains of a native village, but the locals had all been moved. The only signs that they were there were abandoned thatched huts and an old native cemetery. With white washed stone crosses, the grave sites reminded me of the cemeteries in New Orleans. The center of the island had a swamp, and the sweet cloying odor of decaying vegetation and coconuts was pleasant after the sea breezes and salt air laced with fuel oil, we'd been breathing. I supposed the SeaBees would drain it, but I rather liked the way it was. Frigate birds and gooneys, fairy terns and silver gulls had been flitting in and out of the coconut palms, and a stiff ocean breeze made our stay there a delightful interlude.

My diary: "I've been diving for shells on the outer reef and have never seen anything like the beautiful colors these coweries and conchs reflect. The reef seems to take a greater and greater hold on my attention.

"Larry Moorman, Alan Cooney, and I made a bargain with the Skipper of an LCI. For the loan of his small boat we'd trade him some of the shells we'd been gathering. It was about a 14 foot dingy, with one set of oars. He brought us as close to a small palm covered shell island as the draft of the LCI allowed, and lowered our dinghy. We thought the island might not have been been touched by GI's and would have better shell diving than the more closely patrolled Mogmog. Trying to land the dinghy in the surf, we broached. Lunch and the gear we'd packed was soaked. Nothing daunted, we walked the length of our little paradise with .45s at the ready in case any "friends" were hiding in the palms. Assuring ourselves that we were alone, we donned masks and began to look for shells. Turning over coral heads in the shallow water, we were soon loaded with spider conchs and lovely coweries of a dozen species."

"Larry was the one who spotted an octopus in a coral declivity. We swam about it and discussed what should be done. It was decided that I would dive, while Larry and Alan would hold on to a rope tied about my waist. The plan was that I'd attack it with my knife and try to kill it, then take a photograph of our exploit. If it grabbed me, they would pull me ashore. The octopus was not that large, maybe six feet from nose to end of tentacle. Stretched out to his full twelve feet, we figured he'd make quite an impressive photograph.

"I approached him slowly on the first pass, stabbing him with my knife. As he reached out for me, I realized his reactions were slower than mine. Black ink and red blood stained the water. I rose to tell my fearless helpers the day was ours, only to be knocked ass over appetite by an incoming comber. Trying to clear my mask and get back down to finish the task took only a moment, but underwater again, I saw our trophy swimming out to the deep, blood and ink trailing behind." And so, the best laid plans of mice and sailors?

We spent the rest of the afternoon shelling and eating saltwater soaked rations. A great day!

Cleaning sea shells turned out to be quite a chore though. We had to hang them in the sun for a few hours, then blow the dead inhabitant out with a blast of compressed air. Finding a place to hang them in the sun without offending shipmates was always a problem. They could smell like a billy goats ass. I wondered what the heck we'd do with the collection, but we thought it beat drinking warm beer.

Tides were quite a problem on the reef. Several GI's had been drowned. Getting careless could be fatal if you were not aware of shallow escape routes back to the island. Three feet of water on the reef and slack tide could become six feet with a strong set in an hour or so. Breakers on the reef made Waikiki seem pale in comparison. Foaming and crashing into the shallows, light refracted in a hundred blues, purples, and greens, drops of spray looked like diamonds set in a magnificent cloudless South Pacific sky. This was one of the loveliest islands we visited. Or was I just real happy to be alive?

The newly commissioned battleship, *Wisconsin*, now joined us. This gave the task group three *Iowa* class BB's. As the Japanese fleet was destroyed, our force continued to grow. As victory in Europe seemed assured, new aircraft and supplies were dedicated to the war in the Pacific.

12-14- Underway from Ulithi at 0558. We are a part of TG38.2 again. Admiral Halsey is SOPA. Steaming back to Luzon.

12-15- 12-17- We continued our support of carrier strikes against Luzon.

12-18- Ships log: "Typhoon. 3 DD capsized, *Spence, Hull* and *Monahan*. Many men lost. Conducted air and surface search for survivors."

My log and recollections: "Worst typhoon we have been through. Waves mountainous. Huge gray monsters sweeping into our bow. Green water smashed everything on the main deck. One inch armored gun shields on our main deck forward were mashed flat. A giant's hand seemed to be playing with the toys a very puny mankind had created."

I was on the starboard aft refueling station before the worst of the storm hit. The destroyer *Spence* was alongside. We passed several travelers across the gap that separated us. A heavy hawser took a fuel line over, but time after time as our seamen tended the hawser, huge waves would snap the 3 inch line as though it was a thread. As soon as the tending line parted the fuel line would break, and oil would spray out in black spumes until the cut-off could be secured. Lines of seamen struggled in a mad tug of war, but it was no use. The *Spence* would roll and we would pitch and the strain was more than hemp and wire could stand. One line parted and came back like a bull whip, breaking the legs of G/M 2/C C.S. Gearhart U.S.N. Corpsmen carried him to sick bay on a deck so canted, they had to struggle to keep their feet.

Water was knocking us about on the fantail and the main deck forward was even worse. I remember the *Spence* with her bow riding out of a crest as far back as her sound dome. Finally the Captain shouted through a power megaphone, "O.K. Blackjack, (Halsey's and the *New Jersey's* call sign), we'll be O.K." and she sheared off into the mist and spume, never to be seen again. There were eleven survivors from her crew when she ran out of fuel and broached.

I had a watch in Air Defense at noon, and decided since I'd be exposed to the elements, to put on foul weather gear and climb up to my station. There was a ladder on the Starboard side of the mainmast tower and I foolishly decided to use it. The inside route to Air Defense required opening and closing eight or nine hatches, quite a chore even in fair weather. We were in Condition Zed, where all hatches had to be closed to maximize water tight integrity, and I thought climbing the outer ladder the quickest and easiest route. Was I ever wrong.

About half way up the tower, wind and rain were so intense I couldn't open my eyes. I climbed blindly another few rungs and then heard a terrible, rending, crunch. The annometer had torn free of the main yard and was flapping crazily on a piece of armoured cable. I wrapped my arms about the ladder and the ship rolled over so far I looked straight down at foaming swells. Catching my breath, I waited until she righted and climbed a few rungs higher. Waiting until the roll reversed again, I'd manage to repeat the manuever. I clung to that ladder, feeling as though I was about to stream, another pennant in the wind. Finally, climbing and holding fast I slipped over the combing of Air Defense and relieved my watch. He looked at me and said, "You look like the dickens." I don't doubt that I did, and advised him to take the inside passage to his cabin. Never again did I climb that ladder in heavy weather.

The TBS (talk between ships) was coming through in that sharp disoriented way that those channels produced. Carriers were out of control, hydraulic steering mechanisms failing, waves reaching under the unprotected leading edge of flight decks, peeling them back like sardine cans, again and again. The new carriers (post-WWII) have bows that are faired into flight decks, eliminating this problem.

The *Cabot* and the *Monterey* reported fires aboard, and another CV lost steering control and almost rammed a CA. The reports were a few of the very heavy damage inflicted on the Task Group. What the Japanese had failed to do, "Mother Nature" accomplished in a few hectic days. Just imagine destroyers rolling almost sixty degrees. Carrier flight decks with damaged planes being man handled over the side. Fires raging on hangar decks, steering gone, rolls of forty odd degrees on the light carriers, and communications shorting out, gale force winds further compounding the agony of the Fleet. Fires raging, ready service magazines on flight and hangar decks that had to be flooded.

The story of this ordeal was well documented in Captain C. Raymond Calhoun's book: *Typhoon: the Other Enemy*. He states: "As the 18th of December passed into history, the Commander Third Fleet (Admiral Halsey) could not possibly have had any real appreciation of the magnitude of the disaster that had befallen his ships. Not until the 19th did the tragic picture begin to unfold.".

"Three destroyers lost. Major structural damage inflicted on three other destroyers, three light carriers, two escort carriers and a number of destroyer escorts. One hundred and forty six planes lost or damaged beyond repair."

Captain Calhoun's description of the ease with which the *New Jersey* operated in this typhoon does not however jibe with my recollection. The *Jersey* rolled and pitched like a drunken giant. This was a slow roll that felt as the ship shuddered to right itself as though we were on our beam ends. To a destroyer sailor this might sound like nothing, but the huge bulk of this Goliath pounding into waves, was completely different from the buoyant manner in which lighter craft met the challenge. As the *Jersey* shuddered in the huge gray swells, she seemed a Goliath caught in chains that could not be thrown off.

Sadly, much of this damage might have been avoided. The areogropher on the *New Jersey* sent a course and speed to the Fleet that was 180 degrees from a prudent direction. This caused us to sail into the eye of one of the most intense typhoons recorded in the very stormy Pacific's history. The confused information gathered by the aerologist on the *New Jersey* was further compounded by his requests from other elements of the fleet for best estimate of storm center. All estimates were based on local conditions which were widely divergent because of the scattered positions of the Task Groups.

Although the *New Jersey* was not as close to storm center as some elements of the Fleet, the full fury and it's reoccurance as we passed near the eye of the typhoon left an indelible imprint on all hands. No one who was afloat there will ever forget the power and the fury of that storm.

After the post mortem was concluded, there were a lot of very embarrased aerographers. Most knew it was a mistake to proceed into the typhoon, but what Regular Naval Officer would question an order code signed "Black Jack"? Not one!

12-24- The Third Fleet limped into Ulithi Harbor. Destroyer escorts had lost every piece of topside radio and electronic gear. Masts were shortened by sections savaged by winds in excess of 230 knots. Welders like fireflies cut away damaged flight decks and tried to improvise solutions that would make us battle ready. A hundred problems had to be solved. Small craft, life boats and rafts, had been wrenched from davits and smashed beyond repair. The Admiral's Barge was smashed. Another was quickly brought aboard. It was wonderful to see how rapidly damage assessment and repairs were accomplished. American ingenuity and know how at its finest hour.

Admiral Nimitz came aboard for a visit, and his five star flag, incorrectly constructed in the *Jersey's* sail locker as square with the fifth star in the center, flew at the yard. Five stars in a rectangular configuration. The new rank had just been established- Fleet Admiral, there was no precedent.

Christmas Eve was memorable for some additional excitement. An offset shoot was being conducted just outside the harbor with a destroyer as target and a cruiser firing her secondary battery. Suddenly, there was the sound of a badly misdirected five inch round whistling in. It hit on the starboard quarter and penetrated to the mess deck.

By some quirk of fate it failed to detonate. Only one man, a seaman asleep on a mess table, was injured. His foot was neatly severed. Lieutenant George Van Fleet, the ship's Bomb Disposal Officer and a Chief Gunners Mate removed the spent round and dropped it over the side without incident. Had that shell exploded we'd have been burying dead by the score.

To keep in shape some of us made a set of weights and began to work out by the five inch loading machine. Tempers had begun to fray with the passage of time in close contact with one another and this was a good way to ease off.

However our efforts were disrupted by a Communications Officer who began to rib Moorman about his size. Larry made the Fairbanks tremble at around two thirty and was sensitive about his weight. His constant referral to my friend as "the mountain that walked like a man" really got on his nerves. Larry wanted to kick his butt. I managed to calm him down, but assured Larry we'd watch the "Communicator" real close. I was certain we could find a weakness to exploit.

The man was quite a dandy and before long I knew we had him. He had gotten his trousers tailor made as bell bottoms to hide the size of his feet. Larry waited until the "Communicator" was talking to friends in the Wardroom. Lifting his pants legs, Larry smiled and said "My God fellow, you'd be the tallest man on board ship if so much of your legs weren't folded over. I think I'll call you "Foots". That night we had a visitor who abjectly apologized and asked Larry to please not call him "Foots." That was the end of the ragging.

12-25- Christmas carols on the fantail and mail call. Swimming in an ocean that just days before took many a seaman to its gray bosom. Diving for shells on the reefs and dreaming of loved ones half a world away. It was a very sad holiday.

Then, six days alternately working around the clock to square away topside damage and going ashore at Mogmog, untouched by the storm.

12-30- Underway at 0921, course northwest. All ships in our task group restored to combat readiness, bunkers topped off. We had steamed 103,000 miles in 1944. We were seasoned and combat ready.

Chapter 7: China Sea and the Advance on Okinawa

1-1-45- The new year found us at sea and participating in air strikes against Formosa. The mobility of the Fleet and its ability to project air power was proven. Japanese losses were horrendous and the damage to their fleet was impossible for them to repair. Still, sporadic, almost ritualistic incursions of our air space continued.

The *New Jersey* had steamed well over 100,000 nautical miles, and except for a few scattered hits from our own Task Group's AA fire, we were unscathed. The only battle death was a casualty in turret one. A young gunner's mate, cleaning the pit, slipped and fell. Trying to get clear as the turret elevated, he was mashed by the breech mechanism. He died in sick bay of shock, more from the trauma of the experience than from his injuries.

1-3- We were steaming off Formosa. The Cowpens' planes shot down a Betty and an Irving. Floating mines were sighted several times. Strikes had to be discontinued because of heavy weather.

1-4- We were called to alert after alert, but no planes could get past a very effective CAP. The weather continued to worsen and air strikes were called off.

1-5- One of our Kingfishers was smashed in the heavy weather. The main deck was secured again. Green seas washed across us and we rolled heavily, a drunken wallow that never seemed to stop. The small boys really caught hell.

1-6- Supported strikes against air fields on Luzon. Weather was intermittently threatening a typhoon, then changing, permitting renewed air activity.

1-9- *Yorktown* planes splashed a Dinah. 2330- We passed through Bashi Channel between Formosa and Luzon and into the China Sea. Winds of 58 knots buffeted us and there was heavy cloud cover.

Admiral Halsey, ever the showman, called all news people to Flag Quarters and they watched as he announced our passage of the channel to the Japs. "This is Bull Halsey. I'm entering the China Sea with the Third Fleet. We're going to divide the real estate evenly. I want the top half. When I get finished, the bottom half will belong to you." It was dramatic as hell and created headlines.

The Japanese could count the ships on radar as we transitted the rather narrow confines of the passage. Wind and sea conditions made opposition from the air an impossibility. But it was a nice touch, and the press loved it. It was amusing to see correspondents flock to the *Jersey* when Halsey was aboard, but only a few remained when the flag shifted and Spruance came aboard.

Until this penetration, the South China Sea was dubbed the "Forbidden Sea." The waters were also called "Iron Bottom Sound." The might of the Third Fleet made the entry an anticlimax. The Japanese were trapped in their own back yard. Many of the Japanese ships fled, but enough were left to make good hunting for carrier air.

1-10- China Sea, GQ at 0640. A pair of twin-engine planes got into the formation. One was splashed about 2500 yards on our port quarter by an *Independence* CAP. Quite spectacular! The other was shot down in flames on the horizon.

1-11- The weather remained horrible, but sporadic attacks continued. CAP splashed three Jakes. Scuttlebutt was that a large Jap force had been sighted by an Army reconnaissance plane. Admiral Halsey was still hoping for a major surface action. We cruised off Camranh Bay, supporting strikes against the Indo-China coast. The destroyer *English* sank a sampan just before dawn, the sky lighting up as she exploded. We are presently positioned 109-30 east longitude. This was farther west than the *New Jersey* had been to date.

1-12- Air sweeps of Camranh Bay, but the Japs had fled. Bombardment was canceled.

1-13- Weather continued going from bad to worse. Heavy seas made all operations difficult. Refueling the small boys became an impossibility. We had hoped to bombard Camranh Bay in the morning, but weather remained a problem and the bombardment was canceled.

Alerts and GQ all day with single plane attacks by Japs. Why they committed such piecemeal missions was hard to understand. A concerted effort would have proved more productive. Four Jakes were splashed in the vicinity of our Task Group, but none within sight. We were 300 miles from Saigon, one of the largest Japanese bases in the South Pacific.

1-14- DD *Hanks* picked up 5 survivors of a Chinese fishing vessel. Seas continued heavy, winds very strong, blowing spindrift under glowering clouds across our bow. A lone albatross sailed across our wake. Back and forth he soared, held aloft with scarcely a movemnet of his wings. An omen?

1-15- We supported air strikes against merchant shipping out of Hong Kong. The CAP had a field day. Merchant ships and stragglers- a clean up operation. Supply ships and numerous sam-pans amounted to massive tonnage sunk in simultaneous raids on Hong Kong, Amoy, Formosa and Matsou. Damage to the enemy was mounting by the hour, and Jap air loses they could ill afford. All this with minimum loss to the Fleet air arm.

We were at GQ continuously, but the alert status paid off as Jap planes were splashed, and we remained invulnerable. AA fire from enemy bases was reported as heavy, but, the carriers poured in planes and the results were more than satisfactory. Snoopers were on our radar all day long, but none got past the CAP.

1-20- Approaching Luzon Strait at the northern tip of Luzon we exited the South China Sea. At 1000 the General Alarm sounded and bogies showed as small pips of light on radar screens. The CAP was vectored in and another George was splashed. This was followed at 1500 by a lone Dinah, also flamed. Again single plane tactics. At 1630 we picked up a Jap broadcast of our exact position (off Okinawa Gunto) and multiple raids were detected closing. Again the CAP had a field day. Vectored in by CIC (Combat Information Center) they splashed a George, 2 Dinahs, 3 Nicks, 3 Helens, 2 Vals, a Betty and two twin engined bombers that appeared to be new aircraft. The loss on our side- two CAPs making an unorthodox approach to the task group. In all, the final tally showed 16 planes splashed between 1630 and 1930.

The status board in the Combat Information Center is a huge plexiglass grid. Ratings with grease pencils mark and number all bogies and friendlies as the radar screen continues its relentless sweep. The numbered track line of each aircraft establishes an intercept point and the CAP is vectored in for a contact. "Tally - ho!" And another Japanese plane is lost.

1-21- Ships log: "Participated in support of air strikes against Formosa. 0839 Cap splashed a Dinah and a Zero. The *Langley* and the *Ticonderoga* were damaged by enemy aircraft. 1323 *Hancock* damaged by explosion of plane on deck. 1335- The CAP shot down seven more enemy planes. 1934- The *Baltimore* shot down a twin engine bomber. During evening alert the CAP shot down 15 of 18 attacking aircraft."

Even multi-plane attacks were being splashed by our CAP before they reached the screen. Only stragglers were left for the ships anti-aircraft batteries.

1-22- We moved north, striking Okinawa Jima on our way out of the forward area.

1-25- 1605- We anchored in Ulithi harbor. The Fleet looked like it expanded in each new anchorage, new ships joining the Task Groups.

1-26- All hands were ordered aft for muster and change of command. The new skipper was Captain E.T. "Slim" Woldridge. Captain William F. Holden was given a bronze star by Admiral Halsey, who then gave a rousing talk to the crew. He was an unforgettable character- commanding, assertive, positive. The crew responded with cheers to his charisma.

I overheard two signalmen and a hospital corpsman talking on the bridge as we entered the harbor yesterday. The signalmen were impressed with the Admiral's calm demeanor when a Japanese plane seemed headed for the bridge. The corpsman was not. "Hell," he said, "the Old Man ain't brave, he's blind. I gave him an eye test and the old bastard can't see." Take your pick, but I'll tell you one thing, he was a fighter when we needed one badly, and the men of the fleet loved him.

I went to Mogmog in the afternoon, and Alan Cooney and I had another close call on the reef. Those tides are really dangerous. Again, we vowed to be more careful.

1-27 - Halsey and part of his staff left the ship on a troop transport, the General Sturgis, for a Stateside appearance. This to fool the enemy into thinking the Third and Fifth Fleets were two separate entities. The smiles on the faces of the departing Staff showed they thought a week Stateside was a great move. Jean mailed me a news clip a few weeks later. The Admiral and a group of junior officers were photographed living it up in a San Francisco night club.

1-29- Admiral Oscar Badger, COMBATDIV 7 and his staff came aboard.

1-30 to 2-9- The *New Jersey* spent this period chipping away at the accumulation of rust from long months at sea. We were able to get ashore every other day, and the crew enjoyed warm beer and baseball on Mogmog again. With two All American football players, Frank Regan from Pennsylvania University and Charlie Nobel from Duke, we had some great touch football games as well.

I made a friend of the ships diver, Merrill Hardy. A quiet heavy set, East Coast native, he was a man who was superbly qualified and loved his rating. Quite illegally, I persuaded him to teach me to do some shallow water diving. I'd slip back to the fantail in swimming trunks and don the gas mask he had fitted with an air hose. Although he was careful to use the minimum weight in my leaded belt, he used a much heavier load himself. This allowed him to reach depth more rapidly. The belts were ammunition web type for rifle magazines. Lead inserts and a snap buckle to fasten the webbing were our ballast. We'd go over every time we were in port to inspect the zinc bars bolted to the ships hull as protection from galvanic action. This allowed the zinc to erode instead of allowing galvanic action to damage the bronze screws and their shafts.

The screws were huge. Two with five blades and two with four if my memory is correct. I'd stand on a blade and watch as Merrill measured and examined the plates. He was a powerful swimmer and an excessive negative buoyancy never appeared to pose a problem to him. We saw huge sharks swimming in the murk below us, but we'd stand on the blades of the screws and were never bothered by them. What a wonderful thing it was to be young and foolish!

One day I was enjoying the feeling of euphoria that diving creates. The light of the sun filtered down through waters that seemed to stretch to forever. As I glanced down, I was horrified to see a figure on a curving loop of air hose, sinking slowly into the depths. Like a tiny mannequin, Hardy was jerking frantically on his life line. But the signal was dissipated in the loop. I swam over to the vertical section of line and gave four tugs that was the emergency signal to recover the diver. The line came taut and was hauled in. Slowly, ever so slowly the limp figure of Hardy was pulled to the surface. He suffered a mild case of the bends, but an eternal case of gratitude. I received Christmas cards from him saying thanks, until a few years ago. I've tried to contact him at an address in Boston but he has disappeared as quietly as the memory of those wonderful days in the waters under the *Jersey's* hull.

2-10- We were off to support strikes against Tokyo. 0900 We sortied from Ulithi as part of Task Group 58.3. Adm. Forrest Sherman CTG in Essex was ComTask Group.

2-15- This was not a happy day. We were scheduled to return to the States for yard overhaul but the *Iowa* was in greater need. So, we stay... she goes!

The CAP splashed a couple of Bettys and sank a small Jap fishing boat but opposition to the strikes appeared weak.

2-16- Ship's log: "Participated in support of air strike against Tokyo. No opposition. DD *Haynesworth* picked up nine survivors of Japanese fishing boat."

My log- "Destroyers in the screen sank several small pickets. Quite a few snoopers but little action."

2-17- The weather was bad again. Withdrawing, we bucked heavy swells. Reports of strikes against mainland airfields listed over 500 enemy planes shot up during the past two days, most of these on the ground, parked in neat rows.

2-19- Cruising off Iwo Jima. We were between the landing force and Japan. D day at Iwo. AA fire splashed two bandits. We spent most of day at GQ. Snoopers on screen almost constantly until 2100. The Task Group made smoke during evasive action at dark.

It was quite spectacular, smoke billowing, ships weaving in a synchronized dance, the flash of the five inch 38's giving it the look of a giant Halloween celebration. The big problem was the 20mm and 40mm rounds bouncing off our superstructure as ships fired across the formation and the violent evasive action of the Task Group made fire control discipline an impossibility, ships heeling in radical turns, first in one direction then in another. Gun pointers strapped to 20mm mounts tried to keep their feet in heavy seas, it's no wonder so many rounds went astray.

Scuttlebutt had the *Saratoga* taking four Kamikasi hits and the *Bismark Bay* was reported sunk.

2-24- Seas were very heavy. Nine men were injured in a refueling operation while line tending. When a destroyer parted a hawser, the line came back at the fantail like a huge bull whip, lashing across the deck, smashing anything it touched. The sailor who stood in the bight of a line was an accident looking for a place to happen. Broken legs in heavy sea were a sure ticket home.

2-25- I was in Air Defense, the peak of the foremast, on a Condition Three watch. The wind was fierce, screeching through taut rigging.

Sitting in my office some fifty years later, I feel light years away from that stormy scene. We were rolling heavily and trying to refuel a destroyer. Pitching and bucking on our starboard bow, she was joined to us by the umbilical cords of tending hawsers and a fuel line. Waves of solid green water washed over our foc'astle, and as we looked down, a sailor from the line handling party was washed over the side. As he drifted aft, a dozen hands on the main deck stripped off life jackets and threw them to him. He held on to a half dozen, and as he disappeared astern, his position was marked by a small floating island in the swells. Even from the vantage point at the peak of the mainmast, he quickly disappeared. But, it must have been his luckiest day.

A destroyer, the *Erwin*, broached. In the blink of an eye, he was washed onto her deck. Willing hands grabbed him and he was hustled below. The sea mist and the cold waters, lost a young life they were about to claim. The cold waters would have finished him in a few more minutes. As it was, he was in shock for hours after his rescue.

A few days later he was transferred by breeches' buoy back on board the *New Jersey*. He had been so sea sick on the can he wished they'd thrown him back.

We were 450 miles from Tokyo, and gale force winds were part of the daily routine. Refueling continued and air strikes were scheduled for the morrow. The temperature dropped to 42F and after the past year in tropical climate we felt like we were back in the North Atlantic.

2-26-Ship's log: "0040 GQ Unidentified surface craft, gunboat or DD, was caught in the middle of the formation. She was sunk by the destroyer *Porterfield*. A blip on the radar screen one minute, a flash of light as she exploded and sank the next. One officer was killed and 12 men wounded in the crossfire from another ship in the Task Group. Renewed strikes against Tokyo, but again forced to withdraw because of weather."

My log: "Bad weather has gotten even worse. Cold wind and rain. 0100 General Alarm. Two sampans had gotten into middle of the Task Group. Forty mm fire criss crossing ship. A DD took a barrage of 40mm and some casualties. We were really sailing under a lucky star. Tracers passed between our stacks but no one was hurt. Ceiling was about seventy five feet and the superstructure looked like it was in the clouds. The yardarm was lit up by St. Elmo's fire. A weird and beautiful flashing of electrical particles discharged on the rigging. Old sailors held this to be a good omen. I hoped so."

3-1- We supported air reconnaissance over Okinawa and air strikes for next several days.

3-5- 1548- We anchored in Ulithi harbor.

3-11- We had some interesting target practice for the heavy machine guns. Reginald Denny, a Hollywood movie star, brought a team aboard with drones for simulated attacks against the secondary battery. They were little gas powered models like the ones I used to build and fly before the war. But these were radio controlled and had a wing span of ten or twelve feet. The planes were launched from a little ramp on the fantail, and off they'd buzz. At low altitude, twisting and turning in the sunlight, they were a challenging target. The planes were controlled from a little black box and a joy stick that could make them take weaving evasive approaches. The operators were labeled "Peter Pilots" by our "Birdmen," and the name stuck.

The 40mm and 20mm performed beautifully and none of the little yellow drones lasted more than a run or two.

I got a range and bearing from Sky Three on one that splashed near a small island. I hoped I'd get a chance to recover the engine. (We never came back to the area.)

2012- The movie on the fantail was interrupted by a General Alarm. A huge fire ball was lighting up the harbor. It looked like all hell had broken loose. Adm. Halsey insisted the movie operator continue the film. He and a very nervous staff watched the fire works while the rest of us manned our battle stations. This was the sort of thing that made the "Old Man" a legend. He was without fear, and it inspired those he led.

The carrier *Randolph* had taken a hit from a Kamikasi. Another suicide attacker mistook the new coral pier in the harbor for a carrier flight deck. He made a small dent in the surface while joining his "Honorable Ancestors." The *Randolph* was out of action for some time, the glow from her fires silhouetting the Fleet for several hours, but no further attacks arrived.

The planes were launched from a Japanese sub, at least that was the rumor. No surface force was sighted by far ranging search planes in the morning.

3-12- Again the movies were interrupted by GQ. Just a snooper but it sure played hell with the program.

We had swimming parties ashore on Mogmog and a few excursions to adjacent islands. We made friends with some of the LCI boys and they were glad to trade transport for the shells we were collecting.

I was amused, when we recovered one of our bird-men who for the sake of posterity, will remain anonymous. He had flown a patrol and landed near a native village. Now this particular sky-jockey was the ship's stud. He wore pointed boots, and a very sly smile when his plane was hoisted on to the fantail. Looking at the wing, there were two holes on the top side and they didn't go through the bottom. Draw your own conclusions, but the story he told about being shot at was hardly supported by the evidence. This included a grin whenever he looked at his boots.

3-14- 1035 -Underway from Ulithi.

3-15 & 3-16- Underway, with continuous AA practice. We were getting a fine edge on the drills and the results were shown in improved air defense.

3-17- A few snoopers on the outside of the screen, just enough to keep us awake. GQ interrupted sleep and kept everyone tired and edgy.

At quarters in the morning I noticed Huggins, BM1/C with a big bruise on his cheek. When I asked what had happened he said,"Some SOB stepped on me last night."

I had a hard time keeping a straight face, but I replied, "You were probably sleeping in a passage way."

Although frowned upon, the air passage in Officer's Country was a great deal cooler than the second level crew's quarters, and a few venturesome souls would sleep there. I remembered staggering off the mid-watch and hearing a groan and a curse in an athwart ship passage, as I stumbled over an inert form. I was the SOB who had stepped on his face.

Numbers of mines were sighted daily. We passed one close aboard. It was a wonder we didn't have some battle damage at night, but no reports of this.

3-18 & 3-19- Ships log: "Supported air strikes against Kyushu and Shikoku. Many flares dropped by enemy planes. 0605 *New Jersey* fired on *Frances*. Later reported splashed by CAP. 0825 Bomb fell astern of *Bunkerhill*. Plane was splashed by AA fire from *South Dakota*. *New Jersey* pilot rescued downed aviator near Kyushu. *Franklin* hit by suicide plane."

My log: "Bogies on screen since about 0300. Flames in night mark AA fire and further out the work of a very effective CAP. Flares had us lit up as though it was daylight. As many as 20 were burning in air at once. It was really eerie. The surprising thing was the effective work of the lamp lighters and the failure to coordinate the illumination with the attacks. The AA fire was some of the heaviest we'd seen.

"Attacks during the afternoon were spectacular. One bomb just missed the *Bunkerhill*. The plane was splashed by AA fire from the South Dakota and an assist from the CAP of the *Bunkerhill*.

"At 1300 Lt. 'Dilbert' Ethridge (later lost in a postwar crash in an Alaskan white-out), returned with one of the carrier pilots he had recovered in a landing at sea just 15 miles off Kyushu. 1800 flares, AA fire and alerts.

"Four hours sleep in past 48 hours. My ass was dragging. Four CV's took hits, the *Franklin* under tow. The *Intrepid*, the *Enterprise* and the *Wasp* were operational but damage was extensive. Watching these babies wheeling into the wind was heart rending. Smoke poured out like blood from some stricken medieval monster. We stayed near Kyushu while the cripples were trying to retire.

"0744 on the 19th we opened fire on a Judy diving on *Essex*. 0815 opened fire on plane diving on *Bunkerhill*. 0822 *Franklin* under tow by *Pittsburgh*. 1321 we fired on Jill to Port, 1419 fired on Zeke to Starboard. 1801 *Hancock* exploded a floating mine. If you could have seen those carriers after taking a hit you'd never believe they could be battle ready a day later.

"CAP reported splashing 32 planes by 1600. Little sleep but we had the satisfaction of knowing that the Task Group had done its job."

3-22- *Franklin* was now safe. The past days saw the Japs thwarted time and time again as they tried to get at the cripples. The destroyers in the screen rammed and sunk an enemy submarine. We continued to support strikes against Minami Jima and the Ruyukus while screening the cripples.

3-23- Strikes were shifted to Okinawa. Task Groups were reformed after the melee of the past 100 hours. The *New Jersey* was now part of Task Group 58.4 under Adm. Arthur Radford in *Yorktown*. GQ's were again continuous. USS *Monson* exploded another floating mine.

3-24- *New Jersey* joined Task Group 59.7 for the bombardment of Southern Okinawa. The DSM'S cleared the landing area, and as there was no counterbattery fire we secured and withdrew at 1720. We joined Task Group 58.1 under Admiral Clark as CTG with flag on the Hornet.

3-25- This was D day for Kerama Retto. We continued support of strikes against Okinawa.

3-26- We rejoined Task Group 58.4. GQ from 0615 until 2348 but no targets in our sector.

3-27- Targets for strikes shifted further north, covering southern Kyushu and Amani O Jima. Almost constant alerts but no action. The CAP was most effective, splashing five or six bandits a day.

3-29- Air strikes against Kyushu. Two Hellcats and a Zeke blown to hell by AA fire from the *New Jersey*. Another case of hot pursuit on a bad bearing. The whole formation blasted away at the poor bastards.

3-30- Moving south. At 0030 we opened fire on a Betty that had been crippled by night fighters. GQ most of night. "Sleep is just a habit," I told my gun crew. Noticed a funny smile on their faces when I came up for Dawn Alert. They were laughing that I had caught the habit. I couldn't believe it, but I slept through an attack, sleeping under one of the quads that had fired a heck of a lot of rounds that night.

3-31 to 4-1- Continued to support strikes on Okinawa. Long GQ's but not much more than snoopers on the screen. Attacks were sporadic and ineffective.

Cruising in vicinity of Okinawa as part of reserve support force for landings. 0132 Cap splashed a lone Betty. We were at General Quarters again from 0948 till 1955.

4-2- 0409- At GQ, we saw a fireball from the bridge as night fighters splashed a bandit. 2112 I was just off watch when I heard a horrendous scraping noise. The DD *Franks*, scheduled as one of our escorts to Uncle Sugar Able, had side-swiped the *Jersey*. She had been on plane guard and instead of dropping astern and circling to take her place in the screen after launch had been completed, she tried to cut across the formation to speed up her reentry to the screen. Frequently a hot shot DD skipper got away with this, but the *Franks* didn't. Her Captain and Exec were on the Bridge and both were seriously injured. The Captain died enroute to Pearl. The *Franks* was badly damaged, the *Jersey* barely scratched.

4-5- Supporting air strikes against Sakishima Gunto. GQ 0622 till 1940.

4-6- Supported air strikes against Okino Daito.

4-7- *New Jersey* part of reserve force covering the occupation of Okinawa. GQ 0654 until 1919. CAP again splashed snoopers but no concerted attacks were pressed home. We were now part of TG 58.1. The *Hancock* was hit by a Kamikaze. Intermittent firing was seen from the Task Group and air strikes were launched against a Japanese force, sinking a battleship believed to be the *Yamamoto*.

In 1980, I was at a Shinto shrine outside Tokyo, that had a bronze model of the *Yamamoto* in a lovely shaded nook. A grey haired Japanese civilian saw my interest and explained that the *Yamamoto* had been sunk by carrier air during the war. We had quite a chat when I explained I was a part of the TG from which the attack, had been launched. He had been a J.O. on a destroyer that picked up some of the survivors.

We had departed the area with Jap cruisers and destroyers sinking and burning, a major loss to the dwindling Japanese surface navy. Tally reported- 1 BB, 1 CA , 1 CL sunk. 3 DD damaged three more left burning. This force had tried to intercept the transports supporting troop landings but was badly mauled by TG 58. 1. Over 30 planes were reported splashed by our Task Group AA and CAP. A very busy day.

4-8- Rejoined TG 58.3 under Adm. Sherman's flag. Sporadic attacks repulsed at screen. One Nick closed on us to about 6,000 yards, but AA fire made him abort the run and the CAP splashed him.

4-9- During fueling and re-arming the Kingfishers, I was just about ready to catapult the starboard plane when depth charges could be seen going off all over the screen. The launch was scrubbed and a sub contact was pursued by destroyers, while we hauled ass at flank speed, zig-zaging all the way.

4-10- Three DD's needing yard overhaul have been assigned to escort us back to Uncle Sugar Able. Can it be true? For seventeen months the Lord has had his arms around us.

The landings on Okinawa bogged down with the Japanese pushed into a smaller and smaller perimeter, bitterly contesting each square foot of ground. Japanese civilians committed suicide rather than face capture or surrender. The Marine general, commanding forces ashore, needed replacements for the casualties that were suffered. He called for volunteers of ten percent of the officers and men of Marines afloat. I'll never forget what will always be a testimonial to "Semper Fidelis." The entire *New Jersey* Marine detachment, to a man, volunteered. The "chosen" were selected by lot, and one officer and six men off loaded for duty on the still very active line. Now that's dedication. Remember we had been out in the forward area for a year and a half and knew we were heading home for two months of yard time and a reunion with our loved ones.

4-11- A dispatch intercepted from the Japs promised a heavy effort to stop the landings. Our intelligence from interceps was quite an edge.

My log: "At 1130 we went to General Quarters. The word was, a big Jap attack was scheduled. It was no ruse. Planes came at the task force from 1300 until 1900 in an almost constant stream. There was a slight lull until 2330, then the attack recommenced until 0300.

"It was the finest show to date. Eleven planes were shot down by AA fire in our task group. Three were credited to the *New Jersey*. The only casualty was the destroyer *Kidd*, now a war memorial in Baton Rouge, Louisiana. She took a direct hit from a large bomb. Twenty five men were killed and over 60 wounded. She was one of the ships scheduled to escort us to Ulithi enroute home. The "Big E" (the carrier *Enterprise*) was strafed and took a couple of five inch hits from "friendly" AA fire. A few other ships suffered similar damage. We're sticking around to stop the Jap air before it gets to the landing beaches.

"During the night lamp lighters were active but only disturbed our sleep. Most of the illumination was furnished by flaming Jap hecklers."

The *New Jersey* fired one heck of a lot of ammo, and the results were satisfactory but not spectacular. It's hard to claim a kill when the Task Group are all zeroed in on a single plane. I felt sorry for the poor devils- their dedication should never be questioned.

4-12- I was exhausted from standing one watch after another and one of the funniest memories I have are of this night. A young seaman called "Gedunk" (he was a rotund youngster who worked the icecream machine in the ship's galley) was on watch with me as a talker. Our battle station was on top of the number three turret, the ship was darkened and we had enjoyed little sleep the past few days. Gedunk approached me with an idea I couldn't refuse. If I'd turn my head, he'd slip into the galley and get us a pot of hot coffee. Slipping down the face of the turret, opening a hatch on the fantail, he disappeared below deck.

A few minutes later, he was back on station with a steaming pot of "Joe." No cups, but one of the gun crew found a mug that had been used to hold grease to wipe the barrel springs on the 40's. I was offered the first cup, after one of the sailors wiped it out with a dirty rag.

Gedunk smiling asked, "You're the officer, how'd you like the coffee?"

I took a quick sip, and spit it out. Looking at Gedunk, I said, "Damn it man, you forgot the sugar."

"No sir, I just forgot to stir it." The only

thing we found to stir the pot was the swab handle of a little mop, used to clean the latrine bowls.

Gedunk said,"Do you want it with or without sugar?"

O.K. so I grew up thinking you never drink at a public fountain! We drank it sweet!

Gedunk had another claim to fame. He had been a trumpet player in a band led by Louis "Satchmo" Armstrong. He composed a ditty I can't remember completely, but it was sung to the tune of the Wabash Cannonball, a WWII ditty. Went something like this:

Now on the broad Pacific, there's a ship that sails the swells.

She's been from Phil-a del-phi-a, to the Nippon's gates of Hell. And ends-Now when the war is over, and to

Uncle we return— etc.

Hope you'll read this Gedunk, and fill in the rest of it for me.

I can still hear you boogie reveille. Even the Captain enjoyed it.

4-12- My log: "Colors at the dip. President Franklin Roosevelt died today. I had a lump in my throat and there were sad faces throughout the ship. The world has lost a friend. We will win the war! -The peace? Who knows? I have never seen such universal grief. Many a tear has been shed on the *New Jersey* today."

4-14- 1326 We off-loaded our sea-planes and the back up motor for the aircraft crane, then departed in company of the *Enterprise, Minneapolis, Hanks, Hale,* and *Crathen* for Ulithi.

1930- Five minutes of silence and a prayer in the President's memory.

As I sit here reviewing my notes, I find a yellowed plan of the day from 14 April 1945 stuck between the pages of my log. How many of you who read these lines will remember the routine?

PLAN OF THE DAY   SATURDAY

Watch TWO   14 April 1945
Rotation 4-5-6
Work Div. "L"

0430 Reville. Put on flame proof bunk covers.

0450 General Quarters.

0520 Complete rigging starboard side for refueling from tanker at 0600.

0530 New Jersey assumes Relief Seaplane Rescue Duty, Condition Twelve, (2 planes, 20 minutes notice)

Sunrise - Secure from General Quarters

0700 Breakfast.

0800 Muster on stations, make reports to Executive Officer's Office.

1200 Dinner.

1310 Recognition training in Wardroom for Watch One.

1700 Supper.

Sunset Darken ship. Secure from Relief Seaplane Rescue Duty.

(Five minutes after sunset) Evening Alert.

Notes :
1. Water consumption for 12 April 1945 - 20.1 gallons per man.

2. All officers who have not already done so, report to the Executive Officer's Office between 1100 and 1300 for new Identification Cards. This will be the last opportunity to be photographed.

        G.B. Ogle
        Commander, U.S. Navy,
        Executive Officer.

4-15- I attended a memorial service for the President.

4-16- 1415 We anchored in Ulithi Atoll. Adm. Badger shifted his flag to the *Iowa*. The Admiral made an excellent farewell speech to the crew of the *Jersey*, praising her performance and wishing us all God speed and smooth sailing home.

It was a cause of joy to most, but a sad time for others. Several men came to me, hearts broken by wives who hadn't been willing to wait. I felt like closing my ears, but every man needed someone to talk to, and for several of my close friends I was the shoulder to cry on.

4-17 to 4-18- Last days ashore at Mogmog. Had a visit from an old friend from the early days of our cruise, Roy Poorman.

4-19- Underway at 0630. I enjoyed JOOD watches a lot better than GQ. The change in the winds of war was startling. We passed unescorted tankers and freighters heading to bases secured and ready to receive mountains of supplies coming from the States. What a change from a year and a half ago. A screen of frigates would have been patrolling in anti-submarine mode. We were in company with the *Minneapolis*. The three destroyers originally scheduled for escort were all heavily damaged in the savage fighting off Okinawa. Kamikaszes really took their toll of the small boys.

4-21- Heavy weather. A heck of a storm. This one gave the fleet at Okinawa a terrible mauling. We passed within 300 miles of Truk, no longer a threat. We didn't even have a destroyer escort. Storm still raging but every roll taking me closer to my bride. What a wonderful feeling.

4-22- Storm finally abated. Reports of damage to LST's, LCI's, and destroyers in the open harbor were extensive.

4-24- We crossed the International Date Line at 16.00 degrees N, another step closer to home.

4-27- Sighted Diamond Head and moored, starboard side to Ford Island, in Pearl Harbor. The damage from the sneak attack was still evident. The hulks on battleships row bear mute testimony to the efficiency of the attack. Strange how shocked we were then. It just wasn't the gentlemanly way to start a war.

4-28- 1608- Under way! Seattle here we come.

5-4- 0645 Entered Juan de Fuca Strait. Is this a mis-spelled word? A Freudian slip? 1345- We anchored in Rich Passage for the fastest off-loading of ammunition in the ship's history. 1728- We got under way and at 1821 anchored off Puget Sound Navy Yard. Coniferous forests of the Pacific Northwest were quite a change in scenery from the past year. The odor of piney woods filled our brains with thoughts of home. A lone gull circled in an azure sky, his mournful cry seemed a welcome with sad overtones. The fresh salt air, the bright cool weather, the ship alive with sailors bright eyed and bushy tailed. Looked like a litter of puppies just released from the kennel.

5-6- Formalities, "yard-birds" with blue prints, and curious civil dignitaries swarmed aboard, mouths agape at the size of the *Jersey*-everywhere she docked she was the center of the stage. Her size alone didn't explain this. There was a majesty about the *Jersey* and her crew.

More ammunition off-loaded. 0651 underway again, finally moored Port side to, pier 6. Leave commenced. We were scheduled for sixty days yard availability, but Captain Wooldridge cut this back to forty six days. It didn't make him popular with the crew.

Chapter 8: Leave!! Home and Bremerton!

The Navy yard at Bremerton was bustling. Ships damaged in the South Pacific looked like giant beetles covered with ants. Once again welders cables and grease stained footprints on the teak decks. The flicker of welder's torches were a reminder of our days in the Philadelphia Navy yard. But, after a year and a half away from home all we could think about was, "Let's get moving." I was lucky, I was on one of the first leave groups. Twenty three days was not the most popular decision that a new skipper could have made, but we were too excited with thoughts of hearth and home to be disappointed for long.

The ride on the ferry taking us to Seattle from Bremerton seemed to never end. Holding sea bags and standing in the bow, crisp spring winds blowing across the bay, tears streaming from eyes straining to see where we'd dock, no one put their gear on deck for twenty minutes before we docked. Sailors in pea-coats, buttoned against the chill, and officers in dress blues, all straining to sprint for the phones. I was scheduled to fly to New Orleans, but the flight was filled. How I managed to get aboard was pure luck. Even getting a phone call through to my bride was complicated. Lines of G.I.'s were waiting by every booth, jostling with newly arrived sailors and marines fresh from combat. Finally, I had the phone and I heard her voice. Choking, I knew we'd be together soon. Airborne at last, I sat for a flight with a layover in San Francisco and again in Dallas; it seemed planned to eat away more precious hours.

It was the longest trip I ever made. The worry of being bumped by someone with a higher priority for air transport, was another worry. But, in a day and a half, I was in the arms of my loved ones. If my now somewhat faulty memory is correct, the trip took twenty eight hours of flying time and the only place we didn't stop was Atlanta, Georgia. How did they miss diverting for that hub?

The days in New Orleans were a wonderful time, filled with love and laughter. It was great to bathe in showers with an unlimited water supply, and salads - I thought I'd never get my fill of lettuce and fresh vegetables. Sometimes I'd find myself shutting off the water as I brushed my teeth, and feeling guilty if I let the shower run while I was soaping.

The whole country was involved in the war effort. Unlike Vietnam or Korea, there were few dissenters. Those who failed to serve were marked for many years after the war with snide comments and a social stigma.

My mother knitted socks and sweaters for the British Relief Society. My kid brother was a junior in the Tulane N.R.O.T.C. My wife was working for the Navy as a secretary. She had never typed a letter in her life, but soon got to supervise an office filled with girls who could. By that time she had learned to type but couldn't be spared her supervisory tasks to do so.

My Dad was a proud ensign in the Coast Guard Reserve, skipper of a civilian sixty foot yacht, with a crew of five Coast Guard Reserve ratings. Dad's knowledge of the bayous and swamps of the Mississippi River Delta made him a great choice to patrol the coastal bays and estuaries, checking fishing boats rumored to be supplying German submarines in the Gulf of Mexico. Although the rumors persisted, I know of no examples of this activity. Dad loved it, spending every weekend with a .45 strapped to his hip and watching Cajun fishermen with a somewhat jaundiced eye. Giving his crew docking drills and reading "Rocks and Shoals", Rules and Articles for the Government of the Navy, he was always proud of his days in the service of our Country.

It was a time of national unity. The press was supportive, rather than confrontational. The politicians, Democrat and Republican, united behind a bipartisan policy that seems impossible to achieve today. Or has time clouded my memory with only the best of times?

Soon, all too soon, it was over. We were unable to get air reservations back to the ship. However, through a friend of my father-in-law, we got a double berth on the Panama Limited to Chicago, then another double berth on the Northwestern Railroad. Unless you lived through it, you could never believe how congested all transport had become. Buses, trains and planes were booked at one hundred and ten percent of capacity. No matter, though. I tipped the porter to make our double berth into a single and we crossed the continent locked in each others arms. We sat by the window for hours as the train rolled through magnificent midwestern mountain ranges. We ate in dining cars on spotless linens and were served by smiling Pullman porters. It was a world we have bypassed as if it was a dream. Military personnel were treated with a reverence that was at times embarrassing. I have often been shocked, and appalled at the divisive nature that Korea and Vietam engendered. How and why did we lose this bipartisanship? Were our goals and aspirations that much separated from the past? I think not.

Our quarters in Bremerton were a culture shock for a young New Orleans girl reared in a sheltered environment. We shared a two bedroom shack, originally prepared for migratory workers who found the climate too cold and departed for the South. Our house mates were a young, newlywed warrant officer and his bride. Our quarters were separated by paper thin walls. The cooking and dining area had a wood stove, an ice box, a table and a small cupboard. We were issued two teaspoons, two tablespoons, two knives, two dinner plates, two soup bowls, and two cups with a small assortment of pots and pans, all signed for and to be returned to the Navy on day of departure. The two bed rooms were next to one another, and there was a small storage room in back of the kitchen. Since we were off on alternate watches, the girls decided to sleep in the storage room on their night as a single, giving some degree of privacy to connubial bliss. God, my wife will kill me when she reads this, but it was a great time, and almost fifty years haven't dimmed the laughter.

You could tell when a party was in the offing- a parade of young people, walking through muddy streets (it was always raining) carrying glasses, knives and spoons to the site of the festivities. Then there was the problem of heat. We had a cord of wood in back of each shack, but this had to be split before you could get it into the wood stove. I can see Jean in her slippers and a silk bridal robe, chopping kindling to heat our bath water. The water was heated by passing through pipes in the wood stove.

Then there was the ice box. After about a week, Jean said, "I don't know what to do about that darned refrigerator. It keeps leaking all over the kitchen." She had forgotten, we put a sign in the window and had twenty five pounds of ice delivered every other day. The refrigerator was an ice box, and once she learned to empty the pan, no more messy kitchen floor!

Giant redwoods towered above our cabin, and on mild days I'd sit outside with Jean, smoking a pipe and watching an occasional bald eagle circle overhead. The smell of wood smoke from adjoining cabins blended with the odor of pine and spruce trees in the lower stretches of the forest- quite a pleasure after two years of diesel oil and the smoke from weapons fired in anger.

We were standing alternate watches, and every other day I'd have Jean join me for supper in the Wardroom. Now, Captain Wooldridge was a sundowner. He believed in obeying the letter of the law, which led to some rather amusing incidents. After dinner we'd leave for the Officers Club about a mile away and located uphill. The Officers could ride in the ships station wagon, but the wives, who were considered civilians, had to walk. We'd wave to them amid gales of laughter as we rode by, but the looks we got would freeze water. Needless to say this didn't last too long. The order was rescinded and we rode together for the latter part of our stay in the yard.

Saturday nights were celebrated with a Navy band playing Glenn Miller, Benny Goodman and Tommy Dorsey arrangements at the Officers Club. I remember young aviators, faces disfigured by flames in South Pacific air combat- dress blues, campaign ribbons and white gloves doing little to hide the horror that would follow them through plastic surgery and the reconstruction of ears and noses in the months to come. Cute Navy nurses, in uniforms that looked like they had been prepared for a recruiting poster, dancing under soft lights- smiling at those scarred masks, trying bravely to touch the inner man and reconstruct the spirit, often more permanently damaged than the body.

One weekend we chartered a bus and rode to a ski lodge on Mount Rainier. There were nine or ten couples, and I don't think many of them had ever seen a ski. Jean and I had never seen snow, except in Boston and in Portland- that seemed a hundred years ago.

We backpacked picnic supplies from the bus to the foot of the slope and spent the night before a roaring fire in the lodge. We sang "Sentimental Journey" and "I'll Be Home for Christmas." There was a closeness that reflected the months of separation and the realization that we were shortly due to return to the forward area. We sat around in the gathering darkness, finally separating, girls to a dormitory, fellows sleeping in the bunkhouse of the Rangers, now away on their own wartime service. Night sounds- a gray owl hooting, winds whispering through spruce trees, snow softly falling, a white mantle spreading over the land. A full moon shone through the window and I went to sleep dreaming of the past few days- not worrying about tomorrow.

We climbed up the slope of the ski run and picnicked in brilliant sunshine. Cloudless blue skies and trees ladened with fresh powdery snow lent a festive air to what was one of our last days of yard time. Snow buntings in their mottled plumage and horned larks strutted through the new growth of spring grasses.

Frank Regan, the senior Marine Officer and his wife Jean, with my bride and I, walked to the downhill run. I'd never had skis on and Frank, ever the expert, said, "Don't worry- just let yourself go. If you think you're in trouble, sit down."

Well, Frank let off with a whoop and not to be outdone, I followed. What a thrill. We raced in gentle curves for a few hundred yards, speed picking up all the while. The curve began to tighten, and I watched in horror as we slid towards the "Devils Dip". Frank was suddenly airborne and I was in his tracks in moments. I tried desperately to hold the trail, but first one ski, then the next slipped out into open space.

I flew through the air, snow banks and trees flashing by, finally crashing down in powdery free fall, yards downhill. My legs were twisted at a crazy angle, ski boot straps just out of reach. I tried to slip the straps, but I'd slide downhill a little further each time I moved. The sound of water rushing through a little brook was getting closer and closer. I finally managed to get my skies off, with my butt resting about three feet from the icy creek. Using the skis as poles, I staggered on trembling legs back to the trail. I walked down the rest of the way. The girls were smarter. After watching our performance, they walked.

Days flew by and all too soon it was time to leave the yard. We spent the last night together at the Enatai Inn, a small hotel on a hill that overlooked Bremerton. Looking out at the moonlight drenched town, it looked like a Currier and Ives print from the 19th century. The Captain had ordered all hands on board by 2200. Officers by 2400 hours. MP's were ordered to see that all bars were closed at 2100. I had the watch as Officer of the Deck at 2000, so I bid my bride a tearful farewell and returned to the ship.

Enlisted liberty ended at 2200 hours, and I no sooner relieved the watch, when I heard a sound like angry hornets on the dock. The JOOD called from the after accommodation ladder to report several hundred sailors drunk and raising hell on the pier. Shouts of "We aren't coming aboard," and drunken cursing made a crazy pattern on the cold, clear, night air.

I awakened Frank Regan, the Marine Duty Officer, and told him we had a problem on the pier and he'd better break out the "Gyreens." In minutes he was on deck with a lone gunnery sergeant. Buckling Sam Brown belts and carrying night sticks, they descended the ladder to dockside. I can still see him standing there, not a really big man, about 175 pounds, arms akimbo, at parade rest, night stick behind his back. The "Gunny" was by his side, looking as solid as a rock.

Frank's voice boomed out, "Who is the spokesman for this group?" A burly sailor, towering over Frank, stepped forward "I'll speak for the group, Captain." Like a snake the night stick came out and the sailor laid stretched on the pier. "Does anyone else care to speak for the group?" Frank asked. The noise stopped. You could hear a pin drop.

"Pick that SOB up and put him in the Brig. The rest of you get on board." Two sailors grabbed the "Spokesman" and carried his limp form up the ladder. Several hundred now sober and well behaved sailors marched quietly up the after accommodation ladder and the "mutiny" was over.

The next morning as I was eating breakfast, Regan passed by. "Did you log that incident yet, Charlie?"

"No Sir."

"Well, don't. We'll visit the brig after you finish breakfast."

The brig was made of sheet metal, with holes three or four inches in diameter punched through. The unfortunate "Spokesman" was sitting on a stool, covered in vomit. Two Marines were outside with swab handles at the ready. They'd kept that poor sailor's attention during the night with a poke in the ribs, just in case he thought he'd like to go to sleep.

"On your feet sailor." Frank said as we entered. As he came to the closest thing he could to attention, Frank asked in a gentle voice, "Did you learn anything last night sailor?"

"Yes Sir. Don't never be the spokesman, Captain."

"Good, now go take a shower, and sleep this off, but remember-NEVER BE THE SPOKESMAN AGAIN."

Now that's what I consider good WWII discipline. Today, an Ombudsman would probably be shouting to have Regan court martialed, and the "rights" of the sailor would make him look heroic, instead of the butt of laughter, and the nickname- "The Spokesman" that stayed with him during the rest of his service on the *New Jersey*.

The city of Bremerton will never forget the *New Jersey's* last night. Our crew tore up several bars and took them out in the streets for a last drink. Several automobiles were rolled down the hill, clattering a wild refrain in the heart of town. The city fathers sent the word to Long Beach, where we were later denied liberty, fearing another riot from the crew of the *Jersey*. There were twenty seven hundred men in the war time crew and staff. They could make quite an impression on a medium-sized city, and occasionally did.

As dawn approached a dull orange glow, lights of early risers dotted the dark hills that surrounded the city. Here and there, a thin wisp of smoke curled heavenward. It was difficult to believe that we would soon be leaving the sanctuary we had enjoyed. So soon, we knew we'd be separated again from loved ones. The crew separated into excited new shipmates, eager to see the war, and the veterans of the past months who wondered what the next few months would bring. The dull glow of dawn and the shrill call of the bos'n's pipe heralded an end and a new beginning.

6-30-45- We got under way for post-repair trials in Puget Sound. Special sea details were set and the crew mustered at quarters. As the *New Jersey* passed the dock below the Enatai Inn, wives waved from shore and the port side of the ship was lined with sailors, with many a lump in throat. As the girls disappeared from view, we knew we were heading back to the South Pacific, and the War was about to embrace us again.

At 1000 we anchored off Blake Island at the ammo dump. We reloaded ammunition, but not at the same pace we'd exhibited a few short weeks before.

7-3- Underway again, through Juan de Fuca Strait, south bound for Long Beach Naval Shipyard. Summer skies and lush green hills, surf breaking in the shallows, gulls diving in our wake and small skiffs with fishermen waving as we exited.

7-8- We anchored in San Pedro Harbor, all liberty canceled. I managed to get ashore with the guard mail and phoned Jean in New Orleans. We hung on the phone, savoring each moment, knowing it might be a long time before we could speak again. Scuttlebutt filled with rumors as to our next assignment. New VT (proximity fused rounds for the five inch battery) are supposed to be even more effective than the first lot.

7-9- At 0751 we hauled anchor and proceeded to exercises off the coast of southern California. Gunnery drills off San Clemente Island proved our yard modifications, and increased accuracy of gun directors. The old hardware had been having problems with faster Japenese aircraft and Baka bombs, as the war progressed. Particularly troublesome were Kamikazi attacks, Baka bombs with a Japanese, cowboy style, guiding a torpedo like missile to certain death. This, at speeds in excess of the 300 knot limit the old fire control computers were programed to handle.

The ship rolled gently in rather heavy ground swells, a dense fog shrouding a slate gray sea. It was time to get our sea legs back. Quite a few queasy stomachs. There were runs on a measured mile to record the revolutions required to drive the ship at prescribed speeds, and dummy preparations for refueling on port and starboard sides. Gunnery drills for the main battery and simulated air attacks on the secondary battery, kept the Gunnery Department and the "Gun Boss" hopping.

It was the routine of another shakedown, but with a crew now honed by almost two years of action, most in the Southwest Pacific Theater. At 1015 we passed Santa Catalina Island. Slowing to 12 knots we streamed paravanes (a cable towed device to cut the moorings of contact mines in shallow water), probably the most useless piece of deck gear a battleship carried in the twentieth century.

Cdr. R. M. Kiethly, a submarine skipper, relieved Cdr. E. Hahn, who had served as navigator since the ship had been commissioned. The captain was bringing aboard a new group of department heads- the change in command was a transition that allowed for further expansion of a still growing naval presence.

7-10- A copy of the *New Jersey's* deck log for a couple of watches will bring back a lot of memories for many of us: "1200-1600- Steaming as before. 1203 maneuvered on various courses and speeds to catapult two aircraft. 1235 catapulted aircraft 35641 Pilot Ensign A.L. Trecartin, USNR, mission observation. Catapulted aircraft no. 35644 Pilot Lieutenant G. Harris, USNR, mission observation. 1300 changed course to 115 degrees T(pgc). 1312 sounded General Quarters for practice firing. 1325 set condition Zebra throughout the ship. 1331 maneuvered on various courses and speeds to get on station for main battery practice firing. 1434 commenced firing main battery to Starboard. 1521 ceased firing main battery. 1511 recommenced firing main battery to Starboard. 1521 ceased firing main battery. 1524 changed course to 340 degrees T(pgc). 1535 changed course to 090 degrees T (pgc). 1551 changed speed to 15 knots (086 rpm). 1556 changed course to 080 degrees T (pgc). 1558 changed speed to 10 knots (056 rpm).

J.H. Miller , Lieutenant USNR."

"1600-1800- Steaming as before. 1600 commenced firing main battery to Port (these salvos were all being spotted by our aircraft against targets on the San Clemente Island firing range). 1606 changed course to 070 degrees T (pgc). Changed speed to 20 knots (117 rpm). 1610 changed course to 050 degrees T (pgc). 1617 changed course to 090 degrees(pgc). Changed speed to 10 knots (056 rpm). 1621 commenced firing main battery to Port. 1624 completed firing main battery. 1626 set condition modified Zebra third deck and below, condition Yoke second deck and above (this to facilitate first mess). 1631 changed course to 055 degrees T (pgc). 1635 changed course to 090 degrees T (pgc). 1641 secured from General Quarters. Set condition III. 1652 commenced firing 5" battery to port. 1700 Saxton R. D. , F2c 314 68 67, USN punctured right foot when he stepped on a board with a nail in it. Treated in Sick Bay and returned to duty. 1701 ceased firing 5" battery. 1703 changed course to 040 degrees T (pgc). Changed speed to 20 knots (117 rpm). 1710 changed speed to 10 knots (073 rpm). 1712 changed course to 010 degrees (pgc). 1716 commenced firing 5 " battery to) Port. Changed course to 040 degrees (pgc), changed speed to 15 knots. 1732 changed speed to 10 knots (053 rpm). 1731 changed course to 090 degrees T (pgc). 1737 commenced firing 5" battery to Port. 1748 sounded flight quarters. 1755 ceased firing 5" battery. 1756 changed course to 130 degrees T (pgc), changed speed to 15 knots (086 rpm).

E.F. Hayward, Lieutenant USNR."

So it went day after day- we drilled and drilled and drilled- simulated air attacks from planes based in Southern California and towed sleeves for the 20mm and 40mm batteries. Engineering and Damage Control was thinking up new tricks to test the reaction of young men, most of whom had a USNR tattooed on their hearts and souls, longing to get home to drive-in movies and back to being "feather merchants." Sleds were towed by destroyers to practice off-set shoots with the main battery and to furnishd direct targets for the 5" 38's.

As the days passed, there was a gradual tightening of the routine. Firing exercises and torpedo defense drills were continuous. Thousands of rounds were fired, engineering crews shifted steering controls from the bridge to steering aft, where crewmen manned stations that allowed the ship to be steered by manual control in case of battle damage. Casualty and fire drills kept the damage control people busy. Assemblies in the ward room for gunnery officers and the engineers, were a daily repeat to discuss shortcomings.

7-19- We started taking on final supplies and stores. Once more her decks were piled with mountains of gear. Thousands of rounds for the heavy machine guns, stored in ammunition lockers and ready service boxes alongside the 20mm and 40mm gun tubs. The Captain's Mast was no longer filled with AWOL sailors who had overstayed their leave or liberty. We were back to a more orderly seagoing routine.

We took base course 270 degrees true and headed back to Pearl. Sleep that night was fitful. Dreams of family and the pleasures and heartbreak of separations filled our thoughts. I went topside and stood at the bow, watching the Milky Way and a million bright stars that seemed so far away- as far away as the loved ones we were leaving behind. A school of dolphin splashed by, soft shadows in the darkening waters. Evening shadows replaced the sparkle of sunlight and a subdued aura slipped into our beings. The rush of water cleaved by the *New Jersey's* bow whispered a soft and sad refrain that I could still hear as I tossed and turned in my bunk, trying to sleep before relieving the mid-watch..

About this time Larry Moorman and I started a routine that we laughed about at the ship's last commissioning. Neither one of us were drinkers. But- since alcohol was forbidden on board ship and rationed ashore, everyone brought aboard three bottles of whiskey and one bottle of brandy we were allowed to purchase in Bremerton. Our choice had been Boca Chica Rum and a bottle of Napolean Brandy. The rum was used a half jigger at a time mixed with Coca-Cola. Ice was supplied by the third member of our nightly Acey-Ducey game, John Rossie, the A Division Officer. We never did figure out what to mix with the brandy. It sure as hell tasted lousy with Coke.

Chapter 9: The War Moves to Eniwetok

The crew tried to forget the sorrow of parting and in a few days the months ashore seemed light years away. The most difficult time in a man's life is the time of passage- from boyhood to manhood and from hearth and home to the monastic life of seaman and warrior. From the apprentice seamen just out of boot camp to the captain we were all caught up in a flood of memories and of doubts. What did the future hold? Now- generations away, it seems the past is more relevant than the future. A remembrance of times that were the most significant in our lives is stored in the innermost recesses of our minds, relived in dreams. A sailor's white cap seems to be fitted for eternity. Meeting shipmates some fifty years later, the bonds of comraderie seem to have been strengthened by the passage from boyhood to suddenly aged warriors.

The ocean seemed grayer, and more forbidding, as we exited CONLUS. Even the sky offshore had a dull leaden cast. A few sea birds followed softly in our wake, their mournful calls to one another adding to our melancholy. Catching the lift of winds on the slope of an ocean wave, always moving, they seemed imbued with a freedom of spirit that we envied. I followed their random wanderings until darkness hid them in the envelope of night.

Once again we stood watches and heard the clarion call to Air Defense and to General Quarters. The routine again implanted in our minds, sounds we'd respond to in an instant.

7-19- Our ship's log showed "Steaming as before, 16 knots (091 rpm) zigzagging" to complicate a submarine commanders solution based on our course and speed. 2145- "Blew tubes on all steaming boilers." The monotony of open ocean sailing in unthreatened waters finally lulled us to accept the first day of the rest of our lives.

Daily inspection of smokeless powder samples, anti-aircraft drills and main battery exercises filled our waking hours. Aircraft were catapulted, and tracking drills exercised radarmen and gun crews. Engineering casualty drills and deck maintenance kept all hands too busy to think of anything else. Slowly we returned to the other world, a world of watches and alarms, constant drills and quick response to every bell and bugle call.

The ship's log reveals in detail the trials and tribulations of a floating community of some one hundred and sixty officers and eighteen hundred men. Infractions of regulations, the punishments meted out, and the treatment in Sick Bay for the casualties of daily life, all seem mundane: "S1/c D,USNR, AWOL, sentenced by Summary Courts Martial to two weeks in the brig, and a forfeiture of $15.40 per month in pay for a period of two months." "S1/c B, USN, received laceration of right toe while handling 5" ammunition. Treated in sick bay and returned to duty." And then there was the entry -"1810- B. D.A. S1/c USN, received lacerated penis while loading a 40mm gun. Treated in sick bay and returned to duty." I never figured out just how that happened. Wonder what nick-name his shipmates hung around this escapade ?

At 1759 we entered the channel at Pearl Harbor and were moored Starboard side to dock F2. The sounds and smells of the harbor were a reminder of past visits. Diesel fumes blended with a tropical aroma of fruiting trees in perpetual spring. Launches scurried about, transporting us about the greatly expanded base. The signs of the Japanese attack had not been obliterated. The *Arizona's* stark superstructure rising above the still waters was a mute symbol of the massive destruction their attack had inflicted.

The condition of readiness was improved from the December 7th Sunday that seems so long ago. We set Condition ZEBRA third deck and below (that is, buttoned up to prevent flooding in the event of an attack). Ammunition lighters alongside, loading and off loading as our orders required a higher percentage of AP (armor piercing) 16" projectiles.

Went ashore with my room-mate Larry Moorman, for a dinner at Don the Beachcomber's and walked streets crowded with endless lines of Blue Jackets, Marines and GI's, all trying to maximize what we knew was an all too brief respite from tomorrow. Girls and sailors formed a swirl of colorful interaction. Sidewalks were jammed with thousands of young men, all trying to find a date- most of them did.

The next few days were a delightful respite from the regular routine. The ship's complement were veterans of some eighteen months of intensive training and action. They had a confidence in themselves and in the ship that was a bond that has remained in place even now, some fifty years later. It is a union born of war and tempered with the brotherhood that stress and danger forged.

7-27 was a day of liberty for my watch, and Admiral Decker's son Ben, a Junior Officer, Larry Moorman and I took off in a borrowed jeep, courtesy of Admiral Decker. (Ben was killed shortly after the war in a plane crash while qualifying as a Naval Aviator.) We toured the island of Oahu, transported for the moment into a tropical paradise only seen before in our dreams. The roads led through lush fields of pineapples and sugar cane, past homes perched on rocky outcrops, surf breaking on beaches, cliffs verdant with foliage forming a sounding board to a mournful refrain.

Through the Palle, a pass that divides the island's mountainous backbone, we motored in the mist that clouds the pass almost continuously. Just as we peaked, the sun shone through, and stretched on either side was a panorama of gentle hills with fields below, squares laid out in a mosaic painted in the most vivid greens and ochers. With a brilliant blue sky now a counterpoint, it was magnificent. A surreal painting, restful and totally abstracted from the pattern of our lives. The wind in our face, we rolled into Shangrila, Doris Duke Cromwell's palatial estate, now open to a continuous round of parties for all and sundry Officers of the Fleet. The grounds were tended by a staff of gardeners. Gazebos strategically placed to give privacy and an unobstructed view of surf, sand and ocean. The flower beds were colorful beyond reality. Dozens of yard hands pruned every tree and bush, landscaping rook and rill to perfection. We

AV Division poses on the Jersey's *fantail with an OS2U float plane in the background. Standing (L-R): Ralph Slusher, Ed Balley, Alton Faber, Bill Hutchinson, Lt. William Ethridge. Ens. "Willy" Williams, Lt. William Butts, Chief Marion Calder, Flint Hanson, Robert Graham, Ben Flanagan, Jack McSorley, Mark Fletcher, John Selorchac, Harry Press, Ed Gossage, Nelson Boone, Ben Cairns, William Lonsbury.*

Captain's inspection on the fantail was a weekly ritual in port. This one was in Yokosuka Harbor, Japan.

got back to the ship at dusk, the Jeep filled with fruits we'd illegally picked in a transit of the island's farm lands.

7-28- Reveille at 0500 and a breakfast of tropical fruits - papayas and pineapples - bacon, eggs and hot coffee. The Navy was definitely the way to go. But all too soon, we were underway from Pearl for drills offshore. Captain E.T. "Slim" Wooldridge stood on the wing of the bridge, feet planted against the gentle roll of the *Jersey*. The ever-present trades wafted the aroma of the islands for a hundred miles offshore. It must have seemed the zenith of his career. But sailors in the wartime Navy weren't particularly quick to grasp the glory of a moment like this.

Captain Wooldridge was trying to establish himself on the ship and with the crew, and to replace a man like Capt. Carl F. Holden, was not an easy row to hoe. Carl Holden was a complete contrast to Captain Wooldridge. Both men were strong willed and ambitious, but Holden had the rare ability to be a disciplinarian one moment and a hero to all hands the next. Captain Wooldridge seemed aloof and distant to most of us. Especially after cutting a weeks leave out of each watch when taking command in Bremerton.

Now the skipper was a chain smoker, a fact not lost on some of the crew. Some sailor put a wad of toilet tissue in one of the butt kits and liberally doused it with cigarette lighter fluid. The explosion and flame when the Skipper dropped a butt in the kit may not be much compared to a nuclear blast, but the results were comparable. Confusion in the aftermath! The Captain stood there for a moment, a stunned look on his face, then stalked angrily from the bridge. The silence was occasionally broken by a very, very discrete snicker. No one knows who the culprit was, and no mention was made of the incident in the ship's log. To Captain Woldridge's credit, he never mentioned the incident either. With the passage of time he became a warm and well liked Commanding Officer.

At 0821, with pilot aboard, we steamed out to sea again. Bright sunlight sparkled on the ocean and the sound of "General Quarters! Now, all hands man your battle stations." was a grim reminder we were back to wartime discipline-no time for fun and games any longer.

The five-inch battery was exercised, dropping several radio controlled drones, cheers from the 20mm and 40mm gun crews ringing out. The U.S.S. *Rowen*, a DD, took screening station and we launched our "Kingfishers" to scout ahead.

At 1600 hours we secured from anti-aircraft firing, set Condition III and began zigzagging until Evening Alert was completed. Course 270 degrees T and ship darkened for night time security. The Southern Cross was visible once more and the night seemed alive, a full moon, and tropical constellations in the Milky Way bathing the *Jersey* in a soft glow.

7-29- Steaming at 15 knots, we exercised continuously at anti-aircraft drills, 20mm and 40mm guns adding their sharp refrain to the deep boom of the 5 inch 38's. Offset shoots on the destroyer *Rowen* and sleeves for the heavy machine guns towed by planes from Pearl took up much of the day. At 1805 the U.S.S. *Birmingham* and five DD's took station, and a cruising disposition was formed.

At 0610 the *Birmingham* and DesDiv 90 left the formation, proceeding on duty assigned. We spent the remainder of the morning and afternoon on a shore bombardment exercise, and further secondary battery firing on a simulated motor torpedo boat attack. It was this constant training that paid such handsome dividends in the months that followed.

While we were preparing for re-entry into the combat area on this lovely Sunday afternoon, one of those quirks of fate that grace the unlucky was about to occur. Captain Charles McVay, commanding the *Indianapolis* was cruising at routine speed of 15.7 knots, her ETA at Leyte Gulf estimated at 1100 July 31. Having inquired at Guam about an escort, McVay was told it was not necessary, as there were few signs of submarine activity on her track. The Captain was not zigzagging when the Red Gods of War decided to play one last fateful trick on this unfortunate ship. Her last transmission of a fix on her position was received in garbled form and no repeat was requested! Then, she sailed across the path of a Japanese submarine, the I-58, and two of six torpedoes caught her amidships.

In moments, the ship was listing badly, all power lost. Although Mayday was keyed by the ship's radio operator, with the sudden loss of power, the complete transmission was never received. To further complicate the matter the *Indianapolis* was steaming at 16 knots when struck. Tons of water rushed into her ruptured hull. So sudden was her fatal wound that only a handful of flotation rafts were released. Only a third of her 1,200 crewmen survived the next four days- in shark infested waters. Men perished by the score. Dehydration and the merciless sun took a fearful toll. Thus the fortunes of war. A brave captain and a well trained crew were in the wrong place at the wrong time.

7-31- was again a day of anti-aircarft practice. The routine was marred when one of our spotter aircraft was damaged in attempting a Cast Recovery in heavy swells. A Cast Recovery is performed by swinging the ship athwart the line of the wind, creating a brief slick in which a float plane can land. Taxiing into the hookup requires superb timing and a great deal of finesse. Unfortunately, the ocean can play tricks on the most experienced pilot.

A heavy swell pushed the plane into the fantail. Although the aircraft was recovered, a very red faced Junior Birdman climbed out of the cockpit. Another note was pinned to his pillow, "Dear Mom- I wrecked another plane. Please buy lots of war bonds." Launching those float planes and recovering them was one of the trickier assignments on the ship. As a catapult officer I learned to launch at the precise moment of the ships roll, when the upswing was commencing. This made the launch easier on the pilot who flew off with the help of a canted deck.

Probably the closest shave I had during the war occurred during a launch one afternoon. My hands were raised for the second warm-up, and the pilot's head was braced against his headrest. A rating was poised with the firing lanyard in hand, ready for my hands to drop, signaling him to fire a five-inch charge. This would send the plane speeding down the catapult for a launch.

Flames were pouring out of the float plane's exhaust and the motor screamed its call to be hurled skyward. There was a crash, and as I turned my head. The Port aircraft was twisting on the deck, ruptured fuel tanks pouring av-gas across the fantail. A life line had been strung to keep idlers clear of the launch area and a hundred sailors were watching. Knowing that if I dropped my hands the av-gas was going to blow us all to hell, I glanced over my shoulder and saw the officer in charge of the launch, Lieutenant "Rosie" Rosinski, looking at me with that crooked, cool grin of his, and I knew I had control. Watching for what seemed an eternity, the flyer finally turned his head. I slowly moved my hand across my throat, the signal for him to cut his engine. A sigh of relief from all who were watching went up, his engine gave a low growl, and stopped. My shoes, soaked with av-gas, had to be thrown away. One spark, and we'd all have been cinders.

At 1710 we commenced maneuvering for entry into Pearl, and at 1859 hours we were moored as before in the harbour. The watch was shifted from the bridge to the quarterdeck. The night watch topped all tanks with 7858 barrels of fuel oil and 675 gallons of 100 octane aviation gasoline. I kept thinking what a mess we could have had if that AV gas had blown a few days before.

8-1- Liberty was canceled and we stored ship and prepared to get underway. Ammunition ships, and a barge mounted crane came

The 7th Division posed for the Ship's War Log.

along side. A stream of sailors carrying 5" shells and powder canisters transferred their loads to magazines below decks. The day was an all hands evolution- tons of supplies had to be manhandled into stowage compartments and the ship secured for sea.

8-2- At 0700 with Condition Zebra set third deck and below, we sortied once again for the open ocean. The pilot left the ship at 0750, and with the Captain glancing occasionally at the scorched butt kit on the bridge, we left Pearl under a cloudless sky. Gunnery drills for the anti-aircraft battery with the *New Jersey* as guide, we sailed with a screen of four destroyers on a course of 180 degrees T at 16 knots for who knew where.

At 1839 evening alert and course set to 264 degrees T.

8-3 to **8-9**- We steamed in a disembodied world of gunnery drills and damage control exercises. There is nothing more endless than the an ocean and the inverted bowl of the sky.

8-6- the *Enola Gay* dropped the first atomic bomb on Hiroshima. As a recently graduated Chemical Engineer, I didn't understand what the event could mean. Just three short years ago we had been taught a nuclear explosion would start a chain reaction that would destroy planet earth. Now a new technology changed the world forever. When the second bomb, a few days later, reduced the naval base of Nagasaki to rubble, the war was as good as over. Ship's routine continued however, and we maintained full readiness for further engagement.

On the 8th of August at 0653, we sighted Wake Island to starboard in the soft early morning light of sunrise. The ubiquitous boobies were diving into a serene ocean.

At 0815 General Quarters was sounded, and we prepared to launch aircraft for spotting off shore bombardment. This, although we didn't realize it, was to be our last action in the war.

At 0904, with Condition Zebra set we commenced phase one of the bombardment. Closing at 8 knots on a course of 083 T. at a range of 15,000 yards, we commenced firing. The island was a thin strip of ivory colored sand when viewed from Air Defense. The Main Battery, with reduced charges, threw 2,700 pound, high explosive shells at the beleaguered defenders, starting at 16,000 yards. The 5-inch battery, with high explosives, added their fire as the range closed to 12,000 yards. We accomplished very little, but left the Atoll with plumes of dark black smoke curling heavenward. The firing was in two phases, one from 0904 until 1055, after which we retired slightly to recover planes. Firing recommenced at 1309, after replenishing spotter aircraft. Phase two was completed at 1414 with 106 rounds of 16 inch HE and 266 rounds of 5 inch ammunition expended.

At 1660, with Wake dropping astern, we set course 205 degrees T, steaming at 20 knots. Evening alert furnished a sunset that was glorious. Reds and golds and the streaks of the setting sun seemed to portend the declining fortunes of the Japanese warlords.

8-10- We dropped the hook in Eniewetok Atoll, 370 yards South of Berth 421. With 30 fathoms of water and a coral and sand bottom, we were in an island harbor, surrounded by an atoll covered with the impedimentia of war. We secured the ship for port routine.

Men-o-war and their train covered the harbor from horizon to horizon. It was an awesome display of naval power and no one of us who were there will ever forget it. Battleships, cruisers, carriers and destroyers, accompanied by a vast train of supply vessels- cement barges that had been towed across the ocean ladened with every conceivable requisite. LCVPs and motor launches spinning about in the white wake of ships coming and going, their paths etched across a tranquil lagoon. Palm trees on sandy beaches and GI's swimming in the surf gave an aura of security that our dominion of the Southwest Pacific had established. We slept, grateful to Almighty God for his protection, and secure in the knowledge that with His help, we had prevailed.

By 2100 we had received 225 charges of 16" powder, 11,130 rounds of 50 caliber machine gun ammo and a like amount of 20mm rounds, 395 AAC 5" projectiles, 45 H.C. 16" projectiles, and 4720 rounds of 40mm ammunition from the SS. *Durham Victory*, an ammunition ship.

8-10- The Japanese Cabinet offered to surrender.

8-11- This day saw us sortie once more for firing practice. Leaving the anchorage at 1050, we had completed our drills by early afternoon and were steaming in formation with DesRon 50 in an anti-submarine screen comprised of destroyers *Cotton*, *Bronson*, *Healy*, *Gatling* and *Dortch*.

8-13-At 1815 the General Alarm sounded for evening alert and with the ship darkened we steamed on at 24 knots course 280 degrees T picking up a pilot for entering Apra Harbor, Guam. We moored to buoy in berth No. 701 with the port chain in 10 fathoms of water.

8-14-Japan surrendered and the wardroom and crews quarters buzzed with talk of going home. This was a largely Reserve Navy and most felt "It's over. Let me out."

8-15-was declared VJ day and there were divine services with a jubilant firing of star shells at evening alert. After the night settled on the lagoon, our rather somber ship's complement's minds were filled with thoughts of home and loved ones. Shortly, the points needed for release were to be promulgated and the rush to get out had to be tempered with the ships need to retain enough ratings and officers to operate. Democracy survives in spite of our apparent lack of forethought.

Chapter 10: Guam, The Philippines and Tokyo!

8-13- As the new 7th Division Officer I was handed a stack of title B cards by Lt. Reed Weyburn, whom I was relieving. These were to be signed, showing I had inventoried the cards and found that material not a part of the ship's structure was on hand, i.e.- small tools and replacement parts from pots and pans to micrometers. Accepting them was one thing, signing for them was another. I told him I'd sign the cards as soon as I could check the materials they represented. He was rather upset, as the supply officer wanted those cards signed before he left for the States and another assignment. Summoned to the supply officer's office I was asked to sign again.

"I'm sorry Sir, I won't sign till I have a chance to inventory the gear. If you want to sign for this inventory, I'll check it out and sign in a day or two." He frowned, took the cards, and I started checking.

After securing about ninety percent of the gear and assuring myself that it was under lock and key, I found that there was still a heck of a lot of equipment missing. This included extra barrels for the 40mm guns, each weighing some three hundred and seventy pounds, as well as additional tools and other survey-able equipment that was probably never taken aboard. The supply officer asked if I thought the other divisions had a similar set of shortages.

"Hell yes," I told him. With a worried look he convened a meeting in the wardroom and the damndest scavenger hunt in the *Jersey's* history started. Sailors ran about, placing their Division's gear behind locked doors to prevent it changing hands again and again. The final result was a stack of cards six inches high showing equipment unaccounted for. It was surveyed during our next sojourn at sea. Lost over the side in heavy weather?

8-14 to **8-16**- We moored in Apra Harbor, Guam. Got ashore several times. Roamed about in the debris of combat that made every island captured seem alike- Marines and GI's in sun faded uniforms, sweat soaked, a city of Quonset huts with a line of GI's in front of every one, small stores and "gedunck" (ice cream), hot beer - everything the fantastic productivity of American industry could furnish.

When looking at the services our troops enjoyed, comparing this with any of our allies, it was apparent how great our productivity had become, how vast our resources. And the ancillary services- mail, medical and spiritual, in quantities that were limitless. On the perimeter of this activity, foxholes and the surrounding ground were covered with spent small arms shell casings, an odor of dead and decaying flesh still noticeable, a cloying scent that made you rush to the shower when you returned to the antiseptic cleanliness of the *Jersey*. Got into a conversation with a Marine who had been on the first wave- would you believe he was happy he didn't have to be on a ship that might be sunk by Japanese torpedoes? I was glad I wasn't in the first wave with him.

Louis McFall, a Tulane NROTC classmate, came aboard to visit. He brought news from my best friend Jack Gordon, another Tulane University graduate. A few days later, I got word that Jack was missing in action, lost in a midair collision with an Army observation plane. Jack was spotting for the battleship *West Virginia's* main battery- interdictive fire over the ridge of Tinian, in the Mariannas. An Army light plane, called a Moth, flew over the hills and collided with the tail assembly of Jack's aircraft. They both spun into the ocean. The planes were not recovered for several months. Jack was ultimately buried on Tinian.

I got ashore and saw the palm shaded area were the military cemetery had been established. I felt saddened by the distance that separated so many young men who died on distant shores, far from love of hearth and home. After the war, Jack's remains were returned to New Orleans. He was buried not far from the lakefront area where we had flown model airplanes as youngsters. The Navy flyover was a requiem for a mother who had continued to believe her son would return. She held to this hope until the final moments of the graveside ceremony.

The atom bomb had been dropped on Hiroshima on 6 August and on Nagasaki, a Japanese naval base, a few days later. On 10 August an offer of surrender was made by the enemy on condition that Emperor Hirohito keep his throne. On 14 August it was official, and 15 August was declared VJ Day. Formal ceremonies were concluded on the *Missouri* in Tokyo harbor on 2 September.

The *New Jersey* was originally scheduled for the surrender ceremonies, but Congress decided that the choice of the *Missouri* would please President Harry Truman, a Missouri native, and the change was made in an Op-order.

8-17- We sortied from Apra Harbor, Guam at 1055. Sailing with the USS *Patterson*, DD 392, we steamed under now peaceful tropic skies for Manila, refueling enroute from the USS *Banchee*, a tanker, taking on 7,245 barrels of fuel oil.

Refueling at sea, steaming at 15 knots, we threw a line to the tanker, followed by a heavier line. Finally the fuel hose of reinforced rubber was dragged across. Pumping could begin in a matter of minutes and if hostile action threatened, stopped just as quickly. At the same time a destroyer could be hooked up to the other side of the tanker, refueling the screen as the *Jersey* or a carrier was taking its much bigger gulp.

Although the surrender had been announced, we sailed with Condition III watches set. It was a time of jubilation, but we kept our guard up. It was difficult to believe the war was really over. The Japanese had been fanatical warriors. It took a bit of getting used to before we realized they were also the most obedient of citizens. McArthur's decision to let the Emperor retain his throne was the wisest of diplomacies. When the Emperor said the war was over and that there was to be no further resistance- it was over!

8-21- At 0802 a pilot was taken aboard and we moved into Manila Harbor, P. I.

0953- We anchored in Berth 62 in 10 fathoms of water. The sight that greeted us was one of total destruction. The harbor was a forest of masts, attesting to the decimation of the Japanese merchant fleet. Radar tilted at crazy angles on the forepeak of men-o-war. Merchantmen in the shallows had been run aground in a vain attempt to salvage cargo. Sunken vessels by the hundreds were a hazard to navigation, but their military threat had been destroyed. Portholes stared blankly from burned out hulks. The American air power that destroyed this fleet left a legacy of defeat, resting under the sun drenched sky, only frigate birds on aerial patrol. It was quite a sight. We threaded our way into the anchorage.

8-22 to **8-28**- SOPA (Senior Officer Present Afloat) Admiral Raymond Spruance came aboard with his staff. With the Philippines captured, the Japanese fleet in disarray and their best pilots shot down in a war of attrition that had become increasingly one sided, it was difficult to believe the militarists in Japan had refused to admit defeat for so long.

Liberty was granted and we went ashore to see what was left of the battered city of Manila. The main thoroughfare had been renamed MacArthur Thruway and Jeeps raced along in continuous streams. Sam Elliot Morison's Vol XIII "The Liberation of the Philippines" contains a graphic description of the last hours of the battle for Manila.

Of this contest he wrote: "It was too late, all possible withdrawal routes had been cut by General Kruger's Sixth Army. And, as surrender was out of the question to a man of the Admiral's (Iwabachi) kidney, he fought to the bitter end. Manila was fanatically defended from house to house by upwards of 20,000 troops, three fourths of them naval. In the month long battle that resulted, the Japanese defense forces were wiped out almost to a man; the beautiful city of Manila was wrecked, and Intramuros, the old Spanish walled town (in the center of Manila), was reduced to rubble."

Alan Cooney, Moorman and I wandered through fields on the outskirts of Manila. We took pictures of a huge water buffalo with some trepidation. Like our caution with the Japanese, this proved unnecessary. A lad of ten or twelve years, walked up and seizing the ring in the buffalo's nose, calmly walked him to the shade of a battered palm tree.

On the way back to the ship, we were walking down MacArthur Thruway, when an army Jeep screeched to a stop. We were graciously picked up by an Army Colonel named Sutherland. He had been with MacArthur for most of the war and wanted some company. A real nice gent, he took us for a tour of the city and the country side, including an elaborate Chinese Cemetery where some enterprising gals had set up houses of prostitution. Coffins in the walkways and the girls sitting on the stoop waiting for "trade." Another shock to our Judeo-Christian ideas of morality.

In return, we invited the Colonel aboard for supper. It was quite an eye opener for him. Fried chicken, fresh vegetables and the first ice cream he'd had in months. After supper, when the canteen opened, he bought two boxes of cigars and a tube of tooth paste. Smiling from ear to ear as he was leaving the quarterdeck, he turned to Larry and said, "Would one of you fellows want to trade these eagles for those Lieutenant's bars for a few months?" I always thought if you have to die, might as well have your last meal on a white table cloth.

On another day we caught a launch out to Corregidor and viewed the site where our troops had been battered and starved into submission a few short years ago. Quite a contrast to the way we treated a vanquished foe- no death marches, no concentration camps, no torture. The grass was tall and thick and we wondered if the blood of the defenders was somehow nourishing this scar on the earth's surface? There was an eerie silence, only the sound of a bird, invisible in the grass, and the wind rustling tattered palm fronds.

Returning to Manila, we were walking down a side street when I saw a Filipino burning what looked like sheets of stamps alongside a small post office. Being a philatelist, I questioned him. He had been ordered to destroy the overprints and military occupation issues from the days of Japanese dominion. I tried to get him to sell us sheets of each issue, but only persuaded him to give us a few single stamps. We watched in sorrow as he continued to burn this part of philatelic history.

Manila was a city filled with the ghosts of the departed. We walked through the now silent compound of Santo Tomas, where our men had been interned and frequently brutalized. We saw the Malacanan Palace and the Legislative Building, somewhat the worse for wear. The structures gave the appearance of grand old ladies, in reduced circumstances, but very proud.

Everywhere we were followed by children, smiling and with an unquenchable desire for anything 'American.' Can we ever forget, "You got chewing gum, G.I.?" Can you believe how this has all changed in the past few years?

8-28- 0946- After our respite in Manila we got underway at 1200 and passed Tambobo Point to Starboard at 1825. Changed course to 010 degrees T. The bos'n piped "Now all hands darken ship," and General Quarters sounded for the evening alert. As Task Unit 50.1 with the DD 392 (*Patterson*) as escort we headed North by East for Okinawa.

8-30- 1217-We picked up the southern tip of Okinawa and at 1600 dropped the hook in Buckner Bay (Nakagusuku Wan). The harbor, as usual, was filled with American and Allied shipping. We saw an increased British participation in our efforts in the Pacific since VE Day in Europe freed their hands. The British wanted to reestablish their Empire in the Far East and this was the quickest way to accomplish their objective.

I was enjoying my new role as the 7th Division Officer. It was a forty MM heavy machine gun unit with some two hundred men and five gun tubs, each with a 40mm quad and a gyro precessed tracking unit. We protected the starboard quarter against low level air attack.

The ship's routine of drills and periodic launch of the ship's aircraft for observation flights were still repeated regularly. This activity was only interrupted by an occasional trip ashore in one of the *New Jersey's* launches. As the Admiral's Barge Officer, I had the luck to go ashore with the "Boss." This was very interesting as the Admiral had an insatiable desire to eyeball every landing to improve and evaluate the effects of shore bombardment. Although our mission has been to protect the landing sites from the Japanese navy, both Adm. Spruance and Adm. Halsey felt responsible for the hours allotted for softening up island defenses with shore bombardment.

Days passed with drills, polishing bright work and more drills. We were really itching for a change in the routine.

The ship's log reads monotonously "Anchored as before. No comments," watch after watch.

9-13- I was awakened by a seaman shouting in my ear, "Mr. Frank. Wake up, we're going to Tokyo. Cdr. Keithly (the navigator) wants the barge in the water as soon as possible."

It didn't take long. Cdr. Keithly, the *New Jersey's* navigator, an engineering rating and I piled into the skimmer (the Admiral's barge) and with me at the wheel, we roared across the darkened bay leaving the rest of the barge crew shouting from the fantail. We picked up charts from the Harbor Master and raced back to the *Jersey*, already with anchor raised and underway. We were swung aboard with the airplane crane and Cdr. Keithly rushed to the bridge, while I secured the barge on the fantail.

At 1323, on course 052 degrees T and in a gentle rolling Pacific swell, we moved towards the Japanese mainland.

Our destination was Wakayama Wan, Honshu, Japan. Our screen was the destroyer Putnam.

9-15- 0942- We stationed Special Sea Details and entered Wakayama Wan with all hands at General Quarters. 1042 - The anchor dropped and we were in the Land of the Rising Sun as an occupying force. Adm. Raymond Spruance was SOPA (Senior Officer Present Afloat). In berth 54 in 19 fathoms of water, Condition III A on the anti-aircraft battery, we stood at ease.

That first night after a festive supper, we slept soundly. Then, at 0500, the General Alarm sounded and we raced to battle stations. Searchlights illuminated a fleet of small craft with sails filled, course set for our anchorage. As the powerful beams swung from one frail craft to another, sails began to flap and the tiny fleet lost way. Five inch and heavy machine gun batteries trained on them, and they began to mill about in frightened confusion. No one knew what was going to happen next and I don't blame the Japanese for being scared. Finally an interpreter hailed one of the craft to find that we were in their herring fishing ground. The Japanese were told to stand off and a rather humorous incident ended without casualty.

A small Marine detachment went ashore to secure charts of Tokyo Harbor, and returned with the charts and a little Japanese puppy, quickly nicknamed Wakayama. He seemed to take particular delight greeting visitors on the quarterdeck, and became a fixture in that area.

9-16- 0556- We were under way from Wakayama Wan for Tokyo Bay and the port of Yokosuka. Captain Wooldridge was on the bridge and a huge set of colors was flying from the main mast. A wonderful and exhilarating pride in our nation and what it represented overwhelmed us. This was an instant when pride dominated all hands. We were lifted to the highest emotional plateau. Grateful to the Almighty for our deliverance, we were saddened by the memory of so many friends and shipmates who had perished on the way.

0847- Moored to buoy 6 in Yokosuka Naval Base, Tokyo Harbor.

We commenced liberty for my watch the 19th of September and Moorman and I strapped on .45 ACP's and went ashore. The expectation of a possibly violent reception was quickly laid to rest. General MacArthur handled the occupation with flawless aplomb. By retaining the Emperor, he had in effect mandated a complete subjugation of the Japanese citizenry. The strange anomaly to our western minds was the respect the Emperor Hirohito still retained. He was a beloved ruler whose divine right could not be compared with that of European royalty. I remember watching a train approach the station in Tokyo with the Imperial flags fluttering on the engine. Suddenly every Japanese in sight faced away from the track. Bowing low, they stayed bent over until the last rumble of the train had faded away. Such devotion and respect for the Emperor made MacArthur's decisions, mandated by the Emperor, accepted without a murmur. It was the most masterful occupation in military history.

On another occasion, we saw school children being marched about Kamakura with a Russian and a Japanese school teacher waving little Russian flags. We wondered where all this was leading, but not for long. MacArthur instructed the head of the Russian Embassy to have all signs of Russian troops removed and the troops dispatched to their own country. The State Department screamed that he was exceeding his authority, but the General held firm. He was correct, and President Truman stood by his decision. The Japanese did not have to wonder whom to obey. He was the "Supreme Allied Commander" and there will never be a better one. This removed the last doubt in the minds

of the Japanese people as to MacArthur's authority. He was obeyed and revered by the Japanese.

Several hours of walking about the Yokosuka Naval Base, on our first liberty, with Japanese military ratings bowing and smiling at our appearance, was enough to persuade us of the lack of any need to be armed. The following day an order was issued that officers would not carry side arms unless on official duty. Although Moorman and I roamed the country side long before some areas could be considered secure, we never experienced a single hostile act. The little Japanese girls did ask Larry why the United States had sent such giants to occupy their country. Larry told them we were the little ones. The big guys were being kept in the U.S. at stud.

The Yokosuka base was a sprawling complex of frame buildings, relatively undamaged by the bombing. Military hardware was scattered about and we picked up sets of the huge binoculars the Japanese had mounted on the wings of the bridges of their warships. Samauri swords and Arisaka rifles, a thirty caliber, and a fifty caliber machine gun were also smuggled aboard.

Walking into the railway station in Yokosuka, I asked for two tickets to Tokyo, using my Japanese phrase book. The clerk answered in perfect English and we were on our way. We found that on approaching any civilian, a translator would be found in moments, and our slightest wish accommodated. You must remember that for most of us this was really the first contact we had with foreign nationals. The majority of the ship's company had never been more than a few miles from home before the war, including Moorman and me. We felt as though we had been transported into the land of Gilbert and Sullivan.

9-27- An amusing incident occurred while I was OD on a dawn watch. We were moored to a buoy, with a tug alongside in case the wind or tide should cause any danger of collision with vessels moored nearby. The *Nagato*, last of the Japanese battleships afloat, was moored on our starboard quarter. I began to worry as tides caused our bearings to close on the *Nagato*. Calling the JOD at the after accomodation ladder, I requested that the Captain of the tug be advised of the situation and asked to prepare to assist. The word came back that the Captain was sleeping, and had directed that he not be disturbed. I went back to the fantail and ordered the petty officer of the watch on the tug to wake the Captain.

A few moments later a very angry mustang Chief Warrant Officer appeared on deck and proceeded to tell me he didn't consider the matter critical. I ordered him to take station and push the *Jersey* out of the path of the *Nagato*, now only about seventy-five yards away. Reluctantly, the tug began to get underway. The bearing held steady and slowly began to open. I was rather disturbed by the incident and decided to report it to the Command Duty Officer.

Shortly after being relieved, I heard the MC pass the word for me to report to the Captain's cabin. The Marine sentry escorted me into Captain Wooldridge's stateroom where a very red-faced Warrant Officer stood at attention. After exchanging civilities and having slowly savored a proffered cup of coffee, the matter at hand was discussed. The Captain then gave the most thorough "ass-eating" any Warrant Officer in the U.S. Navy ever received, and well did he deserve it. The *Jersey* was a ponderous mass of steel and she needed plenty of time to be moved out of harm's way. Watching her bulk as she was moved in any manner could be intimidating. She required a very experienced ship handler. We had excellent cooperation from the tug from then on.

Chapter 11: Mikado. Homeward Bound!

Larry Moorman and I decided we would make the most of our stay in the Land of the Mikado and we did. Stationery I had picked up in the Admiral's office as a souvenir was called into play over and over again. Passes to restricted areas were never questioned when the stars of a Fleet Admiral adorned the letterhead, signed by a fictitious Captain Carl F. Sherwood, promoted from Commander for his excellent assistance in getting motorpool support for Moorman and myself in prior island forays. Motor transport from the pool were put to constant use and we were grateful to the Captain for his help in getting us into remote parts of Honshu. What could the Navy do if we were caught? Punish us and send us home?

We began a systematic tour of the island. Tokyo, Odawara, Ofuna, Mianoshita, Kamakura and Kitakamakura were but a few of the cities we explored. Beautiful shrines and temples, saffron robed Buddhist monks silently moving through medieval rituals, in a setting of immense grandeur, serenity and beauty bestowed by a thousand or more years of care and worship.

We carried the new C-Rations, quite an improvement over the old K type, and canteens of water from the ship. We sat in isolated nooks and watched the ritual as though it were solely for our pleasure. Ancient bronze bells and the sound of wind chimes were blended with the happy murmur of falling water into ponds stocked with Royal Carp, gold fish that weighed several pounds. Their long silky tails streamed lacelike in bamboo shaded water, stained a rich coffee color by the roots of aged cypress trees.

The bamboo itself was a beautiful counterpoint to the shrines. With stalks as big around as a man's thigh, their lacy fronds towered twenty and thirty feet into the air.

And the Japanese were wild about anything American. A pack of cigarettes could be traded for a silk scroll, hand painted in lovely water colors. We traded for a dozen or more. Woodcuts and ivory carvings were equally beautiful and although the Yen was pegged at 15 to the dollar, trading for anything made in the USA was a game enjoyed by both sailors and the Japanese. The Navy yard was a source of plunder and our crowning acquisition was a Japanese long boat. Beautifully put together, it was requisitioned with the Exec's approval, as a recreational toy for the ship's complement. I felt the best thing to keep my Division out of trouble was to keep them busy in a project they would enjoy. This proved very effective.

The sloop was laying on her beam ends when we first saw her, weather-beaten, but with class written all over her sun scorched hull. I couldn't wait to talk to the Executive Officer, Cdr. Rice. I told the Commander that the crew were just going to get into trouble if some imagination wasn't used to get them working on projects of this nature. I got his instant approval.

This sailboat seemed to be crying for renovation. We hauled her out of the yard, and swung her onto blocks on the fantail. Scraping, sanding, bright work polish and varnish brought her back to her former glory. The machine shop was called into play. A casting to replace the rudder pinion that had eroded was produced in short order. A new set of sheets was fashioned in the sail locker, and we broke a bottle of beer on her bow to christen her "Fairwind".

Tethered to a boom on the starboard quarter, she rode the bay like some ethereal water sprite. Permission was granted to have a day's outing, and a lunch was prepared in the galley for her first American crew. The Seventh Division had done most of the overhaul, so I selected some twenty of the hardest workers for her first cruise.

She was Marconi rigged, with a mainsail and a jib, and the heaviest centerboard I'd ever seen. It took four men to crank the darn thing up. The sweeps were about twenty feet long. She was meant to be rowed as well as sailed. Five thwarts seated ten men at the oars and the cox'n, sat on a little platform in the stern. Never having sailed, but convinced it couldn't be too difficult to master, I went to the ship's library and read for several hours from a primer on sailing. Seemed simple enough, right? Wrong!

The next morning, with idlers manning the rail, and hoots of laughter, we hoisted sail. With a spanking breeze on our stern and joy in our hearts we slipped along the craggy coast of Honshu with me at the tiller.

One lovely scene after another unfolded- tall, wind swept cliffs, stately cypronea japonica (Japanese cypress), gnarled low lying fir trees, and waves crashing on rocks that looked like etchings from ancient wood cuts- beauty beyond description. We stayed well offshore, as I was afraid the charts might not be too reliable. With a 15 knot breeze we covered the water at a spanking spray drenched pace. The feeling of exhilaration was short lived. At noon we hove to for lunch. After a wonderful "horse-cock" and cheese sandwich it was time to come about. God, how I still shudder at the sound of those words.

We tried everything. The *Fairwind* was heeled over with men straining to lift the centerboard and then dropping it as she came into the wind. Over and over we tried, but each time the sails filled, she'd fall off, and we'd be another hundred yards or so further from the *Jersey*. At last, I gave up. Manning the sweeps, we pulled for all we were worth and slowly, oh so slowly, we retraced our course. What had been a glorious down wind stretch became a nightmare. At 2300 hours, exhausted, frustrated and with blistered hands, we secured her to the boom. There were no volunteers for sailing lessons the following morning. But after checking about, I found a Naval Academy J.O. who gave some of us a few lessons and the *Fairwind* was a popular vessel until I left a few weeks later. Who said you couldn't learn anything from the "Trade

School Boys"? I was never in demand again as skipper but then some people are so unforgiving. I have often wondered what was the *Fairwind's* final disposition.

Larry and I then began a series of visits to Tokyo. The rail line and the Emperor's Palace were the only things left untouched by the precision bombing of the city. Miles and miles of leveled debris marked most of the route. Factories and homesites were flattened. The train was loaded to one hundred and fifty percent of capacity, but it ran on schedule. Pushers used their feet to force the last passenger into the cars, holding the hand rails and shouting- train whistles screaming and soot and smoke from the engine compounding our discomfort, we'd board the Tokyo Express at every opportunity. At this point we decided to climb into the cabin of the engine, since it was never crowded. Needless to say, this caused a great amount of shouting in Japanese, but as we held our ground and the train had to leave on schedule, we rode in comfort.

One day we noticed a cave on the outskirts of Ofuna. A lone soldier, peaked cap squared on his head, stood guard. We had to find out what he was guarding. Stories of the bullion that had been found at the end of a dock in the Youkosuka Yard made the solitary watchman all the more interesting. Day after day he stood his solitary vigil, and we watched him as we took the train to Tokyo. Finally we pulled the emergency cord in the passenger car and the train screeched to a stop. As nervous officials scurried about looking for the trouble, Larry and I walked nonchalantly the few hundred yards to the cave. We tried to communicate with the guard, but I had left my phrase book on board so I said, "Oh hell!", and grabbed the little guy by the belt. Pushing him in front of us, we proceeded into the cave. At first it was dimly illuminated by sunshine, but as we proceed and the light faded, an occasional low wattage bulb filled the cave with eerie shadows. The poor little guy started to squirm. Now I'm sure in his mind here were two giants- Larry and I each tipped the Fairbanks at well over 200 pounds- in American uniforms, about to inflict some horror on him. I shouted back at Larry "I can't hold him." With a scream of terror, the little guy wriggled through my legs, knocked Larry aside and was gone. Now the lights went out. With no light, we backed out of the cave, laughing all the way. We were determined to get a battle lantern and return to solve the mystery, but we never did. Each time we passed the spot, the inscrutable guardian of the secret, stood silently watching the train, a faithful minion of the Emperor, doing his duty.

On another foray, we climbed inside the great bronze, Diabutsu, in Kamakura. This magnificent idol is one of the wonders of antiquity, the largest casting in Japan, and a marvel of an early imperial art patron. Surrounded by gardens and lovely bamboo groves- cypress accommodations for the monks who tended the shrine are tastefully woven into the tapestry of this Buddhist temple. It emanated tranquility as the saffron robed supplicants scurried out of our way.

Not too far away by rail, we wandered up a path to the Goddess of Mercy, Kwan Yen, in Ofuna. This huge cement idol stood on a hill overlooking the city- again a feeling of peace. Why did these symbols of reverence contradict the militancy of the Samurai?

The Goddess Kwan Yen, overlooked one of the most brutal prisoner of war camps in Japan and, as well, the Shochiku movie studio, where lovely fables were filmed for the populace.

One of our favorite places to visit, and at the time restricted, was the Hotel Fujia in Mianoshita, high in the mountains, with a view of Fuji (Mt. Fujiama), General Douglas MacArthur had ensconced his wife and son there, as well as a number of the high ranking officers and diplomats of the Axis. These men had escaped by submarine from Europe when Germany fell. They had intended to continue fighting with the Japanese. Mianoshita was an ideal place for their internment. There was only one narrow gauge rail line, and at the time, there was no road to this mountain retreat in the shadow of Fujiama. There was a trail that led over hill and dale to the base of Fuji, and a lovely lookout point for meditation. The weathered cypress pavilion was constructed of pegged cypress boards, and overhung a cliff face, adding to the grandeur of the site.

The little engine that took us up to the hotel grounds was an ancient firetube locomotive, with the boiler on an angle of forty five degrees, to keep it level with the steep grade of the railbed. After alighting one morning, we were watching the swimming pool when Larry remarked that it would be great to go for a dip. General Kesslering, "The Butcher of Warsaw", his wife and daughters were the only ones using the facility, when our Japanese host offered us bathing trunks.

Stuffing our bulk into Japanese bathing trunks, we went down to the pool. I dove in first and thought I'd hit solid ice. Larry asked "Is it

The harbor at Yokosuka was a source of wonder to the Japanese. The endless train of supply vessels, the cruisers and destroyers, the carriers and the hospital ships never seemed idle. Coming and going of "small boys," the sound of the ship's audio and the signals back and forth- blinkers at night, semaphore by day were a grim reminder of what to most Japanese was a time of shame.

Admiral Raymond Spruance on his regular costitutional in Japan.

heated?" I shouted back, "Hell yes!" and as he was airborne, I was halfway out of the pool, convinced that the Germans were really supermen. The water in November was some cold.

As we were leaving the pool after dressing, General Kesslering and family approached on a narrow footpath. I said to Larry, "If that Nazi bastard doesn't give way, I'm going to rearrange his face." To his good judgment, he stepped smartly aside, and would you believe, clicked his bare heels in greeting?

We had become friends with a little child of eleven or twelve who took a shine to us. She was the daughter of the Italian Ambassador and spoke German, French, Japanese, English and of course her native Italian. One day she asked me if I'd like to see her secret place, a nook in a tower that overlooked the city. She led me to a door and a winding set of wooden stairs that took us up thirty or forty feet above the tallest part of the Fugia Hotel. Here she had watched the bombing runs on Tokyo and prayed. The flash of exploding bombs and the red streams of tracers had been terrifying. But she somehow had found solace in her lonely lookout.

It was a beautiful spot, and the ubiquitous Cypranea Japonica towered above us. Ancient tile roofs stretched to the trees, giving the place a medieval appearance. Mist was rising, and there was a feeling of tranquility in the air that I find difficult to describe. A copy of a New Orleans States newspaper had been framed, with a "Robert Ripley's Believe It or Not" column stating - "the longest handlebar mustache in the world" belonged to one of the staff of the Fujia Hotel. I signed the guest log, a huge leather-bound volume on a small table, and returned to the same site and the same misty scene on my fortieth wedding anniversary in 1983. We were having tea in the guest parlor when I remembered the child's secret place.

Although I asked waiters and the manager about the tower, no one seemed to know anything about it. About to leave the hotel, I passed a small cypress door. I knew at once I had found the "place." The stairway seemed to go up to all Eternity. I felt like a participant in an Alfred Hitchcock movie as I climbed the spiral stairway. Reaching the little room at the top, I opened the window, and there it was again. What a strange sensation to look out over those tile and slate rooftops and think how this once serendipitous instant was being relived. Same trees, same mist, but oh, how the world had changed.

Another bit of deviltry Larry and I got into involved cigarettes. The Japanese were wild about American cigarettes and in fact would trade almost anything for a couple of packs. Cigarettes were just six cents a pack for overseas personnel, so Larry and I decided we'd get presents for all of our family and friends in preparation for our return to Uncle Sugar Able. The problem was, only two packs could legally be brought ashore. It was very cold in November and we were dressed in heavy weather gear to go ashore when the idea struck us. Stripping to skivies, we taped arms and legs with cartons of cigarettes and like two monsters from the Black Lagoon, waddled ashore in foul weather gear. Stopped by the ever-alert Shore Patrol, we were told to stand by for the Officer of the Day to be searched. Alone, in a cold waiting room, we wondered what the heck to do. Then the Shore Patrol Petty Officer came back and said, "Sir, if you want to dump them weeds, you can skip the O.D. search." Larry looked at me and shrugged. We went into the next room and disrobed, throwing the cartons down. Two Marines were there, smiling as they sorted Lucky Strikes in one pile, Camels and Old Golds in others. We always wondered if the Duty Officer or those damned Marines were the ones who got to trade those "weeds".

The shortages of sugar and bitter green tea never quite fit our Western palates. But every home we entered proffered the tray with great deference to the American Naval officers. Two beautiful porcelain cups for the visitor, a chipped and sometimes cracked cup to show humility for the host. On one occasion, as we sat stocking-footed and cross-legged on tatami mats, Mama San came in bowing and scraping with three cups. Larry just couldn't take another cup of unsweetened tea, so he waited until Papa San was talking to me and poured the liquid through a crack in the floor. It slowly spread in a yellow stream from under our seats and Papa San saw it. Gesturing furiously at Mama San, the old man drew the wrong conclusion scolding her for her incontinence. Larry and I left sheepishly a few moments later. There was a lighter side to our cruise and we managed to find it as only the very young can.

The baths at Odawara were another place we visited regularly. Along the Inland Sea, old inns with hot baths and wonderful sea food boiled in stoneware were available to the venturesome.

One day we found a ping-pong game in progress in the basement of an inn. As we watched, I was invited to play. I won the first game, but felt I was being conned. Laughing, I told the young Japanese to play a little better. That was my mistake. He beat my brains out to the subdued laughter of his chums.

11-16- Captain E.T.Wooldridge mustered all hands on the fantail for a change of command. He was relieved by Captain E. M. Thompson, U.S.N. and as we stood beneath the shadow of the *Jersey's* sixteen inch guns, silent now and with brass tompions gleaming, I thought back to the commissioning ceremonies in Philadelphia. The original ship's complement had been almost completely rotated to other commands. Young junior officers and another crew of seaman, for the most part in their teens, stood at attention. The new captain would have a chance to leave his mark on a another generation of sailors. Captain Wooldridge had been coolly received, but had won over the crew with firm but consistent discipline. The new skipper would have to go through the same rite of passage. How he would fare would have to be proved. This is how the Navy has functioned so effectively throughout the years.

Weeks passed in a round of day long trips to see as much of Japan as we could. One of the J.O.'s who accompanied us regularly, fell in love with a young woman at a hotel in Odawara. Fraternization was frowned upon, and the course of true love had to be postponed. I understand permission was finally granted after I had departed for the States, but it was a strange feeling to see the star crossed lovers, pining for one another, but held in check by a code of ethics much more rigid than the one that exists today.

The desire to leave the ship and get home was quickly complicated by the number of men seeking a very restricted amount of transport. Five of the plank owners (Charles B. Hoppa, M. A. Larkin, F.M. Milby, Dr. John Moritz and myself) decided we could best accomplish this if we set up a watch in the Radio Shack, and used the advance information gathered to expedite our departure.

The Captain was leaving for an inspection tour of Japanese bases for about a week, and we thought it best to get his permission to leave- if we could find a billet anywhere. This was obtained easily- the Skipper thought it impossible, and the watch was set. Within a few days I was awakened by Milby with a copy of a dispatch saying there were five billets available on the hospital ship *Benevolence*. I jumped up and raced to the crews compartment. Lining up a crew, I requested permission from the Officer of the Deck to test the Admiral's barge. Within moments I was speeding through the night to the huge barracks that housed the Army Captain of the Port. I awakened him and presented him with a request for the billets signed by our old friend (now promoted to Commodore by Larry and myself) Carl F. Sherwood. Later, I gratefully hosted a cocktail party in honor of his promotion, at the Officer's Club in Yokosuka. The Commodore couldn't make it of course, sending his regrets, as a staff meeting interfered. The Captain of the port scratched his head, rubbed the sleep out of his eyes and signed the billets over to us.

Back at the ship, we requested permission from the executive officer to leave. He was a bit reticent to loose any of his rapidly dwindling staff, but we reminded him of the skipper's approval, and were packed and ready on the Quarter deck in a few hours. The barge was waiting, and with hastily said goodbyes, we piled aboard.

How can I describe the lump in my throat as we watched the *New Jersey* recede in our wake? She had been our home for almost three years and those years had been a part of the greatest adventure of the twentieth century. The throb of our motor kept pace with our heart's beat and there wasn't a dry eye as we swung alongside the forward accomodation ladder of the *Benevolence*, homeward bound!

Requesting permission to come aboard, and presenting our recently cut orders, we were standing on the quarterdeck waiting for berth assignments when a group of very irate Senior Officers scrambled out of a launch. Mad as hornets, they demanded that they be assigned those five billets. That was a mistake. Captain Patterson, an old Mustang, wasn't about to be pushed around by a bunch of officers half his age on his Quarterdeck. He advised them that he was preparing to sail, and that if they weren't off the Quarterdeck in the next few minutes, he'd see that they were confined to the brig and re-

Plank owners waiting to board the Benevolence.

turned to Japan for a Courts Martial. They left and the Captain stalked off to prepare to get underway.

How can I forget that trip? The Captain decided to sail the Northern Great Circle route which was the shortest but the roughest ride he could have selected. Heavy weather dogged our every track- seas like gray mountains. Round bottomed, that old bucket rolled and tossed as we forged into the swells under a very slow bell. On some days we were lucky to advance a couple of dozen nautical miles.

Cdr. Moritz, former Senior Medical Officer of the *New Jersey*, thought the time would pass quicker if we'd organize a round robin bridge game. By the time the ante was completed, there were several thousand dollars in a winner-take-all kitty. My partner was David Berliner, a really fine bridge player, and our luck was running strong, with Dave playing most of the hands. It became obvious that we were in a position to win. But fate and my ego got in the way. We bid a slam on the last hand and the Dr.'s Wilson and Moritz doubled. The only way we could have lost was for me to redouble, which I foolishly did. Berliner groaned and I went down two tricks and lost the pot. Berliner is living in Florida and although I've tried to speak to him several times, he hasn't responded to me to this day. Some people are so unforgiving.

About midway to San Francisco the Captain addressed all hands. If anyone was caught in possession of mortar rounds, automatic weapons or unexploded ammunition, he would be sure to see that they were returned to Japan for Courts Martial. GI's had been picking up trophies of battle since long before Hannibal- but some of our "toys" could prove quite lethal, long after the war had ended. That evening, at dusk, I went topside with a Nambu machine gun and several boxes of ammunition and joined half the returnees, as we sadly dumped our trophies over the side. So much for souvenirs.

The heavy weather and overcast skies of the North Pacific gave way slowly to the long rollers and thick ground fog that announced we were nearing San Francisco. Breakfast was bolted down and we manned the rail in a thick ground fog, eyes straining for a first glimpse of shore. The Golden Gate rose slowly out of the mist, and the whistles of small craft welcomed us home. Our commissioning pennant streaming gaily in the wind, we passed under the span and knew we were home at last. A glorious feeling to pass under that landmark and watch the sun rising in all its glory over the hills, burning away the fog and many of the sad memories of classmates less fortunate- men who would never again return.

San Francisco was swarming with recently released troops, and getting out became another game of chance that could take weeks. I was billeted at the Naval Base and had about a one hour ride to downtown 'Frisco to check the progress of my transportation request. Now the gal that manned the desk looked like the answer

Our first sign of home

to me. Every morning I arrived with a bouquet of fresh roses from the flower market and some good old fashioned Southern charm. I got an airline ticket home in four days.

Reflections on those halcyon days reawaken feelings that have been sublimated these fifty years. Heavy weather, dense ocean fogs, typhoons and quiet days of sailing the deep blue Pacific Ocean- days wandering tropic isles in anchorages far from home- they were times in which the good days are subject to total recall- frustration, fear, and loneliness - all are forgotten.

At the 45th reunion of the *New Jersey* in 1988, shortly after she had been recommissioned in the Long Beach Naval Shipyard, a group of shipmates met to renew friendships from those wartime years. A rather old looking sailor came up to me and said, "Sir, you were Ensign Frank?" I smiled and acknowledged that I was. "I was your Messenger of the Watch in Philly." he said. I hated to look in the mirror when I got over the shock.

The high point of the reunion occurred for me when a photographer called for all plank owners (those who had put the ship in commission for the first time) to line up for a group photograph. As hand shakes were being exchanged, with warm greetings to shipmates we hadn't seen for many years, the photographer got on a chair to get the group at a better angle. There were just too many for the lens he was using. "Would some of you please kneel in front." he requested. Captain Jack McCormick was standing next to me and said, "Charlie, these old knees are not up to kneeling any more." So we stood. After taking several shots, the photographer thanked us and stepped down. At that moment he missed the greatest photo of the reunion. Half the kneeling sailors had to be helped to their feet by those who were standing. And so with that, I'll say, "Thanks fellers, for some wonderful memories. It made men of many of us, and we should be grateful to have served."

The Navy fits a white hat for life. I've watched my alma mater, the Tulane University N.R.O.T.C., for many years. Each new class emerges prepared for life by the dedicated cadre of regulars who help "feather merchants" become men and women with their white hats squared away. Let's pray that we'll continue to train the new legions dedicated to the service of our great nation.

Her guns are silent now. Never again will seamen hear the thunderous roar of 16 inch rifles hurling over a ton of high explosives and steel at an enemy over the horizon. Her WWII sailors are graybeards now- grandfathers whose memories of service aboard this grand battleship are the high point of their lives. We were proud of her and proud of our service. We were the lucky ones- the other guy got hit and took the casualties. Planes dropped in flames and ships wheeled in clouds of black smoke, exploding magazines and AV gas - pyrotechnics. How many times I've dreamed of young friends who left Tulane University to die on distant oceans. The litany is a rather long one- headed by Lt. Jack Wintle, U.S.N. - the first casualty of our N.R.O.T.C. instructors. Many more were never to return. The pride in service we all felt was a unique byproduct of a nation united. Perhaps new generations of service personnel will find this testament to our wartime cruise worth remembering.

I will never forget the closing remarks of Captain Warren Hudson, USN commanding officer of the Tulane NROTC at the 50th anniversary banquet in 1993. Watching the bright and shining faces of a new corps of cadets, and the deeply etched faces of shipmates of yesteryear, he reminded us of the Battle of Agincourt 1415, when England and France were locked in mortal combat. Seriously outnumbered, the British, under King Henry V were exhorted: "If we are mark'd to die, we are enough to do our country proud, if to live, the fewer men- the greater share of honor. God's will- I wish not one man more.

"We few, we happy few, we band of brothers. He today that sheds his blood with me shall be my brother: Gentlemen a-bed shall think themselves a'cursed they were not here, and hold their manhood cheap, while any speak that fought with us on this St. Crispin's day."

This is the bond of brotherhood that joins each "JERSEYMAN," "ye happy band of brothers", even to this day!

Captain Charles W. Frank, United States Naval Reserve retired in 1966. His last assignment was Chief Staff Officer for the Surface Group Command of the Eighth Naval District. Surface Division 8-29, which he commanded in 1953, was selected as the best Surface Division in the Naval Reserve. It was awarded the James Forestal Memorial Trophy. Captain Frank has written numerous books and articles on the history of Louisiana duck decoys and on various outdoor related topics.

Entire crew of USS New Jersey *on February 1, 1952 upon return from Korea (submitted by Dana D. Tucker)*

Bibliography

1- *Typhoon, The Other Enemy*, Naval Institute Press, Capt.C.R. Calhoun, U.S.N. (.Ret)
2- Battleship *New Jersey,* Naval Institute Press, Paul Stillwell
3- *Battleships and Battlecruisers*, Chartwell Books, Richard Humble
Salvo Published by the New Jersey 1950-1951
4- The log of the U.S.S. *New Jersey*, Naval Archives of the Smithsonian Museum 1943-1960
5- Personal diary of daily events 1943-1946, Capt. Charles W. Frank, U.S.N.R. (Ret.)
6- War Log U.S.S. *New Jersey* Published by the *New Jersey* 1943-1945
7- Navy Department- Naval History Division (OP 09B9) Ships History Section
8- Naval Historical Center, Washington Navy Yard - Operational Archives
9- *A History of Naval Operations in World War II-* Professor Samuel Elliot Morison
10- *Dictionary of American Naval Fighting Ships*, Office of the Chief of Naval Operations
11- *The Big J- Matriach of the Seas*, Mickey Cooper
12- Coorespondence with Captain Robert C. Penniston, U.S.N.- C.O. USS *New Jersey* August 1969 thru December 1969
13- *A History of Ships Named* New Jersey, Naval History Division of the Office of the Chief of Naval Operations
14- Coorespondence with Captain Edward M. Thompson, U.S.N. C.O. USS *New Jersey* Novovember 1945-August 1946
15- *The Battle of Leyte Gulf-* Edwin P. Hoyt 1972

Glossary

Baka bombs- A torpedo like bomb, with short stubby wings and a small cockpit- housing a Japanese pilot on a one way trip to hell. When dropped from the mother aircraft they could attain a speed of over 600 knots, a speed our primitive fire control computers couldn't handle.
Battery, or back to battery- A term meaning to return a gun after recoil to its original position. i.e.- In a ready to load mode. Slang adaptation- to return to normal in any activity.
Birdmen- Aviators
BB- A battleship.
Betty- A class of Japanese bomber. Japanese planes were identified by Anglicized names to expedite recognition by our lookouts. Zero for a class of fighter aircraft, Jill, Jake, Emily, Dinah, Irving, Tony, and Mike for different bombers, lamp lighters and torpedo planes.
boondocks- A remote area.
bosun's pipe- A nickel silver whistle used by the bosun-mate of the watch- used to call for various ship's activities and to render honors to visiting dignitaries.
CA- A heavy cruiser.
CL- A light cruiser.
CAP- Combat Air Patrol. Planes assigned to deflect and defend against enemy air incursion. Could be a single night fighter or a squadron intercepting a major raid.
CV- A carrier
Condition I- Main battery of 16 inch rifles manned and ready for a surface engagement.
Condition II- Secondary battery of 5 inch thirty eights and heavy machine guns (40mm and 20mm), manned and ready for air defense.
Condition III- A stand by condition of readiness in which one third of the ships complement manned stations necessary for wartime cruising and air defense.
CONLUS- Continental United States.
Chains, the - A pulpit from which the hand lead could be thrown to take soundings when entering a poorly defined port. In the early part of WW II many harbors were only mapped by hydrographers of rather ancient vintage. It was not unusual for a prudent Captain to post a leadsman in the chains to take soundings besides keeping a close watch on the fathometer.
D Day- Designated date of first scheduled landing. Each island could have several dates for phases of logistical support. i.e. - D+1, D+2 etc.
DD- A destroyer.
Dilbert- A comic strip aviator with two left feet. He was portrayed on many a poster to remind our fledgling airmen of the danger in forgetting any of the myriad details of safe flight.
DEVG- Deck or Engineering Volunteer General, the classification used to designate reserve officers qualified for deck or engineering duties.
dogs- Short handles on hatch covers that allowed rapid securing of watertight integrity.
dog wrenches- Pieces of pipe that were placed near hatches to give additional leverage in securing dogs.
DVG- Deck Volunteer General, a reserve officer qualified for deck duties.
ETA- Estimated time of arrival.
EVG- Engineering Volunteer General, a reserve officer qualified for engineering duty.
fantail - the after main deck.
fathometer- An electronic device for measuring depth. Replaced the hand lead by echo sounding, but in the early days of WW II Captains still liked the extra precaution of stationing a man in the chains.
feather merchants- A humorous nick name given to young reservists by lifers.
field day- The day set aside to general clean a ship's living quarters- usually each Friday, followed by Captain's inspection on Saturday.

Frigate- A destroyer sized man-o-war, but lighter armed and with a single screw and much less shaft horse power than a destroyer. Much less costly to put in service for coastal patrol missions, where they did yeoman service.

Gadgets- surface pips or contacts on radar.

gedunk- Ice cream.

Golden Dragons- seamen who had crossed the Equator.

Gyreens- Marines.

Happy hour- A time set aside for entertainment of the ship's crew. Could be a boxing match, a movie, or an open bar in the Officer's Club.

hand lead- A tear shaped, cast lead weight attached to a light line. It could be thrown ahead for soundings in shoal water.

Harpoon- A post-war addition to the re-commissioned *New Jersey* that could be MIRV'ed (Multiple Intercontinental Reentry Vehicle) for 10 nuclear war heads.

IFF- Identification, Friend or Foe. An electronic tag that caused a pip on the radar screen to pulsate, designating a friendly air craft.

JOOD- Junior Officer of the Deck.

Lamplighter- A Japanese plane that dropped magnesium flares to silhouette the fleet at night- increasing vulnerability to torpedo attack.

LCVP- Landing Craft Vehicle or Personnel - a landing craft designed to offload a company of troops or of a tank and support vehicles.

Lifers-Regular Navy enlisted personnel and Officers.

LTA- Lighter Than Air. Blimps, with a non rigid, helium filled bag- they were very silent and effective submarine hunters in coastal waters.

marlinspike seamanship- The ability to handle the various chores of an ordinary seaman. Originally the use of a fid or marlinspike used in splicing lines.

MIRV- Multiple Intercontinental Reentry Vehicle. A means of targeting as many as ten sites with the same intercontinental ballistic missle.

Officers Country- Spaces assigned for exclusive use of commissioned officers and their guests.

OD - Officer of the Deck. The Captain's representative- the primary watch stander for a four hour period.

OS2U- The original Kingfisher aircraft on the *Jersey* was the Vought-Sikorsky OS2U. This plane was ultimately replaced with a Curtis Sea Hawk, a more advanced float plane. Two of these planes were carried on the fantail catapults of the *New Jersey*.

Peter Pilots- A nick name for the operators of radio controlled drones. The reference was phallic, referring to a small control rod used to maneuver the drone.

Pips- The little flashing light on the cathode ray tube that marked a radar contact. Also called blips.

plank owners- A ships original commissioning crew, said to each own a plank of the ship's hull.

Pollywogs- Uninitiated seaman who had not crossed the Equator.

precessed gyro- The effect caused to a spinning gyroscope to resist change in direction. This precessed angle was used to give a proper lead to gunners who were trained to track smoothly in front of an attacking aircraft- the rate of swing increased the precessing pressure and this moment could be translated into a proper lead angle.

pogybait- Candy.

Phalanx- A post WWII 20mm machine gun, multiple barrels capable of spewing out some 3,600 rounds per minute. This weapon was hooked to a computer that allowed it to engage as many as twelve incoming missiles at the same time.

piped aboard- Honors rendered by having the Bos'n of the Watch sound a call on his pipe. Used to render honor to visiting dignitaries both military and civilian.

scuttle butt- Rumors. shakedown- The initial cruise of a Naval man-o-war, designed to test the vessel before sending it to join the fleet.

small boys- Slang reference to destroyers or to yard craft.

spider web sight- The manual sight on weapons, comprised of a series of concentric circles. Used when power failure caused the more accurate electronic gun sights to be inoperative.

special sea detail- Men assigned to duties needed to get a ship underway. Normally used in reference to topside personnel, line handlers, telephone talkers, anchor detail, signalmen, and officers on the Bridge.

stadimeter- A device found on the bridge that was used in station keeping. If the height of a ships mast was known, it allowed the range in yards to be accurately read from a vernier scale.

striker- One who is in training for a higher rating.

spit-kit- A sand filled tube for disposal of cigarette butts.

Shellbacks- Sailors who have crossed the Equator.

swabbies- Slang for sailors.

Tally ho- The cry that pilots used to report an air contact.

TBS- talk between ships- a low frequency means of inter-formation radio.

topped off- Filled to capacity. Used as in "Topping off the fuel oil bunkers."

trade school- The United States Naval Academy.

two blocked- Hoisted to the peak of the mast or to the yardarm. i.e.-"Baker is two blocked." Meaning the signal flag Baker was at the peak of the halyard on the yard arm, and that refueling was underway.

Tomahawk- A surface to air missile- put aboard the *New Jersey* in a 1980s rearmament.

Uncle Sugar Able- U.S.A. in the international signal code of the WW II era.

Wardroon- The space assigned for commissioned officers dining and recreation.

Warrant Officers Country- Berthing spaces and a separate Wardroom for the exclusive use of commissioned warrant officers and their guests.

yardbirds- A derogatory epitaph for idlers and rear echelon personnel, also yard workmen who were usually not up to the Navy's standards of cleanliness and discipline

Photos on this page are courtesy of Stuart Chalkley.

Photos on this page are courtesy of Stuart Chalkley.

Photos on this page are courtesy of Stuart Chalkley.

USS *New Jersey* Veterans

Harry Wolochuk and his best friends, USS New Jersey, *December 1945 at Yokasuka, Japan. (Submitted by Harry Wolochuk)*

USS New Jersey *Ships' Barber Shop. (L to R): Standing, C. Ritchie, R. Hans, Bamboulus, J. R. Caldwell. Kneeling: A. Crabtree, Santiago*

WILLIAM E. ALBRIGHT, was born in Altoona, PA. Entered the U.S. Navy Sept. 9, 1941, MM1/c.

Stations: NTS Newport, RI; NTS Great Lakes, IL; Pier 92 New York City Sept. 9, 1941 to May 28, 1942; USS *Titania* May 28, 1942 to March 25, 1945; Newport News, VA March 25, 1945 to Sept. 9, 1945; USS *Midway* Sept. 9, 1945 to Nov. 7, 1945. Released to inactive duty Dec. 3, 1945; USS *New Jersey* October 1950 to July 1952.

Participated in North Africa Campaign; Asiatic-Pacific; Philippine Liberation, Korean War.

Released from inactive service July 1954 as MM1/c.

Married Betty Albright and has sons Leonard and Robert. He also has three grandchildren.

Retired from Philadelphia Electric Company.

MICHAEL R. ALES, born in Passaic, NJ, Sept. 20, 1958. Entered U.S. Naval Academy July 6, 1976. Commissioned as an ensign May 28, 1980.

Served in the U.S. Navy as surface warfare officer, missile control officer, on USS *Callaghan* (DDG-994) 1981-1984. Boiler Div. officer September 1984-May 1985; Boilers officer May 1985-June 1986 USS *New Jersey* (BB-62); Service School Command, Great Lakes, August 1986-January 1991.

Memorable experience: USS *Callaghan* escorted USS *New Jersey* on her 1983 deployment. Later *Callaghan* was the flagship for the salvage operation of the Korean airliner the Russians shot down. USS *New Jersey* participated in preps for and the first part of the 1986 deployment.

Awarded the Navy Achievement Medal, Humanitarian Service Medal, National Defense Service Medal, three Battle (E), Meritorious Unit Commendation, Sea Service Deployment Ribbon. Discharged Jan. 31, 1991 as lieutenant.

Married to Pamela Beth Ales and they have two sons, Thomas Michael, six years and Joseph Gordon, five years.

Ales is now senior engineer, Ingalls Shipbuilding, Pascagoula, MS. Now lives in Ocean Springs, MS.

WILLIAM L. ALLEN, was born in Vincennes, IN, Jan. 14, 1926. Entered the Navy Jan. 25, 1943 as F1c, M Div.

Stationed at Great Lakes Training Center, USS *New Jersey* May 1943-February 1946.

Awarded Philippine Liberation with two Bronze Stars, American Area, Asiatic Pacific with nine Bronze Stars, Good Conduct and the Victory Medal.

Discharged as F1c Feb. 18, 1946.

Married to Betty Allen and has five children and 13 grandchildren.

Retired after working as lineman for 32 years.

WAYNE A. AMEND, USS *New Jersey* (BB-62), IC2, born Aug. 7, 1933, Kenosha, WI and lived most of his life in Fond du Lac, WI.

Enlisted USN on Sept. 7, 1951 right out of high school. Boot camp and IC "A" School at Great Lakes. Assigned to USS *New Jersey* in May of 1952. Served under for COs during his 39 months on *New Jersey*. Released from active duty on Aug. 18, 1955. Discharged in September 1959. When *New Jersey* was re-commissioned for service in Vietnam, he attempted to re-enlist. Was advised by the recruiter to enter USNR to regain his rate. Remained in USNR from 1968 to 1977. His most significant duty was from 1973-1977 with Coastal River Div. 21.

In December 1977 he transferred to USAR serving for ten years as a tank commander in the 84th Div.

He retired in 1987 with 26 years of service. In 1989 he relocated to Florida. He has been married to his wife, Kathleen, for 34 years. They have two children and four grandchildren.

JOHN ANAYA, S1c, born on Oct. 20, 1926 in Madrid, NM. Joined the Navy on Jan. 16, 1945, and went to boot camp in San Diego, CA. From there he went to Camp Shoemaker in San Francisco, CA in a troop train. Three days later he went on another troop train to Seattle, WA and then on to Bremerton, WA, where he went on board the USS *New Jersey* (BB-62). On Sept. 16, 1945 they left Bremerton, WA to Yokosuka Naval Base in Japan. They were relieving the USS *Missouri* where the surrender of the Japanese occurred. After completing a six month stay in the Tokyo Bay they returned to Bremerton, WA where he was discharged on July 20, 1946.

He went to work at Los Alamos National Laboratory for two years, and then to St. Michaels College in Santa Fe, NM for two years. He was employed by Sandia National Laboratories, retiring with over 40 years of service. He has also served in numerous boards and commissions (e.g., New Mexico Border Commission, New Mexico Investment Commission, etc.) in the last 30 years. His last appointment was made by President Clinton on Feb. 1, 1994 as chairman of the Agriculture Stabilization and Conservation Service State Committee (U.S. Department of Agriculture).

RICHARD E. ANDERSON, was born July 30, 1930 in Rockford, IL. Entered the service Dec. 11, 1950, NTC Great Lakes. Served on USS *New Jersey* (BB-62) from June 1951 to October 1954; Task Force 77 Japan and Korea, 1951 and 1953 cruises to Europe in 1952 and 1954, for midshipmen training.

Awarded the Korean Presidential Unit Citation during the Korean Conflict.

Discharged Oct. 6, 1954 in Chicago, IL as machinery repairman first class.

Married to Millie and they have four sons and one grandchild.

Now retired after 25 years working for VA Medical Center in Minneapolis, MN. Now live in Sun City West, AZ.

JACK W. BAIRD, was born Aug. 21, 1923 in Columbus, OH. Entered the USN Jan. 25, 1943 as chief M Div. Served on USS *New Jersey* May 23, 1943-Feb. 23, 1946.

His memorable experience includes shakedown cruise of USS *New Jersey* and Panama Canal from Kwajalein to Yokosuka Naval Base Japan Sept. 16, 1945.

Discharged Feb. 23, 1946 as chief.

Married to Katherine and they have two daughters, Pam and Cindy and six grandchildren.

Baird is a real estate broker, appraiser and electronic tech.

MICHAEL J. BAKOS, RDSN (Radar), born May 31, 1929, Toledo, OH. Enlisted in organized Naval Reserve, Zanesville, OH, March 26, 1947. Active duty training aboard USS *Haynesworth* (DD-700) January 1949 and USS *Franklin D. Roosevelt* (CVB-42) January 1950. Called to active duty aboard USS *New Jersey* BB-62 Nov. 8, 1950, was aboard for recommissioning at Bayonne, NJ. After shakedown cruise, off to Korea. Stationed on Big J until released from active duty Sept. 25, 1952.

Memorable experiences: *Jersey* crew members receiving a pilot that was shot down and parachuted out of his plane. They were certain he would die when they saw him brought aboard. He was as blue as blue can get from being in the frigid water until picked up. They could hardly believe it when they saw him walking around the ship just a few days later.

Getting hit with shellfire in Wonsan Harbor after firing all night. Daylight brought the return fire.

Standing in the starboard chow line app. 40 miles off Korea operating with the task force when the destroyer on their starboard side hit a mine. Then afterward transferring the bodies to the *Jersey* by highline.

Eating chow in the mess hall with stacks off wooden coffins in the same location sure made a person think.

Stayed in organized reserve until discharged May 31, 1958. Enlisted in Ohio Military Reserve obtaining the rank of a commissioned first lieutenant and commanding officer of the local unit. Still in Ohio Military Reserve.

Worked for Ohio State Patrol as field inspector for six years. Obtained postal service job and retired after 30+ years.

Lives in Cambridge, OH, with wife Bonnie. They have two children, James and Cheryl. They have four grandsons, Chris and Matt Bakos, Isaac and Ethan Forman.

KENNETH BARRIGER, was born Feb. 28, 1925 in Columbus, IN. Entered USN January 1943.

Stationed Great Lakes, went aboard June 1943. Shakedown, participated in all campaigns in the Pacific.

Awarded 11 Battle Stars.

Discharged February 1946 as seaman first, 6th Div. Retired February 1983.

Married to Eva and has five children and six grandchildren

Retired after 40 years at Golden Castings.

RUDOLPH R. BASHA, was born in New York, NY, Sept. 15, 1934. Entered the USN June 30, 1952.

Attended boot camp at Great Lakes, IL; USS *New Jersey*, H Div., November 1952-August 1953; USNH, San Diego; USNH, St. Albans, NY; USNH Portsmouth, VA; U.S. Naval Station, Scotia, NY; USNH, St. Albans, NY; USNS, Lindenwald, Brooklyn, NY; USNH St. Albans.

Memorable experiences: appendix removed on *New Jersey* during battle, 1953. Had to stop 16" guns during surgery.

Awarded United Nations, Korea Service, Presidential Citation, National Defense, China Service and Good Conduct.

Discharged March 18, 1959 as HM2.

He has three children and four grandchildren.

Retired as police sergeant.

LOUIS J. BAUMBACH, USS *New Jersey*, RM2/c, born May 6, 1922 in Newark, NJ. Joined the Navy December 1942. Boot camp in the Great Lakes Naval Training Center. Attended University of Chicago Radio School.

Served in the 5th and 7th Fleet Command TransDiv 26 and 41.

Involved in seven major battles. Hit by a kamikaze on the USS *Callaway*.

Awarded Navy Unit Citation for action against the enemy, air, shore batteries, surface craft and submarine.

Discharged in October 1945, recalled to active duty in September 1950 for duty aboard the USS *New Jersey* until October 1951.

Retired from the American Telephone and Telegraph Company after 37 years as a sales manager.

Married Helen and Lou, have four sons and two daughters and 13 grandchildren and one great-grandchild.

RICHARD WAYNE BEGANDY, USS *New Jersey* (BB-62), LI3/c, born Sept. 20, 1935, Port Vue, PA. Entered Navy July 6, 1954. Discharged June 5, 1958. Boot camp: Bainbridge, MD. First ship: USS *Juneau* (CLAA-119), Deck Force. Second ship: USS *New Jersey* (BB-62). Assigned to EX. Division where he worked in the print shop.

Most memorable experience: When taking on supplies at sea, he joined with some buddies in filching a case of pears. He was caught and taken to the chief master-at-arms. During the interrogation, he refused to name the others involved. The chief admired his loyalty to his shipmates, so instead of a captain's mast, Begandy had to carry the case of pears with him for a week every where he went, to muster, meals, the head and his work station.

When he and his wife attended the New Jersey reunion in Atlantic City in 1984, they were seated at the table with that same chief master-at-arms.

He and his wife live in Massapequa Park, Long Island, NY. She never tires of hearing about his Navy days. At least she says she doesn't. They have five daughters and two grandchildren.

He is currently working in warehousing and transportation.

BOB BELCHER, MRFN, USS *New Jersey* (BB-62), born July 23, 1932 in Tacoma, WA. Joined the Navy December 1950. After boot camp and MR School at San Diego. Was assigned to the USS *New Jersey*, already at station in Korea.

After Korea there was the midshipman cruise to France with a side tour of Paris, then Portugal and Haiti, and of course Gitmo Cuba.

After returning from active duty he transferred to the Navy Seabee Reserve where he advanced to CECS (E-8).

Now retired and still living in Puyallup, WA. (30 miles from the present moorage of the *New Jersey*). He and his wife of 43 years have four children and five grandchildren.

ADRIEN PHILIP BELCOURT, was born in Mohall Feb. 15, 1926. Entered the Navy at Bottineau, ND Feb. 9, 1944. Attended boot camp Farragut, ID, 5th Div.

Served on USS *New Jersey* (BB-62) April 1944, South Pacific.

Memorable experiences include being hit by the worst typhoon to date Dec. 18, 1944 and the seven battles in the Pacific.

Awarded the American-Asiatic-Philippines, and seven battles stars.

Discharged Feb. 21, 1946 as S2/c.

Married Dolores Nov. 28, 1947. Bought farm at Maxbass and still resides there.

He has five children: Ronald, Thomas, Carlyn, Cindy and Mike and 12 grandchildren.

Retired farmer and oil field worker.

HAROLD BURNETT BESS, was born in Pierpont, OH. Entered the USNR May 28, 1943, serving with S Div.

Stationed in Great Lakes, USS *New Jersey*, Gro Pac 13.

Awarded the Navy Occupation Service Asia Clasp, Armed Force Reserve and Philippine Liberation Medal with two stars, NR Merit Ribbon, two stars, American Campaign, Asiatic Pacific with eight stars, WWII Victory Medal.

Discharged as EM1 Feb. 6, 1962.

Married to Lela and has 5 girls, 11 grandchildren and 5 great-grandchildren.

Retired from General Motor Corporation.

WILLIAM H. BETTERMAN, USS *New Jersey* (BB-62), CWT, born Aug. 23, 1919, Staten Island, NY. Joined the Navy July 13, 1938, right after high school. Went through boot camp at Newport, RI Naval Training Station. Normally boot camp was 12 weeks, but because a hurricane came up the coast, things got messed up, he stayed an extra week.

Was then assigned to the USS *Texas* (BB-35) on Nov. 10, 1938. Participated in the Neutrality patrol, also convoy duty, in the North Atlantic. Once during convoy duty, passing by Iceland, icebergs about, sun shining, he could see a blinding snow storm over Iceland.

After supporting troop landings during the African Invasion at the Port Lyautey campaign was transferred to and took part in the commissioning of the USS *New Jersey* on May 23, 1943. Left Philadelphia July 8, 1943 to fight the "Battle of Delaware Bay", endless GQs and drills, with endless in and outs of Norfolk, VA.

Down to Trinidad, shakedown then up to Maine for two months gunnery practice. Visit to Portland, ME Oct. 23, 1943, Boston, MA for four day liberty for some. Norfolk, VA Jan. 1, 1944. January 6, 1944 *New Jersey* headed through the Panama Canal.

Starting Jan. 29, 1944 the *New Jersey* participated in nearly all major campaigns in the Pacific. Winning American Area, Asiatic-Pacific with one Silver Star and four Bronze Stars and two Bronze Stars on Philippine Liberation Battle Ribbons.

On Dec. 18, 1944 the *New Jersey* was hit by the worst typhoon to date while operating off Luzon, three destroyers lost, the operation suspended, the heaviest weather the ship had seen, or was to see, water below decks, and considerable damaged to guns topside.

On Aug. 30, 1945 in Okinawa, left the USS *New Jersey*, transferred to USS *Admiral HT Mayo* (AP-125) for transport to San Francisco, Treasure Island. Then loaded aboard the "Sante Fe" Railroad, cross country to Lido Beach, Long Island, NY, discharged Oct. 3, 1945.

Went to work for C. Edison Nov. 5, 1945 as an oiler in a powerhouse. Thirty-nine years later retired on Sept. 1, 1984 as a general watch supervisor.

He is now living in Staten Island, NY with his wife, they have nine children, eight grandchildren and one great-grandchild.

ROBERT G. BIEBER, USS *New Jersey* (BB-62), RM3/c, born June 19, 1926, at Jersey City, NY.

Enlisted in the Navy at the age of 17, on March 28, 1944. Completed boot camp at Sampson, NY. Assigned to Radio School at Bedford Springs, PA. After graduation, went to Little Creek, VA for amphibious training. Served overseas aboard LCT, LST and LCI. Duty included South Pacific, Philippines and Japanese Occupation.

Discharged in 1946. Married in 1947. A son born in 1949 and daughter in 1950. Recalled to active duty September 1950. Assigned to the USS *New Jersey* at Bayonne, NJ for recommissioning which took place in November 1950.

Served aboard until 1951 and then discharged. Employed by NL Industries for 33 years. Now retired and traveling leisurely.

EARL BIGELOW, was born in Hazelton, IA, April 30, 1941. Entered the USN Jan. 6, 1960. Served as machinist mate first class in M Div.

Stationed on USS *Point DeFiance* LSD-31; USS *Navarro* APA-215, U.S. Naval Station, Subic Bay, Philippines, USS *New Jersey* BB-62, commissioning to 1970; DaNang; Vietnam; Philippines; Panama Canal; Jamaica.

Discharged in 1970. Achieved the rank of machinist mate first class.

Married to Janey and they have one son, Scotty and three daughters, Debby, Tammy, and Pamela. They also have three granddaughters.

Bigelow is an operating engineer, Los Angeles, CA.

JOHN D. BISHOP, was born in Orland, CA March 3, 1919. Entered the service Jan. 10, 1941. Served in the Navy, L Div., as BM1/c.

Attended boot camp, San Diego, CA Jan. 10, 1941-March 10, 1941; USS *Augusta* Atlantic Fleet Jan. 4, 1941-May 6, 1943.

Transferred to USS *New Jersey* early May 1943. Transferred to San Diego, CA July 1945.

His memorable experiences: USS *Augusta*/ HMS *Prince of Wales*. Meeting Churchill, President Roosevelt met on North Atlantic Treaty in Newfoundland.

Participated in the Europe Theater, North Africa, Pacific, Atlantic, Philippines, Marianas, Guam, Iwo Jima, and Okinawa.

Discharged Jan. 16, 1947 as BM1/c. Worked for Boeing in Seattle, WA for 35 years.

Married to Patricia Barton and they have three children and five grandchildren.

He has been retired for 11 years. Volunteers 35 hours a week with Seniors. Drives 15 passenger van and keeps his own home going.

FREDERICK E. BITTING, Cmdr, USN, Chief Engr., USS *New Jersey* (BB-62), 1954-1957, born Jan. 30, 1910 in Philadelphia, PA.

Graduated from high school June 1929. Enlisted Aug. 15, 1929. Boot camp and Machinist's Mate School, Norfolk. Gunboat *Asheville* 1930. Special Service Squadron in Panama and Asiatic Fleet 1932. Monocacy in Yangtze Patrol 1933. *Barney* DD-149, San Diego 1934. Commissioned gunboat *Erie,* New York, 1936 and to Panama. Made warrant machinist February 1941 and to battleship *Arkansas.*

Married in Boston October 1941. Promoted to ensign, temporary, June 1942.

To Brisbane, Australia 1943 as repair officer, escort and minecraft squadrons. Full lieutenant 1944. Commissioned minesweeper *Redstart* in Savannah 1945, as engineer officer. War ended and sent to Japan for sweeping and wound up as skipper. March 1946 returned in minelayer *Adams* as engineer officer. San Diego Naval Base. Received permanent commission. University of Utah 1947, graduated in 1949. Lieutenant commander and to the *Charles S. Sperry* DD-697, as XO. In 1950 to Korea, to Key West, FL for shore duty in 1951. To the *New Jersey* as engineer officer and to commander 1954. *Betelgeuse* AK-260, as CO 1957. Pentagon 1959 and retired 1962. Howard University, Washington, DC, 1963, as plant engineer.

Retired in 1978. Moved to Fair Haven, VT permanently. He has four children, a son and three daughters scattered around the country, three grandchildren, a boy and two girls.

FRANK C. BLAIR JR., (DC), USN, born Aug. 1, 1918, Long Beach, CA. Graduate School of Dentistry, USC. Indoctrination Naval Dental School, Bethesda, MD, December 1942 to April 1943. Precommissioning duty USS *New Jersey* (BB-62), April 1943. After Atlantic shakedown cruises, *New Jersey* went through Panama Canal Jan. 1, 1944 on to seven Battle Stars. Returned October 1944 to USMC Recruit Depot Dispensary San Diego, CA. Discharged December 1945, returning to Long Beach for private dental practice.

Married wife, Ruth, in 1945. They have four children and seven grandchildren.

Serving as one of three original dental officers it is interesting to note: when traveling as guest on the last cruise of *New Jersey* in 1990, he required the services of Capt. Rob Loar, the last dentist of BB-62.

TENNEY BOYER, SN, FA Div., born Decatur, IL on Aug. 12, 1932. Drafted into the Navy on Nov. 20, 1955. Assigned to the "Big J" after boot at the Lakes and a short stay on hospital side. Went aboard at Portsmouth shipyard. Brooklyn Navy Yard (Sand Street) in December 1956 and then to Bayonne in August 1957 for decommissioning. Discharged Aug. 20, 1957.

Married an airline stewardess from Boston and have four children. Reside in Arlington, TX since 1970.

CHARLES C. BREMER, was born in St. Louis, MO. Entered the service in 1942, Div. M, engine room.

Went on *New Jersey* when commissioned to hit Japan.

Participated in all battles and received eight stars.

Discharged January 1945. Married Evelyn Jane and they have four children and nine grandchildren. He is now a retired bus driver.

FRANK D. BRINK, MM2/c, USS *New Jersey* (BB-62), born Feb. 12, 1923, Lawrenceburg, TN. Joined the Navy Jan. 23, 1943, went to Great Lakes Naval Training Station.

Went to Philadelphia Navy Yard, assigned to the USS *New Jersey*. Moved aboard ship the day before commissioning on May 23, 1943. He was assigned to #3 engine room for duty and battle station. Jan. 7, 1944 went through Panama Canal to Balboa, to the Pacific until the surrender of Japan and then occupation forces of Japan Sept. 17, 1945 at Yokosuka. Jan. 29, 1946 headed to San Francisco. He was discharged March 15, 1946. Went back home and worked at Brink Lumber Company for his father and uncle, became part owner of the company. He retired Dec. 31, 1990. He married Jeanette Stumpe from Alabama on July 3, 1951 and they are the parents of three boys, three girls and have ten grandchildren.

BOBBY G. BRITT, USS *New Jersey,* Pfc, USMC, born June 19, 1933, Wesson, MS. Joined the Marine Corps Jan. 2, 1952. Went through Marine boot camp at Parris Island, SC and Sea School at Portsmouth, VA. Was assigned to the *Jersey* in mid summer of 1952 while she was in port for overhaul at Portsmouth Naval Shipyard.

He will always remember the first time they were called to their leaving port stations. For the Mississippi country boy, who had never been far enough from shore that he couldn't swim back, it seemed as if every hair on his head was standing at attention.

Soon after they made a midshipman cruise to Europe with port calls at Cherbourg, France and Lisbon, Portugal.

Spring of 1953 they went through the Panama Canal. Stopped at Long Beach, CA, onto Pearl Harbor then to Japan to relieve the big Mo and took up their duty off Korea.

One day off Korea comes to mind -

This particular Sunday morning was real quiet, the sea was calm as glass, the porpoise were jumping but soon they were called to General Quarters. It seems they were going into Wonson Harbor for a close look at where a destroyer had been hit the day before. As they were easing along between Yodo Island on one side and mainland Korea on the other, they opened fire on them and they took one hit.

It had been said that a ship that size could not maneuver that fast, but he doesn't believe a small boat could have backed down any faster than the *Jersey* did that day.

When the *Jersey* had completed her six months and was relieved by the *Wisconsin,* he transferred to the *Wisconsin* and served as admirals orderly for Vice Adm. Jacco Clark and Adm. A.M. Pride.

He was transferred back to the States in spring of 54 for duty at Treasure Island, CA main gate where he served until he was discharged on Dec. 2, 1954.

He now lives in Wesson, MS. He is a building contractor, backhoe and truck service.

Married to Frances and has two children. His daughter Debbie is 33 and the mother of two beautiful little girls, Devin and Dannielle. His son-in-law is Ricky Brown. His son, David, died Aug. 31, 1985 in a car accident.

CLARENCE J. BROOKS, JR., (JOE), USS *New Jersey* (BB-62), Fire Control Seaman, born June 1, 1927, Washington, DC. Joined the Navy March 1945, went through boot camp at Bainbridge Naval Training Center, assigned to NOB Guam, MI, discharged in October 1946.

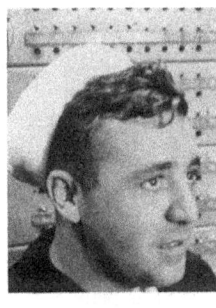 

Joined the active Naval Reserve in October 1947, called to active duty service September 1950 for the Korean War. Assigned to the USS *New Jersey,* FM Div., Bayonne, NJ. After the recommissioning and a shakedown cruise to Cuba the *Jersey* was ordered to Korea.

The highlight of his naval career was on May 21, 1951 at Wonson, Korea, when the *New Jersey* came under artillery fire from Chinese Communist and North Korean batteries. As main battery director pointer he was instrumental in destroying and silencing the enemy gun position. For this and other firing at bridges, railroads and tunnels in the Hungnam, Iwon and Sonjin areas.

He was awarded the Navy Letter of Commendation with Combat V.

Discharged from the Navy in July 1952, returned to civilian life and his job with the Chesapeake and Potomac Telephone Company in Washington, D.C. Retired in 1984 with 38 years service. Lives in Arlington, VA with Margaret his wife of 42 years. He has one son Michael, a detective with the Metropolitan Police Department.

DAILY BROUSSARD, was born in Vermilion Parish April 6, 1924. Entered the service Jan. 26, 1943, seaman first class. Received basic training at Lake Grote, IL.

Served on battleship *New Jersey*. Got on board May 23, 1943. Left Japan in January 1946.

Awarded the Philippine Liberation (two stars), Asiatic-Pacific Area (nine stars).

Discharged Jan. 26, 1946 as seaman first class.

Married and has two sons, one daughter and five grandchildren. Employed as dairyman for 25 years.

He is now retired and belongs to VFW and American Legion.

LARRY W. BROWN, born in Bluffton, IN, Aug. 17, 1936. Entered the USN Aug. 10, 1954.

August 10, 1954 Great Lakes Naval Training Station; November 1954 USS *New Jersey* late 1954; Dental Technician School Bainbridge, MD, 1955-1957, U.S. Naval Academy Anapolis, MD.

Discharged Aug. 16, 1957 as petty officer second class.

Married to Shirley and they have children Bruce, Kimberly and Peggy.

He was a newspaper publisher, *Daily Reporter,* Greenfield, IN.

RUSSELL E. BROWN, USS *New Jersey* BB-62, MM2/c, born July 24, 1924, Urbana, IL. Joined the Navy Jan. 20, 1943, went through boot camp at Green Bay, Great Lakes Naval Training Station. April 1943 was at the Philadelphia Navy Yard and was assigned to USS *New Jersey*. Commissioned USS *New Jersey* May 23, 1943, was in A Div., in the Fwd. Diesel Evaporators. They were on the East Coast until January 1944, went through the Panama Canal and on to their first campaign at the Marshall Islands Jan. 29, 1944.

Nine campaigns later they ended up at Tokyo Bay Sept. 16, 1945, anchored off Yokosuka Naval Base. He was discharged from the Navy at Great Lakes NTS, March 15, 1946.

He worked at the University of Illinois Chemistry Department as a storekeeper for 35 years, retiring in 1981. In 1981 he started the reunions for USS New Jersey Veteran's, Inc. He and his wife Marjorie have been married since Sept. 16, 1947. They have one daughter and one granddaughter. They are happily retired.

LLOYD JOSEPH BUISSON, on Jan. 20, 1943 he enlisted in the Navy as an A.S.S.V. and left for Great Lakes Naval Training Center. After 13 weeks of training and a seven day leave he was assigned to the USS *New Jersey*, 8th Div.

During their shakedown cruise in Trinidad they had night firing of their 5" guns on a surface target. He was on the tugboat that had in tow a target barge. One gun mount accidentally opened fire on the tugboat. Shells straddled the tug and the tug captain ordered "cease firing" by blinker light. He saw firsthand the mighty fire power of the USS *New Jersey* and lived to tell about it.

For 46 years he has been married to Margie and they had seven children (two sets of twins). So far they have six grandchildren. He retired from the telephone company in 1986. They own a 30' 5th wheeler and enjoy traveling all over this beautiful country. Just returned from a four month trip to Alaska and Western U.S.

JOHN E. BURD, born in Harrisburg, PA, Dec. 15, 1932. Entered Jan. 8, 1952, USN, BT3, B Div.

Attended boot camp at Bainbridge, MD, then assigned USS *New Jersey* BB-62, Norfolk, VA, where he was assigned to #4 fireroom and served until his discharge.

Awarded National Defense Service Medal, Korean Service Medal (two stars), United Nations Service Medal, China Service Medal, Korean Presidential Citation.

Achieved the rank of BT/3.

Retired May 1954. Married to Frances and has two children, four grandchildren and two great-grandchildren.

Retired October 1994 after 38 years in building supply business. Still living in Harrisburg, PA area near Hershey, PA.

JOHN BUZENSKI, was born in Norwich, CT, Dec. 25, 1924. Recalled October 1950. Served in Navy M Div. on USS *New Jersey*.

His memorable experience includes fishing for sharks in Gitmo Bay.

His awards include Korean Service Medal (one star), United Nations Service Medal, Korean Presidential Unit Citation Badge.

Retired February 1952 with the rank of MML/2.

He is now retired.

DONALD G. CALDWELL, USS *New Jersey* (BB-62), SN 1st, born Dec. 28, 1930, Catlettsburg, KY. Joined Navy November 1950. Boot camp at Great Lakes, then assigned to USS *New Jersey* in Norfolk. Shakedown operations in Guantanamo Bay, Cuba, in preparation for Far East-Korea. On their way, relieved USS *Missouri* in Honolulu, then on to Pacific, Yokosuka, Japan in 1951. In May they were in Korea area. Before their 16" guns knocked out targets, they got hit three times with one killed and three wounded. His duty was on 40 mm guns. They bombarded off and on for 30 days at a time. The *Jersey* participated in major campaigns all of 1951.

While on the ship he played on the ship's basketball and softball teams. They were Crulant champs in 1952 in Norfolk. Discharged March 1954 then went to work for Allied Chemical then to Saudia Arabia for three years. Now at Aristech Chemical in West Virginia and retiring December 1995.

Married to Mary Adams Caldwell for 43 years. He has three daughters, one son and seven grandchildren.

J.R. CALDWELL, born in Haywood County, Waynesville, NC, Jan. 12, 1930. Served in the Navy, Barber S-3, ship service.

Stationed on battleship, powder room #2 turret, barber in crew, barber shop and officers barber shop.

His memorable experiences include two

trips to Far East Japan, Korea and China 1951-1953. Two trips to Europe, France, Spain, all others 1952-1954. Discharged November 1954 as ship service first class.

Married to Helen and has son David, born 1960, daughter June born 1957. He also has three grandchildren.

He has been an automobile and recreation vehicle dealer for 36 years.

RICHARD "D" CANADAY, JR., born in Atlanta, GA, May 18, 1924.

He entered the USMC Feb. 8, 1943 in Atlanta and went to Parris Island, SC boot camp. From P.I. to Marine Sea School in Portsmouth, VA in March; from Sea School to Marine Barracks in Philadelphia, PA in April; and was assigned to the USS *New Jersey* (BB-62) in May before commissioning ceremonies May 23, 1943. He is a plankowner of the *Jersey*. While aboard, he served as orderly to the ship's captain, executive officer and visiting admirals. He was a 20mm gunner and helped maintain all the Marine-manned 20mms as well as doing other ship maintenance duties required. He left the *Jersey* at Pearl Harbor in the middle of August, 1944. After going to the Marine Barracks at San Diego, he was sent to Camp LeJeune, NC for Artillery School, and then to Camp Pendleton, CA for advanced infantry training. In April, he left Pendleton for Pearl Harbor. The next day he boarded ship in a replacement draft for Okinawa arriving there in late May. He was assigned to the 15th Marine Regt. at the battle of Naha. They moved forward and he was transferred to Fox Co., 2nd Bn., 22nd Regt., 6th Div. (Special Weapons, Machine Gunner). They moved from Okinawa to Guam aboard a landing craft in a violent typhoon.

The point system for discharge had started and he had ample points so he stayed at Guam when the 6th Div. left for Tienstin, China. He returned to the States aboard an oil tanker (*The White Horse*) arriving at New Orleans, LA and then by train to Camp LeJeune, NC where he was discharged Nov. 28, 1945 as a private first class.

He was employed by Plantation Pipe Line Company in the drafting section of the engineering department until his retirement in 1987.

He and his wife Martha were married in November, 1947 and have five children. Three sons and two daughters. The oldest son James joined the Marine Corps, was wounded in Vietnam and received a disability discharge. Their second son served in the Army, but their third son did not serve in the Armed Forces because of his high draft number.

At this time, they have nine grandchildren and one great-grandchild.

BAKER GRANT CARTER, Radarman Third Class, (T) USNR, born in Monroe City, IN, Oct. 3, 1923. He completed high school April 1941, Monroe City, IN. Went to work for S.S. Kresge's Company, Lafayette, IN December 1941 to January 1943.

Joined the Navy Jan. 19, 1943. Boot camp at Great Lakes Navy Training Station.

Was then assigned to the USS *New Jersey* at Philadelphia Navy Yard. They just finished building the *New Jersey*.

Participated in all major campaigns in the Pacific.

Received the Asiatic-Pacific with nine stars, American Area, Victory Medal, Philippine Liberation with two stars.

Was discharged Jan. 26, 1946. His entire Navy career was spent on the USS *New Jersey*.

After the war returned to S.S. Kresge's Co. Lafayette, IN.

He then was transferred to Kresge's store in Lexington, KY. Assigned as store manager in Detroit, MI in 1954. Left S.S. Kresge's and went to work for Sears Roebuck and Company in Highland Park, MI.

After 20 years:

While working at Sears store, a man came into his department and said, "Haven't I seen you somewhere?" He said, were you on the USS *New Jersey?*" Carter related that he was in K Div. The man said he was C.G. Anderson, he had written the Div. Dope - K Div. It was Anderson who slept in the same bunk. Anderson was working for Chrysler there in Highland Park. Small world!

In 1985 retired from Sears Roebuck and Co. after 28 years with store 1490 Troy, MI.

He married a Kentucky girl, Oct. 10, 1954, Inis Jewell Foley, Lancaster, KY.

He's also a member of the American Legion Post 38, Somerset, KY.

They are now living in Somerset, KY near Cumberland Lake.

Moved from Warren, MI to Somerset, KY June 1989.

CHESTER CASARI, was born in Caspian, MI Feb. 3, 1924. Entered the USN Dec. 7, 1942. Stationed at Great Lakes Training Station Dec. 8, 1942-May 19, 1943; USS *New Jersey* May 23, 1943-September 1945.

Casari is a plankowner. Participated in all war-time major campaigns, 3rd and 5th Fleets.

Discharged Oct. 15, 1945 as seaman first class.

Married to Audrey and they have five children and ten grandchildren.

Now a retired teacher/high school principal.

JOSEPH CATINO III, was born in Newark, NJ, April 25, 1947. Entered the Navy Jan. 3, 1967. Served in USNR, BT3, B Div. #2 Fireroom.

Stationed in Long Beach, CA; Bremerton WA (homeports). Also tour of Vietnam 1968-1969. Attended boot camp, Great Lakes Naval Station.

Memorable experiences include liberty in Japan, Philippines, Singapore, Hawaii; crossing the equator.

Awarded the Republic of Vietnam Campaign Medal, Combat Action Ribbon, Vietnam Service Medal with two Bronze Stars, National Defense Service.

Discharged Jan. 2, 1973 as BT3.

Married to Janet and they have a son, Joseph and daughter, Jennifer.

Catino is outside plant engineer for Bell Atlantic-New Jersey, Inc.

FREDERIC A. CHENAULT, entered USN June 1932. Served as commander and executive officer.

Served on the USS *New Jersey* 1953-1954. Served in WWII and Korea. Retired Sept. 1, 1965 as captain, USN.

He is now retired.

ARTHUR F. CHMELIK, JR., USS *New Jersey* (BB-62), Radioman 3/c, born Dec. 12, 1926, Oak Park, IL. Joined Navy Dec. 13, 1944. Boot camp in San Diego, CA 44-627. Radio School in Los Angeles. Transferred from Treasure Island to receiving station in the Southern Philippines. Transferred to the PCS 1403. Returned to States and was discharged July 1946. Recalled for Korean duty aboard the *New Jersey*. Saw duty off Korea, September 1951. Returned to the States by way of Panama Canal. Transferred to USS *New Port News* for two months before discharge on Oct. 7, 1952. Spent 37 years as a sheet metal worker from Local 73 in Chicago.

Retired on Jan. 1, 1990 and moved to Scottsdale, AZ. They raised five children, (three boys and two girls), and have six grandchildren, (three boys and three girls).

He was awarded the Asiatic-Pacific National Defense, WWII Victory, Korean Service and United Nations Service Medal.

WILLIAM J. CLIFFORD, USN, USS *New Jersey* (BB-62), WT1/c, born March 16, 1925, New York, NY. Joined the Navy March 27, 1942, went through boot camp at the Newport, RI Naval Training Station.

Clifford was then assigned to the USS *Texas* and convoy duty in the North Atlantic with trips to Murmansk, Russia. After supporting troop landings at Oran in the North African campaign, he was transferred to and took part in the commissioning of the USS *New Jersey* May 23, 1943.

The *New Jersey* participated in nearly all major campaigns in the Pacific starting Jan. 29, 1944 in support of air strikes at Kwajalein and ending with the dropping of the anchor at Yokosuka Naval Base Sept. 16, 1945. He was entitled to the Asiatic-Pacific Medal, nine stars, European Theater Medal, one star, American Theater Medal, one star, Philippine Liberation Medal, two stars. He was discharged from the Navy March 23, 1946.

He joined the Naval Reserve Nov. 17, 1947 while attending Fordam University and was recalled to active duty Sept. 5, 1950 because of the Korean Police Action. He served as a WT1/c on the USS LST 602, USS *Weiss* APD 135, and the USS *Mellette* APA-156. He was released from active duty March 8, 1952.

He was appointed to the New York Fire Department on Jan. 1, 1953, attained the rank of lieutenant and was retired on Dec. 9, 1980 because of a fire-related injury.

He lived in Wantagh, NY with his wife and two daughters and was the proud grandfather of three. He passed away on Veterans Day, Nov. 11, 1993 at the age of 68.

GREGORY M. COFFMAN, GMG1 (Ret), was born in Connellsvill, PA Dec. 13, 1942. Entered the USN Dec. 22, 1961 and retired Aug. 1, 1986.

His memorable experiences include combat patrol on PBR Mekong River and Song Vam Sat River, RVN.

Awarded Bronze Star Medal with Combat V, Navy Good Conduct Medal, Purple Heart Medal, National Defense Medal, Vietnam Service Medal, Vietnam Gallantry Cross, Vietnam Campaign Medal with 60 Bar, Vietnam Medal of Honor 1st class, Civilian Action Medal, Sea Service Ribbon, Battle "E" Ribbon, Combat Action Ribbon, PUC Ribbon, MCU Ribbon, Surface War Device, Small Boat Device, Rifle Expert Medal, Pistol Expert Medal.

Assignments: Boot camp, RTC, NTC, Midway, NIOTC, FT 116 Div. 551, TF-117, T131-5, ARG-4, LST 902, ACB-1, AD-15, RTC Staff, BB-62 G-4 Div. (1984-1986).

Discharged Aug. 1, 1986.

Married to Rose M. Wilson Aug. 13, 1983 at NTC, San Diego, CA.

Presently working as apartment manager in San Diego, CA.

ARTHUR J. COLERICK, USS *New Jersey* (BB-62), BM2/c, born March 19, 1923, Woonsocket, RI. Joined the Navy Jan. 3, 1941.

Attended boot camp at Newport, RI. Assigned and participated in commissioning of USS *Antaeus* (AS-21) Baltimore, MD June 1941 to March 1943.

The *Antaeus* serviced and supplied submarine bases, tendered submarines from Coco Solo, Panama to sub bases in the North Atlantic, routinely traversing through what is remembered as 'Torpedo Junction.'

Transferred to and took part in the commissioning of the USS *New Jersey* (BB-62) May 23, 1943. Assigned to a deck division, the 6th and introduced to the 40mm antiaircraft gun quads.

Stayed aboard the *Jersey* while it was in the Pacific, and Yokosuka, Japan until it returned to the West Coast and he was transferred to the Fargo Building, Boston, MA for discharge April 8, 1946.

Self-employed in the restaurant business for several years and then employed for many years in the production control and purchasing departments of a major textile machine manufacturer.

He lives with his wife in Warwick, RI and is retired. They both enjoy traveling.

PHILIP RICHARD COUGHLIN, (P.R.), AM1/c, Aviation Unit, BB-62, born in Syracuse, NY Feb. 9, 1924. Joined the Navy Feb. 9, 1941. Attended boot camp at Newport, RI, Aviation School, NS Jax; PBY Sqdn. VP-41 in Caribbean, commissioned NAS Pax River; assigned to present at commissioning of USS *New Jersey* in May 1943. Served aboard from then through Okinawa Campaign. Detached for flight training, commissioned ensign and then discharged. Finished Syracuse University and University of Pennsylvania. Graduated with DDS degree. Practiced dentistry 1952 until present.

His hobbies include flying, building airplanes, model ships and airplanes (including six foot model USS *New Jersey*), scuba diving and motorcycling. Married and has three children and continues to work full time.

He is a member of the USS New Jersey Vets, Inc.

MERLE LEROY COX, JR., USS *New Jersey* (BB-62), S1/c, born June 16, 1931, in Washington, DC. Joined the Navy Feb. 14, 1951, went through boot camp at the Great Lakes Naval Training Station. Was then sent to the Brooklyn Navy Receiving Station in New York City, for assignment.

Next he was assigned to Fasron 104 Air Detachment in Port Lyautey, French Morocco, N.W. Africa. He arrived in June 1951.

After a tour of duty in Morocco, he was assigned to the USS *New Jersey* (BB-62), 1st Div., in November 1952. April 5, 1953, they arrived in Yokosuka, Japan, to begin the ships second tour of duty in Korea. A short time after arriving in Korea, he transferred to the 5th Div. Armistice was signed July 27, 1953. He spent the rest of his time serving in the USS *New Jersey*, and was discharged Jan. 13, 1955.

He returned home and joined his father in the family retail memorial business and took it over when he retired in February 1968. He has one son, two daughters and three grandchildren.

JACK D. CRANDALL, born at Ostrander, OH on Oct. 20, 1933. Joined the Navy in September 1951 and was discharged in August 1954. Boot camp at the Great Lakes Naval Training Station. Went aboard the USS *New Jersey* on March 1952 and was discharged from the *Jersey*. Served in the 1st Div. as a gunners mate seaman first class.

Employed 40 years as a design engineer for Ford Motor Company, and has not retired yet. Married with two grown children and four grandchildren. He resides in Grosse Ile, MI.

HAROLD E. (GENE) CRUMLEY, was born in Scott County, IL, April 16, 1931. Entered the USN, Oct. 10, 1951. Attended boot camp in Great Lakes. Served as ME2, R Div.

Stationed on USS *New Jersey*, 1952-1955.

His memorable experiences includes being

aboard ship when the Korean War ended. Saw many foreign ports and had many great shipmates.

Participated in the second Korean cruise.

Released Sept. 10, 1955 as metalsmith second class.

Married to Pauline and has two sons, David and Gary, four grandsons, Scott, Troy, Jonathan and Brandon.

Crumley is the owner of a welding/repair shop in East Peoria, IL and has 12 employees.

RONDLE D. CRUMP, was born Nov. 2, 1931 in Lenoir, NC. He entered the USN Jan. 9, 1951.

Attended boot camp in New Port, RI January 1951 to April 1951. On board USS *New Jersey* April 1951 to November 1954.

His memorable experiences include taking a direct hit in Wonson Harbor, 1951 and almost being captured by North Koreans on a train spotting mission somewhere north of Wonson.

Awarded the National Defense, Good Conduct, Asian Theatre, and two Battle Stars.

Discharged Nov. 22, 1954 as E2c.

Married to Anna and they have one son, one daughter and two grandsons.

Presently he is designing and building machinery and equipment for a manufactured home company.

FRANK DAVILA, L3c, USS *New Jersey* (BB-62), born April 20, 1935, New York City. Enlisted Navy April 21, 1952. Attended boot camp in Bainbridge, MD.

Assigned to USS *New Jersey* and worked in the engineering department in M Div. as fireman. Main Engine Control as throttleman.

Participated in numerous bombing raids along North Korean Coast, February 1953.

Transferred to Ex Div. and worked in print shop and printed the *Jersey Bounce* newsletter.

Awarded the Good Conduct Medal, National Defense Service Medal, Korean Service with three Battle Stars, United Nations Medal, Korean Presidential Unit, China Service Medal.

Released from Navy April 1956. In Naval Reserve until discharged in 1960.

Married Nancy Shields Nov. 22, 1953 in Gettysburg, PA. They have four children: two sons Daniel A., Michael F. and two daughters, Melanie J. and Kelly Ann. They also have eight grandchildren: Daniel A. Davila, Catherine Davila, Rebecca Brillhart, Jacob McGuire, Benjamin McGuire, Eliza Ann Davila, Jonathan Davila, and Lauren Davila. Presently living in York, PA.

Davila is an avid hunter, fisherman, woodworker and boater. Works at Intelligencer Printing Co., Lancaster, PA as technical sales rep. He has been with the company for 30 years.

JAMES D. DAVY, born Feb. 28, 1948 Anaconda, MT. Entered service September 1965. Served in Vietnam 1967-1969 and on various ships and at various stations until reporting to pre-com USS *New Jersey* in 1981. He served on board until December 1983 leaving the ship at Beruit Lebanon. Retiring in 1988 as a master chief he now works for the V.A. He is a member of both The Battleship Historical Museum Society and the USS New Jersey Veterans, Inc and is a member of various other veterans groups.

Decorations and awards include four Bronze Star Medals, with Combat V, two Purple Heart Medals for wounds received in combat, the Meritorious Service Medal, four Navy Commendation Awards. The Army Commendation with Combat V, the Navy Achievement Medal, Combat Action Award, two Presidential Unit Citations, two Navy Unit Commendations, the Navy Expeditionary Medal, Meritorious Unit Commendation, five Good Conduct Awards, three Navy Battle "E" Awards, four Vietnam Service Awards, Sea Service Deployment with three stars, Overseas Service with two stars, Vietnamese Gallantry Cross, Republic of Vietnam Civic Action Unit Citation and Republic of Vietnam Campaign Ribbon.

He is married to the former Yvonne White of Torrance, CA, has a daughter and three grandchildren. He and his wife now reside in Mertle Creek, OR.

GORDON J. DECORSEY, USS *New Jersey* (BB-62), BM2/c, born July 3, 1924, St. Paul, MN. Joined the Navy July 8, 1941, went through boot camp at the Great Lakes Naval Training Station. Was then assigned to the USS *Savannah* and convoy duty in the North Atlantic. After supporting troop landings at Oran, in the North Africa campaign was transferred to and took part in the commissioning of the USS *New Jersey,* May 23, 1943.

After some good Philadelphia liberty and a shakedown the *New Jersey* participated in nearly all major campaigns in the Pacific starting Jan. 29, 1944, in support of air strikes at Kwajalein and ending with the dropping of the anchor at Yokosuka Naval Base (the heart of Japan) Sept. 16, 1945.

He was discharged Oct. 15, 1945, Minneapolis, MN. Went to work for the Department of Defense, U.S. Air Force Base, Minneapolis, MN. Later transferring to the Naval Weapons Station, Seal Beach, CA where he retired July 1986. He is now living in Sacramento, CA with his wife, who served with the U.S. Marine Corps, Hunter College, NY, 1942-1943. They have one grandson, two sons. One son is retired from the U.S. Air Force.

MYRON S. DEMPSEY, JR., born Aug. 6, 1920, Peabody, MA. Joined the Navy Nov. 7, 1939. Boot camp at Newport, RI. Assigned to USS *Texas* doing convoy duty in the North Atlantic and supporting troops in the North Africa Invasion. Transferred to and took part in the commissioning of the USS *New Jersey*.

Discharged on Dec. 15, 1945 in Boston. However, Uncle Sam requested 29 cents from him as overpayment for travel from Bremerton, WA. Became a chef on GI Bill.

Awarded the European African Middle Eastern Theatre Medal, WWII Victory Medal, American Theater Medal, Philippine Liberation Medal with two stars, Asiatic-Pacific Theatre Medal with one star, Good Conduct Medal and the American Defense Medal.

Now retired, and enjoying the fishing and sunshine in Florida.

VALENTINE FRANK DEPEPPO, was born May 26, 1918 in Brooklyn, NY. He enlisted in the US Navy as Apprentice Seaman on May 11, 1937 and was discharged May 16, 1941 as a MM/2c. After the attack on Pearl Harbor, Depeppo re-enlisted at NRS, New York, NY. He served aboard the USS *Maumee*, USS *Philadelphia*, and USS *New Jersey* and achieved the rank of MMC/1c. Depeppo retired from the Navy after 11 years regular and 20 years reserve in 1969.

He received the African Campaign w/1 star, American Theater w/1 star, Asiatic-Pacific w/9 stars, Philippine Liberation w/2 stars, and the World War II Victory medals.

He has worked in the restaurant and tavern business with his brother, worked as Assistant Supervisor for the Census Bureau of New York, and as a clerk for the Richmond County Courthouse.

JOSEPH G. DICORCIA, USS *New Jersey* (BB-62), born Sept. 11, 1927, Jersey City, NJ. Enlisted in the Navy December 1944. Called to duty March 1935. Went through boot camp at Sampson Naval Training Center and amphibious training at Pearl Harbor. Transferred to Yokosuka Naval Base and assigned to the 2nd Div. of the USS *New Jersey* September 1945.

Released from active duty July 1946 but served with the Reserves. Recalled to active duty November 1950 and requested "The Big J". Came aboard in Bayonne, NJ prior to her recommissioning. Assigned to the 4th Div., later transferring to the Q (Signal Gang).

Released from active duty in 1952 earning the rate of QM3 in the Reserve in 1953.

Retired as an administrative specialist after 37 years with Public Service Electric and Gas Company in 1988. Married the former Doris Browning in 1948 and has five children and eight grandchildren. Now residing in North Arlington and Ocean City, NJ.

JOSEPH A. DINELL, boarded the *Jersey* May 1943 in Philadelphia, PA. Served with 9th Div.

After a 22 day leave he was shipped out to the Brooklyn Navy Yard for guard duty. This consisted of armored car duty in New York and the chasing of prisoners in the Navy Yard. Discharged on points on February 1946.

A humorous thing happened when Charles Downing was learning to play his guitar and really getting on everyone's nerves. His bunk was next to George McNultys and two bunks below Dinells and he would sit there and plink on those strings for hours. Ed Gundersen was walking by Downing when he reached down, pulling the guitar from Downing and breaking it over his head. The look on Downing's face was something to see.

A frightening experience happened when Dinell was walking back through the ship when a 5" shell, from the *Iowa*, came through the deck and into the head and blew a sailors leg off below the knee. That was Dinell's first experience with the reality of the war.

He left the *Jersey* August 1945 in San Diego, CA.

After his discharge he went back to the steel mill for five years but decided to go to college. Bought a gas station and sold it after one year. Joined the police department for 13 years and decided to go to Texas and start a business. Left Texas after a couple of years and was offered a job with May Company as assistant director of security for Washington, DC, Maryland and Virginia.

After ten years at this job he left to go back to Texas and start his own cleaning plant. He had a nice business for about eight years and the economy in Houston hit bottom and he sold out for a deal he couldn't turn down. He moved to Fort Worth and managed his son-in-law's plant for seven years. He and his wife Toni are in good health and are enjoying their three daughters Deborah, Jody and Kris and their children: Michael, Dinell, Nicole, Anthony, Madeline and Aubrey. Their son Joseph died in 1975 at age 13.

He keeps busy doing odd jobs for his daughters and keeping his home in good shape. Stays in contact with Alvin Trachok, who lives in Johnstown, PA and was also on the *New Jersey* with him.

ROBERT F. (DING) DINGMAN, USS *New Jersey* (BB-62), EM2/c, born Nov. 12, 1947, Syracuse, NY. He joined the Navy on Feb. 23, 1967 in Syracuse. Went through basic training at the Great Lakes Training Center and also EM "A" School in Great Lakes. In September, 1967, Bob (along with three of his fellow classmates, Noah Bleigh, Jr., Bruce Edelman and Don Barge) reported to his first duty station, Philadelphia Naval Base as part of the nucleus crew responsible for the recommissioning of the battleship *New Jersey*. Bob served on the *New Jersey* from that time until it's decommissioning in Bremerton, WA in December, 1969. He reported on board as an EMFA and left as an EM2 two years, three months later. While on the *New Jersey,* Bob worked as an electrician in the Distribution Gang. He first worked in #3 Engine and Fire Rooms and then in Forward and After Diesel. After decommissioning the *New Jersey* in Bremerton, Bob was assigned to the USS *Hoel* (DDG-13). He reported to San Diego but after a month was flown over to WESPAC to find his ship. He followed the *Hoel* from Japan, to Okinawa, then Da Nang, RVN and finally to Subic Bay, Philippines, before reporting on board. Three weeks later the *Hoel* set sail for San Diego. Bob finished his Navy career on the *Hoel* and was discharged on Nov. 5, 1970.

Bob returned to civilian life in Albany, NY. Attended Hudson Valley Community College and then started work at General Electric Co. in Schenectady, NY. In 1978, he joined the engineering firm of Rist-Frost Associates, in Glens Falls, NY. In 1983, he was promoted to his present position as CADD manager and senior electrical designer at Rist-Frost-Shumay Engineering, in Laconia, NH.

Bob lives in Laconia with his son, Mark, 13 and his daughter, Sara, 10.

Shipmates are encouraged to contact "Ding" in Laconia, NH.

HUGH G. DIXON, USS *New Jersey* (BB-62), turret captain first class, born Indianapolis, IN, Oct. 14, 1924. Grew up in Ft. Lauderdale, FL. Enlisted in the U.S. Navy Dec. 18, 1941. Attended boot training in Norfolk, VA. Served on USS *Woodcock*, USS *Erie*, in the Panama Canal Zone.

Assigned to the USS *New Jersey* at the Philadelphia Navy Yard, before commissioning, as GM3c turret #2 (2nd Div.).

Left the ship in Tokyo Bay to come home for discharge Dec. 21, 1945.

Worked on automobiles and small airplanes in Broward County, FL. Flew crop duster aircraft in Mississippi four years.

Married Bettie Joe Barrett in Indianola, MS on Oct. 29, 1950. Worked as mechanic on automobiles, welding shop, small airlines, and National Airlines, until joining Eastern Airlines as mechanic on June 1, 1955. Retired from Eastern Airlines Feb. 1, 1987 as a maintenance inspector. He lives in Miami, FL.

He has two sons, Ralph and Paul and one daughter, Judy. He also has seven grandchildren. Bettie passed away Nov. 29, 1994.

DONALD B. DONAGHY, USS *New Jersey* (BB-62), Hospital Corpsman 3/c, born April 16, 1930, New Bedford, MA. Joined Navy Nov. 16, 1947, boot camp Great Lakes. A School Great Lakes, Naval Hospital Bethesda, MD, 22nd Marines, Quantico, VA, USS *New Jersey,* January 1951. Shakedown in Gitmo then to Korea for Big "J's" first Korean Tour. Following duty in *New Jersey* completed Navy career serving in submarines, amphibs, shore duty in Hawaii, aerospace facility, Johnsonville, PA working with the training of the first group of astronauts. Capped off 21 years of naval service with an extended tour on a destroyer during Vietnam Conflict. Piped over the side July 28, 1968 as chief hospital corpsman. Continued in Medical Administrative Field as deputy director of an Alexandria, VA based Medical Association, transferred to Associations Medical Liability Insurance carrier becoming vice president of company prior to retirement.

Married in 1949 in Groton, CT to Mary (who wrote all those wonderful letters while aboard *New Jersey*). They have two sons, their oldest

CHARLES S. DOUGHERTY, USS *New Jersey* (BB-62) EM1/c, born Oct. 29, 1920 in Decatur County, IA. Enlisted in the Navy, Nov. 7, 1942; Des Moines, IA.

Attended boot camp Great Lakes, IL. Assigned to USS *New Jersey*, Philadelphia, PA before commissioned. He was an original crew member. Participated in all battles from time *New Jersey* went to Pacific until left *New Jersey* to come back to States and to go to school Camp Perry, VA and EIC School, Washington, DC.

Discharged at Washington, DC Sept. 27, 1945. Retired construction electrician in 1979.

Lived in Yuba City, CA for 35 years. Married to Margaret for 53 years. They have one son, two grandsons and three great-grandchildren. He is now working on his genealogy in retirement.

SAMUEL M. DRURY, was born March 19, 1924 in Atkinson, GA. Reared in Brunswick, GA by a widowed mother from the age of nine. Joined the Navy on his 17th birthday. Trained at Norfolk, VA. Boarded USS *Albemarle* in May 1941, a seaplane tender. They housed crews and tended seaplanes while the base was being built at Argentia, Newfoundland. Shifted to south Atlantic Islands and Brazil. After two years transferred to Philadelphia, PA for USS *New Jersey* draft, a plank owner, was gun captain on 40mm gun on the starboard side of captains deck. Left ship at Okinawa. Mustered out Oct. 3, 1945. Migrated to Toledo, OH. Finished his education and received his high school diploma from Waite High School in 1946.

Worked for Pur Oil/Union Oil for 21 years and owned and operated a night club for 21 years with Juanita, his wife of 44 years. Lived in California for nine years. Retired in Bradner, OH with Juanita. They now go to all of the reunions. Juanita was Russ Brown's secretary for the first four reunions and at present trying to get an auxiliary together for the wives of the men of the USS *New Jersey*.

WILLIAM F. DUMOULIN, USS *New Jersey* (BB-62) S1c, born on Sept. 20, 1923 in Taunton, MA. Joined the Navy on Oct. 28, 1942. Went through boot camp at Coddington Point, Newport, RI.

Later assigned to Philadelphia Receiving Station and became "plank owner" as part of the USS *New Jersey* commissioning crew.

On May 23, 1943, assigned to C.S. Div. (Communications Signal). Served aboard vessel during complete combat tour in Asiatic-Pacific area, ending in Tokyo Bay in November 1945. Discharged on Jan. 6, 1946.

Among various occupations in civilian life, merchant seaman and painting contractor.

Residing in Taunton, MA with his wife Evamae. They have two children, Mark and Mona, and two grandsons, Joshua and Jacob Cross.

Retired in 1985, enjoying the grandchildren and world travel with spouse.

Many episodes of the *Jerseys* combat record in WWII are indelibly etched in his mind, but none more so than the bombardment of Mille Island in the Marshall Island Group.

The date was March 18, 1944 and in company with their sister ship *Iowa*, they were sent on "practice bombardment" of that island, neutralizing shore installations in the process.

They proceeded to shell the target for two hours with the 16" main batteries providing the fire power from long range. Things were uneventful until the ship closed to 19,000 yards whereupon the secondary 5" mounts commenced firing, only to be answered by stiff counterfire from shore batteries.

Enemy shells flew everywhere, between the "stacks" and over the ship from port to starboard, causing geysers of water to erupt close to the vessel as they struck the sea.

One of their men on the 11th level swore he could read the lot numbers on the incoming shells and asked to be relieved from his station. Though the situation was grim, a little humor somehow crept into it as the "Chief" told him to stay put as it wasn't any better on the signal bridge where the rest of the C.S. Div. had it's battle station.

To this day he can hear the firing observers words over and over again … "flash from the beach Sir - bearing … flash from the beach Sir - bearing … "

They ended the engagement in the afternoon, unscathed but the *Iowa* suffered two superficial hits on her port side.

The C.S. Div. normally had quite a few comedians but during and after the action there were no laughs or joking. Basically they were a sober and scared group, regarding themselves as very lucky to be in one piece and thanking God for it.

He is certain that all personnel exposed topside that day share his memories despite the passing of 50 years. If there are some things in this life that remain stubbornly integrated in the human psyche, then for the men of the *New Jersey* it has a name — Mille.

JAMES R. EDENFIELD, GM2/c, USN, born Lake City, FL, Oct. 27, 1919. December 13, 1941 enlisted in the Navy at Tampa, FL.

December 30, 1941 sworn in the Navy, Macon, GA.

December 31, 1941 NOB Norfolk, VA, boot camp, Platoon #5.

Assigned to USS *Pollux* Jan. 24, 1942.

Survived the sinking of USS *Pollux* at Newfoundland, Feb. 18, 1942. Spent two weeks in hospital at Argentia NOB, survivors leave.

Receiving station Boston, MA, April 30, 1942; August 13, 1942, Receiving Station, New York; Sept. 10, 1942, USS *Brooklyn* CL-40, convoy duty, invasion of North Africa; April 24, 1943, R.S. Philadelphia; May 23, 1943, USS *New Jersey* BB-62, plank owner, 1st Div.; Sept. 19, 1944, Naval Repair Base, Adv. GM and Elect. Hyd School; Dec. 21, 1944, N.A.D. Hawthorn, NV VJF Fuses (School); March 18, 1945, AQERU # Navy #926, NAD Guam, M.I.; Sept. 6, 1946, USS PC1149; Feb. 28, 1947 USS *Latona*.

Discharged Oct. 7, 1947 at Alameda, N.A.S., CA as GM2/c.

Awarded the Asiatic-Pacific with four stars, American Area, EAME (one star), WWII Victory Medal, and Good Conduct.

Married and has four children and five grandchildren.

He was an aircraft mechanic for 10 years with Boeing Vertol; 25 years Atlantic Aviation Corp., Wilmington, DE. Retired November 1984.

DAVID S. EDWARDS, FC2, was born Dec. 11, 1969 in Pendleton, OR. Entered service July 17, 1988, USN.

Attended boot camp in San Diego. Basic Electricity and Electronics School in San Diego.

FC "A" School in Great Lakes; USS *New Jersey* November 1989-Feb. 8, 1991; MK 86 "C" School in San Diego; USS *Belleau Wood*, USS *O'Brien*.

Awarded Battle "E" on USS *O'Brien*, National Defense, Good Conduct, Southwest Asia for Southern Watch; Armed Forces Expeditionary; Sharpshooter Pistol, Marksman Rifle, Sea Service.

Discharged Nov. 1, 1994.

Resides in San Diego with his wife and daughter. Currently stationed on USS *McKee*. Currently going to school to become a paramedic.

GEORGE H. ELWOOD, was born in Hancock, NY, May 19, 1927. Entered the U.S. Navy May 1945.

Stationed at Sampson Naval Base. Aboard two ships USS *Laurens* and USS *Audubond*; Camp Shoemaker and Treasure Island, CA; Samar, P.I.; USS *New Jersey* September 1945 to August 1946 as S1/c (storekeeper disbursing).

His memorable experience: Persons in disbursing office, T.S. Mullaney, Paul Allen, Bob

Moodie, Harold Harp, Guy Van Hess, Paul Scott, Rod Crock, Bill Ellis — others Jim Farrel, Bill Fanning.

Awarded the WWII Victory Medal, Asiatic-Pacific Ribbon.

Discharged as S1/c, Aug. 3, 1946 in Bremerton, WA.

Married to Ann and has children, Charles, Thomas, Barbara, and granddaughter Teri.

He graduated from Rutgers University and Fordham Law School. He is now an attorney.

WILLIAM R. ESSELSTEIN, USS *New Jersey*, GM2c, born in Corning, OH, Sept. 10, 1923. Joined Navy Jan. 27, 1943, went to Great Lakes for training. From there to Philadelphia where he boarded the *Jersey* in May 1943. Participated in Pacific campaigns until discharge in January 1946. Married and has two sons and twin daughters. His oldest son, 1st Lt. Harold Esselstein was killed in a helicopter crash, Bill never recovered from this loss. Bill looked forward to all the reunions.

Taken from a local paper

A QUIET HERO

The people of Corning lost a friend and quiet hero on Aug. 8, 1992 when he died from a heart attack. Esselstein received little formal recognition in his lifetime, but if there was ever an underestimated individual in this community, he was that. Esselstein was community worker for his family, kids, for his church and American Legion. He was a quiet guy who faithfully sat at the top row to cheer Miller basketball team home or away, even his sons' careers had long passed. He was gentleman, coal miner, a World War II veteran, and a man who faithfully worked the land on his farm on Chapel Hill. He will be missed.

He leaves his wife of 46 1/2 years, three children, eight grandchildren and four great-grandchildren.

ROBERT E. FARR, USS *New Jersey* (BB-62), MM1/c, born Feb. 20, 1923, Fort Wayne, IN, joined the Navy Jan. 20, 1943. Went through boot camp at the Great Lakes Naval Training Station. Was then assigned to the USS *New Jersey* as pre-commissioning crew, left the ship on Jan. 21, 1944.

One of the first jobs aboard ship was to check all shaft alleys and engineering spaces for saboteurs as there were still workmen aboard. After shakedown cruises and final inspections he was transferred. He also served aboard USS *Apollo* (AS-25) submarine tender in the South Pacific. After being discharged the first time, was called back in and served aboard USS *Salisbury Sound* (AV-13) seaplane tender again in the South Pacific.

Campaign ribbons earned were Good Conduct Medal with one star, Asiatic-Pacific Medal, American Theater Medal, Victory Medal, UN Ribbon, Korean Service Medal, China Service and Occupation Service (Asia Clasp).

Was discharged in Seattle, WA on Sept. 26, 1952. After discharge, he worked at International Harvester in Fort Wayne, IN then moved to Port Townsend, WA in 1956. He began work there in an auto-body shop and retired from there in 1985. He worked 15 years as a volunteer firefighter, over 20 years as a volunteer police officer and deputy sheriff, as a motorcycle officer most of the time. He and his wife are both retired and living in Port Townsend, WA. They have one son, two daughters and seven grandchildren.

GLENN M. FISHER, S1/c, was born Feb. 3, 1931, in Roanoke, VA. He joined the Navy in September of 1948, went through boot camp at the Great Lakes Naval Training Station and was then assigned to Bayonne, NJ and the Brooklyn Navy Yard. He was transferred to the USS *New Jersey* at the time of her recommissioning in 1950 and served on her in the 3rd Div. during the Korean Conflict. His medals include Good Conduct, United Nations and Korean with two stars.

Discharged in July, 1952, he went to work for American Viscose Corporation until 1957 and then for McKesson Drug Corporation until his disability in March, 1992. At that time, he became a fortunate and grateful heart transplant recipient and now spends a lot of time promoting organ donation. He and his wife, Eleanor, still live in Roanoke. They have two children and four grandchildren.

Glenn says, "It was an honor to serve on and be a part of BB-62's history and her distinguished career." He would like to get back in touch with his shipmates in the 3rd Div.

JAMES A. FLOOD, *see page 98.*

WILLIAM C. FOGAL, (BILL), born in Brookfield, OH, Nov. 28, 1925. Reared in West Middlesex, PA until entering U.S. Navy on Jan. 18, 1943 at Pittsburgh, PA.

Went through the Great Lakes, NTS for boot camp. Was stationed at Philadelphia Navy Yard and assigned as part of the commissioning crew of the USS *New Jersey* on May 23, 1943.

Served aboard the *Jersey* during the shakedown and participated on all of the major campaigns in the Pacific. He was discharged from Seattle, WA in Jan. 31, 1945.

Worked for Westinghouse Electric Corp. for 26 years.

Married in 1948 to Lela for 43 years until death.

Remarried in 1992 to Barbara, a widow, together they have eight children and 10 grandchildren.

They have lived in CO since 1978. They are retired and enjoy traveling about the country.

He and his hobbies are being a handyman and woodworking.

EDWIN M. FOGELSON, was born in Franklin, NJ, Nov. 1, 1927. Entered the service, USNR, V-6, Dec. 30, 1944 and Nov. 10, 1950.

Stationed at Navy Training Station, Sampson, NY; USS *Croatan* CVE-25; USS *Corregidor* CVE; USS *New Jersey* (BB-62); Nov. 20, 1950-July 19, 1952.

His memorable experience: When on USS *Croatan* they were acting as troop ship and brought back all of Gen. Patton's belongings from France. Also when the USS *New Jersey* dropped anchor in Wonson Harbor and they were fired on by the North Koreans. He was not to far from the crewman who was killed.

Awarded the American Campaign Medal, EAME Campaign Medal, WWII Victory Medal, National Defense Service Medal, Korean Service Medal with two Battle Stars, United Nations Service Medal, Republic of Korea Presidential Unit Citation.

Discharged July 6, 1946 as F1/c. July 19, 1952, CSSN. U.S. Naval Reserve in 1966.

Married to Marilyn for 41 1/2 years. She died on Dec. 21, 1993. They had sons: Dr. Brian D. and Scott. Daughters: Renee'L, and Sondra L. Grandsons Stephen and Daniel and a granddaughter, Catherine (Katie).

He retired from sporting goods business in Newton, NJ in 1987. Member of Battleship New Jersey Museum Society since 1976. Past president of USS New Jersey Veterans, Inc. Reunion coordinator, secretary/treasurer. Member since 1981. Living in Port Orange, FL since 1988.

CHARLES W. FRANK, A/S, V-1, 1939, graduate Tulane NROTC 1943. Served and was a plank owner on USS *New Jersey* May 1943-December 1945. Fifth Divs. JO, then 7th Div. officer. Starboard catapult officer, and deck watch officer. Continued in the surface naval reserve. Won district competition as C.O. Naval Reserve Surface Div. Large 8-29, 1950, 1951, and 1952. His division won National Naval Reserve Competition in 1952 (628 divisions competing).

Awarded the James Forrestal Memorial trophy. Commanded the Naval Reserve Surface Battalion 8-1 and finally served as chief staff officer Group Command 8th Naval District. Retired with rank of captain and 26 years of satisfactory federal service.

LEO S. FRATIS, TM3/C, born Nov. 19, 1931, Philadelphia, PA. Served aboard USS *New Jersey* (BB-62) from 1952 through December 1953. He was in the 1st Gunnery Div., and later transferred to the Communication Div. Summer of 1952 went on a midshipmen cruise to Cherbourg, France, Lisbon, Portugal and Cuba. Left March 1953 for Korea, where they were involved in numerous coastal shelling attacks. Other places visited were Hong Kong, Sasebo and Yokosuka, Japan, Hawaii, and Panama.

He was awarded the National Defense Service Medal, Korean Service Medal with two Battle Stars, Presidential Unit Citation, and China Service Medal.

Following his discharge, December 1953, returned to work at the Frankford Arsenal, Philadelphia, until it's closure March 1977. Transferred to Picatinny Arsenal, Dover, NJ served as deputy to the Command Inspector General until retirement June 1989. He lives in Stroudsburg, PA with his wife Barbara. They have two sons and a daughter.

DONALD M. FROST, was born at Bar Harbor, ME May 18, 1927. Entered WWII Dec. 15, 1944. Korea, Oct. 1, 1950. Served in the Navy as FN1/c, Eng. Div.

NTS Sampson, NY 16 weeks; Basic Eng. at Gulfport, MS eight weeks; USS *Change* AM-159; USS *Invade* AM-254, during WWII. Reserve call up for 10 months on USS *New Jersey*.

He got married on call up. Took part in recommission. Aboard when shelled at Wonson. Regular WWII Asia-Pacific Medals. Wonsan Bay incident. Received one Bronze Star in Korea.

Discharged from WWII July 29, 1946 and Korea July 25, 1951. Achieved the rank of FN1/c.

Married to Mollie and has children Nykki, Paula and Thomas. Grandchildren of Nykki's, Christopher and Michelle.

Retired from a tele-comm job in a laboratory, working part-time at that job. He is also a Ham Radio operator "KI WJY".

CHARLES E. GASSER, was born in Owensboro, KY, Dec. 6, 1932. Entered the U.S. Marine Corps July 8, 1950. Also served in the U.S. Air Force, 0311, 2nd Div.

Stationed at Paris Island, Korea, Hqs. EUCOM, Paris, France, Henderson Hall, Camp Lejeune, Armed Forces Pol., Washington D.C.; Manzano B. Albuquerque, NM; Lindsey Air Station Wiesbaden, Germany; Joint Chiefs of Staff-Pentagon, Washington, DC.

Awarded the Korean Campaign, Good Conduct Medal, Navy Occupational Service Medal, National Defense Service Medal, United Nations Service Medal, AF Longevity Service Award with one Bronze Oak Leaf Cluster.

Retired July 31, 1970. Joined U.S. Capitol Police Force, August 1970. Retired November 1992.

Married to Mary L. Gasser and they have two sons, Dwaine and Neal. Gasser died Dec. 2, 1993.

RICHARD E. GEORGE, USS *New Jersey* (BB-62), EM1/c, born June 4, 1925, Los Angeles, CA. Joined the Navy March 27, 1943, went through boot camp at San Diego NTS. Attended Electrical School at the University of Minnesota (four months), followed by eight months of training in Shipboard Interior Communications at the Navy Yard, Washington, DC.

Joined the *New Jersey* crew in September, 1944, at Pearl Harbor. The ship participated in many major campaigns as Admiral Halsey's flagship. In May, 1945, the *New Jersey* returned Stateside for major overhaul at Bremerton, WA. They sailed from Bremerton in July, then after war's end, dropped anchor in Tokyo Bay for occupation duty until February, 1946.

He was discharged April 18, 1946 at San Pedro, CA, then graduated from UCLA School of Electrical Engineering in 1950. Following a 40-year career, specializing in the design and development of electrical measuring instruments and systems, he retired in July 1990 from the Fluke Corporation of Everett, WA. He now resides in Las Vegas, NV with is wife, Hilda. They have one son, a financial consultant with Merrill Lynch, and two grandsons.

CHARLES E. GIBB, RMC, Flag Allowance COMSEVENTHFLT, USS *New Jersey* (BB-62), 1953. Born Nov. 16, 1926, Rochelle Park, NJ. Joined the Navy Dec. 13, 1943. After Radio School in Boston, was assigned to the USS *Laub* (DD-613) and experienced combat operations in northern Italy in WWII. During peacetime, he served on USS *Portland;* COMSEVENTHFLT (USS *New Jersey);* USS *Hector;* staff, COMDESRON 5.

Commissioned as a lieutenant jg in the Navy in 1963. He served with Beach Jumper Unit One. Received the Navy Commendation Medal, with Combat V, for his action as officer in charge of a special operations unit in Vietnam in 1965. Later served as the operations officer for Commander Special Warfare Group Pacific. The last tour of duty he was assigned as the communications officer, USS *Little Rock* (COMSIXTHFLT). Retired as lieutenant in 1969.

After the Navy, he went to college and graduated from three universities, obtaining his Ph.D in 1976. He later was a consultant for local governments. Now, in his retirement years, he writes novels, completed two, but has yet to be published. He is now living in San Diego with his wife, Yvonne. They were married 45 years in 1995.

JAMES B. GOSSETT JR., PHM3/c, born Nov. 7, 1925, Atlanta, GA, joined the Navy on his 17th birthday, November 1943. Went through

boot camp in Bainbridge, MD Hospital Corp. School, Bainbridge, MD. Duty stations U.S. Naval Hospital Quantico, VA and assigned to the *New Jersey,* September 1943. Served and participated in all campaigns from the Marshall Islands to Tokyo, Japan. Was one of the youngest sailors aboard ship at the age of 17. Discharged March, 1946. Recalled to active duty June, 1951. Served with the 2nd Marines during the Korean War. Discharged November 1952.

Had already joined the Atlanta Fire Department May in 1947. After Korean War, returned to the Atlanta Fire Department and rose through the ranks to division chief. Retired after 35 years with Atlanta Fire Department. Appointed as Public Safety Director for the City of Douglasville, GA. Retired from the position March 1991. Lives in Douglasville, GA with wife of 48 years. Has one son who served with the Navy Sea Bees in Vietnam. His son is now with Fulton County Fire Department. He also has one granddaughter who resides with him and attends Mercer University.

DONALD E. GRANT, born July 15, 1925 in Manchester, NH. Raised in Hillsborough County, NH.

Enlisted in the Navy June 1942 on graduation from high school. Trained at USN Construction Battalions Training Center, Camp Peary, VA. Received Advanced and Combat Training at USMC Camp LeJeune, NC.

Joined 14th USNCB (SeaBees) at Camp Parks, CA (1943), and shipped out to USMC Air Station at Ewa, Oahu. Made beachheads with 3rd Marine Div. on Eniwetok, Saipan/Tinian (1944) and Okinawa (1945) Islands. Served as Hqts. Co. Clerk and Armory Keeper (on Okinawa) until war's end. Discharged as GM2/c in April, 1946.

Attended University of New Hampshire 1946-1948. Married November 1947 and worked in light electronics industry while continuing education. Re-enlisted in the Navy during the "hard times" and served aboard the USS *Dayton* CL-105, USN Submarine Base at New London, CT and the *New Jersey* (1950-1952); (S-2 Div./GSK, Trunk 5). Participated in the Korean campaign and a European cruise (Haiti, France and Portugal). Discharged in October 1952 and went to work in USAF missile systems at Raytheon and Avco Corporations before joining NASA in 1986. Currently traveling the world out of the NASA Flight Facility in Wallops Island, VA where he worked in the Safety Department as a rocket fuels specialist. No intentions of retiring.

Memorable experiences: (1) Studying the local culture whereever he was. Even in the Pacific Islands. Everywhere was so different from New Hampshire. (2) Photographing the nine-gun salvos off Wonsan, Korea. He has a color slide that won all competitions for years.

Awarded the Pacific Theater with three stars, Unit Commendation with two stars, WWII Victory, Korean Campaign and GCM with star.

He and his wife Barbara have raised seven well-traveled children of their own and a dozen or so foster/troubled children. Two of four sons have served in the military: Mike on the USS *Saratoga* and Doug with the 3rd Div., USMC. All are in engineering, including one daughter who is a corporate VP.

WAYNE K. GREENLEAF, was born in Passaic, NJ, March 15, 1945. Entered the USNR March 19, 1962 and served as drilling reservist. Served on USS *New Jersey,* 4th Div. officer (lieutenant jg.).

USS *New Jersey* September 1967 to July 1969 (pre-commissioning and duty afloat).

USS *St. Louis* July 1969-March 1970 (pre-commissioning and duty afloat).

As drilling reservist after active duty.

He had several commands both in New Jersey and Pennsylvania.

All awards related to USS *New Jersey* Vietnam deployment.

Retired Sept. 1, 1992 with 30 years. Captain.

Married to Loretta and has children, Wayne Jr., Dawn, Alyson and Tara.

Presently Human Resources manager Jersey Center Power and Light Co., Morristown, NJ.

Now living in Rumson, NJ.

BRUCE F. GREER, USS *New Jersey* BB-62, Storekeeper 3rd Class, born Aug. 23, 1930, Nashville, TN. Joined Navy June 20, 1951. In boot camp NTC San Diego, CA. Was assigned to naval overseas Air Cargo Terminal, Tokyo, Japan. Spent two years shore duty. Most of this time was during the Korean Conflict. Oct. 12, 1953 he was transferred to the USS *New Jersey* along with four other buddies Del Karnes, Jim Moore, Charles Murray and Lonnie Starr. Returned to States via Pearl Harbor, Long Beach, Panama Canal, GITMO and Norfolk, VA and some leave. Made cruises to Vigo Spain, Cherborg, France. Along with midshipmen from the Naval Academy he left the *New Jersey* June 2, 1955 for discharge from the Navy. Spent four years in inactive Naval Reserve for a total of eight years.

Retired from Wilson Sporting Goods after 30 years in 1985. Retired from Chapman Drug after six years. Married and has daughter and two grandchildren.

ORAL A. HARDY JR., ENDFN, was born Aug. 22, 1927 in New Vineyard, ME. He enlisted Aug. 24, 1944, left for boot camp Sept. 29, 1944, NTC, Sampson, NY, then to the Navy Training Center (Basic Eng.) in Gulfport, MS.

Oral went aboard the USS *Denebola* (AD-12) February 1945, working in the boiler room until she was decommissioned Spring of "46". He was transferred to the LST 707, working as an electrician's helper until her decommission in June 1947. He received a honorable discharge July 14, 1946, but remained in the Navy Reserves.

Oral was recalled Sept. 29, 1950, when he went aboard and recommissioned the USS *New Jersey* (BB-62). He worked with small boats and refrigeration until again receiving an honorable discharge May 22, 1952, from the Navy.

He received the Korean Service Ribbon with one star and the United Nations WWII Victory, American Theater and the Asiatic-Pacific medals.

Oral was married June 18, 1949, and has two sons, a daughter and three grandchildren. He is enjoying retirement after 20 years as head custodian at a local high school. He is a member of the VFW and The American Legion. He enjoys upholstery and craft projects.

Memorable experiences:

"The difference between a fairy tale and a sea story ... A fairy tale starts with — "Once upon a time" and a sea story starts with —"This is no B.S."...

A day to remember . . . was the first day aboard the *New Jersey* (BB-62), recommissioning at Bayonne, NJ for Korea. Three of them went from Boston to Bayonne that day. After being on the AD-12, a rebuilt banana boat with three or four holes and on a LST, they went sightseeing on the BB-62. They got lost bigger than hell, down inside #1 turret and into #2 with all open rounded compartments. Four decks down, they found a phone and called the quarter desk. Their own division First Class was O.D. and top rank of the 150 men on board at that moment. He asked what frame # they were at - but there was no # showing under the new paint. He was real kind by sending a Gunner's Mate Stricker down to find them. The Stricker handed him the end of a string with instructions to rewind the string as they followed it back to the quarter deck. The Gunner's Mate was quickly out of site. They did as instructed reaching the Quarter Deck with a six pound ball of string. They received a round of applause for a job well done from all personnel waiting on the Quarter Deck.

It was well worth the razzing for the remainder of the trip. They always had a drink waiting at every bar from Bayonne, Brooklyn, Gitmo, Panama, Hawaii, Japan, San Diego, and Portsmouth, VA. He found it hard to believe, half way round the world and back, he would meet someone from the original 150 men.

HAROLD W. HARMON, USS *New Jersey* (BB-62), Ensign, Ltjg, born Feb. 23, 1928, Lexington, SC. Enlisted in the Navy January, 1946 and completed boot camp in San Diego. He served in the deck force aboard the USS *Arequipa* (AF-31) in Japan and China. He was discharged in November, 1947. He entered the NROTC program at the University of South Carolina and graduated on Jan. 26, 1953 with a degree in Mechanical Engineering and was commissioned ensign. He reported aboard the USS *New Jersey* in Norfolk in February and the ship left immediately for Korea. The combat tour in Korea included the winter and spring offensive periods in 1953. The *New Jersey* fired the last shot, from a U.S. Navy vessel, in the Korean War, on July 27, 1953, in Wonson Harbor. He served on the *New Jersey* two years in the Gunnery Department as the Sixth Div. officer. He was also qualified as officer of the deck underway and in port.

Upon his release from active duty in February, 1955, he continued his service in the Naval Reserve for 29 years. He was promoted to the rank of captain on July 1, 1977. He served in many key assignments and had four commands. The last major command was as commander of the Atlantic Fleet Training Command 107. He also served three years (1978-1981) on the staff of the Naval Reserve Readiness Command Region Seven, Charleston, SC. He retired on June 30, 1984.

During his active and reserve career Capt Harmon has been to sea on 17 Navy ships. The ship that he continually admires the most and had the most profound effect on his career, in the areas of patriotism, motivation and discipline, was the USS *New Jersey*. His awards include nine service medals and several citations and commendations.

His civilian career of over 38 years, was spent at the Savannah River Plant, Aiken, SC. The plant made major nuclear components for the hydrogen weapons. The first 34 years was with E.I. DuPont and he progressed from engineer to area superintendent in various management positions. The remaining four years with Westinghouse as manager of a project liaison group. He retired Sept. 30, 1993.

Capt. Harmon married Retha Black Harmon on Dec. 5, 1953 while serving aboard the *New Jersey*. They have three children: Melinda in Charleston, SC; Cynthia Harmon Yascavage and Michael in Aiken. The Harmons have lived in Aiken, SC 38 years.

FLOYD P. HARRISON, USS *New Jersey.* (BB-62), S1/c, born Oct. 18, 1927, Picayune, MS. He grew up in Baton Rouge, LA. Joined the Navy in June of 1945, with basic training at San Diego, CA. He took amphibious training at Coronado, CA. His amphibious unit broke up in Japan and on Dec. 3, 1945 was assigned to the 3rd Deck Div. of the *New Jersey*. The ship left for Stateside in late January. It spent time in Long Beach, CA and Bremerton, WA. He left the *New Jersey* for discharge on July 24, 1946.

After discharge he enrolled in Louisiana State University where he stayed until 1953. He then went to the University of Maryland. He stayed there until retirement in 1990. He then moved to Central Virginia.

He and his wife, Betty, have three children, two boys and one girl. Both boys served in the military.

There are two grandchildren.

ROBERT F. HARRISON, was born in Pineville, KY, Sept. 29, 1920. Entered the USN, as GM1/c, V Div.

Stationed at Great Lakes; USS *Texas* (BB-35); USS *New Jersey* (BB-62); Advance Gunnery School; USS *Topeka* (CL-67); San Diego Destroyer Base, USS PC-1134; Philippine Sea Frontier duty in Shanghai.

Memorable experience: 600 mile trip up the Yankzer River on PC 1134 March 1946.

Awarded Asiatic-Pacific with seven stars, Philippine Liberation with two stars, American Defense, Bronze Area, American Area, EAME with one star, WWII Victory Medal.

Discharged Jan. 11, 1947 as GM1/c, USN. Married Feb. 19, 1949, widowed April 17, 1992.

Owns a small golf shop since 1980.. Sold Ford autos for 25 years. Commercial fisherman for seven years.

WILLIAM P. HARVEY, S3/c, born in Wheeling, VA, April 8, 1925. Joined the USN on Dec. 26, 1942. Went through boot's at the Great Lakes Naval Training Station, CO 114-G.E. Miller - C.S.P. CO, Com'd. From boots, where his first assignment was steam cleaning garbage cans, he was assigned to the Philadelphia Naval Station to await the commissioning of the USS *New Jersey*. Philadelphia was the best liberty town in the U.S. Was proud to be a part of the commissioning crew, May 23, 1943. Worked in G.S.K. amid ship first, then was transferred to Prov. Aft, later. The S. Div. had a hard working

crew. His first battle station was 20mm. Remember the day one little 20mm brought down a "Betty". Coming out of nowhere. Last battle station was the forty's by the crane, aft. Vividly remember the first kamikaze plane, burning badly, still trying to get to them or the *Iowa*.

His most memorable day was the day they used Mille Atoll for target practice. As the shells were splashing close by, he was in hiding, behind #3 turret. Left the beautiful lady in December 1944, awaiting the securing of Okinawa. Was one of the first 25 Navy men assigned to the island. They were sent there to start a N.S. Depot. The Army tried to kick them off, but Nimitz saw to it they stayed. It was N.S.D. #3256, Okinawa. Was on the island when the typhoon hit in 1945. It devastated the island. Had the privilege to visit the *New Jersey* while she was anchored in Buckner Bay. Finished his war days on the island, but one of those chosen to be froze, and was sent to Treasure Island, in the dispersing office. Got to like San Francisco as a liberty town, also. Was discharged on March 3, 1946 from Shoemaker, CA. His parents had moved from Cuyahoga Falls, OH, to Stanford, CT, so he crossed country by train.

Not liking Connecticut, he returned to Akron, OH to marry Eva Youtzy on July 10, 1948.

They have four children, and seven grandchildren. Retired as a life member of the International Brotherhood of Painters and Allied Trades, after almost 40 years at the glazing trade. After retiring, they moved from Cuyahoga Falls, to Mount Gilead, OH. Found employment with McDonalds Restaurant in Mt. Gilead, as a host and counter person. Really enjoying his work, and the people of Morrow County. Will always be grateful for having been picked to serve on such a great ship. His prayer is now to see her sleep in peace.

JOHN J. HAYES, USS *New Jersey* (BB-62), Lt(jg), born Feb. 27, 1944 in Detroit, MI. Joined the U.S. Naval Reserve in April, 1966. After graduating from Michigan State University with a BA degree, reported for active duty in August, 1967 at the Officer Candidate School in Newport, RI. Volunteered for and assigned to USS *New Jersey* in October, 1967.

Attended various Navy schools until reporting aboard USS *New Jersey* in March, 1968 at Philadelphia, PA. Served as a Secondary Btry. plotting room officer and FA Div. Junior Div. officer. Later assigned as Weapons Department administrative assistant. From September, 1968 to April, 1969 took part in USS *New Jersey's* shore bombardment of North Vietnamese and Viet Cong positions. Released from active duty in October, 1969 at Bremerton, WA where USS *New Jersey* was being mothballed. Retired from the U.S. Naval Reserve in 1988 with the rank of commander.

Earned a MA degree from the University of Michigan in 1971 and a MBA from Michigan State University in 1976. Presently an accountant for the state of Michigan. Divorced, resides in Williamston, MI with sons Mark and Mike who are both high school students.

KENNETH A. HOBBS, RDSN (USNR), born Oct. 30, 1929, Indianapolis, IN. Joined USNR, August, 1947; activated January, 1951, and assigned to the 3rd Div. of USS *New Jersey*. Transferred to Radar School, Norfolk, in April; rejoined New Jersey in Yokahama in August; assigned to K Div. Participated in Korean operations until ship relieved December, 1951. Summer of 1952 took the NROTC cadets to France and Portugal. Discharged October, 1952 as radarman third class.

Graduate of the University of Miami in 1957, spent 10 years in insurance reporting, followed by 25 years with First Federal Savings & Loan Association, Miami, FL, retiring in 1987 as assistant vice president-accounting. Spent two years with Bloc Development; now volunteer at Wayside Baptist Church, destroyed during Hurricane Andrew in 1992, and is now almost completely rebuilt. Happily married for 37 years, three children, two grandchildren, and living in Miami, FL.

STANFORD G. HOLSONBACK, born April 6, 1925 in Langley, SC. Served in USN, April 7, 1942-Dec. 6, 1945 as electrician's mate third class.

Attended boot camp in Norfolk, April-May 1942; Electrician's School, June-September 1942; USS *New York,* September 1942-May 1943; USS *New Jersey,* May 1943-July 1945; U.S. Naval Communications Annex, Washington, DC, September-December 1945.

Memorable experience aboard USS *New Jersey:* On April 2, 1945, about 2130, while on watch as bridge electrician, orders were given to him to turn on the side lights, (green on starboard and red on port). The destroyer *Franks* was changing position, but was on a collision course with them and the distance was closing rapidly! It was almost dead ahead and seemed almost parallel to them. Just after he had turned on the lights and checked to see that they were burning and was about to report they were, there was a tremendous banging at the bow, and sparks flying upward. The apprehension rose, since he didn't know at what angle they had collided. He was relieved to learn that injuries on the *Franks* were at a minimum-but-their skipper died a day later. His death was not caused by combat, but still in the line of duty. Skill, responsibility, and alertness are always a must - even though the events seem routine. Hats off, to all of you who did a great job!

Attended college, 1947-1951; Seminary, 1951-1954. Served as minister 30 years from 1954-1994. Public school teacher 1958-1983.

Now retired living in Augusta, GA. His wife Marianne is a retired physician's assistant. Chaplain of USS New Jersey Veterans, Inc. since 1986.

His hobbies include, travel, reading naval histories, health spa, and vegetable gardening.

JOSEPH A. HOPKINS, USS *New Jersey* (BB-62), YN3, born April 18, 1925, Akron, OH. Joined the Navy, Jan. 8, 1943, went through boot camp at Great Lakes Naval Training Station. Was assigned to USS *New Jersey* May 23, 1943 to the 5th Div. as a gunner's mate striker. After scrubbing decks, wiping bulkheads became striker for yeoman. Assigned as chaplains yeoman. Promoted YN3. Participated in the famous Turkey Shoot and all operations until transferred on Feb. 3, 1945 to Fleet Replacement Pool Okinawa.

Re-enlisted on Okinawa Jan. 4, 1946.

Retired from U.S. Navy July 1962. Believe to be one of the first to receive Captain's Mast from Capt. Carl Holden while serving on the *Jersey*. Loss of three liberties which the captain excused when ship arrived in Trinidad for shakedown cruise before departing to the Pacific Theater.

Now living in Hainesport, NJ enjoying ten grandchildren and three great-grandchildren.

GEORGE F. HOPWOOD, USS *New Jersey* (BB-62), EM1/c, born March 28, 1920, New York, NY. Joined the Navy, Nov. 9, 1942. Went through boot camp at Great Lakes Naval Training Center. Assigned to USS *New Jersey*. Attended the commissioning of the USS *New Jersey* on May 23, 1943. Enjoyed many good Philadelphia liberties and shakedown cruises and on Jan. 6, 1944, they squeezed through the Panama Canal. Participated in all major Pacific campaigns starting Jan. 29, 1944, with the Kwajalein operation and ending with the dropping of anchor at Yokosuka Naval Base, Japan, Sept. 16, 1945.

His most memorable experience was Dec. 23, 1944, as he was talking with a group of shipmates while at anchor in Ulithe, just forward of the starboard catapult, he was advised by a passing shipmate that he had received mail. At which time the entire group broke for mail call. Moments later a five inch shell went through the deck at the exact spot where they were standing. Had it not been for the letter he received from his sweetheart, Marie, they would have all been casualties. On May 16, 1995, he and Marie will be celebrating their 50th wedding anniversary.

Discharged Oct. 18, 1945.

Worked for New York Telephone Company, 35 years and retired December 1979.

Residing in Mesa, AZ. They have four sons, Thomas, George, James, Martin and five grandchildren.

JOHN R. HORAN, was born in Brooklyn, NY, March 27, 1924. Entered service Nov. 13, 1942. Served in the USNR, C.S. Div.

Stationed at NTS Great Lakes, 1942; NTS Signal University of Chicago, 1943; USS *New Jersey*, 1943.

His memorable experience includes serving on the best ship in the U.S. Navy.

Awarded the American Theatre, Asiatic-Pacific, one Silver and four Bronze Stars, Philippine Liberation, two Bronze Stars, Victory Medal and the Good Conduct.

Discharged Jan. 11, 1946 from Lido Beach, NY as SM3/c.

Married to Mary and they have a daughter Sharon, and grandchildren Brett and Brandon.

Retired after 40 years with Getty Oil Company.

GEORGE MATT HOWARD, born in Pittsburg, KY, June 11, 1923. Entered the Navy, January 1943. Served in USNR, 5th Div., on USS *New Jersey*.

Stationed in Great Lakes Training Station; Philadelphia Navy Yard. Commissioned *New Jersey* and assigned aboard ship. Left ship in Bremerton Navy Yard, August 1945. Transferred to Norfolk Navy Yard, Shore Patrol duty until December 1945.

His memorable experience includes the war in the Pacific.

Discharged December 1945 as gunners mate third class.

Married to Tootsie and they have four sons, six grandchildren.

Howard attended college on the GI Bill. He is a doctor of chiropractic. Practices every day except Sunday.

ALVA RAY HUDSON, born Nov. 23, 1924 in Raymondville, TX.

Joined the Navy Nov. 10, 1942. Went through boot camp at Great Lakes Naval Training Station.

Was assigned to U.S. Naval Yard Jan. 9, 1943 as S1/c, which is the Armed Guard and Merchant Marine ships. He boarded the SS *John D. Archbold,* a Merchant Marine oil tanker Jan. 31, 1943. They made five trips across the North Atlantic delivering oil to Glasgow, Scotland through Nov. 24, 1943.

He boarded the USS *New Jersey* Nov. 24, 1943 at Portland, ME. They crossed the Panama Canal Jan. 7, 1944 to the South Pacific. They were in all major campaigns until the surrender of Japan.

He rated two Silver Stars for the European operation, two Silver Stars for the Philippine operations, and nine Silver Stars for the Asia operation. He left the *New Jersey* Dec. 14, 1945 at Tokyo and was discharged Jan. 12, 1946 at Camp Wallace, TX. He married Evelyn Bolton July 10, 1948 at Kingsville, TX. They have three daughters, six granddaughters and one grandson.

He retired Jan. 1, 1994 and now lives at Valley Mills, TX.

DALE M. HUDSON, USS *New Jersey* (BB-62), PNA2, USNR-R, born Oct. 3, 1934 in Stuart, FL. Attended the University of Florida from 1952 until 1955. Graduate of Florida School of Banking at University of Florida 1972. Went on active duty in January 1955 in the U.S. Navy serving on the *New Jersey* for two years with cruises to the Caribbean, Northern Europe and the Mediterranean, participating in the NATO sea exercises with the 6th Fleet, and taking midshipman from Annapolis for two summer training cruises. Served aboard the USS *Tills* (DE-748) and USS PC-1078 during reserve cruises to South America and Caribbean.

In his 38 year career in banking, he worked in every area of the bank, specializing in his earlier years in the operational areas. Has extensive knowledge of the many aspects of investment management. Continuing in his career in banking as chairman of the First National Bank and Trust Company of the Treasure Coast, president of Seacoast Banking Corporation of Florida, president of South Branch Building, Inc. and is a director of Suite 100 Investment Services, Inc. Currently he is serving on the board of directors of the Florida Bankers Association.

He devotes much of his free time to community services and St. Mary's Episcopal Church including past senior warden, currently serving on the Vestry and is past president of Saint Michael's School serving on the Board of Trustees for 17 years. He married the former Mary Jane Thurlow in 1961 and they have three children: Dale, Jr., Jane, and Stephanie.

He is past commodore of the board of governors of the Snug Harbor Yacht Club. Past secretary/treasurer of the Crossroads Yacht Club, a member of the Stuart Sailfish Club and the United States Power Squadron and the USS New Jersey (BB-62) Veterans Association.

CHARLES A. HUNTINGTON, Engineman/Fireman, born April 11, 1934, in Chicago, IL. Entered the Navy, May 14, 1951. Stationed at Great Lakes Naval Training Station. Falt Act, Yokosuka, Japan, two years; USS *New Jersey* A Div. He participated in no battles.

Awarded the National Defense Service Medal, United Nations Service Medal, Korean Service Medal.

Discharged April 6, 1955 at Navsta, Norfolk, VA.

After leaving the Navy he moved to Chicago and went to work for International Harvester. He worked there until 1961. He then went to work for the Chicago Fire Department. He's still working for the Chicago Fire Department as a fire engineer. He'll retire in three years.

He and his wife have been married for 39 years. He has two sons, two daughters and six grandchildren.

THOMAS R. IHNKEN, USS *New Jersey* (BB-62), QM2/c, born Oct. 31, 1933, Staten Island, NY. Joined the Navy on May 1, 1952. After boot camp at Bainbridge, MD he was assigned to the *Jersey* and was on board during the second cruise to Korea in 1953.

His duties in the Navigation Div. included assisting the navigator in planning and directing the ships course. Special duties included: Sea and Anchor detail, helmsman and helmsman while refueling/replenishing at sea.

One memorable day was May 27, when the ship was in Wonsan Harbor, Korea and was fired on from North Korean gun emplacements ashore. Captain Welson on the bridge shouted, "All engines aboard flank, Commence firing to starboard." With that all starboard 5" mounts and the 16" guns started firing.

He left the *Jersey* in April 1956 and was discharged. In 1958 he went to work for IBM and 33 years later retired.

He is now living in Pompton Plains, NJ with his wife of 34 years, Ann. They have five children and five grandchildren. Tom enjoys all sports, plays golf and has been a New York Giant football season ticket holder since 1956.

DELNO B. JACKSON, born Hendersonville, NC July 3, 1927. Entered the service Aug. 1, 1944, serving in the U.S. Navy. Assigned Amphibious Force, Asiatic-Pacific Area.

Stationed on USS LST 17, USS *New Jersey.*

Awarded Asiatic-Pacific with nine stars, American Area, WWII Victory Medal.

Discharged June 4, 1946.

Married and has three children, five grandchildren, four great-grandchildren.

Retired carpenter, traveling the USA.

DWIGHT S. JACOBS, JR., USS *New Jersey* (BB-62), FC2/c, born Aug. 20, 1924 at Star City, WV. Moved to Zaneville, OH 1935. Joined the Navy February 1943. Went through boot camp at Great Lakes, assigned to (BB-62). Took part in commissioning of (BB-62) May 23, 1943. Sent to Fire Control School on the (*Wyoming*). Returned in June and was assigned to Sky I (pointer) until February 1946. Discharged at Great Lakes and moved to Long Beach, CA.

Married his lovely wife, Fayann Johnson, November, 1946. They have two children, four grandchildren and four great-grandchildren.

He worked as a baker, restaurant manager

and owned two large restaurants. Now retired and attended the 50th reunion of (BB-62) and all commission and decommissioning of BB-62 on the West Coast. A very proud plank owner holding four Battle Ribbons, containing 11 stars and the Good Conduct Ribbon. (37 points).

Member of New Jersey Veterans, Inc.

JOHN C. JARRELS, was born in Mt. Crawford, VA, March 8, 1932. Entered the service Oct. 14, 1952. Served with the U.S. Navy, SA, 6th.

Stationed in Norfolk, VA. March 5, 1953, left and arrived at Yokosuka Naval Base, April 6, 1953. Joined 7th Fleet. Served in Korea action until truce signing July 23, 1953 (12:17 p.m.). Returned to Norfolk September 1953. Served one month on USS *North Hampton;* transferred to USS *Des Moines* until discharged Sept. 28, 1956.

Involved with shore bombardments cutting enemy rail lines. Vice Adm. J.J. Clark present at truce signing.

Memorable experience: Returned to Norfolk, they traveled through the Panama Canal. They got stuck and pieces of cement rolled on the deck from the locks. He has a piece of the cement as a souvenir.

Awarded Syngman Rhee Citation, Navy European Occupation, Good Conduct Medal, China Service, National Defense Ribbon, Korean Service Medal, and United Nations Service Medal.

Discharged Sept. 28, 1956 as SH3.

Worked for Reynolds Metal Company for 38 years. Retired Jan. 7, 1994. Married to Helen, a registered nurse. They have four married daughters, five grandsons, and two granddaughters.

Jarrels performs volunteer work in church and community. Enjoying life!

WILLIAM D. JARVIS, was born in Jersey City, NJ, April 9, 1923. Entered service January 1943, serving in the U.S. Navy, 2nd Div.

Stationed at Great Lakes Training Station in 1943; Philadelphia N.S. 1943.

His memorable experience includes commissioning of USS *New Jersey* (BB-62); plankowner); entering Tokyo Bay.

Awarded nine Battle Stars. All documented-history. Achieved the rank of BM2/c.

He was discharged January 1946.

Married to Catherine and they have sons, William III and Richard and four grandchildren: Richard, 22; Jennifer, 20; Jessica, 16; and Lauren, 4.

Jarvis was employed 37 years in law enforcement and retired as chief of police in 1988, township of Lyndhurst, NJ.

LINCOLN D. JEANES, USS *New Jersey* (BB-62), Lt(jg), born Feb. 13, 1931, Shreveport, LA. Sworn in as midshipman Sept. 21, 1948, completed NROTC training at University of Texas. Ordered to USS *New Jersey,* and from Aug. 4, 1952 to March 1, 1954, participated in Springboard at Guantanamo, and 7th Fleet Ops (Korea), as 5th Div. JO, including preparations for an ambush of the North Korean coastal railway train; (the train didn't run that night!). Underwent flight training at NAS Pensacola from March 10, 1954 to Aug. 7, 1954. Ordered to USS *Caperton* (DD-650) as first lieutenant and assistant gunnery officer, during Northern European cruise then Sixth Fleet Ops.

He was authorized the National Defense Service Ribbon, Korean Service Ribbon, China Service (extended), and Occupation Service (European Clasp). Released from active duty to Ready Reserves (July 10, 1955).

Attended Harvard Medical School, and later trained in Neurosurgery at John Hopkins. Engaged in private practice of Neurosurgery until 1978. More recently worked as emergency room physician at Fort Stewart, GA and in primary care at naval hospital, Jacksonville. Divorced, one son, one daughter.

HARRY M. JONES, born in Houston, TX, Nov. 12, 1923. Entered the service Jan. 10, 1943. Left home Jan. 16, 1943. Served in the U.S. Navy. He was in 7th Div. for about nine months, then he went into SS Div. He went through boot camp at Great Lakes Naval Training Station.

He was on the *New Jersey* when she was commissioned May 23, 1943 and left her on Sept. 21, 1945. He was discharged Oct. 17, 1945.

He was awarded all the awards/medals the *New Jersey* participated in January 1944 to 1945.

Retired Nov. 15, 1984. He and his wife Marjorie have been married 54 years and have two sons, Joe Ray and Gregg. They also have four grandsons: Joe, Jeff, Gregg and Jimmy. All are fine boys. They also have two great-great grandsons, Hunter and Brent.

LESTER JONES, S1/c, USS *New Jersey* (BB-62), born Feb. 22, 1922, Laurel County, KY. Joined the Navy Nov. 19, 1942. Completed boot camp at Great Lakes. Went on the *New Jersey* when it was commissioned. Reported aboard ship May 23, 1943. Stayed aboard for the duration of the war. The *New Jersey* participated in all major campaigns in the Pacific, Iwo Jima, Okinawa, Marianas, Western Pacific, Philippines, Formosa, South China Sea, Tokyo, to the occupation of Japan at the end of the war. The *New Jersey* was the flagship for Adm. Halsey part of the time.

Decorations: Oak Leaf Cluster, Philippines Liberation with two stars, American Area Campaign Medal, Asiatic-Pacific Campaign Medal with nine stars, Good Conduct Medal and WWII Victory Ribbon. He was discharged Nov. 11, 1945.

Jones married May 17, 1946. They have celebrated their 43rd anniversary. He is a Baptist and a 32nd Degree Mason. Worked for the L&N Railroad, serving as an apprentice boilermaker and boilermaker for six years. Then worked for the Navy at Naval Ordnance, Louisville, KY as a metal fabricator and supervisor until retirement April 16, 1981. He is now enjoying retirement, fishing, woodworking, and traveling.

LAWRENCE A. KALAKAUSKIS, USS *New Jersey* BB-62, BT1/c, 1967-1969, born Aug. 22, 1940, Cambridge, MA. Enlisted U.S. Navy, Oct. 1, 1957. Attended boot camp, San Diego, CA. Served on USS *Porterfield* DD-682, BT-B School, Philadelphia, PA; USS *Haverfield* DER-393 (Guam, MI); USS *Alfred A. Cunningham* (DD-752); YNG-16 Bremerton, WA; USS *New Jersey* (BB-62); BT-B School, Philadelphia, PA; USS *Constellation* (CVA-64); USS *Tuscaloosa* LST 1187; D.A.T.C. San Diego, CA; USS *Southerland* (DD-743).

Participated at QUEMOY-MATSU, Formosa Straits, Taiwan Evacuations 1958-1959; Vietnam veteran 1965-1973. Served In-Country Republic of Vietnam with the 134th Assault Helo Sqdn., 1st Air Cav., U.S. Army, January 1970 as Starboard M-60 machine gunner with two younger Army brothers in same squadron.

Retired from 20 years active service as chief boiler tech. 5, October 1977.

Employed by San Diego Gas and Electric Company as power plant operator. Residing in

San Diego, CA with wife Donna Rae, three sons, two daughters, five grandchildren.

One son, Henry A., served in Iran Ship Blockade, and participated in the Persian Gulf War with the 1st Force Recon., U.S. Marines, corporal. The September 1994 USS *New Jersey* 7th Annual Reunion at the San Diego, CA Hanalei Hotel was hosted and co-chaired by Larry (Ski) Kalakauskis.

FRANCIS W. KEENAN, joined the Navy in May 1943 and went to Great Lakes Naval Training Station for boot camp. He was in Co. 119.

Went to Philadelphia Naval Yard. Assigned to the USS *New Jersey* (a brand new ship).

He was a member of the commissioning crew.

On shakedown cruise they went to island of Trinidad. He found it to be quite a place.

They then left East Coast, and went through the Panama Canal. It was a very exciting trip.

They then went to the Pacific War Zone and he took part in nearly all major campaigns.

When the war with Japan ended, they went to the Yokosuka Naval Base, then to Tokyo Bay to watch the signing of the surrender of the Japanese Government.

Stayed on USS *New Jersey* until May then the ship returned to the USA, then to Great Lakes Training Station, to be discharged May 1946.

Awarded the Asiatic-Area Ribbon, Asiatic-Pacific Area Ribbon with nine stars, Philippine Liberation Ribbon with two stars, WWII Victory Ribbon, Good Conduct Medal, Philippine Liberation Medal, Philippine Presidential Unit Citation Badge.

Married in 1954. They have four children, (three sons and one daughter).

Keenan was a stationary engineer at a hospital in Saginaw, MI.

Retired in 1990. They have a farm, which they still live on and farm.

Enjoying going to USS *New Jersey* reunions. They also do a lot other traveling. At this time they are planning a trip to Ireland for two weeks.

RICHARD H. KERR, LCDR, USN, (Ret), was born in Edgerton, WI, June 24, 1926. Entered the U.S. Navy Nov. 8, 1943.

Served in LCT 1049 from April 1944 until December 1945 and participated in the invasion of Okinawa. During the Korean conflict served in the USS *Kenneth Whiting* (AV-14). Between then and Vietnam served in two heavy cruisers, the USS *Rochester* (CA-124) and the USS *St. Paul* (CA-73). During Vietnam served in the USS *New Jersey* (BB-62) as the admin. officer from November 1967 until decommissioning in December 1968.

Retired from the U.S. Navy as a lieutenant commander June 30, 1973 following 30 years service.

Awarded various campaign ribbons for WWII, Korea and Vietnam. Additionally was awarded the Navy Good Conduct Medal with one Silver Star, and the Navy Achievement Medal and the Combat Action Ribbon for service aboard the USS *New Jersey.*

Married with three children and 12 grandchildren.

Semi-retired, working as computer consultant for small Christian ministry.

BERNARD J. KLEIN, was born June 18, 1924 in Chicago, IL. Entered the service Jan. 23, 1943. Served in the Navy, L Div., living quarters A307L.

NTS Great Lakes, IL; USS *New Jersey* (BB-62), May 23, 1943.

Awarded the Good Conduct, Philippine Liberation with two stars, American Area-Asiatic-Pacific with nine stars, Good Conduct.

Memorable experience includes the typhoon of 1944.

Discharged Jan. 26, 1946 as coxswain.

Married to Mae and they have one son, three daughters, and five grandchildren.

Retired truck driver.

CLIFFORD H. KNUDSEN, USS *New Jersey* (BB-62), BT1/c, born May 21, 1921.

Recalled to active duty 1950, recommissioned and served on the USS *New Jersey* commencing shore bombardment in Korea. Relieved from Korea, returned to Norfolk, VA in 1952. Authorized to wear Korean Service Ribbon with one star. Honorable discharge June 3, 1953.

Enlisted in the United States Navy in Providence, RI, 1942. Completed recruit training in Newport, RI. Served on the USS *Denver* (CL-58) 1942-1946. Cruiser in the South Pacific during WWII. Ship was shelled, torpedoed and bombed. Ship was decommissioned in the Philadelphia Navy Yard in 1946.

Earned the American Area, WWII Victory, Good Conduct, Asiatic-Pacific, Philippine Liberation Navy Unit Commendation and the Japanese Occupation.

Served on the USS *Kline* (APD-120) and the USS *Hopping* (APD-51) during 1946-1947. Served on the USS *Corry* (DD-817) during 1947-1948. Honorably discharged Sept. 2, 1948.

He was married in 1952, moved to Alligerville, NY with his wife. He has five children, eight granddaughters and two grandsons. He is still fully employed in a supervisory position with the Ulster County Department of Public Works.

He is an active member with the VFW Post 8959, a member of the American Legion, Alligerville Fire Company, the USS Denver Reunion Association and the USS New Jersey Reunion Association. He enjoys traveling throughout their great country, his family and telling his Army son-in-laws what they missed on the high seas.

ANDY KOEHLER, was born in Chicago, IL in 1945. He graduated from the University of Illinois in August, 1967 and entered the US Navy in October, 1967.

Koehler served aboard the USS *New Jersey* from 1968-1969 as a DK2 during the Vietnam War. After the *New Jersey* was decommissioned, he served on board the USS *Bridget* (DE-1024) from 1969-1970, and the USS *Albany* (CG-10) from1970-1971. He was discharged in August 1971.

His most memorable experiences were his combat action during Vietnam and the first man on the moon in July 1969. He also served on board with President Nixon's son, David Eisenhower. When the *New Jersey* was decommissioned, Koehler was the only sailor transferred to Captain Peniston's next ship, the *Albany.*

Koehler has always been a bachelor and he works for the Water Department in the city of Kewanee, Illinois.

FREDERICK E. LANDIS, was born in Hartford City, IN (Oct. 9, 1922). Entered the service, Nov. 14, 1942. Served in the USN, SR S.

Boot training, Great Lakes, IL; USS *New Jersey* (BB-62); NOB, Norfolk, VA; USNR, Muncie, IN; USS *Howard W. Gilmore* AS-16, USS *Petrel* ASR-14, U.S. Navy Recruiting Station, Indianapolis, IN; USS *Brown* DD-546; USS *Brain* DD-630; USS *Prairie* AD-15.

Retired from the U.S. Navy and went to work for them in Civil Service for another 17 years.

He volunteered for a battle station topside on 40mm anti-aircraft guns because he said if someone hit him he wanted to see them.

Well, one night they were under attack along with other ships, including the USS *Hancock* CV. The *Hancock* sprayed the *Jersey* with anti-aircraft fire while firing at one of the attacking aircraft that flew into their sector.

Unknown to him his younger brother was on the *Hancock.* When they went into their favorite island for a rest his brother came over to visit with him. When the guys in the division found out he was off of the *Hancock* they wanted to throw him overboard in a jokingly way.

Retired from USN, Aug. 1, 1966 as SKC.

Married to Margaret E. Landis, and they have two sons, Paul F. Landis, and Roger E. Landis. They also have four grandchildren.

WARREN G. LATISLAW, EM1/c (T), born in Benton Harbor, MI, May 24, 1923. Entered the Navy Jan. 25, 1943.

Served on USS *New Jersey*. Participated in all battles that the *New Jersey* was in from 1942 to 1946.

Awarded the Victory Ribbon, Asiatic-Pacific Theater with nine stars, Philippine Liberation with two stars, American Theater and the Good Conduct Ribbon.

Honorably discharged Jan. 28, 1946 in Great Lakes, IL.

Lived in Zion, IL, 1946 to 1985. Retired from Johns-Manville Corp. He was a machinist with Johns-Manville for 35 years. Later moved to Constantine, MI to their home on the St. Joseph River.

Married Doris Evelyn Davison, March 28, 1953. He has one son, Larry Warren and two grandsons, Casey and Jake.

Enjoying their retirement, living on the river, and spending their winters in the Rio Grande Valley of Texas.

JOSEPH WILSON LEVERTON, JR., born in Baltimore, MD, Jan. 26, 1909 to Joseph Wilson Leverton and his wife, the former Clara Belle Robinson. Going to school in Washington, DC, he had his heart set on joining the Navy. With an appointment to the Naval Academy, he graduated with the Class of 1931.

His career spanned 35 years with duties in the USS *Augusta*, the destroyers *Tucker*, *Wasmuth* and *Laffey*, the *New Jersey*, *Fremont*, and *Truckee*. Shore duties took him to PG School at Annapolis, the War College in Newport, the Industrial College in Washington, and other jobs in DC and Norfolk. Advancement to flag rank came in 1959 with an overseas assignment to Japan as COMDESFLOT One. That interesting year was followed by responsible duties in OP06 at the Pentagon and as deputy chief of staff to CINCLANT in Norfolk. A severe heart attack in June of 1964 forced him into early retirement.

There were still 22 more good years of travel and family visits and civic activities. He never lost his love for the Navy, and relished all contacts with former classmates and shipmates. One thing he took pride in was the excellent way the USS *New Jersey* was mothballed under his supervision. He always said that was the reason the Navy took the Big J back into commission first, ahead of her sister ships.

He died Sept. 6, 1987 in the hospital at Pinehurst, NC, leaving his wife, the former Helen Bell of Atlanta, and four daughters: Joan Covell, Joyce Mauney, Kim Maher, and Debi Willis. There are now eight grandchildren and three great-granddaughters, all proud of Bill's life and accomplishments.

FREDERICK H. LINDER, was born December 7, 1924 in Lawrence, MA. He entered the Navy on February 2, 1943. Linder went aboard the *New Jersey* in early 1944 at Bremerton, WA as an AMM3/c.

His most memorable experience was during one of his first battles, at Wake Island. The Japanese fired at the ship and a 6" or 8" shell showered him with water on a miss. Suprised, he shouted: "Hey, they're firing at us!" A nearby CPO replied: "What the hell did you think they would do?"

Linder received the WWII Victory, Asiatic-Pacific, American Theatre, and Good Conduct Medals. He left the Navy in 1950.

Linder is married and has seven children, 22 grandchildren, and four great-grandchildren. He is currently retired.

LEONARD "RICK" LOERZEL, was born in Chicago, IL, Nov. 4, 1949. Entered the USN, July 15, 1968, seaman apprentice, Supply Div.

Stationed aboard USS *New Jersey* (BB-62) April 1969-October 1969. Final duty station; WSMR, New Mexico, January 1972-July 1976.

Duty stations: Great Lakes Naval Station, July 1968 to October 1968; NTC San Diego, November 1968 to January 1969; Treasure Island, San Francisco, January 1969 to April 1969; USS *New Jersey* (BB-62), April 1969 to October 1969; USS *Savage* (DER-486), October 1969 to December 1969; USS *Dale* (DLG-69), January 1970 to June 1970; NTC San Diego, June 1970 to July 1970; USS *Dehaven* (DD-727) July 1970 to January 1972; Naval Ord Missile Test Facility, WSMR, NM, January 1972 to July 1976.

His memorable experiences include was being assigned to *New Jersey*. After reading the history of the *New Jersey* you could almost feel Adm. Halsey's (and others) presence.

Discharged July 1, 1976 as YN1.

Married to Kathleen and they have one son, Jeffrey and a grandchild, Kyle, two years.

Worked in parts technical department/desktop publishing for Isuzu Motors America.

BOYD E. LONG, SKC, SS, born in Bowling Green, OH, June 29, 1929. Entered the service March 2, 1948, Nav. Comm Sta., USS *Southerland* DDR-743, Navy Prov. Ground, Dahlgren, VA; USS *New Jersey* (BB-62); Nav Res. Station, New London, CT; USS *Joseph K Taussing* (DE-1043); USS *Grand Canyon* AD-16; USS *Fort Mandan* LSD-21; Sub School, New London, USS *Irex* SS-482; Sqd. 8, Sqd. 2; USS *Billfish* (SSN-676). Served in the Korean War.

Awarded Good Conduct, 6th Award, China Service, Korean United Nations, American Defense.

Married and has eight children.

Retired today from Navy and Public School and he goes to Florida during the winter months.

JESSE J. LONGWORTH, USS *New Jersey*, S1/c, born April 9, 1924. Joined the Navy at age 18 on Jan. 25, 1943 in Dayton, OH. Went through boot camp at Great Lakes Naval Training Station.

Longworth was assigned to the USS *New Jersey* April 1943. He was in K Div. (Radar). His job at battle stations was G.S. Talker. He manned headphones and relayed information from Combat Information Center to a lieutenant commander who was the assistant gunnery officer. His General Quarters Station was Sky Aft. From this advantage location they could see everything that was happening on the starboard, port and aft sides. When the ship returned to the States at Bremerton, WA in May 1945, he became ill and was transferred to the hospital. Later ending up at the Convalescence Hospital in Sun Valley, ID. He remained there until discharged Jan. 18, 1946. After service, he attended the University of Louisville and Wittenberg College majoring in accounting. Later he opened an office and was self-employed real estate/insurance broker. He remained in that occupation until he retired in 1976 at age 52.

He and his wife Joan have five children and seven grandchildren. They still reside in Dayton, OH.

J. PETER LOUGHAN, enlisted in the regular Navy on July 9, 1942. He went to Newport,

RI for six weeks of boot camp and four months of class A Fire Control School for four months in Washington, DC in January 1943.

On completion of school in Washington he was transferred to Philadelphia in April, 1943 as crew member of USS *New Jersey* in the FA Div.

The FA Div. had the responsibility of maintenance and operation of all the AA batteries fire control equipment.

The ship was commissioned on May 23, 1943. After a shakedown cruise to Trinidad and training off the coast of Maine, the ship headed south and passed through the Panama Canal and entered the Pacific on Jan. 8, 1944.

Awarded the American Theatre, Asiatic-Pacific Theater, Philippine Liberation Medal, Philippine Presidential Unit Citation, Victory Medal, Japan Occupation Medal, 11 Battle Stars.

He was a crew member during the major Pacific operations in 1944 and 1945. He remained on the ship during occupation of Japan through Jan. 29, 1946.

He was advanced in rate to chief fire controlman on Jan. 1, 1946.

Left the ship in May 1946 to attended Advanced Fire Control School in Washington, DC.

He left the Navy Nov. 1, 1946.

Worked for IBM for 35 years and retired on March 1, 1986.

Married to Josephine and had three daughters and four grandchildren.

STANLEY C. (PETE) LUNDY, born Dec. 25, 1923, married same day in 1943, Brooklyn, NY. Joined the Marine Corps Feb. 2, 1943. Attended boot camp at Parris Island, Sea School, Norfolk, VA. April 1943, assigned to USS *New Jersey* May 4, 1943. Participated in action against the enemy until transferred to Brooklyn Navy Yard on June 30, 1945. Discharged Sept. 10, 1945 as a corporal.

While standing orderly duty on the bridge for Captain Holden he gave him a black eye by responding to a light reflecting on the water, he neglected to close his blackout curtain all the way as he was leaving his quarters. He was facing the ocean, turned and lunged at the curtain hitting the skipper. The skipper never held it against him. Lundy was his chauffeur in Philadelphia and Pearl Harbor. While at Pearl spent three days at Admiral Nimitz cottage with the skippers cook and many other officers (some of Admiral Halsey staff). While on the beach, the Marines standing guard duty would salute him (he was in a bathing suit), when they saw him in his corporal stripes they gave him hell.

He spent 38 years in the Fid & Surety Bond business. The last 19 years with American Re-Insurance Company, now located in Princeton, NJ as V.P. and F&S Bond manager. Married to Dorothy. They just celebrated their 51st wedding anniversary. They have two daughters, Chris and Nancy, and one granddaughter, Kaitlin. They all reside in Manchester, CT.

RAYMOND LYLES, born in North Carolina September 18, 1932. Entered the service April 1954, U.S. Navy, RM3, C Div. Stationed in Norfolk, VA.

Discharged in 1955. Married to Betty H. Lyles.

Employed as vocational director, Rutherford County Schools, Spindale, NC.

LAWRENCE E. LYNCH, USS *New Jersey* (BB-62) chief shipfitter, born June 20, 1921 at Hazleton, IN. Joined the Navy September 1939 at Evansville, IN. Went through boot camp at Portsmouth, RI and was assigned to the USS *Texas* in November 1939. Served in Atlantic and North African campaigns was transferred to USS *New Jersey* May 23, 1943 and took part in commissioning May 23, 1943. Participated in S. Pacific operations, starting Jan. 29, 1944.

He took great pride in his service aboard BB-62 and serving under Bull Halsey when he was aboard. He left the ship at Bremerton, WA, June 14, 1945. One thing he remembers was that on their shakedown cruise they had shipmate crushed to death during elevation of big guns. In Philadelphia Naval Yard he was much impressed with the pride, dedication and love, the Navy Yard Crew expressed during his six months duty working with them.

JAMES A. MALONEY, SN, USS *New Jersey* (BB-62), joined the Navy on a (kiddy cruise) in July 1950. Boot camp at the Great Lakes Naval Training Center (Company 210).

After radioman school at Norfolk, VA, was assigned to the *New Jersey* for three years during both Korean tours of duty. Served in C Div. as an RMSA carrying messages to the bridge in 1951. In N Div. on the signal bridge in 1952. And in FN Div. as an electrician on the 40mm guns in 1953. Honorably discharged in December 1953 upon returning to Norfolk from Korean tour #2. After discharge lived in Miami, FL. Was a police officer/lieutenant in Dade County until retirement. Now living in Florida Keys with wife Mayda. Is an active member and past flotilla commander of the U.S. Coast Guard Auxiliary. One of five children is presently serving in the U.S. Navy SeaBees.

While serving on the USS *New Jersey*, he remembers that each morning after chow he would wander down to the radio shack and tune in his favorite country western station on one of the many short wave radios there. One day, as they were entering Norfolk harbor, he followed his routine and tuned the radio. Promptly came the captains voice over the intercom shouting "What happened to my tug boat communications"? Needless to say he lost that privilege.

Places that he remember as a sailor on the *New Jersey*: The crowd sleeping on the floor at night behind the radios in the transmitter room, (one of the only air-conditioned rooms on the ship at that time). Watching the ship go through the Panama Canal from a small radio compartment high up in the superstructure. The tiny radio room inside the 16 in. thick walls on the back of the Main Bridge where he spent many hours at General Quarters. The hammocks strung on the mess deck when they carried troops to Korea.

EDWARD S. MARTIN, was born March 15, 1921 in Amsterdam, NY. He enlisted in the Navy Jan. 10, 1939 and completed basic training at Newport, RI.

He became a plankowner of USS *St. Louis* in April of 1939. The *St. Louis* was flagship for Adm. Greenshade when USA transferred 50 destroyers to the United Kingdom.

St. Louis passed through the Panama Canal on the way to Hawaii and Philippines. The ship returned to Hawaii on Dec. 2, 1941 and survived the Japanese attack on Pearl Harbor Dec. 7, 1941.

After duty around the Aleutians he was transferred to precommissioning crew of USS *New Jersey* in Philadelphia. He was a plankowner.

He was a crew member throughout all the Pacific campaigns and occupation of Japan. He was advanced in rate to chief fire controlman in 1944.

On Jan. 10, 1946 he was transferred from Yokosuka, Japan to recruiting duty in Albany, NY.

He was discharged from the Navy on March 10, 1948 and was employed by IBM for 35 years.

Ed was the recipient of American Theatre, Asiatic-Pacific, Pearl Harbor, European Philippine Liberation, Philippine Presidential Unit Citation, Victory Medal, Occupation Medal, two Good Conduct Medals, 13 Battle Stars.

He passed away in May of 1993.

JAMES CLARENCE MARTIN, Chief Petty Officer, USN, (Ret), highest rank warrant officer.

J.C. was born in Bethel, NC, Pitt County. He received his formal education in that city and county.

After his school years he entered Government Service in 1939 and enlisted in the U.S. Navy May 21, 1940, and received his naval training at the Norfolk Naval Base, Norfolk, Virginia. He had a varied and interesting naval career. He served on many naval ships and stations, including the USS *Jarvis*, USS *West Virginia*, USS *Nechess*, USS *Sperry*, USS YMS 431, USS *Boston*, USS *Fargo*, USS *Macon*, USS *New Jersey*, and the USS *Alstead*. He also was the skipper aboard a Navy Diving Tender Station at the Naval Weapons Station, Yorktown, Virginia, and skipper of a Navy Y.W. station at the Norfolk Naval Base, Norfolk, VA.

Other assignments during his career included duty at the U.S. Naval Station, Camp Perry, VA; U.S. Naval Air Station, Norfolk, VA; U.S. Naval Air Station, Chincoteague, VA; U.S. Navy Base, Greene Cove Springs, FL; U.S. Naval Weapons Station, Yorktown, VA; and the U.S. Naval Mine Warfare School, Yorktown, VA.

On Dec. 7, 1941, he was at Pearl Harbor, HI, aboard the U.S. Pacific Fleet flagship the USS *West Virginia*, a battleship. The *West Virginia* was sunk by the Japanese attack on Pearl Harbor, his ship the *West Virginia*, received seven torpedoes and two bombs. Following the Japanese raid on all naval ships and stations in Pearl Harbor he transferred to the USS *Tennessee*, another battleship, for several weeks and then transferred to the USS *Nechess*. This assignment didn't last long, as the *Nechess* was sunk in late January, 1942, in the South Pacific Ocean by Japanese submarines after a running battle for several hours. During the remainder of WWII, he was aboard several other ships of the Navy that saw action and sunk in battle in the Pacific Ocean. After the war, he was aboard one of the first ships to enter Tokyo Bay with the battleship *Missouri* for the signing of the Japanese Peace Treaty.

During the Korean War, he saw action in Korea, aboard the battleship USS *New Jersey*. This time his ship was not sunk, but came under gun fire several times by North Korean planes and shore batteries.

After retirement from the Navy with credit of 20 years, he transferred to in-active duty in the Navy Fleet Reserve to complete his 30 years naval service. After his retirement of 20 years, he initiated a second career with the U.S. Government when he entered Civil Service as a Marine navigation-seamanship instructor for the U.S. Army at Fort Eustis, VA. He fully retired from U.S. Government Service in 1973, with 34 years Federal Service, this time from the U.S. Army Civil Service at the age of 56 years old.

Participated in following battles: Pearl Harbor during the Japanese attack on Dec. 7, 1941; Wake Island, Midway, American Defense, Asiatic-Pacific, Europe-Africa-Middle East, China, WWII Occupation of Japan and Philippine Liberation, Guam, Iwo Jima, Okinawa, Korea and many more.

Awards/Medals received: All the battles as list above along with the Good Conduct Medal, Presidential Unit Citation and participated in nearly all major campaigns from Pearl Harbor on Dec. 7, 1941 to Japan in the Pacific and in Tokyo Bay when the peace treaty was signed by the Japanese, September 1945.

Since his retirement from the Navy and Federal Service he is now in his third career, this time with Peninsula Funeral Home, Inc. in Newport News, VA.

ARNOLD H. MILLMAN, USS *New Jersey* (BB-62), born Nov. 6, 1928, Providence, RI. Entered the regular Navy, June 24, 1946. Attended boot camp, Bainbridge, MD Co. 4567. Served on USS *Wisconsin* (BB-64).

Goodwill cruise to South America through Panama Canal; "Crossing the Line"; becoming a "shellback"; Midshipman cruise to England, Scotland, Norway, etc.

Served on 13+ reserve training cruises to Panama, Cuba, etc. Decommissioned USS *Wisconsin* (BB-64) in 1948. Inactive Reserve 1948-1950. Recalled to active duty to recommission the *New Jersey* (BB-62) for Korean Conflict.

Served in Korea and Japan, 1950-1952. In 1952 went back to inactive reserve and was discharged in 1953.

Every day was a memorable experience for him.

Awarded the WWII Victory Medal.

Married Marilyn Donkin, November 1952. They have on son and two grandsons.

He is a construction superintendent (active). They live on their 40 foot motor yacht, six months of the year.

J.W. MIXON, was born in Collinsville, MS, Nov. 15, 1925. Entered the U.S. Navy Sept. 14, 1943. Served on the USS *New Jersey*, 3rd Div., (is turret three). He served 2 1/2 years on the *New Jersey*.

Attended boot camp at Bainbridge, MD and then went to Norfolk, VA. He loved to tell the things that happened on the *New Jersey*. J.W. said that he had to learn to walk again after 18 months on water.

Awarded the Victory Ribbon, Philippine Liberation with two stars, Asiatic-Pacific with nine stars and the American Area.

Discharged March 21, 1946 as seaman first class in New Orleans, LA.

Married to Sarah Lee and they have a son David, two daughters, Cherryl Ann and Myra Gaye and six grandchildren, Beau, Jason, Dave, Pam, Paula and Kelli.

J.W. and his best friend drowned in small lake May 13, 1991. His family believes he drowned trying to save his friend. He had been retired four and one-half years as supervisor for Owens Corning Fiberglass Company.

JOSEPH MURRAY, USS *New Jersey* (BB-62), EM2/c, born Feb. 7, 1922 Wyndmoor, PA. Joined the Navy Aug. 5, 1942, went through boot camp at Newport, RI.

Then assigned U.S.N.T.S. Iowa State College, Ames, IA and Treasure Island, CA, for electrical training before being assigned to USS *New Jersey* April 25, 1943 before its commissioning on May 20, 1943. After its shakedown, then to the South Pacific where it became the flag ship of Task Force 58, participating in all major campaigns until Aug. 9, 1944 when he was transferred at Pearl Harbor. He was notified that on June 10, 1945, his brother Thomas PhM3/c was killed on Okinawa, while assigned to the 1st Marine Div.

He was later honorably discharged on Sept. 14, 1945. He joined the Philadelphia Police Department and retired as sergeant after 26 years. He is now living in Philadelphia, PA with his wife Rebecca. They have two sons, one daughter, five grandchildren and one great-grandchild. One son is retired from the U.S. Marine Corps.

WILLIAM O'NEILL, USS *New Jersey* (BB-62), YN3, born June 9, 1936, Trenton, NJ. Enlisted in the Navy on his 18th birthday. Went through boot camp at Bainbridge, MD. He was then assigned to battleship *New Jersey*. Went aboard just when she came back from Korea. Went to many different ports in the Mediterranean and was aboard for almost two years, until they decided to decommission her in 1956.

He had a choice of staying aboard or taking shore duty. He opted to go to SACLANT in Norfolk, VA. He stayed there until he was discharged from active duty in May of 1958. While aboard ship he worked in the damage control office.

Some of his memorable times occurred when they were under way and a bunch of guys would take their sleeping blankets and sleep under the 16" guns.

After leaving the Navy he went to work as a steamfitter and welder for local union #9 out of Trenton, NJ. Retired after 35 years at the age of 56.

Moved to Springhill, FL where he now resides with his beautiful wife Marion. He has three children, four step-children, and six grandchildren.

CHARLES OWEN, joined the Navy January 1943. Went to Great Lakes, IL and was in Camp Green Bay, Co. 121. From boot camp he was assigned to the USS *New Jersey* and served there until Jan. 1, 1946. Left the ship while she was anchored at Yokosuka, Japan. He then went back to Great Lakes for discharge, Jan. 22, 1946.

He married the same year and has three children, nine grandchildren and one great-grandchild.

He started and managed Owen Wholesale Produce until he retired in 1986, turning the business over to his two sons.

He now resides at Citrus Hill Golf Club.

MICHAEL J. PAZIENZA, AMM3/c, born July 10, 1921 in New York City. Joined the Navy on Aug. 27, 1942. Went to boot camp in Newport, RI.

His first ship was the USS *Vulcan*. He met the ship in Reykjavik Island in December 1942. After the ship returned to the U.S. he was transferred to the USS *New Jersey* in May 1943. He took part in the commissioning and the shakedown cruise, off the Caribbean. He also took part in all the Pacific campaigns, until the war ended, and was on his way home from Yokosuka Naval Base in Japan. Discharged in New York on Oct. 18, 1945.

He went to school at the Academy of Aeronautics in November 1945 and received his Airman's License, in December 1947. Went to work for United Airlines in January 1948.

On January 1951, recalled into the Navy and served on the carrier *Antietum* and took part in one full tour in Korea campaign and again returned from Yokosuka Naval Base and discharged in New York February 1952.

He went back to work for United Airlines and retired after 39 1/2 years. He is a member of USS New Jersey Veterans, Inc. and a plank owner in the Navy Memorial in Washington, DC.

He is celebrating his 50th wedding anniversary on June 10, 1995. He has three children and five grandchildren.

ROBERT C PENISTON, Capt, USS *New Jersey* (BB-62), born Chillicothe, MO, Oct. 25, 1922. Attended grade, high school, Wichita, KS and University of Wichita. Entered U.S. Naval Academy in June 1943. Graduated June 5, 1946, class of 1947. Masters degree Stanford University 1958. Naval War College graduate 1962.

Initial assignment aboard *New Jersey*. Served in destroyers *Putnam, Cone, Willis A. Lee, Nicholas* (executive officer), *Savage, Tattnall;* guided missile cruiser *Albany;* Presidential Yacht *Williamsburg* during presidency of Harry S Truman.

Commanded *Savage* (DER-386), *Tattnall* (DDG-19), *New Jersey* (BB-62), and *Albany* (CG-10). Had heart rending task of decommissioning *New Jersey* Dec. 17, 1969.

Served ashore at Recruit Training Command, Great Lakes; two tours in Bureau of Naval Personnel; aide to President Naval War College; J-3 on staff CINCLANT/ CINCLANTFLT; director Naval Education Development, Pensacola.

Married and has two children and three grandchildren. Retired June 1, 1976. Joined the staff of Washington and Lee University, Lexington, VA.

EDWARD PEREGRIN, S1/c, born Thayer, IL Nov. 3, 1923. Joined the Navy Jan. 25, 1943. Went through boot camp at Great Lakes Naval Training Station.

After boot camp, assigned to USS *New Jersey* at Philadelphia Navy Yard. Commissioned the *New Jersey* May 23, 1943. Left Philly July 8, 1943, on to Norfolk, then the Caribbean and Trinidad on shakedown cruise. Went through Panama Canal on Jan. 6, 1944 for Pacific. First strike in Marshall Islands, Jan. 29, 1943 also participated in most all major campaigns in Pacific. Anchored at Yokosuka Naval Base, Sept. 16, 1945.

Discharged from Great Lakes, Jan. 28, 1946.

Married and living with wife in Divernon, IL. They have a son, daughter and two grandchildren. Also hosted six foreign exchange students.

One of the most memorable experiences in Pacific was the typhoon of Dec. 18, 1944. At that time lost three destroyers and damaged most ships in task force.

HENRY P. PETIT, USS *New Jersey* (BB-62), BM3/c, 5th Div., born March 28, 1932, Brooklyn, NY. Enlisted Nov. 14, 1950. Attended boot camp at Great Lakes. Assigned to USS *New Jersey*, March 1951 for Korean Conflict. Promoted to BM3 1952.

1952 attended Salvage Diving School, Bayonne, NJ. Assigned to aka *Achrana* 1953.

1954 assigned to Bayonne Naval Station Master at Arms.

Discharged September 1954.

Appointed to New York Police Department Feb. 1, 1955 and retired July 1975.

Entered private sector July 1975 Republic Insurance Company as senior claims investigator.

Retired as claims manager of their New York Metropolitan District Office January 1989.

Resided in Brooklyn, NY, from birth to 1963. Moved to Deer Park, Long Island until 1989. Moved to Deltona, FL with his wife of 42 years, Joan (Holmes). They have three children, Diane Cruciata, Henry P. Petit, and Janis Sokolowski and nine grandchildren, all residents of Florida.

ROLLAND A. PITTENGER, was born July 16, 1932, in Newton, NJ. Entered the Navy Feb. 21, 1952. Served as GMSN, 7th. Stationed on USS *New Jersey* (BB-62) for two years and *Des Moines* for two years.

Awarded the National Defense Service Medal, Korean Unit Citation, China Service Medal, Korean Service Medal, UN Medal.

Discharged Jan. 31, 1956 with the rate of GMSN.

Married to Carol and they have three children, Cheryl, Dale and William. They also have a grandson Derek.

Employed in maintenance department for the school system.

PAUL B. PLAMONDON, USS *New Jersey* (BB-62), GM1/c, born May 22, 1921, Denver, CO. Joined the Navy Aug. 21, 1942. Went through boot camp at San Diego Naval Station. Attended Gunners Mate School at Great Lakes and advanced to Gunnery School in San Diego. Took part in the commissioning of the USS *New Jersey*, May 23, 1943.

After going through the Panama Canal, participated in nearly all campaigns in the Pacific starting Jan. 29, 1944 in support of air strikes at Kwajalein and with dropping anchor at Yokosuka Naval Base (Japan) Sept. 16, 1945.

He was mount captain of a 5" 38 cal. twin gun mount with the greatest bunch of men he's ever known, who were capable of firing 38 rounds (19 per gun) per minute, consisting of a 54 pound projectile and a 32 pound powder charge.

Discharged Oct. 14, 1945, Bremerton, WA. Worked 39 years in the Denver area as pattern and model maker, retiring in 1984.

Married 47 years to the same woman "Miss Denver 1940". They have three children and seven grandchildren.

Plamondon plays golf, a lot of pool and attends many of his grandchildren's sporting events.

MICHAEL PLATOW, machinist mate chief, born Oct. 18, 1913, Shenandoah, PA. Joined USN, Feb. 21, 1938. The USS *Honolulu* commissioned, one year tour to Honolulu, HI. USS *Williamsburg* formerly the Presidential Yacht. USS *Arkansas* Brooklyn Navy Yard, Scotland, Africa, Casablanca.

October 1941, training in Connecticut. March 1943 Philadelphia Navy Yard, USS *New Jersey* commissioned, served on board throughout war in Pacific.

September 1945, USS *West Virginia*. March 1946, USS *Rochester*. February 1948, Quincy,

MA, USS *Manchester*. November 1950, Philadelphia Navy Yard under Commander R. Knox, one year.

1951, Bath, ME. USS *Timmerman,* experimental ship.

1956, decommissioned the USS *Timmerman,* received master at arms, ships FLAG.

1957, USS *Kennedy,* Boston, injured.

August 1, 1958 temporary retirement.

Permanently retired June 1, 1963.

Awarded the American Theatre Medal, American Defense Medal, WWII Victory Medal, National Defense Service Medal, EAME Medal, Good Conduct Medal, Pacific Campaign Medal.

Retired to Florida in 1964 and now residing in Seminole, FL with wife, Phillippa.

After his retirement, he attended as many USS *New Jersey* reunions as possible. It was at the Nashville reunion in September 1992, that Michael Smith, also attending reunion, introduced himself and announced, "Hi Dad, "I'm your son". Mike Smith had not been told who his father was until recent years and then started to search for him. It was only upon his mother seeing an announcement of the reunion of the USS *New Jersey* in a magazine, that she told Mike his father had served upon that ship during the war. It was an emotional event to say the least.

Some amazing facts were revealed. Mike Smith, who knew nothing about his father or his naval career, joined the Navy as a young man, became a machinist mate, did not make a career of the Navy but did work in the Philadelphia Navy Yard until a transfer this year, due to the downsizing of the yard. Michael Walter Smith was born June 27, 1944. It was 48 years before Mike Platow knew he had a son, his only child. They visit as often as possible now.

BART J. PORPORA, USS *New Jersey* (BB-62), B3/c, born Dec. 3, 1932, South Ozone Park, Queens, NY. Joined the Navy, May 8, 1952 and went to boot camp at the Bainbridge Naval Training Station, Bainbridge, MD. Upon graduation, was assigned to the USS *New Jersey* and reported aboard Sept. 5, 1952, Pier 7, Norfolk, VA. This was his assignment until April 1, 1956 when his tour of duty was completed.

June 1, 1957 he was married to his lovely wife Jean. They were blessed with two children, John, born July 4, 1961 and Maryellen, born July 20, 1963. Jean, his wife of 33 years passed away in 1990.

He spent 24 years with the New York City Department of Sanitation and rose through the ranks to assistant borough superintendent and retired in 1993. He is now living in Dobbs Ferry, NY.

1994 was a busy year for Bart, both of his children were married.

JAMES A. POWELL, BT2, born Aug. 27, 1924, Augusta, GA. Joined the U.S. Navy November 1942. Went through boot camp in Norfolk, VA. for three weeks and then assigned to the Machinist School in Norfolk, VA in October of 1942. In January of 1943 was assigned to the USS *Texas,* made a short cruise escort to Europe and then was assigned, to the USS *New Jersey* (BB-62). To the Baker Div. Boiler Room #3 in the last part of April 1943. During this time he took part in the commissioning of the USS *New Jersey* (BB-62) on May 23, 1943. Was then on a shakedown cruise and training until January 1944. He was aboard the USS *New Jersey* (BB-62) until August 1945.

When the war was over he came back to the United States from Tokyo Bay, on a troop ship. Re-enlisted in the Navy for six years. He was in many a battle in the South Pacific, he also was on many ships during his Navy career of 17 years. Some of his most memorable times were: Serving under Admiral (Bull) Halsey; the typhoon Sept. 3, 1944 and the big typhoon of Dec. 18, 1944. When the fleet lost three destroyers. After the war he went back to school at the Philadelphia Naval Base and then served aboard the USS *Albany* (CA-123). Then the USS *Missouri* (BB-63). In 1947 he had the pleasure of meeting then President Harry S Truman, when the USS *Missouri* (BB-62) brought him and his staff back to the United States from South America. The President and his staff were initiated before crossing the equator heading north.

Next he was transferred to the USS *Fargo* (106). Served aboard for two years in the Mediterranean for occupation duty. Was then transferred to the USS *Shey* (DM-30), after that the USS MSO 422. In 1952, he served aboard the USS *McGowan* (DD-678), during the Korean War for nine months. Then continued on around the world cruise and returned to the U.S. in 1953 at Charleston Naval Base.

He received an honorable discharge from the U.S. Navy on Feb. 4, 1959, with physical defects to his left foot. During his successful Navy career he earned 11 Campaign Ribbons with 11 stars and a Good Conduct Medal with four stars.

After several weeks of rest went to work for the state of Georgia and retired from the state Jan. 31, 1983, after working for 25 years.

He is now 70 years old and he and his wife have settled down in Evans, GA. They are enjoying their time with their grandchildren and lots of fishing. Life has been exciting for him and he hopes it will continue to be for many more years to come.

MICHAEL F. PRIME, USS *New Jersey* (BB-62), ships serviceman 2nd class, born Oct. 13, 1948, Watertown, NY. Joined the Navy, Sept. 28, 1967. Went through boot camp at the Great Lakes Naval Training Center. Was then assigned to the USS *New Jersey*. Went to San Diego Naval Station, in January 1968 for pre-commissioning detail. In April 1968 went aboard the Big "J" in Philadelphia, PA at the Philadelphia Naval Station. Put *New Jersey* in commission in April of 1968. Went out for refresher training and then made the transit from Norfolk through Panama Canal and arrived in home port of Long Beach, CA. In September 1968, deployed to West Pac and on the gun line off of Vietnam. Had port visits in Subic Bay, Yokosuka Japan and Singapore. Finally returned to Long Beach in May of 1969.

Got word that Big J was to be decommissioned in December of 1969. In September they sailed to Bremerton, WA for decommissioning. He left Bremerton in the middle of December for three weeks leave and then reported to the USS *Bradley* (DE-1041), home ported in San Diego. He made two more deployments to Vietnam in the next two years.

He was separated from the Navy in July of 1971 and returned home to Syracuse, NY. He worked 10 years for the post office and in 1984, he joined the Oswego County Sheriff's Department. In 1975 he joined the Naval Reserve and in October of 1995 will have 20 good years. He started as a ships serviceman and in 1987 he switched over to master at arms. Made first class in 1989 while drilling at NRC Syracuse.

He married a wonderful lady named Bonnie. They have two children, Denise and Michael Sean and they reside in Fulton, NY.

CHESTER R. RADER, USS *New Jersey* (BB-62), F1/c, born Oct. 28, 1926, Richland County, OH. Drafted into service Feb. 12, 1945, USNR, and went through boot camp at the Great Lakes Naval Training Station. Was then assigned to USS *New Jersey* (BB-62) M. Div. at Bremerton, WA in April 1945. On board ship they were in Hawaii, Wake Island, bombardment of Eniwetok, Guam, Manila, Okinawa and to Yokosuka Naval Base4 in Japan to relieve the USS *Missouri* after the treaty with Japan was signed.

One of his most memorable experiences was the Pacific typhoons and liberty in Japan and the islands.

He was awarded the Pacific Campaign Medal with one star and WWII Victory Medal. Discharged July 11, 1946 at Bremerton, WA.

Worked for the Westinghouse Corporation for eight years then for the Ohio Department of Transportation for 28 years. Retired Feb. 29, 1988.

He and his wife Miriam Wolf Rader live in Mansfield, OH. They have a daughter living in Sacramento, CA, a son and one grandson.

LESTER R. RADER, USS *New Jersey* (BB-62), F1/c, born Oct. 28, 1926, Richland County, OH. Drafted into USNR, Feb. 12, 1945. Went through boot camp at the Great Lakes Naval Training Station. He was then assigned to USS *New Jersey* (BB-62) in M Div. at Bremerton, WA in April, 1945. On board ship they were in Hawaii, Wake Island, bombardment of Eniwetok, Guam, Manila, Okinawa and to Yokosuka Naval Base in Japan to relieve the USS *Missouri* after the treaty with Japan was signed.

One of his most memorable experiences was the Pacific typhoons and liberty in Japan and the islands.

Was awarded the Pacific Campaign Medal with one star and WWII Victory Medal.

Discharged July 11, 1946 at Bremerton, WA.

Worked as an auto mechanic for 43 years. He is now retired and resides in New London, OH.

Married Patricia R. Ingmand Rader and she passed away December 1990.

He has four children, Stephen, Roger, Mark and Paula and four grandchildren (three girls and one boy).

LEN RAFF, USS *New Jersey* (BB-62), EM1/c, born May 20, 1920, Brooklyn, NY. Enlisted in the Navy, Sept. 30, 1941. Attended boot camp in Newport, RI. Attended Electricians School (Hadley High School), St. Louis, MO, in 1941.

Assigned to USS *Joseph Hewes* 1942. Boat school in New Orleans to learn to run Higgins invasion boats. Took part in invasion of North Africa Nov. 8, 1942. Ran troops into the beach in LCVP (USS *Joseph Hewes* torpedoed and sunk, Nov. 11, 1942 at Fedala, Morocco).

Assigned to battleship USS *New York*. Assigned to USS *New Jersey*. Took part in the commissioning of the USS *New Jersey* May 23, 1943. Through the Panama Canal Jan. 7, 1944 to join the Pacific Fleet. Participated in all major campaigns in the Pacific until the end of the war on Aug. 14, 1945.

Discharged Oct. 18, 1945.

Worked as a projectionist on SS *America*.

Went to work for CBS News in 1949 as a news editor. He is now divorced.

He has one terrific daughter, Susan, who is a news reporter in Hartford, CT. Now living in New York City and New Fairfield, CT and still working for CBS-TV News.

JOSEPH E. RICHTER, was born in Brooklyn, NY. Entered the service March 26, 1951, U.S. Navy, regular. Attended boot training in Newport, RI, Co. 206; U.S. Naval Torpedo Station Gould Island, Newport, RI; USS *New Jersey*.

Served three years on the BB-62.

Participated in several offenses in Korea. Received Presidential Unit Citation, Korean and Formosa Blockade.

Discharged March 24, 1955 as lithographer third class.

Married to Barbara and they have three children and nine grandchildren.

Richter is a retired educator and is now teaching at CCNY, Department of Secondary Education.

PAUL E. ROBBINS, USS *New Jersey* (BB-62), GM3/c, was born in Fremont, IA, on Feb. 15, 1925. He went to boot camp at the Great Lakes Naval Training Station before joining the Navy on Jan. 21, 1943. A few months after joining the Navy, on May 23, 1943, he took part in the commissioning of the USS *New Jersey*. Paul, and the *New Jersey,* left Marshall island on Jan. 29, 1944, and participated in nearly every campaign until the *New Jersey* dropped her anchor at Yokosuka Naval Base (in the heart of Japan) on Sept. 16, 1945. During this time in the Pacific,

Paul met up with three of his brothers, in brief but happy reunions.

He was discharged on Feb. 19, 1946. He is now retired and lives in Omaha, NE, with his wife, Mary. They have four children and one grandchild.

MANUEL ROCHA (MANNY), was born Jan. 17, 1927 in Stockton, CA. He enlisted in the USN in January 1944. Boot camp was at Sampson, NY; Amphibious training at Little Creek, VA; picked up LSM-30 at Galveston, TX in July 1944. He saw action at Lingayen Gulf, Okinawa and Japan.

Back to the States after some leave, reassigned to duty as master at arms, Pearl Harbor receiving station in 1946. Reported aboard USS *New Jersey* (BB-62) in 1947. Onboard the *New Jersey* he made cruises to Scotland, Norway and England with 1,000 midshipmen and about 800 crewmen 2nd Div.

He received an honorable discharge in November 1947 as BMG3 and returned as an aircraft engine mechanic helper at NAS Quonset Point, RI in 1948. He was then transferred to NAS South Weymouth, MA and retired as aircraft inspector in 1982. He worked as a field service technician for Beech Aerospace from 1984-1987; was a police dispatcher for the Raynham Police Department in 1988; worked with U-Haul sales and service from 1989-1990 and retired in 1990.

Manny spent 34 years in the Naval Air Reserve and retired as CPO (ADC).

He married Beatrice in 1948 and they have one child, Lynn. He was the founding president of the National LSM Association from 1989-1992.

WALLACE N. SAIN, USS *New Jersey* (BB-62), S1/c, born in Washington, DC Feb. 13, 1925. Began boot camp at Great Lakes Naval Training Station on Nov. 3, 1942. Was then assigned to Purdue University for electrical school. In 1943, was assigned to the USS *New Jersey* at Philadelphia Navy Yard. Took part in the commissioning on May 23, 1943. After some good Philadelphia liberty and a shakedown cruise to Trinidad, B.W.I., the *New Jersey* went to Boston, Portland, ME and Norfolk Navy Yard, then to the Pacific via the Panama Canal. They participated in nearly all of the major campaigns in the Pacific, starting Jan. 29, 1944, in support of air strikes at Kwajalein, and ending with the dropping of the anchor at the Yokosuka Naval Base (the heart of Japan), in September 1945.

He was discharged from Bainbridge Naval Station, MD, Jan. 28, 1946. For several years, in Washington, DC, working in plumbing, steamfitting, and timekeeping for an automobile dealership.

From 1951 to 1952 was back in the Navy, serving on the USS *Wisconsin* (BB-64). Following three midshipmen cruises to Edinburgh, Scotland, Lisbon, Portugal, and Halifax, Nova Scotia, saw action in Korea and was discharged from the USNR in 1954.

In 1953, began 37 years of managing duckpin and tenpin bowling centers, mainly in the Metropolitan Washington, D.C. area, until retirement in 1990.

He has two daughters, four grandchildren, and lives in Waldorf, MD. Staying active and loving retirement.

J. ROBERT SAUPPEE, USS *New Jersey* (BB-62), FC2/c, born Feb. 3, 1927, Reading, PA. Joined the Navy December 1944 and boot camp, at Sampson, NTC, NY. Then assigned to the USS *Missouri* (BB-63), which was already in the Pacific. He was aboard at the time of the formal surrender of Japan. In Tokyo Bay, Sept. 2, 1945. He was discharged April 1946. He joined the Naval Reserves, and was called back into active duty November 1950. He was assigned to the USS *New Jersey* (BB-62), still in mothballs, in Bayonne, NJ. The USS *Wisconsin* (BB-64) was going to relieve the *Missouri*, in Korea, got stuck in the mud, on the Hudson River, the *New Jersey* got a hurry up call to relieve the *Missouri*. While in Korea, he had some good liberties, in Japan, with his buddies. He was discharged again, April 1952.

He was an area salesman, for Walker Manufacturing Co., Racine, WI (exhaust systems), traveling, Pennsylvania, New Jersey, Maryland and Delaware. Retired in April 1989.

Sauppee lives in Reading, PA with his wife Madeline. They have four children, 16 grandchildren and two great-grandchildren.

FREDDIE E. SCAGGS, was born Aug. 25, 1928. Entered the Navy August 1948, Ship Service (barber), S-3 Div.

Stationed at Great Lakes, Bayonne, NJ; USS *Putman* (DD-757); USS *Salem* (CA-139); USS *New Jersey* (BB-62).

He feels it was an honor to serve on such a great ship.

Served in Korea in 1951 and received the United Nations Service Medal and Korean Service Medal with one star.

Discharged July 1952 as SH2

Married to Inez and they have three children and seven grandchildren.

He owns a barber shop that has been in business for 105 years.

DANIEL J. SCANLON, USS *New Jersey* (BB-62), F1/c, born April 17, 1924 in Buffalo, NY. Joined the Navy Aug. 11, 1943. Went through boot camp at Sampson Naval Training Center, attended Iowa State College for electrical training and thence to Hawaii. Served temporary duty on the USS *Indiana* and was assigned to USS *New Jersey* in May 1944.

He served in all the major battles the *Jersey* was involved in during the war in the South Pacific.

Dan was discharged March 15, 1946 and returned to Buffalo and worked for Niagara Mohawk Power Company for 35 years. In 1950 he married and subsequently raised eight children. He is now retired and still living in the Buffalo area. Dan and his wife have 15 grandchildren and enjoy traveling cross country in their van. One son is in the Navy as a flight engineer out of Tinker AFB in Oklahoma.

JOHN D. "JACK" SCHAAR, USS *New Jersey* (BB-62), RM2/c, born May 9, 1923 Mahanoy City, PA. Enlisted in the Navy Nov. 24, 1942, and went through boot camp at the NTS Bainbridge, MD. Was then assigned to Naval Radio School in Auburn, AL and upon graduating second in his class was transferred to the

Philadelphia Navy Yard to await the commissioning of the USS *New Jersey,* May 23, 1943.

Jack may have been one of the first crewmembers to get married while aboard. He was given a 48 hour leave to get married to his high school sweetheart on June 5, 1943.

He served on the *New Jersey* for 28 months through all its WWII campaigns and finally departed the ship while at anchor at Yokosuka Naval Base, Sept. 30, 1945.

He was discharged Oct. 17, 1945, Bainbridge, MD. Went to work for his father, a Buick dealer in Mahanoy City, PA. He succeeded his father and in 1962 took over the business, retiring late 1989.

Jack's wife died in 1991 and he is now living in Barnesville, PA. He has a daughter and two grandsons. His hobby is amateur radio, holding Amateur Extra Class License WZ3D.

MICHAEL A. SCHAPPAUGH, SH3, USNR, born March 3, 1946, Lincoln, IL. Joined the Naval Reserve, Dec. 6, 1966, St. Petersburg, FL. Transferred to USS *Darby* (DE-218), April 1, 1967.

April 1, 1968 transferred to active duty San Diego.

May 2, 1968 transferred to USS *Hooper* (DE-1026), San Diego. Made one midshipman cruise summer of 1968.

August 31, 1968 transferred to USS *New Jersey* (BB-62). Sailed five days later for Subic Bay and Vietnam.

December 16, 1968 advanced to SHL3, crossed equator (great experience). Upon return to Long Beach, CA he made one more midshipman's cruise and was later part of the decommissioning crew.

Awarded National Defense Service Medal, Vietnam Service Medal with two Bronze Stars, Vietnam Campaign Medal, Navy Unit Commendation Ribbon, Combat Action Ribbon.

Discharged from active duty, Dec. 2, 1969 as SHL3. While on duty with *New Jersey* his duties included storeoom management and laundry. Schappaugh stated that words cannot describe the experience of the ship and all that ecompassed it. It truly was an experience of a lifetime.

Divorced and has no children.
Employed by Florida Power Corp.

GERALD W. SCHMIDT, RM3/c, born Oct. 2, 1924 in Alton, IL. Inducted into U.S. Navy on Jan. 25, 1943. Served as radioman aboard USS *New Jersey*. Participated in all the battles the *New Jersey* was involved in during WWII.

Memorable experiences: The *New Jersey* returned to the States in May 1945. His first leave since assigned to the *New Jersey* and to his surprise when he arrived home, his three brothers were also on leave for the first time. Two of them were Marines and the other one was in the Navy also. They had not all been together for over three years. They had quite a reunion.

Another memorable experience was a chance meeting with one of his brothers in Hawaii.

Awarded the Good Conduct Medal, American Area, Victory Medal, Asiatic-Pacific with nine stars, Philippine Liberation with two stars, Point System Discharge.

Discharged Feb. 19, 1946.

Married to Bonnie and has four children (three sons and one daughter) and nine grandchildren.

He attended Quincy University and worked at Olin Industries as an industrial engineer in the Winchester-Western Division until he retired in 1987. He is now enjoying retirement, playing golf and traveling.

PAUL WILLARD SCOTT, SK2/c, USS *New Jersey* (BB-62), born Sweet Home, AR. Inducted April 1944 Little Rock, AR. Participated in seven battles. Discharged April 1949 at Receiving Station U.S. Naval Base (R) Charleston, SC.

Received following awards: American Area Campaign Medal, Asiatic-Pacific Area Campaign Medal, WWII Victory Medal, Philippines Liberation Ribbon, and Good Conduct Medal.

He is married and has two sons. Worked on family dairy farm prior to induction, and one year following discharge. Employed by Aluminum Company of America for 33 years. Retired as crane operator in January 1986. Presently enjoying retirement. Interested in antiques and has two antique cars.

RAYMOND P. SHERTEL, USS *New Jersey* (BB-62), SN1, born Jan. 30, 1929, North Bergen, NJ.

Joined U.S. Naval Reserve June 1947, received training at U.S. Naval Reserve Training Station, Jersey City, NJ. Called to active duty Oct. 30, 1950 and reported to USS *New Jersey* at Bayonne, NJ. He served on the USS *New Jersey,* first Korean tour as SN1-5 Div. He was projectile man on five inch Mount I.

Discharged at Norfolk, VA on June 5, 1952. Went to work for Public Service Electric and Gas Company in New Jersey.

After 38 years retired as chief lineman and is residing in North Bergen, NJ with his wife Dorothy. They have four children and six grandchildren.

PAUL W. SIEGERT, was born in Yonkers, NY Aug. 19, 1943. Entered the USNR, Oct. 3, 1966, YN-3, assigned to administration and captain's office, X Div.

Served on the USS *New Jersey* 1968-1969.

Assigned to 5" magazine in combat; educated at Riverdale Country Day School (1958-1961); Wesleyan University (Middletown, CT) 1961-1965; New York University School of Law (1972-1974) JD Degree.

Escorted Penelope Plummer (Miss World from Australia) when she came aboard with the Bob Hope Show in 1969; Was known as a good gambler (won $8,000 on their R&R trip from Japan to Singapore; helped Capt. Snyder conceal the fact that the 40 millimeters gun tubs were converted to small swimming pools.

Discharged Oct. 2, 1972 as YN-2.

Married to Margaret (divorced 1990 after 22 years of marriage). Has a son, Clayton, attends Trinity College (Hartford, CT); daughter Anne attends Wesleyan University (Middletown, CT). Son Evan in high school. He's a lawyer with Jung and Siegert, New York, NY.

LEROY ALBERT SIEKMAN, born Sept. 30, 1924 in Chicago, IL. Entered the Navy Feb. 9, 1943, SSM (C) 2/c, SS.

Stationed USNTS, Great Lakes, IL and USS *New Jersey*.

Awarded American Area, Victory Ribbon, Philippine Liberation with two stars and Asiatic-Pacific with nine stars.

Siekman was discharged Feb. 19, 1946 as SSMC2/c.

He is married to Mary. Now retired from USS Steel living in Crete, IL. He has made six trips to Europe. Member of two Folk Dance groups and musical ensemble. Performs in U.S. and Canada.

EDWARD PEARL SIX, S1/c, USS *New Jersey* (BB-62), joined the Navy at Des Moines, IA in 1942 and went through boot camp at the Great Lakes Naval Training Station. He was then assigned to the USS *Livermore* and out of Receif, Brazil to Casa Blanca, came back to New York and was then transferred to the USS *New Jersey* where he took part in the commissioning of the USS *New Jersey* on May 23, 1943.

They participated in nearly all major campaigns in the Pacific. They were the first ship to have lookouts. He was in "L" Div. He was on duty when they ran into a typhoon and lost three destroyers. Also they were under Jap attack at night and were able to read a paper from the flares they were dropping. Went into Tokyo after the Japanese surrender.

He left ship from Tokyo to Seattle and from there to Minneapolis, MN where he was discharged from USN Personnel Separation Center and from naval service on Oct. 15, 1945.

He was in Long Beach when they commissioned the USS *New Jersey* at Long Beach Naval Yard. He did not see anyone from L Div. During his time on the USS *New Jersey,* he ran around with a guy named Buck and Six would like to hear from him.

Six retired from the Maytag Company, Newton, IA in 1976 after 30 years of service.

WESLEY J. SMITH, was born May 27, 1935 in Midland, MI. Entered the U.S. Navy June 1952, BT2/c, B Div., #3 Fireroom, Oil Lab, M.A.A.

Stationed on USS *New Jersey* (BB-62) 1952 through 1956. Again as reservist, 1984 in Lebanon. During Desert Storm served aboard an AD in Persian Gulf.

Awarded Navy Unit Commendation, Navy E Ribbon, Navy Good Conduct, Navy Reserve Meritorious, Navy Expeditionary Medal, China Service Medal, Navy Occupation Medal, National Defense Medal, Korean Medal, Navy Reserve Sea Service, South Korean Presidential Unit Citation, United Nations Service Medal, and SW Asia Clasp, Kuwait Liberation Medal.

Discharged from active duty May 5, 1992. He now resides in Freeland, MI with his wife Patricia. Smith is retired.

J. EDWARD SNYDER, JR., was born in Grand Forks, ND, October 1924. Entered the Navy June 1941. Served as CO on *New Jersey* during Vietnam activation.

Other stations include: USS *Arkansas, Pennsylvania, California, Macon* and *Toledo*; DD *Holder* and *Heerman*.

CO, DER *Calcuterra,* DD *Brownson,* BB *New Jersey,* nuclear bomb development Los Alamos, NM; MIT Post Grad Nuclear Physics; Polaris Rentry body officer at SP and Livermore; Exec and Spec Asst to ASN (R&D), COMTRALANT oceanographer of the Navy.

Most memorable experience: *New Jersey* off Vietnam; battle of Surigao Straits (last surface battle).

He was awarded four Pacific Battle Stars, four Legion of Merit, one Legion of Merit with Combat V, elected to National Academy Engineering. Parsons Award for Scientific Achievement, American Defense Medal.

CARLO SPOTO, was born in Brooklyn, NY, Nov. 27, 1922. Entered the Navy Nov. 19, 1942, seaman first class, 5th Div.

Stationed at Great Lakes Naval Station. Participated in all major campaigns.

His memorable experience includes Marianas "Turkey Shoot, 1944; Typhoon October 1944; Shore leave in Nagasaki and Hiroshima; seeing damage of atomic bomb.

Discharged Jan. 11, 1946 as S1/c.

Married to Josephine and they have a daughter, Rosemarie and grandson, Christopher.

Worked for U.S. Immigration for 33 years and is now retired.

GEORGE C. STEGMANN, USS *New Jersey* (BB-62), F1/c, (M Div. #2 Engine Room), born Feb. 20, 1928, New Rochelle, NY. Joined the Navy July 5, 1946, (#227-31-65) survived boot camp at Bainbridge, MD, and went on to Engineering School at Great Lakes Naval Training Station. Transferred to Bremerton, WA to join

the crew of the *Jersey* in dry dock in February 1947. Ship transferred from Pacific to Atlantic, after picking up additional crew, cruised to Europe and back. Then began the first decommissioning of the *Jersey* in Brooklyn Navy Yard in late 1947. After decommissioning, discharged in July 1948.

After discharge, went to college, obtained a BME degree, and a scholarship for post graduate studies. Married in 1964 with two children (an architect and a pastry chef), one grandchild to come. Presently retired after 40 plus years in engineering, construction and finally research; now beginning to enjoy the good life, traveling and volunteering.

ALBERT STEINWEHE, MM3/c, born Des Plaines, IL, Jan. 3, 1924. Entered the USN Jan. 26, 1943.

USS *New Jersey,* May 23, 1943, plankowner. Boot camp, Great Lakes Naval Training Station. Participated in nearly all major battles in Pacific, 11 Battle Stars, Good Conduct Medal, all Pacific Medals.

Discharged March 15, 1946.

Worked after discharge, license plumber Local 130, Chicago, IL.

Married May 8, 1948. They have three children, (one boy, two girls), four grandsons and four granddaughters.

Retired and enjoying fishing trips with his wife of 46 years, taking care of some of the grandchildren.

JOSEPH W. STEVENS, USS *New Jersey* (BB-62), Teleman third class, assigned to "Charlie" Div., born Nov. 30, 1932, Bloomington, IN.

Joined the Naval Reserve Reserve Unit at Indiana University February 1950. Enlisted in the regular Navy June 1950 and went through boot camp at the Great Lakes NTS. Upon completion, assigned to Teleman Class "A" Technical School at Norfolk, VA. Upon graduation, assigned to the USS *New Jersey* (BB-62) as a SA, while still in the Brooklyn Naval Yard October 1950. Took first shakedown cruise to Guantanamo Bay Cuba, then off to Korea for the winter of 1950 and early 1951 tour. After Korea, made the midshipman cruise to England and Norway. Reassigned to USS *Missouri* (BB-63) and made Teleman 2/c and off to Korea 1952-1953 tour. After Korea, made midshipman cruise to Brazil. Returned to Norfolk and discharged November 1953. Re-enlisted in the Navy, June 1954 and sent to Naval Instructors Training School Class "C", Great Lakes, IL. Upon graduation, assigned to the USNRTC Navy Armory, Indianapolis, IN, as stationkeeper instructor and served three years as instructor in the communications field. Made 1/c Teleman. Discharged June 1957 and re-enlisted in the United States Air Force as technical sergeant in the Communications Field. Served tours of duty in Japan, Germany, Vietnam and Scott AFB, IL.

Retired from USAF as CMSgt (E-9) October 1972 at Richards Gebaur AFB, MO. While in the Air Force awarded the Air Force Commendation Medal twice, the Air Force Meritorious Service Medal and the Legion of Merit Medal.

In 1981 he graduated with a BA degree from Upper Iowa University. Since 1976 he has been a self-employed locksmith and was certified as a master locksmith in March of 1988 by the Associated Locksmiths of America. He resides in Marissa, IL (near Scott Air Force Base, IL) with his wife, the former Lydell Westerman Peck. They have two grandchildren, a son (Kendell), and a daughter (Nancy).

WILLIAM M. STEVENS, RDCS, USN, (Ret), USS *New Jersey* (BB-62), born Oct. 30, 1930, Cincinnati, OH moved to family farm at Verona, KY in 1931.

Joined the U.S. Navy, Jan. 13, 1948, went through boot camp at Great Lakes Naval Training Station. Was assigned to USS *Okaloosa* (APA-219). 1949 transferred to USNCICTTC Beavertail Point, Jamestown, RI; August, 1951 transferred to USS *Wisconsin* (BB-64) Korea deployment; May, 1952 transferred to USS *New Jersey* (BB-62) as radarman second class; January, 1955 transferred to USS *Northampton* (CLC-1) as radarman first class; June, 1956 transferred to Great Lakes Naval Training Center, Recruit Training Command as a recruit company commander; January, 1958 transferred to USS *Northampton* (CLC-1); November, 1960, transferred to Staff Commander Cruiser Div. Four as radarman chief; June, 1962 transferred to USS *Little Rock* (CLG-4); February 1963 transferred to Naval Research Laboratory Chesapeake Beach, MD; August, 1965 transferred to USS *Truxton* (DLGN-35) as senior chief radarman; November 1965 transferred to USS *Belknap* (DLG-26); May, 1967 transferred to Naval Amphibious Warfare Center, Little Creek, VA. August 17, 1967, retired and transferred to Fleet Reserve.

He is now living in Verona, KY with his wife Ann on the family farm.

ROBERT A. ST. GERMAIN, born in Madison, ME, Nov. 9, 1930. Served with the U.S. Navy, M Div., MM3/c. Served Jan. 2, 1948 to Jan. 2, 1952.

Served aboard USS *Worcester* for three years. Served aboard USS *New Jersey* Jan. 1, 1951 to Jan. 1, 1952.

He received the Korean Medal from USS *Worcester* and USS *New Jersey*.

Discharged Jan. 1, 1952 as MM3/c.

Married and has two children, Debra and Laura and six grandchildren: Alex, Nicholes, Corey, Andrew, Sahra, Racheal.

St. German is self-employed in sewing machine sales and service.

WILLIAM L. STIFF, was born in Oak Grove, VA, July 1, 1928. Entered the U.S. Navy March 9, 1953.

April 8, 1953 to March 1, 1956: active duty; USS *New Jersey;* (1st Div. J.O.; Aux. Machinery Off.; ABC Defense officer) Reserve duty: Inshore Undersea Warfare Div. 5-2 (C.O. three years).

He had many memorable experiences throughout the USN/USNR years.

Awarded the National Defense Service Medal, Korean President Unit Citation, Korean Service, United Nations, China Service, European Occupation, Naval Reserve Medal.

Separated from active duty March 1, 1956. Retired (USNR) July 1, 1988. He achieved the rank of captain.

Married to Betty and they have children, Karen, Timothy and Charles and grandchildren, Kaitlin and Christ.

Retired professional engineer. His hobbies include golf and flying.

HENRY M. STRUB, III, USS *New Jersey* (BB-62), Personnelman third class, born Nov. 5, 1946, Winston-Salem, NC. Enlisted U.S. Navy March 29, 1966. Attended boot camp at Great Lakes Naval Training Center.

Served on USS *Stoddard* (DD-566), July 1966-April 1968; USS *Bausell* (DD-845), April 1968-August 1968; USS *Bridget* (DE-1024), August 1968; USS *New Jersey* (BB-62), September 1968-December 1969.

Awarded the Navy Unit Commendation Ribbon with one Bronze Star, National Defense Service medal, Republic of Vietnam Campaign Medal with Device, Vietnam Service Medal with three Bronze Stars, Combat Action Ribbon, and Battle Efficiency "E".

Separated from active duty Dec. 3, 1969 - PN3, USNR. Discharged March 29, 1972.

Bachelor of Arts Degree, Mars Hill College, May 1972.

Married Maria O'Neal Strub, October 1989.

Currently: Microstation PC CADD design draftsman (self-employed) as well as contracted to Burlington, Ind. Corp. Engineering Dept. in the same capacity.

HUGH F. TAYLOR, was born in Cleveland, OH, April 29, 1931. Entered the U.S. Navy Aug. 29, 1950, Shipservice S-3.

Attended boot camp (Great Lakes), USS *Gloucester* PF22, Feb. 1, 1951 to May 1951; (Came aboard USS *New Jersey* by high line May 1951); USS *New Jersey* May 1951 through June 8, 1954.

His memorable experience includes (Sea of Japan Search for two ditched Navy jets in fog at night they didn't find 1951); (1952 visit to Fatima Portugal); (1953 signing Korean Peace Treaty).

Awarded U.N. Service Medal, Korean Presidential Unit Citation, National Defense Service, Good Conduct, China Service, Korean Service with two stars.

Discharged June 8, 1954 as SH-3.

Married to Ellen for 42 years. They have seven children and 17 grandchildren.

Taylor is a draftsman and field engineer for Arch Metal Fabrication Company.

DONALD L. TERRY, GM3/c, U.S. Navy, was born May 17, 1926, in Salt Lake City, UT. Joined the Navy June 16, 1943. Boot camp at Camp Hill Naval Training Station, Farragut, ID. Graduated NTS for gunner's mate, Farragut, ID. Flt. Ser. School, Adv. Gunners Mate, San Diego, CA (Sub. Base). Served as shore patrol in San Francisco, Tokyo and Bremerton, WA. Went on board the USS *New Jersey* at Majuro in May of 1944 as a gunners mate third class in the Main Btry., Turret Two.

Served there until the end of the war. Honorably discharged March 23, 1946. Married Moiselle Tracy on June 26, 1948. They have four children, six grandchildren, six step-grandchildren and four step-great-grandchildren. Retired after 40 years as a patternmaker for Buehner Concrete Company.

CHARLES P. THOMMEN, SR., GM1/c, USS *New Jersey* (BB-62), born June 10, 1922 in Baltimore, MD. Attended school in Baltimore, MD. Enlisted in the Naval Reserve in Baltimore in 1940. Called to active duty on Jan. 16, 1941.

Served from 1941 to March 1943, 10th Naval District in San Juan, PR and Submarine Base, St. Thomas, VI March 1943, transferred to Philadelphia Navy Yard, assigned to USS *New Jersey* (BB-62).

Participated in nine major engagements in the South Pacific as mount captain on Twin 5; 38 gun mount 4th Div.

After discharge in October 1945, joined the Baltimore Police Department in October 1946 to Dec. 2, 1971. Retired as detective lieutenant in Robbery Squad. Received 35 commendations on various cases solved.

In 1972 employed by the dstate of Maryland as instructor of Driver Rehabilitation Clinic. Later as an investigator for the Maryland Motor Vehicle Administration and then transferred as court commissioner for Anne Arundel Co., MD. Retired in 1982.

Member of USS New Jersey (BB-62) Veterans organization and USS New Jersey BB-62 Historical Museum Society.

RUBIN PATRICK THORNTON, was born in Houston, TX, Sept. 27, 1941. Entered the service October 1961, serving in the U.S. Navy.

Stationed on USS *New Jersey* (BB-62) (December 1967-August 1969); shore duty, U.S. Naval Station, San Diego (August 1965-December 1967); USS *Mt. McKinley* AGC-17 (August 1962-August 1965); U.S. Naval Air Station New Iberia, CA (January 1962-August 1963). Attended boot camp, San Diego (October 1961-January 1962).

His memorable experiences include crossing the equator the second time on board USS *New Jersey*. Discharged August 1969 ad ET1 or E-6.

Married to Earnestine and they have daughter Rudyne A.

DOD, USN Civilian, Logistics Management Specialist, NAVSTAR GPS and SHF SATCOM programs.

LOUIS J. TOTH, was born in Petersville, PA, Aug. 23, 1923. Entered the service Feb. 12, 1943. Served in the Navy, S1/c, L Div..

Stationed at Sampson Naval Training Station, Philadelphia Naval Base. Participated in all campaigns with the 3rd and 5th Fleets.

His memorable experience includes the typhoon in December 1941.

Participated in the American Campaign, Asiatic-Pacific Campaign, and received WWII Victory Medal, Philippine Liberation, nine Battle Stars, Asiatic-Pacific, two Battle Stars.

Discharged April 22, 1946 from Philadelphia Naval Hospital.

Now residing in Zionsville, PA with his wife. They have two children. Retired from Mack Truck Inc., after 42 years service. Enjoys gardening, taking care of six acres.

ANTHONY R. TRAMAGLINI, USS *New Jersey* (BB-62), MM3/c, born June 12, 1924, Newark, NJ. Joined the Navy Jan. 9, 1943. Went through boot camp in Great Lakes Naval Training Station. Was transferred to Philadelphia Navy Yard and the USS *New Jersey* before the commissioning. Participated in almost all major campaigns in the Pacific up to the surrender of Japan.

Discharged March 15, 1946. Tony retired from the New Jersey Division of Motor Vehicles 1988. He enjoys his home at the Jersey Shore, plays tennis and fishing.

Tony is the past commander of the VFW and is presently quartermaster. He enjoys the USS New Jersey reunions where he meets his shipmates and is a member of the USS New Jersey Museum Society.

He married Gerry Donatiello May 2, 1948. They have a daughter Lisa, and two grandchildren Melissa and Marc.

Tony and Gerry live in Belleville, NJ, and have a summer home at the Jersey Shore.

DANA DE WITT TUCKER, USS *New Jersey* (BB-62), was born on Feb. 13, 1931, St. Louis, MO and enlisted in the Navy on Dec. 30, 1950. He completed his boot camp training (Troop 007) in San Diego, CA in March 1951. He was first assigned to the USS *Burlington* PF-51 from the April 1, 1951 until June 6, 1951 at which time he was then transferred to the *New Jersey* in Sasebo, Japan. He was on the *New Jersey* from June 1951 until mid-August 1954 at which time he was transferred to "shore patrol" duty in Norfolk, VA where he was discharged as an SK2 on Oct. 27, 1954. The *New Jersey* was sent to Korea on three separate occasions for six month stints. There were also two midshipman "six week" cruises to Europe during those three years. He spent time in Paris, Cherbourg, Amsterdam, Rotterdam, Brussels, Weisbaden and Copenhagen while in Europe. When in Korea the *New Jersey* spent most of its time bombarding the North Koreans in Wonsan Harbor and other strategic points, while only being hit once.

When in Norfolk, he spent all his free time at the USO clubs, the YMCA and other community locations where weekly dances were constantly held. During his tenure on the *New Jersey* he won the Norfolk City Table Tennis Tournament in 1953, and the Virginia State Championship in 1954. The *New Jersey* bowling team won the "Bat-Crulant" bowling tournament all four years, and Dana was the only Jerseyman to be on that team all four years. He still has his original bowling shirt (though it doesn't fit now). He also became a professional bowler, and was able to achieve 17 perfect 300 games in his bowling career which expanded over 30 years. He now plays tennis in lieu of bowling or golf. He and his wife (Carlene) love to play double deck pinochle and bridge.

He completed his undergraduate work at Omaha University in 1957, and his graduate studies at Golden Gate College in San Francisco in 1962. He attributes his accomplishment of obtaining an MBA degree at night school to his wife Carlene whom he married in June of 1958.

He met Carlene at Macy's in San Leandro, CA in August of 1957, and they have three children, Dana, Scott and Alycia. He worked for General Motors in Oakland, CA for almost three years, for Aerojet-General (General Tire & Rubber) in Sacramento, CA for almost 12 years, and W.R. Grace in Reno, NV for almost nine years. Dana and his wife were in business for themselves for over seven years from 1973 through 1980 in the largest retail shopping center in Reno. He now lives in Sparks, NV and is retired. Dana's wife plans to retire sometime in 1995. He and his wife wish nothing but health and happiness to all ex-*New Jersey* shipmates especially those on the *New Jersey* between 1951 and 1954. Dana also wishes nothing but the best to all ex-shipmates of the USS *New Jersey*.

LARRY D. TURNER, was born in West Manchester, Preble County, OH. Entered the U.S. Navy January 1943, CM2/c, R Div.

Stationed in Great Lakes January 1943 and on board the USS *New Jersey* May 1943.

Participated in 11 battles.

While in the Pacific on the USS *New Jersey* he is aware of only one incident concerning a shell hole put in the deck. It was due to a five inch shell while they were anchored on Thanksgiving Eve in 1944. He was awakened about 2300 hours to help repair it. He waited on a shipfitter, Louwickie, to weld the studs and fasten the teak deck down. Finally, Turner grew tired of waiting and ended up welding and laying the deck in a slight rain.

Later he and Rodgers, a coxswain, had the midnight shift. They were told when they went on duty that they were in a storm and the watch before them had not closed the armored hatch near #3-16" turret. The water was rushing back and forth across the deck from 12-24 inches deep. Finally they dogged it from the top side and then wondered if they would make it back down.

They sat on the gunshield of the 20mm for a time. They thought they could make it to the manholes. One was fairly close, the other not so close. Then he saw the ship sort of even up and he turned to tell Rodgers that he was going for a manhole. He was already gone. So, Turner went through the hole like he was shot! After getting down, Turner could not find Rogers. Suddenly, while looking for each other, they almost collided.

Discharged Oct. 8, 1945 as CM2/c.

Married to Jeanne and has stepchildren Daniel, Barbera, and Chris Howell.

Retired as carpenter/cabinetmaker. Managed retail lumber company approximately 40 years.

JAMES R. VAUGHAN, was born Jan. 3, 1921, Mt. Vernon, NY. Entered WWII in July 1942, and Korea in September 1950.

Served in USNR. Attended boot camp, Newport, RI. N Div. Destroyer *Benson* (DD-421) (WW-II); N Div. USS *New Jersey* (BB-62) (Korea).

Destroyer Div., #7 Atlantic and North Atlantic, Convoy Escort 1942-1944; Mediterranean Fleet until October 1944; V-12 Naval Aviation 1944-1945.

Memorable experiences: Gela, Sicily, Salerno, Italy; invasions: invasion of Southern France; sunk subs Atlantic and Mediterranean; 1st ship to bombard European mainland; Published a book USS *Benson* DD-421 "The Bitchy B", the complete life of the *Benson* from his personal daily dairy requested by the crew of DD-421; bombardment of Korean coast in Korean war.

Awarded the Korean Presidential Unit Citation, EAME with six stars, United Nations, American Defense, Korean Service with two stars, Navy Good Conduct, WWII Victory Medal, American Campaign.

Discharged December 1945 from WWII and July 1952 from Korea.

Achieved the rank of QMQ2.

Married to Anne and they have daughters, Ellen, Jean, Lauren and three grandsons and one granddaughter.

Retired NYNEX Corp (New York Telephone Company) after 40 years. Former captain LaGrange Fire Department; police officer Town of LaGrange Police, 28 years to present.

JAMES WALLACE VAUGHN, was born in Greensboro, NC, Jan. 5, 1924. Entered the U.S. Navy Nov. 10, 1942. Served as GMGC gunnersmate, 5th Div. aboard USS *New Jersey*.

Stationed on various ships during WWII, Korea and during peace time.

His memorable experience includes firefight offshore Vietnam, fall of 1968 on *New Jersey*, Mount 55.

He received Navy Achievement Medal with Combat V, 14 ribbons various battles: Guadalcanal, Marshall Islands, Philippine Campaign, Iwo Jima.

Discharged January 1947 and re-enlisted February 1950. He was discharged as E-8 senior chief petty officer.

Married to Clara Brackett Vaughn. They have two sons, two grandsons and two granddaughters.

Today he is "Wishing he was back on board the *Jersey*."

H.R. VIERKANT, was born in Chemnitz, Saxony, Germany April 1, 1925. Entered the U.S. Navy Jan. 25, 1943.

Stationed at Great Lakes Naval Station Jan. 25, 1943-March 30, 1943; USS *New Jersey* April 15, 1943-April 21, 1946.

His memorable experience includes the impressive commissioning ceremony on fantail of USS *New Jersey* May 23, 1943. March 18, 1944, during "practice" bombardment against Mille Atoll in Marshall Islands, Japanese shells came so close that some crew members swore they could read the serial numbers of the Japanese shells.

Awarded the American Area Ribbon, Asiatic-Pacific Ribbon, one Silver Star, four Bronze Stars, Philippine Liberation Ribbon, two Bronze Stars, (total of nine).

Participated in entire USS *New Jersey* cruise May 23, 1943-April 21, 1946.

Discharged April 21, 1946 with the rank of S1/c.

Married to Alice and they have two sons and four grandchildren.

He is retired and living in Daytona Beach, FL.

HERBERT WILLIAM VOSS, was born in Chicago, IL, July 15, 1917. Entered the service May 1942. Served in Navy, 5th Div. and General Quarters Station as 40mm shell handler.

Stationed in Great Lakes, Norfolk, VA and USS *New Jersey*.

His memorable experiences include most all of his experiences on board the *New Jersey*.

Received awards for all battles aboard the *New Jersey*.

Discharged as SC2c October 1945.

Married to Gladys and they have one son and two grandsons.

He is now retired and living in Florida and Dowers Grove, IL, part-time.

ANDREW J. WADE, USS *New Jersey* (BB-62), AMM1/c, born Sept. 12, 1925, Citra, FL. Enlisted in the Navy Oct. 9, 1942 with boot camp at Naval Training Station, NOB, Norfolk, VA. First assigned to USS *Dauntless* and then USS *New Jersey* for it's commissioning May 23, 1943. After the shakedown the *New Jersey* headed to the Pacific where they participated in nearly all major campaigns starting Jan. 29, 1944. The anchor was dropped at Yokosuka Naval Base, Sept. 16, 1945. The war over, the *New Jersey* docked at Bremerton, WA where he was discharged Nov. 15, 1946. Assigned to the 5th Div. then M. Div.

On Jan. 14, 1948 he re-entered the Navy assigned to NARTU-NAS JAX. Transferred to Patrol Sqdn. VP-1 Whidby Island, WI. Participated in the Korean War. Had three transfers from Whidby Island to Memphis to Whidby Island. He was discharged Jan. 31, 1957. Employed by Fairchild, Inc. St. Augustine, FL 1957-1958.

Civil service NAS JAX 1958 until retirement June 1, 1982.

He'll never forget when the captain announced the death of Franklin D. Roosevelt, the laughing at Tokyo Rose radio broadcasts and the day the war ended.

Received the American Theater Campaign, Philippine Liberation (two stars), Asiatic-Pacific Campaign (nine stars), WWII Victory, Japanese Occupation, Korean Service with one star), Air Medal.

He has two sons, two grandsons and one

granddaughter. He and his wife, Lucille, live in Orange Park, FL. They travel, fish and do volunteer work.

JAMES B. WAGONER, ET1, USS *New Jersey* (BB-62), born June 28, 1929 in Whitehead, NC. Attended elementary school in Laurel Springs and high school in Sparta, NC. Entered in the Navy in 1947 and attended recruit training in San Diego, CA. After recruit training, attended Electronic Material School at Treasure Island, CA.

Served aboard the following ships and stations: Navy Weather Central, Kodiak, AK (1948-1950); USS *New Jersey* (1950-1952); NAS North Island (1952-1954); USS *Fort Snelling* (LSD-30) (1954-1956); Navy Station Coco Solo, Panama Canal Zone (1956-1958); Navy Officer Postgraduate School, Monterey, CA (1958-1959); Fleet Training Group; Guantanamo, Cuba (1960) and disability retired with the rank of ET1 (1960).

After retiring, worked as supply clerk at Alleghany Memorial Hospital, Sparta, NC 1965-1969.

Member of USS New Jersey Veterans Association, Battleship New Jersey Historical Museum Society and American Battleship Association.

DAVID J. WARD, CS3, USS *New Jersey*, born March 29, 1948 in Clinton, CT. Joined the Navy September 1967. Attended boot camp, Great Lakes, IL. Assigned USS *New Jersey*. Attended recommissioning April 6, 1967, Philadelphia, PA. Participated in Vietnam Campaign.

Transferred to USS *Worden* in July of 1969. Discharged December 1969.

Employed by the town of Clinton, CT as maintenance engineer for it's police department for 15 years.

A former firefighter for 23 years in Clinton. Attaining the rank of assistant chief.

Published writer of short stories.

GEORGE W. WASELESKI, was born in Bayonne, NJ. Entered the Navy January 1943, MM2, M Div.

Attended boot camp in Green Bay, WI. Plankowner, USS *New Jersey*. March 1943 served aboard until November 1946.

All his memorabilia, diary, day one to discharge, donated plus five foot model of ship to Battleship New Jersey Historical Museum Society.

Discharged November 1946. Married to Claire and they have five children, two grandsons and two granddaughters.

Today he is on R&R and catching up, and fishing.

JACK ADRIAN WATSON, was born April 10, 1925 in Burlington, NC. He joined the Navy, 6th Division on April 6, 1943 in Baidbridge, MD. Watson served on the USS *New Jersey* from July 30, 1943 to Feb. 6, 1946 as a GM2/c.

His most memorable experiences were the Marianas Turkey Shoot and sailing into Tokyo Bay at the end of the war. He received the Asiactic-Pacific Campaign, American Campaign, World War II Victory with nine combat stars, Occupation Service, Philippine Liberation with two stars, and the Good Conduct Medals.

He is married to Norma S. Watson and has one daughter and seven step-grandchildren. He is now retired and is doing more than he has to.

CLIFTON L. WENTWORTH, was born in Danvers, MA, March 22, 1928. Entered the Navy September 1945. Served in U.S. Naval Reserves.

Stationed on USS *New Jersey* (BB-62) (7th Div.); USS *Brush* (DD-745); USS *Newman K. Perry* (DD-883); USS *McCaffery* (DD-860).

Awarded the Korean Service, United Nations, Korean Presidential Unit Citation, American Theater, Asiatic-Pacific Victory, American Defense, China Service, Navy Occupation, Philippine Independence Medal.

Memorable experience: the operation of the *New Jersey* during the two days of May 20 and May 21, 1951 their first taste of action. The ship entered the harbor of Wonsan to support a LST that was taking enemy fire from shore batteries and two DDs that were involved in a gun duel. Their ship fired most of the night and into the morning of the 21st. Shortly after the morning meal the ship was taken under fire by the enemy shore guns that were hidden behind a small hill. The awesome fire from their five inch and 16 inch guns that destroyed the enemy guns will always remain in his memory. Most important was the fact that the ship received several direct hits but suffered very little damage but three of their men were wounded and Robert Osterwind, a member of the 7th Div. was killed while manning one of the after 40 mm guns. On the return of their ship to the States the crew donated several thousand dollars, in his memory, to the Damon Runyon Cancer Fund.

Last October he met an ex-crewman that was on one of the DDs in the harbor that day. When he learned Wentworth had served on the *New Jersey* he thanked Wentworth for saving their ass that day. Small world.

Discharged March 1953 as BMSN (leading seaman).

Married to Monica and they have daughters Jane (Dec) and Joann, also granddaughters Alison and Brianna.

Wentworth is a police officer doing building restoration.

ROBERT J. WESTCOTT, SR., born in Bridgeton, NJ, March 18, 1922. Enlisted Oct. 13, 1942. Attended boot camps at Great Lakes.

Served on USS *Constellation*, USS *New Jersey*. Stationed on the *Jersey* May 23, 1943-Oct. 7, 1945. Served with CR Div.

Achieved the rank of radio technician.

Served all major campaigns from Jan. 29, 1944 to dropping the hook in Tokyo bay off the Yokosuka Naval Base, Sept. 16, 1945.

Awarded the WWII Victory Medal, American Campaign Medal, Asiatic-Pacific Campaign Medal with one Silver Star and four Bronze Stars, Philippine Liberation Medal with two Bronze Stars, Philippine Presidential Unit Citation Bar.

Discharged Oct. 17, 1945.

Enlisted the Naval Reserve May 23, 1947. Discharged from the Naval Reserve April 30, 1965 with the rank of CPO radioman.

He had two children at time of enlistment. Three more after coming home, two boys, three girls. Lost oldest son in Navy Nov. 8, 1967 serving on the USS *Northampton* CC-1, RM2/c in Navy seven years Robert J. Westcott, Jr. age 26. Lost wife, Doris M. Westcott, Feb. 5, 1993, married 52 years.

Employed in the radio, television electronics service. Retired in 1981. Just service for family and amateur radio friends. In radio from 1937, amateur radio call - W2MAS.

DEWARD WHITEHAIR, JR., USS *New Jersey* (BB-62), BMSN, born Jan. 6, 1930 Oxford, WV, joined the Navy Nov. 14, 1950. Went through boot camp at the Great Lakes Naval

Training Station. Was then assigned to the 2nd Div. aboard the USS *New Jersey*. Serving two tours of duty in Korea with Task Force 77, operational forces in Western Pacific, concentrated chiefly in Korean waters.

Most memorable experience was the truce signing at Panmunjon. Participated in several battles.

His medals and citations received include: Good Conduct Medal, National Defense Medal, Korean Medal with two stars, United Nations Medal, Korean Presidential Unit Citation, and the China Service Medal.

Honorably discharged Sept. 10, 1954 RECSTA NS NORVA. Next 38 years he worked for Hope Gas, Inc. Retiring Jan. 1, 1987 as manager of residential and commercial marketing. He and his wife live seven months in Glenville, WV and five months in Titusville, FL. They have two sons and four grandsons.

JOHN R. WILLIAMS, was born in Kent, OH, Feb. 24, 1924. Entered the service Jan. 20, 1943, USN, SM3/c, Signal Div.

Stationed at Great Lakes Naval Station, Philadelphia Naval Yard, USS *New Jersey*.

His memorable experience occurred when the USS *Jersey* was bombarding Truk. He watched a torpedo pass between the USS *Iowa* stern and the *Jersey* bow. Discharged Oct. 17, 1945 in Toledo, OH as signalman third class.

Married Geri and they have three daughters, Laura, Janet, and Joyce.

Retired after 47 years in retail hardware business.

RAYMOND WINTERS, was born in Bellow Falls, VT Jan. 1, 1935. Served in the Navy, Engr. Dept, Deck, S1 Div. Entered July 7, 1952.

Served on the USS *New Jersey* (BB-62), September 1952-March 1954.

For five months, blew a good part of North Korea into dust spring and summer of 1953.

He had a great overall time on the "Big J".

He was awarded the Korean Presidential Unit Citation, Presidential Unit Citation, Korean (two stars), United Nations, China Service, few others but can't remember.

Divorced, and has children Raymond and Marisol and has grandkids, Priscilla, Cristina, Timmy and Samantha Rae.

Employed as transportation engineer, Hess Oil, Bayonne, NJ. (truck driver).

ROBERT CARL WIRZBACH, was born in Dubuque, IA, Feb. 21, 1921. Entered the service Aug. 2, 1942, serving in the Navy, Fire Control, FC2, FA Div.

NSNTS, 16 weeks basic training, Great Lakes, IL, 1942; USNTS, 14 weeks Fire Control School, Great Lakes, IL, 1943; DES Base, San Diego, CA, Fire Control Service School Maintenance, 1943 (16 weeks); USS *New Jersey* Plankowner, May 23, 1943-Nov. 20, 1944; Navy Yard Washington, DC, Advanced Fire Control, 25 weeks 1945; NTS, Newport, RI, 1945; USN Personel Separation Center, Minneapolis, MN. Discharged December 1945 as FC2.

New Guinea Operations, Hollandia Landings, April 1944; Marshall Island Operations, Jan-March 1944; Asiatic Pacific Raids, Feb-May 1944.

Married to Mildred M. and they have children: Robert, Thomas, Janet, Susan, Karen and Jean. They also have 13 grandchildren.

He retired as electrician after 45 years.

HARRY G. WOLOCHUK, S1/c, did his boot training at New Port Rhode Island, September 1943.

After he completed 10 weeks, he went to Norfolk, VA N.O.B. in December 1943. He went to Boston, went on board at night, raining like hell, didn't know where he was. He went top side in the morning and to his great surprise he was aboard the USS *New Jersey*. Next day they sailed and headed for Norfolk again. Three days later they headed South for Panama.

They joined the USS *Iowa* and went through the canal. The rest is in the book.

ROBERT L. WOODS, WO-1, T Div., born July 5, 1922 in Grinnell, Powshiek County, IA. Grew up in Center Point, Linn County, IA. Enlisted in the Navy Aug. 29, 1940. After boot camp and Radio School, to USS *Altair* (AD-11). Was in Bermuda, BWI on Dec. 7, 1941. Then to USS *Stack* (DD-406) and to South Pacific. To new construction USS PC-623 in 1943, and back to southwest Pacific. At end of war was on USS PC-492 as station ship, Brunei Bay, Borneo.

To teletype school, then to Bikini A-bomb test on LST-817.

To technician school, then USS *Putnam* (DD-757) in 1948. To Europe, then was the first USN ship to fly the United Nations flag during the Palestine/Israel/British changeover. To AFSWP in 1949. When appointed warrant officer, to USS *New Jersey*. After Korea, back to AFSWP. Retired from the USS *Forrestal* (CVA-59) on Nov. 1, 1960.

After working for a Motorola Service Station in Wichita, KS, for three years, moved to Ava, MO and started his own business. Retired and sold business after 24 years. He and his wife Vi (Violet) are both retired. He has four children, six grandchildren, and one great-grandsons.

HAROLD F. WRIGHT, was born at Belvidere, IL, June 8, 1923. Entered the service Jan. 23, 1943. Served in the Navy, FC3/c, FM.

Attended boot camp in Great Lakes, and stationed on the USS *New Jersey* the remainder of the time.

On the same ship from May 23, 1943 until Dec. 28, 1945.

Discharged Jan. 28, 1946 as FC3/c, and retired Jan. 1, 1984.

Married to Shirley. They have four children, 13 grandchildren, and two great-grandsons.

Retired (fishing).

JOSEPH M. WYNNE, USS *New Jersey*, EM2/c, born Aug. 15, 1931, Boston, MA. Went through boot camp, Newport, RI. On Jan. 10, 1951, was assigned to USS *New Jersey*. Spent all his four years service time on USS *New Jersey*.

Earned the China Service Medal, National Defense Medal, Good Conduct, Korean Service Medal, Navy Occupation Medal, United Nation Service Medal, Korean President Unit Citation.

He was discharged Nov. 24, 1954 Norfolk, VA. Went to work for Local #103 IBEW Boston as a construction electrician.

After 40 odd years he has retired to Deltona, FL where he manages and plays senior softball. From June to October, he enjoys his summer home in York Beach, ME.

He is married to his wife Margaret for 41 years. They have nine children and 11 grandchildren.

JAMES A. YATES, JR., S1/c, born Jan. 31, 1935, Martha's Vineyard, MA. Entered service May 1, 1952, USN.

Attended boot camp Bainbridge Naval Training Station, MD.

Stationed on USS *New Jersey* (BB-62) L Div.

Fought in the Korean War.

Awarded the National Defense, Korean Service (two stars), United Nations, China Service, Korean Presidential Unit Citation Medal.

Also served on USS LST-528, USS LSMR-520, USS *Randall* APA-224.

Released Jan. 4, 1956.

Honorably discharged April 30, 1960.

Employed at Pratt & Whitney Aircraft Middletown, CT, 25 years.

Retired as a machine shop foreman.

In retirement now living in Beverly Hills, FL.

Married to Patricia and has two sons, two daughters, and five grandchildren.

EDWARD F. ZAREMBA, SR., USS *New Jersey* (BB-62), born Sept. 16, 1924, Everett, MA, joined the Navy January, 1943, went through boot camp at Great Lakes and was assigned to the *New Jersey* April 1943, a month before she was commissioned on May 23, 1943.

He was assigned to Division 4 for a week or so when he was transferred to a new division, Division L. After a year and a half he was accepted into Div. M after the overhaul in Bremerton, WA May 25, 1945.

As fireman first class, arrived at Yokosuka, Tokyo Bay on Sept. 16, 1945, his 21st birthday. He left the ship Jan. 1, 1945 to go Stateside for discharge which was Jan. 28, 1946.

He is now retired and lives in Atkinson, NH with his wife Eleanor and most of their children nearby. They have four children, seven grandchildren and still counting.

GEORGE W. ZIEGLER, was born in New York City. Entered the U.S. Navy Jan. 21, 1941, GMC, 5th Div.

Attended boot camp, Newport, RI. Other stations include: USS *Texas* 1941-1942; NIM Schenectady, NY; NTsch, Detroit MI; RINM, Minneapolis, MN; USS *New Jersey;* ATSch, Washington, DC; USS ATA 185; R/S New York, NY; USS *Honolulu;* USS *Tangier,* NRB, New Orleans, LA.

Awarded the American Defense ("A"), American Area, Asiatic-Pacific (11 stars); Philippine Liberation (two stars); WWII Victory Medal, Good Conduct (one star); EAME Campaign Ribbon (one star).

Discharged Jan. 21, 1947 as chief gunners mate, USN.

Married to Mary and they have five children and 10 grandchildren.

He is now retired.

JAMES M. ZUBERT, 1st Div., USS *New Jersey,* BM1/c, born June 4, 1922 in Brooklyn, NY. Joined the Navy December 1941. Went to boot camp, Rhode Island. Was assigned to the USS *Texas.* Convoyed the first American troops to England, January 1942. Operated with the USS *New York,* carrier *Wasp,* USS *Philadelphia,* USS *Brooklyn,* USS *Quincey,* early in 1942. Also with English Navy out of Iceland convoy duty. Was in on the landing in North Africa, Casablanca.

Transferred to the USS *New Jersey* April 1943. Went through all the campaigns. Stayed on the *New Jersey* until he left the Navy December 1946. Met his wife in 1943, a small town girl. Married on leave June 11, 1945.

Went to work for E.I. DuPont, worked 36 years then retired.

He still lives in Pitman, NJ. He has one son, an ex-Marine, one daughter and three grandchildren.

WILLIAM H. ZUEHLKE, was born in Appleton, WI, April 19, 1915. Entered the U.S. Navy in 1941.

Stationed on USS *South Dakota* in 1942; USS *New Jersey* 1945; commanding officer of USS LST 43 in 1943; USS *Neosho* 1942; USS *Neches* (1941).

His memorable experience includes two ships being sunk from under him.

Retired in 1945 as lieutenant commander.

Married to Muriel Mae Zuehlke.

He died on July 12, 1994.

JAMES A. FLOOD, was born July 4, 1944 in Philadelphia, PA. He entered the USN in June 1965. He attended QM school in Newport in 1965 and served on the USS *Wright* (CC-2) from 1965 to 1967; T.A.D, USS *Laffey* (DD-724) 1966; and the USS *New Jersey* 1967-1969 and achieved the rank of QM2. He received all the usual medals from serving during the Vietnam era.

His most memorable experiences were being under fire off the DMZ and a storm off Japan when they took a terrific wave. The wave hit with such force that it bashed in the QM deck shack door on the main deck by Turret II, cleaned the place out of all furniture, gouged everything off the bulkheads, and set off every alarm on the ship.

Flood was discharged in June 1969 and he is currently working as a Maritime Artist.

Taking time out for a photo. (Courtesy of Len Raff.)

USS *New Jersey* (BB 62) Roster

The following roster was provided to the publisher by USS New Jersey Veterans, Inc. It was the most current version available at press-time.

- A -
ABERCROMBIE, ROBERT
ADAMEK, RAYMOND
ADAMS, FRED
ADAMS, JAMES
ALBRIGHT, WILLIAM
ALCAMO, THOMAS
ALES, MICHAEL
ALLEN, HARRY
ALLEN, PAUL
ALLEN, SYLVESTER
ALLEN, WILLIAM
ALLISON, LYNN
ALLMAN, NORMAN
ALMASIAN, HAMPTON
ALTIZER, WILLIAM
ALTZ, CARL
AMEND, WAYNE
ANAYA, JOHN
ANDERSON, CLYDE
ANDERSON, RICHARD
ANDERSON, RICHARD
ANNASE, NICHOLAS
ARTHUR, DARWIN
AUSTIN, CLIFFORD
AZZOLINA, JOS

- B -
BABB, DEWEY
BACICH, GEORGE
BADGETT, WILLIAM
BAILEY, DALE
BAIRD, JOHN
BAKER, MYERT
BAKOS, MICHAEL
BALDWIN, ROBERT
BALOG, GEORGE
BALOGH, STEPHEN
BARKER, DAVID
BARKLEY, BERNARD
BARNHOLDT, WILLIAM
BARR, DELBERT
BARRIGER, KEN
BARTELS, WILLIAM
BARTHOLOMEW, JOHN
BARTUSCH, WILLARD
BASELICE, JOHN
BASHA, RUDOLPH
BAUGHMAN, ROBERT
BAUMAN, BERNARD
BAUMBACH, LOUIS
BEAMER, DAVID
BEAULIEU, MARC
BECKER, FRANK
BEDNAR, JOS
BEGANDY, RICHARD
BELCHER, ROBERT
BELCOURT, ADRIEN
BENATOR, MAX
BENDIT, MARVIN
BENDORF, WILLIAM
BENNETT, HARRY
BENSON, WILLIAM
BERGER, BARRY
BERNIER, NORMAN
BERRY, JAMES
BERRY, ROBERT
BERTEL, VERNON
BESS, HAROLD
BETTERMAN, WILLIAM
BIANCHI, ANGELO
BIEBER, ROBERT
BIEBER, ROY
BIERMAN, JAMES
BIGELOW, EARL
BISHOP, JOHN
BITTING, FRED
BLACKMAN, ROBERT
BLAIR, FRANK
BLAKE, DEAN
BLANKS, JOSEPH
BLOCK, RONALD
BLOODWORTH, WILLIAM
BLUMENTHAL, BOB
BODISH, GEORGE
BOLAN, JOHN
BONATELLI, LOUIS
BONNER, FRED
BORMOLINI, JOHN
BOSETTO, DOMINIC
BOSICH, JOS
BOSTWICK, E JAMES
BOWLING, HUBERT
BOWNDS, BILLY
BOYD, JOHN
BOYER, TENNEY
BOZEK, FRANK
BRAGG, JOHN
BRANDENBURG, E H
BRANHAM, JOHN
BRATTIN, SHERMAN
BRAULT, EVERAL
BRAUN, WALTER
BREMER, CHARLES
BREWINGTON, RONALD
BRIEN, ROBERT
BRIGGS, ALBERT
BRINK, FRANK
BRINK, WILMONT
BRINSON JR, LINWOOD
BRITNER, GEORGE
BRITT, BOBBY
BRITTON, JACK
BRITTON, RICHARD
BROOKHOUSER, BILL
BROOKS, CLARENCE
BROUSSARD, JOS
BROWN, BRENDAN
BROWN, FRANCIS
BROWN, JACOB
BROWN, LARRY
BROWN, ROBERT
BROWN, RUSSELL
BROWN, VICTOR
BROWN, WILLIAM
BROWN, WM
BROWN JR, CURTIS
BRUCE, THOMAS
BUCHANAN, GORDON
BUCK, ESTER
BUCKINGHAM, RICHARD
BUDER, HAROLD
BUDNIK, ANDREW
BUISSON, LLOYD
BUONAIUTO, ANTHONY
BURD, JOHN
BURNS, ROBERT
BURRUS, LYLE
BURTON, GERALD
BUSH, LAROY
BUSHER, JAMES
BUSHNELL, CLYDE
BUSSE, BLAINE
BUTTS, CARL
BUZENSKI, JOHN
BYRNES, JOHN

- C -
CAHILL, JAY
CALDWELL, DON
CALDWELL, HERSCHEL
CALDWELL, J R
CALHOUN, RICHARD
CAMERON JR, WILLIAM
CAMPBELL, PATRICK
CANADAY, RICHARD
CAPOBIANCO, ANTHONY
CARBER, FRANK
CARDAMONE, RUSSELL
CARLSON, FRANK
CARLSON, RICHARD
CARPENTER, DONALD
CARRICK SR, EUGENE
CARROLL, JOHN
CARTER, BAKER
CASARI, CHESTER
CASHION, RUSSELL
CATES, ELLIOTT
CATHERS SR, THOMAS
CATINO III, JOSEPH
CATTERTON JR, C M
CAUZ, ANDREW
CEMPA, RICHARD
CERESOLI, ROBERT
CESARIO, SAM
CHALKEY, STUART
CHAMBERLAIN, WILFRED
CHAPMAN, ALBERT
CHASTAIN, LYLE
CHAVEZ, E L
CHEETHAM, KENNETH
CHENAULT, FRED
CHESNUT, DENNY
CHESTNUT, GEORGE
CHESTNUT, JIM
CHINNOCK, R L
CHMELIK, ARTHUR
CHRISTOPHER, ROY
CICHONE, WILLIAM
CIESIELCZYK, FRED
CIPRIANO, THOMAS
CLAEYS, ROBERT
CLAY, DWAIN
CLIFFORD, WILLIAM
CLINE, HARRY
CLOUGH, VICTOR
CLOWER, ROBERT
COCHRANE JR, JOHN
COFFMAN, GREGORY
COLDWELL, ALAN
COLE, ROBERT
COLERICK, ARTHUR
COLES, HAROLD
COLLINS, ARTHUR
COLLINS, DONALD
COLLINS JR, RUSSELL
COMBS, WILLIAM
CONKLIN, KENNETH
CONLAN, JACK
CONNELLY, JOS
CONNOLLY, JAMES
CONRAD, WILLIAM
CONTI, CARL
CONZATTI, JOHN
COOLE, DAN
COOPER, MICKEY
COOPER, WALTER
CORBY, CARLTON
CORRADO, ANTHONY
CORRY, JOHN
COSBY, TOM
COSSE, CLAUDE
COTTRILL, WILLIAM
COURY, HERB
COWDEN, SID
COWELL, STANLEY
COX, B A
COX, LEO
COX JR, MERLE
CRABTREE, EDWARD
CRAIG, JACKIE
CRAWFORD, CHASE
CRAWFORD JR, LEON
CREEDON, DANIEL
CRILLEY, PAT
CROCOLL, WM
CRONCE, MERRIL
CROUSE, ART
CRULL III, WILLIAM
CRUMLEY, HAROLD

CULLEN, FRANCIS
CULP, JOHN
CUNNINGHAM, DONALD
CUNNINGHAM, JAMES
CUNNINGHAM, ROSE
CURCIO, SAL
CURCIO, SAL
CUSTER, ROLLAND

- D -

D'AMICO, T J
DAIGLE, ROLAND
DALTON, E J
DANEKER, GARY
DANGLER, HARRY
DANNELLEY, RAYMOND
DARBY, ALLAN
DAVILA, FRANK
DAVIS, HAROLD
DAVIS, MARVIN
DAVIS, WALDEN
DAVIS JR, IRVING
DAVY, JAMES
DAWES, CLARENCE
DAY, ROBERT
DAYBERRY, JOHN
DECESARI, ALFRED
DECKER, CHARLES
DECORSEY, GORDON
DEGRIPP, GEORGE
DEHN, ROBERT
DEITRICK, THELMA
DEMPSEY JR, MYRON
DENNY, J R
DESMOND, LOUIS
DESTARKEY, DONALD
DEVLIN, ED
DEWHURST, ROBERT
DEZELAR, RICHARD
DICORCIA, JOSEPH
DIERKS, JERRY
DIETL JR, FRANK
DIGIROLAMO, SAM
DILLON, GARVEESE
DILLON II, DONALD
DIMARIA, JOS
DINELL, JOSEPH
DINGMAN, ROBERT
DIPENNTINA, EMIL
DIXON, HUGH
DODEZ JR, ROY
DOERR, ROBERT
DONAGHY, DONALD
DONAHUE, BRENDAN
DONLON, JOS
DONOFRIO, FELIX
DORAN, BILL
DORFF, CHARLES
DORRIS, ROBERT
DOSTER, EMMETT
DOUGHERTY, CHARLES
DOUGLASS, NATHAN
DOWNING, WILLIAM
DRUMP, RONDLE
DRURY, CURTIS

DRURY, SAM
DUBEL, ROBERT
DUCHON, DAVID
DUDEN, ROBERT
DUGAN, WILLIAM
DUGAN JR, JOS
DUMOULIN, WILLIAM
DUNCAN, THOMAS
DUNHAM, JAMES
DUTCH, JOHN

- E -

ECKERT, GEO
ECKERT, LEROY
ECKERT JR, LARRY
EDENFIELD, JAMES
EDWARDS, DAVID
EDWARDS, DONALD
EGGLETON, DONALD
EISBRENER, JOHN
ELGIN, RUSSELL
ELLIOT, RANDOLPH
ELLIOT, RUSSELL
ELLISON, JAMES
ELWOOD, GEORGE
EMIG, WILLIAM
ENGLEBERT, ROY
ENRIGHT, FRANK
ENRIGHT, JOHN
EPPERSON, JAMES
EPPLER, NORMAN
ESSELSTEIN, JEAN
ESSER, RICHARD
ESTES, E FLORINE
ETHIER JR, GEO
EVANS, FRANCIS
EVERNHAM, LAWRENCE

- F -

FAFARD, OMER
FAGAN, HARRY
FAIRFAX, G DALE
FALCON, WILLIAM
FALLER, WALTER
FALSO, VINCENT
FARR, ROBERT
FAULKNER, JAMES
FELLURE, LESTER
FERGUSON, BILL
FERGUSON, ROBERT
FERGUSON, WILLIAM
FERRY, CHARLES
FIELDS, FLOYD
FILLHART, NED
FILLMORE, JOHN
FINBY, MARK
FISHBACK, JAMES
FISHER, GLENN
FISHER, WILLIAM
FLAHERTY, EDWARD
FLETCHER, RAYMOND
FLOOD, JAMES
FLORIDA, MICHAEL
FLYNN, ROBERT
FOGAL, WILLIAM

FOGELSON, BRIAN
FOGELSON, EDWIN
FOGELSON, SCOTT
FOLEY, DONALD
FORD, JOHN
FORTUNA, FREDERICK
FRANK, CHARLES
FRATIS, LEO
FREECE, STEWART
FREEMAN, JOHN
FRENCH, LARRY
FRIEND, CLARENCE
FROST, DONALD
FULKS, ROBERT
FUNK, JOSEPH
FURST, VINCENT

- G -

GABBERT, FRED
GAFFORD, R DALE
GALLAGHER, JOHN
GANDOLF, RICHARD
GARCIA, TOM
GARRISON, ALBERT
GASSER, LU
GEORGE, RICHARD
GERBER, DONALD
GERMAINE, RAYMOND
GERVAIS, DONALD
GIBB, CHARLES
GILDEA, JOHN
GILL, HAROLD
GILLES, BERNARD
GLENN JR, WALTER
GOHLKE, MARTIN
GOLDING, RICK
GOLDMAN, STUART
GOLDSTEIN, DAVID
GOLEMBIEWSKI, HENRY
GOODPASTURE, L H
GOODRICH, GEORGE
GORTON, MICHAEL
GOSSETT JR, JAMES
GRAHAM, PHILLIP
GRAHN, ROGER
GRANT, GARRETT
GRASSO, ANTHONY
GRAVES, ROBERT
GRAY, GERALD
GREEN JR, JOHN
GREENWOOD, JOHN
GREER, BRUCE
GRETZINGER, AUGUST
GRIEDL, MELVIN
GRISCHUK, MICHAEL
GROGINS, MALCOLM
GROSSMAN, EDWARD
GROVES, EDWARD
GROW, HUBERT
GUEST, ADA
GUFFEY, CARL
GUINN, RAY
GUND III, GEORGE
GURNARI, JOHN
GUTHRIE, DONALD

- H -

HAACK, EDWARD
HAGAR, LEONARD
HAGEN, WILLIAM
HAGOPIAN, EDMUND
HAINES, GREGORY
HALL, LEMUEL
HALL, ROBERT
HANBA, FRANK
HANLE, KENNETH
HANNAN, PATRICIA
HANNON, GERALD
HANS, C RONALD
HANSEN, DONALD
HARDY JR, ORAL
HARLAMERT, LEROY
HARLEY SR, MARTIN
HARMON, HAROLD
HARP JR, ROBERT
HARPER, HOWARD
HARRIS, FRANK
HARRIS JR, JOHN
HARRISON, FLOYD
HARRISON, ROBERT
HART, WM
HARTLEY, WILLIAM
HARVEY, ARCHIE
HARVEY, WILLIAM
HASTINGS, JOHN
HAUSER, DONALD
HAYES, ELMER
HAYES, JOHN
HAYES SR, MARTIN
HEGELMEYER, W J
HEININGER, HOWARD
HEISER, HAROLD
HEMRICH, CHARLES
HENNIGHAUSEN, FRED
HENRY, RUSSELL
HENSIEK, SCOTT
HERMAN, JACK
HERMAN, JACK
HERWEG, JAMES
HESELTON, L R
HESNOR, THOMAS
HICKS, ERNEST
HICKS, ROBERT
HIGGINS, JOHN
HILBERT, WELDON
HILL, BERT
HILL, EDGAR
HILL, EDWARD
HILL, JAMES
HILL JR, GEORGE
HILTS, GEORGE
HIMES, JAMES
HINES, ALBERT
HOBBS, KENNETH
HOFFMAN, JAMES
HOFFMAN, JAY
HOKE, RONALD
HOLLERBACH, FRANK
HOLLINGSWORTH, TOM
HOLSONBACK, STANFORD
HOOD SR, DONALD

HOOPER, ELDON
HOPKIN, GLEN
HOPKINS, JOS
HOPWOOD, GEORGE
HORAN, JOHN
HOSICK, JOSEPH
HOWARD, GEORGE
HRENCHIR, CHARLES
HUBER, DON
HUCKENPOELER, W B
HUDAK, JOE
HUDSON, A R
HUDSON, DALE
HUDSON, GEORGE
HUDSON, TIM
HUGHES, ROBERT
HUGHES, ROBERT
HUNT, WILLIAM
HUNTINGTON, CHARLES
HUTH, EDWIN

- I -
IACONO, TONY
IHNKEN, TOM
IRETON, CHARLES
IREY JR, JOHN
IRVING, GARY
IVIE, RALPH

- J -
JABLON, LEONARD
JABLONSKI, CARL
JACKSON, DELNO
JACKSON, EDWIN
JACOBS JR, DWIGHT
JACOBUS, CHARLES
JAROSCH, DAN
JARRELS, JOHN
JARVIS, WILLIAM
JASON, WILKER
JEANES JR, LINCOLN
JENKINS, REX
JOHNSON, CONRAD
JOHNSON, FRANK
JOHNSON, GEORGE
JOHNSON, GEORGE
JOHNSON, LESLIE
JOHNSTON, JOS
JOHNSTON, RONALD
JONES, ARTHUR
JONES, HARRY
JONES, HENRY
JONES, JAMES
JONES, JAMES
JONES, LESTER
JONES, ORA
JULIAN, PETER
JULIOT, JAMES

- K -
KACHAROS, MELVIN
KADERLI, RONALD
KALAKAUSKIS, LAWRENCE
KANTOR, TED
KAPUSHINSKI, WILLIAM

KARAWAY, VICTOR
KARNES, DELBERT
KASTNER, FRED
KATZZ, DOUGLAS
KEEGAN, JOHN
KEENAN, FRANCIS
KEHOE, RAYMOND
KELLY, MICHAEL
KELVER, CECIL
KERN, BILLY
KERR, R H
KESSLER, WALTER
KESSLER, WALTER
KEY, CLARENCE
KIMMEY, FRED
KINES, EDWARD
KINES, EDWARD
KING, JAMES
KIRK, RAYMOND
KIRKPATRICK, ROBERT
KISER, MAYBELLE
KISLIN, RICHARD
KLEIN, BERNARD
KLIMAS, TONY
KLINE, DONALD
KNIGHT, BOB
KNOLL, ROBERT
KNOLL SR, RICHARD
KNUDSEN, CLIFFORD
KOBERNICK, ARNOLD
KOCHER, JOHN
KOEHLER, ANDREW
KOETS, FLOYD
KORMAN, GILBERT
KORNDORFFER, J R
KREUTZ, EMIL
KRICK, JOE
KRIEGER, WILLIAM
KROLL, HOWARD
KRUEGEL, JACK
KRZYZEWSKI, PETE
KURZ, NORMAN

- L -
LABAT, PIERRE
LADD, JOSEPH
LAGUARDIA, JOHN
LAMADRID, JOHN
LANDGRAFF, RICHARD
LANDIS, FREDERICK
LANE, LAVERNE
LANE, WM
LANEY, FREDERIC
LANKFORD, HUBERT
LANNAN, WILLIAM
LANOUX, LESTER
LARWINSKI, CHESTER
LASLEY JR, GLENN
LATISLAW, WARREN
LAUATO SR, VINCENT
LAUDER, DONALD
LAVINE, ROBERT
LAVINE SR, JOHN
LAWRENCE, ABE
LAWRENCE, JOHN

LAWRENCE, MITCH
LEE, DENNIS
LEE, DON
LEE, JOHN
LEONARD, ONEIL
LEVERTON, HELEN
LIAN, ROBERT
LINDNER, FRED
LINES, DONALD
LITTLEFIELD, FRANK
LIVELY SR, JAMES
LOCKHART, BILLY
LOCKIE, THOMAS
LOCKWOOD, WILLIAM
LOERZEL, LEONARD
LOMANTO, RICHARD
LOMBARDO, FRANK
LONG, BOYD
LONGWORTH, JESSE
LOTSPEICH, JAMES
LOUGHAN, JOHN
LOVE, LEONARD
LOVECHIO, ROSE
LUNDY, STANLEY
LUSSIER, JOSEPH
LUTZ, GEO
LYDON, JAMES
LYLES, JAMES
LYLES, RAYMOND
LYNCH, LAWRENCE

- M -
MACK, ANGELO
MAGYAR, KENNETH
MAISEL, GORDON
MAITLAND JR, ROBERT
MALKOVICH, RICHARD
MAMROTH, ELLIS
MANGUN, DONALD
MANLEY, CHARLES
MANNA, FRANK
MANRING, JERALD
MARLATT, PAUL
MARLER, THOMAS
MARMELZAT, WILLIAM
MARRIOTT SR, WM
MARRO, JOHN
MARRO, JOHN
MARTELLO, GEO
MARTIN, ADEE
MARTIN, JAMES
MARTIN, RICHARD
MASSIE, GREGORY
MASTERS, WALTER
MASTROGIAOVANNI, A J
MATHUS, HOWARD
MAZA, RAFAEL
MAZUR, MICHAEL
MCCANCE, FRANK
MCCARTHY, JOHN
MCCORMICK, JOHN
MCDONNELL, JOSEPH
MCDOWELL, RICHARD
MCENTEE, JACK
MCFARLAND, JAMES

MCGINTY, MIKE
MCGOWAN, JOSEPH
MCGRANE, JOHN
MCGUIRE, CHARLES
MCGUIRE, EDWARD
MCINTYRE, JOHN
MCKENNA, JOSEPH
MCLANE, JAMES
MCLEAN, MARVIN
MCMALL, FLOYD
MCMALL, FLOYD
MCSORLEY, JACK
MEADOWS, PAUL
MEHLING, JULIA
MENDITTO, MICHAEL
MESZKO, RICHARD
MEYER, LEO
MICAS JR, HENRY
MICHAEL, ROBERT
MIDDLETON, DONALD
MILLER, GARY
MILLER, GERALD
MILLER, JOHN
MILLER, LEAMAN
MILLER, RICHARD
MILLER, ROBERT
MILLER JR, JOSEPH
MILLHOLEN, GERALD
MILLIGAN, R
MILLMAN, ARNOLD
MININCHIELLO, ARTHUR
MITCHELL, JIM
MITCHLER, ROBERT
MIX, LELIO
MIXON, SARAH
MOHNMAN, HAROLD
MOODIE, ROBERT
MOORE, KEN
MOORE, ROBERT
MOORE, TRAVIS
MOORE JR, LEWIS
MOORMAN, LOUIS
MORGAN, CARROLL
MORGAN JR, EDGAR
MORITZ, JOHN
MORRISON, LEON
MORRISON, MERLE
MOSS, JAMES
MULFORD, HOWARD
MULLEN, GERALD
MULLER, JOHN
MULLER, ROGER
MULLER, WILLIAM
MUNROE, CHARLES
MUNSEY JR, ROBERT
MURPHY, JOHN
MURPHY, JOSEPH
MURRAY, CHARLES
MURRAY, JOSEPH
MURRAY SR, ROBERT
MUSCENTE, SAL

- N -
NAVALANEY, JOE
NEESON, PAUL

NEUMANN, JOHN
NEUMANN, LEO
NEWELL, BERTRAM
NEWKIRK, LEROY
NEWKIRK, LEROY
NEWS, JOHN
NEWTON, JOSEPH
NICHOLAS, CARL
NICKOLS, JAMES
NIEDZWIECKI, JOHN
NIELTOPP, ROBERT
NORLEY, RICHARD
NOTHDURFT, JACK

- O -
O'BRYEN, DALE
O'CONNOR, BERNARD
O'MARO, JOHN
O'NEILL, JAMES
O'REILLY, JOSEPH
O'ROURKE, JAMES
O'SULLIVAN, JOHN
ODOM, WARD
OEHME, CHARLES
OHANLON, JAMES
OLEARY, JAMES
OLKOWSKI, WALTER
OMMERMAN, VERN
OOSTERINK, ROGER
ORGAN, LEONARD
ORLANDO, JOHN
OWEN, CHARLES
OWNBY, JAMES

- P -
PACE, CHARLES
PAGLIALONGA, A
PARKER, JACKSON
PARMELEE, ROBERT
PARSHALL, NORMAN
PASCERI, VINCENT
PAULCHEL, RALPH
PAULINO, FRANK
PAZIENZA, MICHAEL
PEARSON SR, GLENN
PELLETIER, KENNETH
PENISTON, ROBERT
PEREGRIN, EDWARD
PERRY, CHESTER
PERRY, THOMAS
PETERS, ALLEN
PETERSEN, DONALD
PETRUS, THOMAS
PETSKY, ROGER
PETTY, FRANK
PHILLIPS, SHERMAN
PICKEL, MELVIN
PIECZYNSKI, HENRY
PINGRIN, PAUL
PITTENGER, ROLLAND
PLAMONDON, PAUL
PLANK, FAY
PLANTZ, GERALD
PLATOW, MICHAEL
PLATT, RON

PLESS, WILLIAM
POFFENBARGER, GARLAND
PORAMBO SR, JOSEPH
PORPORA, BART
PORTER, ROSS
POST, PETER
POTTER JR, ALLIE
POTTLE, CECIL
POWELL, JAMES
POWER, RICHARD
PRIBILIA, ROBERT
PRICE, RAYMOND
PRIME, MICHAEL
PRITCHARD, NELSON

- Q -
QUANTZ, JAMES
QUIMBY, WILLIAM
QUINLAN, CORNELIUS
QUINN, DONALD
QUINN, JAMES
QUINN, ROBERT

- R -
RACINE, GERALD
RADER, CHESTER
RADER, LESTER
RAFF, LEONARD
RAGONE, FRANK
RAHN SR, FRANK
RAINE, ROB
RAKOCY, MICHAEL
RANDOLPH, JACK
RAPONE, P J
RATLIFF, DONNIE
REED, FREDDIE
REIHING, THOMAS
REILLY, THOMAS
RELLEVA, JOHN
REQUARTH, WILLIAM
RESCORLA, DONALD
RESSO, RAYMOND
RESTEGHINI, ALFRED
REYNOLDS, DONALD
RFAHS JR, FREDERICK
RHOAD, EDWARD
RHOADS, DONALD
RICHARDS, LLOYD
RICHARDS, RAYMOND
RICHTER, JOS
RICKERT, GARY
RICKLEY, HOWARD
RIDDLE, CLYDE
RINGWOOD, JOHN
RIPLEY, FRED
RITACCO, LOUIS
ROBBINS, PAUL
ROBBINS, RALPH
ROBERSON, BILLY
ROBIE, WM
ROBINSON, FRANK
ROBINSON, GEORGE
ROBINSON, MARSHALL
ROBINSON, MERLIN
ROCCO SR, JOS

ROCHA, MANUEL
RODER, CHARLES
ROSS, ROBERT
ROSSIE, LUCILLE
ROTH, GEORGE
ROXBURGH, KENNETH
RUDDEROW, JOHN
RUDY, CHARLES
RUPERTUS, LEROY
RUPP, BRYAN
RUPP, JORETTA
RUSCOE, WALTER
RUSSELL, JOHN
RUSTICK, RONALD
RUTAN, JOHN
RUTHERFORD, ROBERT
RUTTEN, RICHARD
RYAN, ROBERT
RYAN JR, HENRY

- S -
SABLESKI, JEROME
SACCO, PETER
SAIN, WALLACE
SALA, ANTHONY
SAMSOE, LEE
SANDBERG, RALPH
SANDERS, NORWIN
SARNICOLA, PAT
SAUDE, FRANK
SAUNDERS, FRANCIS
SAUPPEE, ROBERT
SAXON SR, RICHARD
SAXTON, RICHARD
SCAGGS, FREDDIE
SCANLON, DANIEL
SCHAAR, JOHN
SCHACHT, CHRISTIAN
SCHAPPAUGH, M A
SCHATZMAN, JIM
SCHEIDER, WILLIAM
SCHELLE, ARTHUR
SCHEPERLE, RAYMOND
SCHMIDT, RICHARD
SCHRANK, ARTHUR
SCHRODERUS, ROBERT
SCHULTZ, EUGENE
SCOGINS, RALPH
SCOTT, ARTHUR
SCOTT, PAUL
SCOTT, ROBERT
SCOTT JR, R L
SCROOPE JR, HENRY
SELLAR, GERALD
SEMSAK, JOSEPH
SENA, CARMEN
SHARP, GEORGE
SHEA, THOMAS
SHEEHAN, STEPHEN
SHERLERLE, RAYMOND
SHERTEL, RAYMOND
SHULTS, WARREN
SHURTZ, FRED
SIEGERT, PAUL
SIEGMUND, WARREN

SIEKMAN, LEE
SIMADIRIS, ELIAS
SIMON, STEWARD
SINNOTT, JOSEPH
SISON, IRVING
SIX, EDWARD
SKOCIK JR, JOHN
SKOLFIELD JR, JOHN
SLADEWSKI, ERWIN
SLOANE, CHESTER
SLOCUM, ROBERT
SMITH, ARTHUR
SMITH, CLARENCE
SMITH, IRVIN
SMITH, MICHAEL
SMITH, PHILLIP
SMITH, RAYMOND
SMITH, RICHARD
SMITH, ROBERT
SMITH, WESLEY
SMITH, WILLIAM
SMITH JR, CHARLES
SMODIC, VINCENT
SNOW, ROSS
SNYDER, TOM
SNYDER JR, WALTER
SONNTAG, HARRY
SORRENTINO, VICTOR
SOSNOWSKI, WILLIAM
SPIERER, ARTHUR
SPIVEY, V EDWARD
SPORER, ERNEST
SPOTO, CARLO
SPRENG, ERNEST
SPRENG, RAYMOND
ST GERMAIN, ROBERT
STADNIK, CHESTER
STAHLMANN, ROBERT
STALEY, CHARLES
STANKEWICZ, ROBERT
STEEN, LAWRENCE
STEGMANN, GEORGE
STEINEBACH, WILLIAM
STEINWEHE, ALBERT
STEM, LEE
STERN, HARRY
STETINA, JOSEPH
STEVENS, FRANK
STEVENS, JOSEPH
STEVENS, WILLIAM
STIA SR, SAM
STIAK, FRANK
STIBOL, JOHN
STIFF, WILLIAM
STILLWELL, PAUL
STONE, CHARLES
STONE, RICHARD
STORM, JOHN
STOUT, MELVIN
STRANDLUND, ARCHIE
STRUB III, HENRY
SUCY, JAMES
SULMA, EDWARD
SUMMERALL, JAMES
SUSANEK, GEORGE

SVILAND, MARC
SYERS JR, PAUL
SZOSTAK, JOHN

- T -
TALBOT, EDWARD
TALBOT JR, GRANT
TANZER, FRANK
TAYLOR, HUGH
TAYLOR, JOHN
TEEHAN, PHIL
TELFER, GEORGE
TERRY, DONALD
THARP, ION
THELANDER III, PETER
THIEMANN, DARRELL
THOMMEN SR, CHARLES
THOMPSON, ARTHUR
THOMPSON, PHYLLIS
THORNTON, RUBIN
TIERNAN, WILLIAM
TIERNEY, KEVIN
TODD, DAWSON
TOMLINSON, MOY
TOTH, ANDREW
TOTH, LOUIS
TOUZIN, KEITH
TOWNSEND, DON
TRACHOK, ALVIN
TRAMAGLINI, ANTHONY
TRAPANI, SAM
TRECARTIN, ALLEN
TRIMMEL, ANDREW
TRIPPLE, EDWARD
TROTTIER, BERTRAND
TRUMAN, JOHN
TUCKER, DANA
TUCKER, R D

TUCKER, SAMUEL
TURDO, ANGELO
TURNER, LARRY
TUSSING, RICHARD

- U -
UNDERHILL, EDWARD
UTTER, PATRICK

- V -
VAN NOSTRAND, DAVID
VAN PORTFLEET, GORDON
VAN PORTFLEET, GORDON
VANLEAR, GLEN
VANNOSTRAND, DAVID
VANSICKLE, JOSEPH
VAUGHAN, JAMES
VAUGHN, J W
VAVRA, ELVIN
VIERHELLER, ART
VIERK, EDWARD
VIERKANT, H R
VINCZE, RICHARD
VOSS, HERBERT

- W -
WADAS, ALEXANDER
WADE, ANDREW
WADJA, EDWARD
WAGNER, DAVID
WAGNER, DONALD
WAGONER, JAMES
WAKELAND, EDWIN
WALKER, GEORGE
WALKER, MARVIN
WALLACE II, TOM
WALSH, JOHN
WALTER, NORMAN

WALTER, RICHARD
WALTERS, JERRY
WALTERS, ROBERT
WALZ, THOMAS
WARD, DAVID
WARD, WILLIAM
WARMAN, CLYDE
WARNER, CURTIS
WASELESKI SR, GEORGE
WATSON, JACK
WEAVER JR, VICTOR
WEBB, FRANK
WEBER, VINCENT
WEEKS, CORBIN
WEGNER, ALBERT
WEISGERBER, MARCUS
WELLS, WARREN
WENTWORTH, CLIFTON
WERBISKY, RICHARD
WEST, THEODORE
WESTCOTT, ROBERT
WESTPHAL, CHARLES
WHITACRE, EDWARD
WHITE JR, JAMES
WHITEHAIR JR, DEWARD
WHITEHAIR JR, DEWARD
WHITLOCK, GEORGE
WHITLOCK, JERRY
WILDSIN, CLETUS
WILEY, HAROLD
WILLENBORG, HENRY
WILLIAMS, CARL
WILLIAMS, JOHN
WILLIAMS, ROBERT
WILLIAMS, THOMAS
WILLIAMSON, HARRY
WILSON, DONALD
WINDHORST, ROBERT

WINKELMAN JR, VAL
WINTERS, RAYMOND
WIRZBACH, ROBERT
WISE, ROBERT
WITT, DALE
WOLOCHAK, HARRY
WOLPIN, RICHARD
WOOD, JAMES
WOODMAN, WAYNE
WOODS, ROBERT
WOOLLEY JR, GEORGE
WOOSLEY, BALLARD
WRIGHT, HAROLD
WYNNE, MARGARET
WYNNE, MARGARET
WYSOWSKI, WALTER

- Y -
YEAGER, JOHN
YOUNG, RUSSELL
YOUNG SR, JOHN
YUHAS, EUGENE

- Z -
ZAHLAWAY, J M
ZAREMBA SR, EDWARD
ZAZZARINO, MICHAEL
ZENTGRAF, WILLIAM
ZIEGLER, GEORGE
ZIELINSKI, WILLIAM
ZIMMEL, MARVIN
ZIMMERMAN, JOHN
ZIMMERMAN, MATT
ZIPP, LAWRENCE
ZUBERT, JAMES
ZUEHLKE, WILLIAM
ZULESKI, TED

Index

A

Abhau, Ltcdr. W.C. 23
Addy, Ed 39
Amani O Jima 46
Amoy, China 18, 44
Anchor Hill 11
Apra Harbor, Guam 31, 33, 53
Argentua, Newfoundland 23
Atkeson, John C. 9
Atlantic City, NJ 3

B

Badger, Adm. O.C. 17, 37, 44, 47
Bailey, J.A. 11
Baird, Bruce 34
Bakos, Michael J. 2
Balley, Ed 51
Bamboulus 65
Baton Rouge, LA 46
Bayonne, NJ 10, 15
Beirut, Lebanon 15
Beneke, Tex 29
Berliner, David 58
Berttheard, Jennings 18
Bigelow, Earl 9
Blackwood, Herb 25
Blair, Dr. Frank 3
Blake Island 49
Boone, Nelson 51
Boose, Ens. 24
Boston, MA 3
Boston Navy Yard 23
Bremerton Naval Yard 14
Bremerton, WA 4, 10, 13, 15, 47
Brooks, Charles S., Jr. 9
Brown, Russell 3
Butts, Carl 3
Butts, Lt. William 51

C

Cairns, Ben 51
Calder, Chief Marion 51
Caldwell, J. R. 65
Calhoun, Capt. Raymond 43
Camden, NJ 8
Camranh Bay 44
Carney, Adm. "Mick" 31, 35, 39
Caroline Islands 26
Chalkley, Stuart 62, 63, 64
Cherbourg, France 12
Cherry Hill, NJ 3
Chongjin 11
Churchill, Winston 31
Clark, Adm. 46
Cole, Bob 37
Connally, Chief J. 19, 20
Connolly, Adm. 9
Cooney, Alan 24, 37, 42, 44
Corregidor 54
Crabtree, A. 65
Cromwell, Doris Duke 50
Cromwell, N.C. 34
Cruise, Lt. 24
Cuisner, 2nd Lt. 24

D

Dancy., Lt. Charles 23
Dart, Ben 34
Davis, Lt. D, III 23
Decker, Adm. 50
Dinell, Joseph A 10
Dorsey, Tommy 29, 48
Draemel, Rear Adm. Milo F. 8
Dunning, Allen L. 8
Dzekon, Joseph H. 11

E

Edison, Charles 8, 16
Ellice Islands 25
Elwood, George H. 3
Eniewetok Atoll 25, 33, 52
Erickson, Louis 25
Ethridge, Lt. William 45, 51
Evans, Lt. Jim 17
Eves, Capt. E.T. 35

F

Faber, Alton 51
Flanagan, Ben 51
Fleet, Lt. George Van 43
Fletcher, Mark 51
Fogarty, Capt. William M. 9, 16
Fogelson, Edwin M. 3
Ford, Lt. (jg) 24
Forest, Francis X. 8
Formosa (Taiwan) 10, 38, 43, 44
Forrestal, James 8
Frank, Charles W. 16, 24
Ft. Mitchell, KY 3
Funafutti 25

G

Gasser, Charles 3
Gearhart, C.S. 42
Geisendorf, Fred 25
Glenn, Walter L., Jr. 9
Goode, Father J. 34, 39
Gordon, Jack 34, 53
Gossage, Ed 51
Graham, Robert 51
Greason, 1st Lt. E.H. 24
Guadalcanal 28
Guam 10, 31
Gulf de Paria 22
Gulf of Tonkin 12

H

Haakan, King 9
Hahn, Cdr. E. 49
Halsey, Adm. "Bull" 9, 15, 17, 19, 29, 30, 31, 34, 35, 36, 37, 40, 41, 42, 43, 44, 45, 54
Hampton Roads, VA 18, 22
Hans, R. 65
Hanson, Flint 51
Hardy, Merrill 44
Harpster, Dave 25
Harris, Lt. G. 49
Hayward, Lt. E. F. 50
Hicks, Leo 25
Holden, Capt. Carl F. 8, 9, 16, 21, 22, 23, 37, 51
Honshu, Japan 54
Hope, Bob 13
Hoppa, Charles B. 58
Huffman, C.O. Leon 9
Hungnam 11
Hutchinson, Bill 51

I

Inchon 12

J

Jackson, Maurice 25
Jersey City, NJ 14
Johnson Island 35
Juan de Fuca Strait 47, 49

K

Kaafjord, Norway 23
Kalakauski, Larry 3
Kalmagak 11
Katz, Vice Admiral Douglas 3, 9
Keithly, Cdr. 54
Kesslering, General 56
Kiethly, Cdr. R.M. 49
Kimball, Capt. William 18
King, Adm. Ernest 8
Kitchel, Bill 35, 36
Klein, B.J. 14
Kojo 11
Koltun, Allen 34
Korea 7, 10
Kruger, General 53
Kurita, Adm. 40
Kwajalein Atoll 25, 26
Kyushu 10, 11, 46

L

Laird, Melvin 13
Landers, Ltcdr. Matt 24
Larkin, M. A. 58
Lebanon 7, 14
Lee, Adm. Willis 17, 32
Leedom, Lt. Craig 27
Leonard, O'Neil 3
Leverton, Joseph W., Jr. 9
Levy, David 37
Leyte Gulf 10, 51
Liberty State Park 4
Lill, Allen 34
Lisbon, Portugal 12
Long Beach, CA 3, 12, 14, 15
Long Beach Naval Shipyard 16, 49
Lonsbury, William 51
Luzon 10, 39, 41, 42, 43

M

MacArthur, Gen. Douglas 30, 37, 39, 54, 56
Majuro 25, 26, 29, 30, 33
Manila 40, 53
Manus Island 35
Marianas 10, 25
Martin, Harold M. 11
Martin, James C. 3
Matsou 44
McCain, Adm. 41
McCorkle, Capt. Francis D. 9, 11
McCormick, Capt. Jack 17, 21, 25, 34, 59
McCormick, Jerry 34
McDowell, Cdr. Pete 16, 35
McDowell, Richard 3
McFall, Louis 53
McFarland, James 39
McLean, Adm. 9
McMahon, Lt. Gregory 24
McSorley, Jack 51
McVay, Capt. Charles 51
Melson, Charles L. 9
Menocal, Capt. George L. 9
Milby, F.M. 58
Miller, Lt. J. H. 49
Miller, Stu 25
Milli Atoll 27
Milligan, Richard D. 9
Millman, Arnold 11
Minami Jima 46
Minor, Billy 37
Mitchell, Billy 7
Mitscher, Adm. Marc 31
Mogmog 37, 42, 44, 47
Moorman, Larry 19, 35, 37, 42, 50, 55
Morison, Adm. Sam Elliot 29, 38, 53
Moritz, Cdr. 58
Morse, George 17
Mrozinski, Lt. Roman 9
Munsey, Robert, Jr. 3
Murphy, Joseph Francis 27

N

Naples, Italy 18
Nashville, TN 3
Nelson, Adm. Horatio 35
New Guinea 28
New York Shipyard 18, 19
Nimitz, Adm. 29, 34, 38, 43
Nobel, Charlie 16, 44
Norfolk, VA 3, 11, 12
Nultemeir 25

O

O'Donnell, Edward J. 9
Ogle, Cdr. G.B. 25, 47
Okinawa 10, 38, 45, 46, 54
Olendorf, Adm. 39, 40
Osterwind, Robert 11
Ozawa, Adm. 40

P

Palau 29, 33, 36
Pammunjon 12
Panama Canal 8, 12, 14, 24
Parker, Ens. Robert 16, 23, 24, 34
Patterson, Captain 58
Peabody, Eddy 41
Pearl Harbor 7
Peniston, Capt. Robert C. 9, 13, 14, 17
Peters, Malcolm 37
Philadelphia Naval Yard 8, 12, 15, 16, 19, 20, 23
Ponape 30
Poorman, Roy 47
Port of Spain 22
Port Said 18
Powers, Dick 3
Press, Harry 51
Prima, Louie 31
Puget Sound Naval Yard 15, 47
Pusan 12

Q

Quincy, Massachusetts 18

R

Raat, Lt. Benny 24
Rasmusson 25
Reagan, President Ronald 3, 14
Regan, Capt. Francis 24, 44, 49
Reynolds, Harry 17, 18, 20, 25
Rhee, Syngman 12
Ritchie, C. 65
Rockland, Maine 20
Rogers, Tim 25
Roosevelt, President Franklin 47
Roosevelt, President Theodore 18, 20
Rose, Cdr. Rufus 16
Rosinski, Lt. 52
Rossie, John 17, 19, 22, 25, 50
Rota 10
Ruyukus 46
Ryuku Retto 38

S

Saipan 10, 31, 32, 33, 37
Sakishima Gunto 46
Samar 37
Sampson, Lcdr. 24
San Bernardino Strait 39
San Clemente Island 49
San Diego, CA 3
San Francisco, CA 10
San Pedro Harbor 49
Santiago 65
Sasebo 11
Schaniel, J.E. 11
Schatzman, James J. 3
Schwartz, Ralph 34
Selorchac, John 51
Sherman, Adm. Forrest 25, 44, 46
Sherwood, Capt. Carl F. 55, 58
Slusher, Ralph 51
Smith, Keely 31
Snyder, Capt. Edward, Jr. 9, 12
Songjin 11
Spencer, Lt.(jg) R. 12
Spencer, Ltcdr. E.C. 23, 24
Spizer, David 34
Spruance, Adm. Raymond 9, 10, 15, 17, 25, 30, 33, 34, 43, 53, 54, 57
Stafford, Ed 25
Stassen, Harold 33

T

Taylor, Ltcdr. E.W. 23
Thompson, Capt. E.M. 9, 17, 57
Tinian 10, 31, 34, 53
Topham, 2nd Lt. Al 24
Trecartin, Ens. A.L. 49
Truman, President Harry S. 10, 53
Tucker, Dana D. 60
Tucker, Ronald 9
Tuffanelli, Lt. George 11
Turchin, Ens. Robert 24
Tyree, Capt. David 9, 10, 11

U

Ulithi Atoll 37, 41, 42, 45, 46

V

Vietnam 7, 12

W

Wakayama Wan 54
Walsh, John 3
Washington, George 20
Weyburn, Lt(jg) S.M. 24
Williams, J.B. 11
Williams, "Willy" 51
Wintle, Lt. Jack 59
Wolochok, H.G. 11, 65
Wooldridge, Capt. E.T. 9, 17, 44, 51, 54, 55, 57
Wouk, Herman 17

Y

Yeager, Lt(jg) John 24